The Tamil V

The Tamil Veda

Piḷḷāṉ's Interpretation of the Tiruvāymoḻi

John Carman and
Vasudha Narayanan

THE UNIVERSITY OF
CHICAGO PRESS
Chicago and London

John Carman is the Parkman Professor of Divinity, professor of comparative religion, and director of the Center for the Study of World Religions at Harvard University.
Vasudha Narayanan is associate professor of religion at the University of Florida.

The University of Chicago Press, Chicago 60637
The University of Chicago Press, Ltd., London

Printed in the United States of America

98 97 96 95 94 93 92 91 90 89 5 4 3 2 1

(∞) The paper used in this publication meets the minimum requirements of the American National Standard for Information Sciences—Permanence of Paper for Printed Library Materials, ANSI Z39.48-1984.

Library of Congress Cataloging-in-Publication Data

Carman, John Braisted.
The Tamil Veda : Piḷḷāṉ's interpretation of the Tiruvāymoḻi / John Carman and Vasudha Narayanan.
p. cm.
Bibliography: p.
Includes index.
ISBN 0-226-09305-0. ISBN 0-226-09306-9 (pbk.)
1. Tirukkurukai Pirāṉ Piḷḷāṉ. Āṟāyirappaṭi. 2. Nammāḻvār. Tiruvāymoḻi. I. Narayanan, Vasudha. II. Title.
PL4758.9.N3155T5329 1989 88-39888
294.5′95—dc19 CIP

To Ineke and Ranga

Contents

Preface

This book is a study of a Hindu commentary, the first work paraphrasing and interpreting Nammāḻvār's devotional poem in Tamil, the Tiruvāymoḻi. The poem is sometimes called the Tamil Veda, because South Indian worshipers of Lord Viṣṇu (the Śrīvaiṣṇavas) consider it equal in sanctity to the Sanskrit scriptures revered by all Hindus. This first commentary was written between 1100 and 1150 C.E. by Tirukkurukai Pirāṉ Piḷḷāṉ, the cousin and disciple of the community's greatest theologian, Rāmānuja.

Piḷḷāṉ's commentary provides the earliest unmistakable evidence of a central feature of the Śrīvaiṣṇava tradition: the flowing together of the Sanskrit and Tamil traditions of devotion to Viṣṇu as the Supreme Lord. Although it is unusual for a Hindu group to consider a text in any language but Sanskrit to be scripture, this community refers to its own theology as *Ubhaya Vedānta:* the "dual Vedic theology," that is, the theology based on both the Sanskrit and Tamil Vedas.

Rāmānuja wrote only in Sanskrit and made no direct references in those writings to the Tamil hymns of Nammāḻvār. In the traditional biographies, however, Rāmānuja is said to have commissioned Piḷḷāṉ to write a commentary on the Tiruvāymoḻi. Whether or not that story is historically accurate, it is evident that Piḷḷāṉ's commentary contains phrase after phrase close to or identical with the language of Rāmānuja. This is one of the reasons for the new mixed language of this commentary, which is Tamil in its grammatical structure and in many of its verbs but is full of Sanskrit nouns and adjectives. The two streams of tradition clearly come together in this work. Piḷḷāṉ understands many of Nammāḻvār's verses in the light of Rāmānuja's theology, but conversely, Piḷḷāṉ's understanding of Rāmānuja's philosophy of the Vedānta is affected by the sentiments in the Tamil hymns.

It is not difficult to find an outline of Rāmānuja's theology in Piḷḷāṉ's comments. It is more challenging to try to see clearly where Piḷḷāṉ differs from Rāmānuja and why. The Śrīvaiṣṇava tradition has preserved Tamil comments on Nammāḻvār's verses attributed to Rāmānuja as well as stories about Rāmānuja and Piḷḷāṉ. It therefore regards Rāmānuja as Piḷḷāṉ's teacher and is not concerned with the question of Piḷḷāṉ's originality. That question is, however, a puzzling one for the modern historian. Still more intriguing is the question of the extent of the unacknowledged influence of the entire āḻvār tradition on Rāmānuja's Sanskrit writings.

In our earlier studies we have both recognized that the writings of Rāmānuja's immediate disciples can provide the key to understanding Rāmānuja's link with the earlier poet-saints called the āḻvārs as well as with the teachers two centuries later whose divergent emphases led to a widening split in the Śrīvaiṣṇava community. The writings of these immediate disciples are still read in both the Teṅkalai and Vaṭakalai branches of the community, and they provide many clues to the relation (and apparent distance) between Rāmānuja's teaching and those of his most famous successors, Piḷḷai Lokācārya and Vedānta Deśika.

These direct disciples wrote both in poetry and prose, both in Tamil and in Sanskrit. Piḷḷāṉ committed to writing the tradition of discussing and paraphrasing the Tamil verses of the Tiruvāymoḻi in a highly philosophical and Sanskritized Tamil. In doing so he crystallized a new mixed language that reflected the mixing of Sanskrit and Tamil traditions in ritual and social institutions, as well as in the community's theological reflection.

John Carman's study of the polarity of supremacy and accessibility in Rāmānuja's concept of God in *The Theology of Rāmānuja* includes a brief treatment of some important themes in the writings of Rāmānuja's immediate disciples. The same subject is explored at much greater length in Vasudha Narayanan's recent book, *The Way and the Goal: Expressions of Devotion in the Early Śrī Vaiṣṇava Tradition,* which is the first of two volumes dealing with the growing distinction between bhakti and prapatti in the Śrīvaiṣṇava tradition. Bhaktiyoga and prapatti come to be understood by both the later schools as distinct means to salvation, the former the path of disciplined meditation in loving devotion to the Lord, the latter a total surrender to God and reliance on God's unmerited grace. Both schools opt for prapatti, but they differ somewhat in their interpretation of it and even more in their assessment of bhaktiyoga. The two schools continue at times to use bhakti in a wider sense, and in reference to the goal of communion with the Lord as well as the means to that goal. Both schools claim the authority of Rāmānuja and all his predecessors, both Sanskrit and Tamil, for their interpretations.

Whereas traditional scholars of both schools affirm the identity of their views with all their predecessors back to the undivided community and beyond, some modern scholars have emphasized either the difference between Nammāḻvār and Rāmānuja or the gap between Rāmānuja's teachings and the positions of the two schools three hundred years later. Our position lies between that of the traditional scholars and the more extreme challenges of modern scholars, for we see both continuities and discontinuities in the large number of Śrīvaiṣṇava writings during the three hundred years after Rāmānuja. Some positions more apparent in later writings are already anticipated in Piḷḷāṉ and his contemporaries, a fact that supports both the later schools' affirmation of their faithfulness to Rāmānuja's total teaching, in Tamil as well as in Sanskrit. Nevertheless, there are differences from one generation to another, and even authors in the same generation are often quite distinctive.

Piḷḷāṉ's commentary was followed a generation later by a longer commentary on the same hymn, and two generations later by two much longer ones. Until very recently both Teṅkalais and Vaṭakalais considered all four commentaries to be authoritative. The differences between (and sometimes within) these commentaries could be more easily tolerated than divergent interpretations of the Sanskrit scriptures, since the Tamil hymns were considered to deal, not with *tattva*, "reality as such," but with *anubhava*, "spiritual experience." In recent years one part of the Teṅkalai tradition has tended to ignore Piḷḷāṉ's commentary. This neglect may be a sectarian Teṅkalai response to a Vaṭakalai claim that the line of succession from Rāmānuja begins with Piḷḷāṉ rather than with Parāśara Bhaṭṭar.

The positions taken by Piḷḷāṉ in his commentary suggest that the split between Teṅkalai and Vaṭakalai had not yet taken place. Yet it seems to be this very commentary, standing at the point of confluence of Tamil Vaiṣṇava and Sanskrit Vaiṣṇava theology, that starts to pose questions that are not evident in either previous stream, that is, Nammāḻvār's Tamil poetry or Rāmānuja's Sanskrit prose. The questions raised in Piḷḷāṉ's Sanskritized Tamil paraphrase of Nammāḻvār's Tamil verses appear, not as polemic, but as expressions of a perplexity that the commentator assumes is the poet's own.

Our indebtedness to a number of recent scholarly contributors will be acknowledged in our notes. We do want to recognize the debt we both share to our common teacher (at different times), Dr. K. K. A. Venkatachari, and especially for his help to us in India in April and May of 1983. We have benefited from Dr. Venkatachari's survey of the Śrīvaiṣṇava literature in Sanskritized Tamil, as well as from his collaboration with Dr. David Kaylor on a brief interpretation of the Tiruvāymoḻi. We are also indebted to Professor A. K. Ramanujan, both for his personal encouragement and for making available his poetic translations of selected verses of the Tiruvāymoḻi contained in his *Hymns for the Drowning*. Our recognition of the importance of Rāmānuja's disciples has been stimulated by Robert Lester's denial of the authority of several writings attributed to Rāmānuja. Though we disagree with Dr. Lester's conclusions, we appreciate his focusing some important issues in Śrīvaiṣṇava history.

We have also benefited from Friedhelm Hardy's substantial book entitled *Viraha-Bhakti (The Devotion of Separation)*, the most recent scholarly effort to demonstrate radical differences where the tradition sees only continuity. We shall try in this study to dispute Dr. Hardy's conclusion that the Śrīvaiṣṇava tradition has misunderstood and reinterpreted Nammāḻvār.

The two of us come from different religious backgrounds: Vasudha Narayanan grew up in the Śrīvaiṣṇava Vaṭakalai tradition, John Carman in the

Protestant Christian community in India and the United States. We share, however, a strong common interest in making available the devotional riches of the Śrīvaiṣṇava tradition to students of religion in all parts of the world. We believe in the value of a historical approach that recognizes both continuities and discontinuities in the ongoing development of the Śrīvaiṣṇava tradition, and of all religious traditions. We have found it easy to agree on the historical questions with which our study deals and indeed on our basic understanding of Piḷḷān's interpretation of bhakti as both longing for God and belonging to God.

We write in different styles, which we have not tried to homogenize, and we have each taken responsibility for different parts of this book. Vasudha Narayanan is responsible for all the translations of both poem and commentary and wrote the first draft of chapters one, two, four, and twelve. John Carman wrote the first drafts of the remaining chapters and of this preface. We have gone over all the drafts together, greatly aided by the painstaking copy editing of Helen Schultz, Andrew Rasanen, and Joanna Barry; and the extensive suggestions of Professors D. Dennis Hudson, Glenn Yocum, and Francis X. Clooney, S.J. We are most grateful for the typing of Helen Schultz, Peggy Schnoor, and Andrew Rasanen. We also want to express our appreciation to Andrew Rasanen for all his help on the index. We want to acknowledge the financial support we have received from the National Endowment for the Humanities and the Ford Foundation through the Social Science Research Council, and from the American Institute of Indian Studies.

We are very grateful to Mr. and Mrs. V. R. Rajagopalan of Madras for their generous help in India. Finally, we want to say a public thank you to our spouses, Ineke Carman and Ranga Narayanan, for their patience and encouragement.

While this study focuses on Piḷḷāṉ's commentary, we intend it to contribute to the exploration of Śrīvaiṣṇava history before and after Piḷḷāṉ's time. We should like to encourage others to undertake a new kind of historical study of all the major Śrīvaiṣṇava commentaries on the āḻvārs' hymns. We hope that this examination of one traditional commentary may increase our modern understanding of the process of retrieval and translation going on in so much Hindu commentary and in other religious commentary as well. It is Nammāḻvār's poem, not any later commentary, that bears the epithet of "the Tamil Veda." It is Piḷḷāṉ's interpretation, however, that first shows us a community of Hindus ascribing to a poem in their mother tongue the sanctity of the Sanskrit Vedas and thus finding in those Tamil words the same saving truth of the Vedas.

Notes on Translations

The translations in this book form an integral part of our discussions on the Tiruvāymoḻi and its earliest commentary, so some explanation of the choice of verses and style of translation is necessary.

Our choice of verses for Part Four was governed by several considerations. The Śrīvaiṣṇava community has its own selection of twelve decads (known as the "Temple-Tiruvāymoḻi") that are chanted regularly during home and temple liturgies. Four of the decads in Part Four (1.1, 1.2, 6.10, 10.10) are drawn from this corpus and are of philosophical and liturgical significance to the community. Others, like 6.3, were chosen for their theological importance, while some, like 10.3, were selected as examples of love poems in which the poet speaks from the viewpoint of a girl separated from her beloved. In 7.9, Nammāḻvār speaks of his poems being revealed by the Lord; other sets like 9.8 describe pilgrimage centers. We chose some decads because they were intrinsically interesting; others, because Piḷḷāṉ, the commentator, perceived them as crucial to Śrīvaiṣṇava thought or said something in his exegesis that we thought illustrated his style or reflected his preoccupations. Thus Part Four is a show case, not only for Nammāḻvār's poems, but also for Piḷḷāṉ's commentarial style and theological interests.

Nammāḻvār's Tamil poems maintain the conventions of earlier classical poetry, whereas Piḷḷāṉ's comments are in heavily Sanskritized Tamil (maṇipravāḷa) and include long stretches of Sanskrit phrases drawn from Rāmānuja's philosophical and devotional works. Unfortunately, the differences in style between Nammāḻvār's Tamil poetry and Piḷḷāṉ's formal scholastic prose in maṇipravāḷa (a difference that is so obvious in the original) can only be hinted at in the English translation. To some extent, this distinction is comparable to one in English: the difference between Anglo-Saxon and Latin derivatives. Our translations make some use of these two styles of English.

Piḷḷāṉ writes in long complex sentences, which in most cases we have split up into smaller units in order to make the comments more readable. In some places, however, we have tried to retain the intensity that Piḷḷāṉ achieves by building several phrases and Sanskrit compounds into one long sentence. Although these sentences are written as prose, they sound almost like a Sanskrit Gadya (prose-poem). We have tried to convey the litanylike quality of these comments and remain faithful to the commentator's style by retaining the length of the sentence but spatially dividing it into smaller units. Thus we have tried to suggest in a visual format the rhythms that are so apparent when one hears Piḷḷāṉ's prose.

The first words of all lines in any verse in the Tiruvāymoḻi usually rhyme, as is seen in the following verse (for which both a literal and a literary translation are given):

Eṇ perukku an nalattu
Oṇ poruḷ—īṟu ilā
vaṇ pukaḻ nāraṇaṉ
tiṇ kaḻal cērē.

Endless numbers good
bright object—no end
bounteous/praise fame Nāraṇaṉ
certain feet reach.

Infinitely good
dazzling goal.
Without end,
his glorious fame.
Reach
Nāraṇaṉ's secure feet.

(1.2.10)

The poet also makes extensive use of alliteration and we did not attempt to reproduce either the rhyme or alliteration in our translations. Nor could we imitate the *antāti* ("end-beginning") style of Nammāḻvār, a style by which the last word of every verse becomes the first word of the next.

The question of how literal a translation should be is one that can be discussed at length; the problem is compounded in Tamil where words sometimes have several meanings. Nammāḻvār sometimes repeats the same word in the beginning of every line in a verse, using the same word with different meanings, instead of his usual rhyme. Consider the following verse:

uḷḷam urai ceyal
uḷḷa im mūṉṟaiyum
uḷḷik keṭuttu, iṟai-
uḷḷil oṭuṅkē

thought word deed
are these three

think; destroy -God
inside/heart shrink/submit

Just reflect:
thought, word, and deed,
you have these three.
  Destroy them.
Submit yourself
  to the Lord's embrace.

(1.2.8)

The word *uḷ* has been used as "thought," "are," and "think" in the first three lines. The occurrence in the fourth line is more problematic, and the word may mean "inside," "heart," or "mind"; *oṭuṅku* may mean "restrain," "subservient," "shrink," "shrivel," "reduce," or "to close, (like the petals of a flower)." One could translate the line as "shrink/contain/reduce/ yourself inside the Lord's heart/mind." We have translated it as "submit yourself to the Lord's embrace." Other words are more complex; *ari,* for instance, has more than fifty-three meanings, including "emerald," "horse, "Viṣṇu," "snake," "frog," "anklet," "garland," "smoke," and "sun." Fortunately, the meaning of Tamil words is generally more fixed, but it is obvious that even the most literal translation involves decisions about meaning, intention, and context. The Śrīvaiṣṇava tradition has made specific suggestions as to what "correct" interpretations may be allowed. Since the Tamil lexicon occasionally cites these commentaries as the authorities and sources for the meanings of some words, it does not help in determining what the words mean in the verses which were written centuries before the commentaries. We have sometimes diverged from the commentaries when the Tamil words lend themselves to a different grammatical arrangement and alternate interpretations from those that the classical commentaries suggest. These instances have been explained in the notes.

The Tamil word *tiru* (Sanskrit: *śrī*) may indicate the name of the Goddess Lakṣmī or mean "sacred" or "holy." We have translated it both ways, but have occasionally used "sacred" even where the commentators see a reference to the Goddess. We have retained the various names and epithets of Viṣṇu that the poet or commentators use, as well as specific references to various myths, because these usually form an integral part of the poet's and commentator's associative framework. These Tamil names include Kaṇṇaṉ (or Kaṇṇā, vocative) for Krishna, which Nammāḻvār frequently uses. They have been retained in the translation, instead of being changed to the more familiar Krishna, to emphasize the Tamil character of the verses and the intimacy of the relationship between the poet and the Lord. However, we have rendered the names of Brahmā and Śiva/Rudra by their more commonly known forms, rather than, for instance, switch between "The Four-faced One" and "Ayaṉ" (<*aja*) in the case of Brahmā. In most cases we have tried to keep to the structure of the verse, except in those cases where the connections between the segments of the verse could only be made clear by reversing the order.

Since the heavily Sanskritized Tamil prose of Piḷḷāṉ's commentary is so different from Nammāḻvār's older Tamil poetry, we are translating what is almost a "translation." This makes us all the more cognizant, not only of the problems connected with our translation, but also the common challenge facing all commentators and translators: to convey a close approximation of meaning in a different linguistic medium and in a different cultural environment. Foreign words are like holograms, each part containing a whole picture, a whole culture; but they remain unrecognizable patterns of whorls until illuminated by the coherent light of a translation or discussion which organizes them into clear three-dimensional images. But no matter how lucid the picture, invariably there is some detail that has been lost, some nuance that has been missed in the process of reconstitution, and this is to be regretted. Piḷḷāṉ, the commentator, re-created the meaning of the poem, illumining it with scriptural and textual light from Tamil and Sanskrit sources. Like Piḷḷāṉ, the authors of this book have lived in two cultures; and like him, we have tried to interpret a work done in a different era to an audience that has different ears and different concerns. The translations, we hope, reflect our understanding of the original texts, our commitment to make the reconstituted version resemble the original as closely as possible, and to make the re-creation intelligible and accessible to a late twentieth-century audience.

Vasudha Narayanan is responsible for the translations of āḻvār poetry, commentarial literature, selections from *The Splendor,* Vedānta Deśika's poems, Maṇavāḷa Māmuṉi's *Upadeśaratnamālai,* and the Sanskrit hymns of Yāmuna, Kūrattāḻvāṉ, and Parāśara Bhaṭṭar. John Carman translated all passages from Rāmānuja, except where noted. We have both gone through all our translations together and have revised them extensively. All other translations used have been acknowledged in the text or the notes. The principal edition of the Tiruvāymoḻi used in this book is *Śrī Tivyap pirapantam:* vol. 4, *Tiruvāymoḻi,* edited by Tamil scholars and published by Murray and Co., Madras, 1956. Śrī S. Kiruṣṇasvāmi Ayyaṅkār's edition of the *Bhagavad Viṣayam* (10 vols. Madras: Nobel Press, 1924–1930), which contains Piḷḷāṉ's *Six Thousand,* was used for the translation of the commentary.

Works that are part of the Sanskrit or Tamil canon of Śrīvaiṣṇavas are printed in Roman type. Other sacred writings and revered books, including both the commentaries and the hymns of the ācāryas, are printed in italics.

Part One
The Two Streams

1

Ubhaya Vedānta: The Confluence of Tamil and Sanskrit Scriptures

The Scriptural Heritage of the Śrīvaiṣṇava Community

The devotees of Viṣṇu and his consort Śrī became organized as a religious community in South India about the time of Rāmānuja (circa 1017–1137 C.E.), the most important Śrīvaiṣṇava teacher (ācārya). This community considers both Sanskrit scripture and the Tamil songs of the twelve mystics revered as āḻvārs (seventh to tenth centuries C.E.) as the basis for its theology. The word *āḻvār* is traditionally derived from the Tamil root *āḻ* "deep" and the title *āḻvār* "one who is immersed in the love of God" was used by the Śrīvaiṣṇava community after the eleventh century C.E. to refer to the twelve poet-saints who had composed hymns in praise of the Lord Viṣṇu. Because the Śrīvaiṣṇava tradition prided itself on its twofold heritage and held the Tamil poems of the āḻvārs to be equal to the Sanskrit Vedas, its religious thought came to be called the system of the Dual Vedānta (Ubhaya Vedānta), and even today, the honorific title, "One who advances [the cause of] the Dual Vedānta," is used as a formal prefix to the names of Śrīvaiṣṇava men. We shall begin our discussions of the Dual Vedānta by studying the early history of the Tamil Veda in the Śrīvaiṣṇava community and by focusing on the importance of a poem called the Tiruvāymoḻi, composed by Caṭakōpaṉ (Nammāḻvār) in the ninth century C.E.

The Śrīvaiṣṇava tradition contains elements from the culture that developed around the river Gaṅgā in Northern India (a culture that wrote principally in Sanskrit) as well as from the culture of the Kāvēri basin in the South, where Tamil flourished. We may perceive the Gaṅgā and the Kāvēri civilizations forming the cultural and geographical analogue to Athens and Jerusalem as the joint ancestors of a new way of thinking. The complexities of the Hellenistic and the Hebraic heritages seen in western thought are paralleled in the twofold inheritance of the Śrīvaiṣṇava culture. Like the literatures of Athens and Jerusalem, the Sanskrit and Tamil literatures perpetuate two distinct ways of perceiving the universe and a human being's place in it; and the Śrīvaiṣṇava tradition is the product of these two ways of thinking.

The scriptural authorities of the early Śrīvaiṣṇava community are both the Sanskrit canon and the Tamil works of the āḻvārs. The Sanskrit literature includes the Vedas, the Upaniṣads, the Bhagavadgītā, the two epics, several Purāṇas, the Dharma Śāstras, the Brahma Sūtra and some āgamic texts. The Tamil devotional poems of the āḻvārs are seen as parallel to the Vedas. Specifically, the Tiruvāymoḻi, whose title means "sacred word of mouth" or "word of sacred mouth," [1] is one of the four works of Nammāḻvār and is frequently referred to as the Tamil or Drāvida Veda. It is clearly the understanding of the Śrīvaiṣṇavas that the Vedas have been revealed in Sanskrit and in Tamil. The Tamil Veda is not an imitation of the Sanskrit Veda or even a translation; it is considered to have been revealed through the twelve āḻvārs and primarily through Nammāḻvār, a poet-saint who lived between the eighth and ninth centuries C.E. The message of both Vedas is considered to be the same and later theologians went to elaborate lengths to show how their ideas parallel each other.

Nāthamuni, the first Śrīvaiṣṇava teacher, is said to have called the Tiruvāymoḻi the Tamil Veda.[2] Such a claim was significant in the tenth century C.E. because no vernacular language had hitherto been held to be the medium of revelation within Hinduism; no other work had been called a Veda. For the first time in Hindu consciousness, hymns in a language other than Sanskrit were considered to be revealed. The claim was also unique in that none of the teachers in the Śrīvaiṣṇava community felt that they were rebelling against Sanskrit tradition; nor did they hold either Veda to be inferior to the other. In the Śrīvaiṣṇava tradition, we see a confluence of two rivers: the coming together of Sanskrit and Tamil cultural traditions and religious literatures.[3]

The Tamil Veda [4]

Over the last two thousand years in the Hindu tradition, several works have been honored with the title Veda or considered to be an upaniṣad. The Bhagavadgītā is said to be an upaniṣad, the Mahābhārata is called the fifth Veda,[5] and some purāṇas have been claimed to be as good as, or better than, the Vedas.[6] It may be argued that the acceptance of the Veda or of a substitute is an important characteristic of the Hindu tradition as a whole and that calling the Tiruvāymoḻi a Veda fits into this accepted pattern. The difference between the other Sanskrit works and the Tiruvāymoḻi, however, is remarkable, because this is a vernacular work and not part of an accepted epic like the Mahābhārata or even a recognizable genre like the purāṇas. The Tiruvāymoḻi is a unique poem, confessional in tone and passionate in spirit, and not quite like any Sanskrit work of the period.

One of the most popular hagiographical works of the thirteenth century, *Guruparamparāprabhāvam* (*The Splendor of Succession of Teachers,* henceforth referred to as *The Splendor*), describes the circumstances which led to the initial revelation of the Tiruvāymoḻi and other works. According to this work, Viṣṇu in all his glory appeared in front of the poet, who was in deep meditation, whereupon Nammāḻvār sang four poems born from his intense enjoyment of visualizing the Lord and his devotees. The four works, says *The Splendor,* are the four Vedas, and the Tiruvāymoḻi is the last and most important of these poems.[7]

The second revelation is described in a later chapter in the same book. The songs of the āḻvārs, *The Splendor* tells us, became lost to human beings and so had to be revealed for a second time: by the poet Nammāḻvār to the first teacher, Nāthamuni, around the tenth century. *The Splendor* narrates his efforts in recovering the lost poems:

> Some Śrīvaiṣṇavas came from the Western country, worshiped [the Lord] Maṉṉār [that is, Viṣṇu] and with grace chanted the Tiruvāymoḻi song [that begins with the words] "O nectar that never satiates. . . ." [TVM 5.8).[8]] Nāthamuni heard this; with great joy he asked them, "You said that these are ten verses out of a thousand; do you know the entire work?" They replied, "We only know these ten songs." [Nāthamuni] then asked, "Is there a sacred text in your land? Are there minstrels to sing it?" They replied: "We only know this; we don't know anything else." [Nāthamuni] gave them holy water and articles blessed by the Lord and bade them farewell. Thinking that this sacred work should be known in the land of Tirukkurukūr where Nammāḻvār lived, he went to that sacred city. He worshiped the āḻvār and the celebrated Lord. He bowed before Śrī Parāṅkuśadāsa, the disciple of Maturakavi āḻvār and asked, "Are there people here who chant the Tiruvāymoḻi? Do you have the sacred texts?" He replied, "The Tiruvāymoḻi and other sacred works have been lost for a long time. My teacher Maturakavi graciously taught me the sacred poem called 'The Short Knotted String.' Our teacher said that if one were to go in front of [Namm]āḻvār alone and with focused thought and subdued senses meditate on his sacred feet, chanting 'The Short Knotted String' repeatedly for twelve thousand times, the āḻvār would be delighted." Nāthamuni bowed down, paid his respects, and prayerfully requested that he be taught the sacred poem. Śrī Parāṅkuśadāsa graciously taught it, reciting with pleasure. Nāthamuni, reciting it, sat under the sacred tamarind tree in front of the āḻvār. With restraint he meditated repeatedly on the poem "The Short Knotted String" twelve thousand times. The āḻvār, pleased with Nāthamuni . . . , asked him . . . , "Why do you meditate so intensely on me?" Nāthamuni submitted, "I want you to take pity on me and [teach] me the Tiruvāymoḻi and other sacred works." The āḻvār, pleased, graciously gave Nāthamuni eyes of divine knowledge. . . . Just as the Supreme Lord graciously gave [the āḻvār] "wisdom and love to cut

> all sorrow" [TVM 1.1.1], he gave Nāthamuni the "three secrets," the Tiruvāymoḻi and the other three thousand verses, the truth of all philosophies, and the secret of the eightfold yoga.[9]

The poems of the second revelation are collectively called the Nālāyira Tivyap Pirapantam (The Sacred Collect of Four Thousand Verses, henceforth The Sacred Collect). Nāthamuni, it is said, instituted the chanting of verses from the The Sacred Collect alongside the Sanskrit Vedas, which alone had been traditionally recited, both in home and temple worship.

This use of the The Sacred Collect alongside the Sanskrit Vedas, as well as statements of the later ācāryas, reinforces the idea that the entire collection of āḻvār poems is the Tamil Veda. The living tradition of the Dual Vedānta is seen most dramatically in rituals. When, for example, the processional image of the Lord is taken through the streets, a group of Śrīvaiṣṇavas chanting the Tamil Veda goes in front of the deity and a group chanting the Sanskrit Vedas follows behind.[10] Also, during daily worship, the Śrīvaiṣṇava switches from Tamil to Sanskrit frequently, and at weddings, funerals, and annual ancestral rites, selections from The Sacred Collect are recited.[11]

Śrīvaiṣṇava theologians state that the poems of the āḻvārs contain the essential meaning of the Sanskrit Vedas. Consider the following statements of Vedānta Deśika, a thirteenth-century theologian, who likens the ten āḻvārs to the ten incarnations of Viṣṇu:

> We clearly understand the unclear Vedas from the songs of joy woven like beautiful Tamil garlands by Poykai [and all the other āḻvārs]. Through them, the Vedas are made manifest all through the world. In the form of Parāṅkuśa, Parakāla [that is, Nammāḻvār and Tirumaṅkai āḻvār], and others, the Lord made ten new incarnations. Like clouds gathering moisture from the ocean and pouring it down as rain for the welfare of all, the essential parts of the meaning of the Vedas were gathered and given to all in a language which everyone was qualified to know.[12]

While all the works of the āḻvārs are said to consistute the Tamil Veda,[13] sometimes specific poems are singled out for that distinction, especially the Tiruvāymoḻi of Nammāḻvār. The Śrīvaiṣṇavas tend to uphold all these statements as conveying the importance of individual works; but on the basis of the number, frequency, and quality of references to that effect in later commentaries, poems, and independent works, we can say that, while all of The Sacred Collect is considered to be revealed, the Tiruvāymoḻi and its author have a special status in the Śrīvaiṣṇava community.[14] In declaring the Tiruvāymoḻi to be *the* Veda, the Śrīvaiṣṇava community stressed the revealed nature of the work and implied that it contained the same themes and concerns as the

Sanskrit Vedas. In a larger sense, it was quite clear that it was not a literal translation of any single Sanskrit work with which it was compared. The notion of translation itself as an attempt to convey the meaning of words or sentences in more or less literal and exact terms seems to have been alien to Hindu theologians. The vernacular versions of the epics (for instance, the Tamil *Rāmāyaṇa* of Kampaṉ or the Kannaḍa work of Pampa) were free renderings of the story as a whole. The poet, writing in his mother tongue, used his poetic license broadly and sometimes included new incidents. However, unlike the Tamil and other vernacular renderings of the Rāmāyaṇa and the Mahābhārata, which followed the main story line of the Sanskrit versions, the Tiruvāymoḻi does not follow the structure of the Vedas, though later theologians went to some length to show that some of the contents were similar. Just as the Sanskrit Vedas were never directly translated into any other language, the Tiruvāymoḻi was also never translated from Tamil. The first undertaking in this direction came only in the nineteenth century when it was rendered into Sanskrit. Instead of translations, the Śrīvaiṣṇava community used other ways to interpret, understand, and spread the message of the poem. Piḷḷāṉ, the first commentator on the poem, rendered certain words and phrases literally into Sanskrit and later theologians also elucidated the verses with Sanskrit phrases. The Tiruvāymoḻi was also summarized in both Sanskrit and Tamil verse; in the thirteenth century, Vedānta Deśika summarized it in Sanskrit verse and called his poem "The Gem-Necklace of the Meaning of the Tamil Upaniṣad" and in the fifteenth century, Maṇavāḷa Māmuṉi wrote the *Tiruvāymoḻi Nūṟṟantāti*. The format of this poem is similar to the Tiruvāymoḻi and the gist of the "thousand verses" is given in a hundred Tamil verses which are connected in structure and content.

The basis for regarding the Tiruvāymoḻi as a revealed text comes from the work itself. Nammāḻvār claims that the Lord sings about himself using the saint as an instrument.

> What can I say of the Lord
> who lifted me up for all time,
> and made me himself, everyday?
> My radiant one, the first one,
> My Lord, sings of himself,
> through me, in sweet Tamil.
>
> (7.9.1)[15]

While the acknowledgment of the Tamil works as the Vedas goes back to Maturakavi āḻvār and to Nāthamuni, according to the Śrīvaiṣṇava tradition, other ācāryas repeated and perpetuated this notion in the laudatory verses that they prefix to the hymns.[16]

The Commentaries

According to tradition (see chapter 5), Rāmānuja authorized his cousin Tirukkurukai Pirāṉ Piḷḷāṉ, the son of Śrī Śaila Pūrṇa, to write a commentary on the Tiruvāymoḻi. In the next generation, Nañjīyar wrote a commentary on the Tiruvāymoḻi and the Tiruppāvai; till the time of Periyavāccāṉ Piḷḷai, in the thirteenth century, no other commentary on any work from the Sacred Collect was committed to writing.

The writing of a commentary on the Tiruvāymoḻi marks a new epoch in Hindu literature. While commentaries were frequently written in Sanskrit for Sanskrit literary and religious works, the commentarial tradition in Tamil began only about the eighth century C.E.[17] No Hindu religious work in the vernacular had been deemed worthy of a written commentary, although a strong oral tradition on the Tiruvāymoḻi had probably existed even before Piḷḷāṉ committed one to writing for the first time.[18]

Why was the commentary committed to writing in the late eleventh century C.E.? From *The Splendor* as well as from the later commentaries on the Tiruvāymoḻi, we know that Yāmuna, Rāmānuja, and several other ācāryas commented upon it orally and that this oral tradition existed prior to the writing of the Piḷḷāṉ's commentary. Nāthamuni, the first ācārya, is said to have divided the Tamil poems, setting some to music and others to recitation. The Śrīvaiṣṇava community understood this to be an act that emphasized the equivalency of the poems to the Sanskrit Vedas. *The Splendor* says that just as the legendary sage, Veda Vyāsa, divided up the Sanskrit Vedas into udātta and anudātta,[19] so Nāthamuni set the Tamil poems to divine music and divided them into icai (music) and iyal (chant). The act of setting them to a form of music and chant like the Vedas and introducing them into liturgy was itself a ritual commentary on the poems, one which emphasized the equality of the Sanskrit and the Tamil Vedas. Nāthamuni is said to have transmitted the proper chanting of the Tiruvāymoḻi to his disciples and *The Splendor* specifically mentions that one of them, Uyyakoṇṭār, was given the task of disseminating the Tiruvāymoḻi and the other works of the āḻvārs.[20] The oral commentarial tradition must have become popular by the time of Yāmuna and his opinions have been preserved in the longer written commentaries on the Tiruvāymoḻi.

It was Rāmānuja who gave permission for Tirukkurukai Pirāṉ Piḷḷāṉ to record the commentary for the first time and we may speculate about the reasons which made him endorse this task. It is possible that Rāmānuja wanted the opinions of the earlier ācāryas to be preserved for posterity, and committing the texts to writing ensured that they would not be forgotten. He may have also believed that the comments and opinions of earlier ācāryas would add to the flavor of the community's understanding of the poems. According to *The Splendor,* there had been an earlier incident in Rāmānuja's life which, we believe, may have led to his decision to record the commentary. Apparently, while learning the meaning of the Tiruvāymoḻi from Tirumālai Āṇṭāṉ, Rāmānuja differed from his teacher's interpretation of the verses several times, offering alternate explanations. After Rāmānuja offered a different interpretation for 2.3.4, his teacher ceased his instruction, saying that these were mischievous explanations, which he had not heard from Yāmuna. The stalemate was resolved by another disciple of Yāmuna, Tirukōṭṭiyūr Nampi, who reconciled the teacher and disciple by proclaiming that *he* had heard the alternate interpretation from Yāmuna. What is interesting to note is that Rāmānuja's position had to be vindicated by another teacher's recollection of Yāmuna's commentary, and there was no text against which to check it. *The Splendor* goes on to say that at a later time, Tirumālai Āṇṭāṉ again hesitated to accept a certain interpretation, but Rāmānuja said that he was a disciple of Yāmuna as the legendary Ekalavya was a disciple of Droṇa: a student who learnt from a master in spirit, without actually ever being in his presence.[21] So, even when there was no witness to attest that Rāmānuja's opinion had been stated earlier by Yāmuna, the community assumed that whatever Rāmānuja said would have been said by or at least permitted by Yāmuna. *The Splendor*'s account of Rāmānuja's learning the Tiruvāymoḻi gives us a glimpse of the transmission of the poem, which, at this stage, still seems to have been on the model of private tuition rather than public oration to a Śrīvaiṣṇava audience. The commentarial tradition certainly did become that in later years and we hear of large audiences listening to the ācāryas' exposition of the Tamil poems.

Rāmānuja's permission to allow the commentary to be written, therefore, may have stemmed from his desire to preserve all possible alternate opinions in writing, so that later generations might know that these opinions, and others within reason, were admissible. Similarly, by not writing the commentary himself, Rāmānuja made sure that the line of commentaries on these hymns, which were meant to be experienced and enjoyed by all, would keep growing. Rāmānuja's comments were considered authoritative and would have been held to be the final word on a topic; and it seems probable that the teacher wanted to encourage a chain of commentaries, rather than establish one set of correct interpretations. Usually commentaries preserved the correct interpretations and opinions on a text; interestingly enough, the commentaries on the Tiruvāymoḻi preserve a diversity of opinions. However, it is important to note that the diversity of the opinions did not at any time involve important theological issues pertaining to the supremacy of Viṣṇu, his "wholly auspicious nature," and so forth, but usually reflected the flavor of the teachers' enjoyment of the poem.

The recording of the commentary also allowed for the elaboration of doctrine and the strengthening of the understanding of the Dual Vedānta. The need to interpret and comment arises when something is not self-evident. The language of the Tiruvāymoḻi itself was easily understandable; the concept that had to be communicated to the audience was something already present by virtue of Nāthamuni's incorporation of the hymn into liturgy: that this poem was equivalent to the Sanskrit Veda. One of the principal tasks of the commentarial tradition seems to have been the establishment of this concept. The commentaries are directed to an audience which is familiar with both the Sanskrit Vedas and Tamil verses. The lengthiest comments occur either when there are issues of doctrinal importance to be proclaimed or when there are parallels in Sanskrit literature; we see important examples in the comments on 1.1.7 and 4.10.1 where the supremacy of Viṣṇu is emphasized. Here, there are long lists of quotations from Sanskrit Vedas and later literature; the written commentary records and preserves these lists of quotations, thus reiterating the notion of the Dual Vedānta. An important part of the commentator's agenda seems to have been the highlighting of this concept and proclaiming the authority of the Tiruvāymoḻi. By both verbal and ritual comment, therefore, the Tiruvāymoḻi was exalted as the Tamil Veda.

Piḷḷāṉ's commentary is called the *Āṟāyirappaṭi* or the *Six Thousand Paṭi*s, while later commentaries are called the *Nine Thousand Paṭi*s, *Twelve Thousand Paṭi*s, *Twenty-four Thousand Paṭi*s and the *Thirty-six Thousand Paṭi*s. The numbers refer to the number of paṭis, a literary unit of 32 syllables. Thus, Piḷḷāṉ's commentary has 32 × 6,000 syllables and was numerically modeled on a Sanskrit work of the same length, the Viṣṇu Purāṇa. This self-conscious modeling is, of course, significant in the twofold Sanskrit-Tamil tradition.[22]

Piḷḷāṉ's commentary highlighted and articulated certain ideas that challenged traditional norms of Hindu culture without rebelling against them. The very fact that he wrote a commentary on a hymn that was in Tamil and had been composed by a person who was believed to have been from the Fourth Class was an unprecedented act. The writing of the commentary challenged two claims made by traditional Hindu society: the belief in Sanskrit as the exclusive vehicle for revelation and theological communication, and the importance of the hierarchical class system which denied salvific knowledge to the Śūdra. This latter point was openly refuted by Piḷḷāṉ's assumption that Nammāḻvār was the ideal devotee who is always at the Lord's feet, whose name, in fact, was synonymous with the Lord's grace. The close connection between Nammāḻvār and divine grace is articulated by a ritual included in Śrīvaiṣṇava temple practice. A silver crown engraved with the feet of the Lord is placed on the head of every devotee; the feet symbolize the grace of the Lord, and the crown itself is called Śaṭhāri, which is a name of Nammāḻvār. The first written reference to this ritual, significantly enough, is in Piḷḷāṉ's commentary.[23]

Piḷḷāṉ wrote his commentary in maṇipravāḷa, a new hybrid language of communication used in Śrīvaiṣṇava circles. *Maṇipravāḷa* means "gems and corals" or "pearls and corals" and refers to a combination of Sanskrit and

Tamil. Unlike other forms of maṇipravāḷa,[24] the Śrīvaiṣṇava variety always retained Tamil grammar and endings even though the sentences were heavily interspersed with Sanskrit words. The language of the commentary itself gave the message effectively, proclaiming the equivalency of the Sanskrit and Tamil languages and literatures. This style of communicating—in speech and in writing—flourishes even today in the Śrīvaiṣṇava community.

The importance given to vernacular languages only grew in India after the twelfth century C.E., following the South Indian precedent. Hinduism, which prides itself on its self-conscious continuity with the Vedic Indo-European culture—ultimately going back to the primal moment of creation—owes more to its Dravidian genes than is formally acknowledged; thus, one can conceive of Hinduism itself as a product of cultures for which we can use the shorthand names Indo-European and Dravidian: the cultures of the Indus and Gangetic plains, on the one hand; the Kāvēri and the Vaikai, on the other.[25]

The Śrīvaiṣṇava tradition as recorded in the maṇipravāḷa commentary of Piḷḷāṉ and as practiced today can be seen as a striking product of the languages and cultures that grew up around the rivers Gaṅgā and the Kāvēri. The Śrīvaiṣṇava community articulates the terms of the dual heritage clearly, but in the process of accepting two models of thinking, moves away from the primary concerns of both and sets its own priorities. In our search for the beginnings of this dual heritage, we shall focus on the Tamil Veda: the Tiruvāymoḻi and its first maṇipravāḷa commentary, the *Āṟāyirappaṭi* or *The Six Thousand,* written by Tirukkurukai Pirāṉ Piḷḷāṉ, a disciple and cousin of Rāmānuja. We hope that this study will aid in the exploration of Śrīvaiṣṇava history and will be a first step in a new kind of historical study of all the major Śrīvaiṣṇava commentaries on the āḻvārs' hymns.

The Serpent and the Eagle: Tamil and Sanskrit Literatures in Praise of Viṣṇu

In myth and iconography, temple worship and popular calendar art, Viṣṇu is represented as being served by an eagle, Garuḍa, and a serpent, Ananta or Śeṣa. Just as the serpent and the eagle are combined in iconography and theological reflection, the Śrīvaiṣṇavas combined the Tamil and Sanskrit languages and heritage in the formation of a new maṇipravāḷa style of communication as well as a whole new way of life. Garuḍa is the mount on which Viṣṇu travels, and his image is directly in front of the inner shrine in most Śrīvaiṣṇava temples. On the other hand, in many temples, Viṣṇu is depicted as reclining on a giant five-headed serpent. In some pictures, Viṣṇu rides Garuḍa whose talons hold a serpent—a picture which gives the theological message that the deity is all-pervasive (viṣṇu), simultaneously present in the aerial and terrestrial realms. Garuḍa and Ananta symbolize that ancient polarity between the celestial and earthly forces.

In Śrīvaiṣṇava mythology, the two creatures, antagonistic even in early

Hindu tales,[26] are reconciled in the common goal of serving Viṣṇu. The very first paragraph of Piḷḷāṉ's *Six Thousand* commentary says, ". . . the Lord with all auspicious attributes shows his generosity to the serpent, Garuḍa and others. . . ."[27]

In Sanskrit literature, Garuḍa is the personification of the Vedas and wisdom;[28] on the other hand, the serpent Ananta (literally, "without end") symbolizes eternity. The term *ananta* might well be applied to the continuous, "endless" line of commentaries in which the community relives and re-experiences the emotions of the āḻvārs. Sanskrit literature, on the other hand, is perceived as embodying one truth for all time—after Rāmānuja's commentaries on the Bhagavadgītā and the Brahma Sūtras, no Śrīvaiṣṇava wrote another commentary on them.[29] One may carry the analogy a little further: just as Viṣṇu harnesses the celestial and terrestrial forces for his service, the Śrīvaiṣṇava utilizes Sanskrit and Tamil literatures in worship of the deity. Just as his Lord rides the eagle to travel to distant places to help his devotee,[30] the Śrīvaiṣṇava uses Sanskrit to communicate with theologians all over India. But Viṣṇu, in the privacy of his temple at Śrīraṅgam, the heart of Śrīvaiṣṇava culture, reclines on the coils of the serpent which is his couch, warm and intimate as one's favorite armchair. And so too, in the familiar milieu of "the Tamil land, where musicians and devotees can sing and proclaim about the Lord who is wonderfully auspicious" (1.5.11), the Śrīvaiṣṇava uses Tamil, the language that he is most accustomed to, in expressing the joys of serving the Lord like the paradigmatic, eternal servant, Śeṣa-Ananta. Commenting on the polarity between Garuḍa and Śeṣa, Heinrich Zimmer says: "This is paradox with a reason; for Vishnu is the Absolute, the all-containing Divine Essence. He comprises all dichotomies. The Absolute becomes differentiated in polarized manifestations, and through these the vital tensions of the world process are brought into existence and maintained."[31] For the Śrīvaiṣṇava community, it is this Viṣṇu who brings into existence the Sanskrit and Tamil Vedas; these, then, form the basis for its theology and shape its world view.

2

The Āḻvārs and Their Sweet Tamil Songs

Introduction

The Tiruvāymoḻi is a complex and powerful composition. It begins and ends with triumphant notes of union between the Lord and the poet. For about a thousand verses there are separations, patient and anguished expectations, longing, missed meetings, gentle unions, brisk happy lines, exhortations to the world at large, and slow melancholy passages. And yet the end is reached with a sense of majestic inevitability, a sense that thwarted expectations are finally fulfilled with grandeur and grace.

Perhaps the closest analogy to the experience of reading the Tiruvāymoḻi would be the emotional and intellectual satisfaction, both sensuous and sublime, that one may derive from auditory participation in a Beethoven symphony or a complex rāga. Like the musical composition, the Tiruvāymoḻi makes demands on its audience; complex themes lead the audience through a long journey of latent and articulated expectations, resistances, delays, and uncertainties. Leonard Meyer, in *Music: The Arts and Ideas,* says that sometimes an uncertainty is slight and evanescent, as when a chromatic note is introduced within a central cadential progression or when the portamento of a violinist delays the arrival of a substantive (expected) tone ever so little. At other times uncertainty may reach heroic proportions. The tremendous impact of the new theme, when it arrives, is clearly a product of the uncertainty of the antecedent situation.[1] One could use similiar terminology to describe the Tiruvāymoḻi. The uncertainties of the (expected) meetings with the Lord provoke behavior in Nammāḻvār varying from quiet longing to anxious frenzy. When the Lord finally arrives, the relief and impact are felt in brilliant clarity. The power of the Tiruvāymoḻi, at least in part, lies in witnessing this journey of Nammāḻvār. A tonal progression or theme which moves in an expected way without deviation or resistance is said to be a musical cliché quite banal in its information value. Value in music seems to have "something to do with the activation of a musical impulse having tendencies toward a . . . definite goal and with the temporary resistance or inhibition of these tendencies."[2] We suggest this analogy as one mode of apprehending the grandeur of the Tiruvāymoḻi. Like a piece of sophisticated music, the pace of gratification is slow in the Tiruvāymoḻi. There are many distant departures from the certainty and repose of the tonic note (or state of union in the Tiruvāymoḻi) and lengthy delays in the fulfillment. The tonal repertory of Nammāḻvār is scintillating.

The analogy with great music need not stop here. Three aspects of musical enjoyment—the sensuous, the associative, and the syntactical characteristics—would be applicable to the Tiruvāymoḻi. Just as in music, where brief musical events on a higher architectonic level are part of larger musical sections, so in the Tiruvāymoḻi each verse is part of ten verses; this becomes one segment in a block of a hundred verses, and ten sets of these are eventually linked by content and themes in physical and structural blocks. This chapter will present some of the connections and weaving patterns by presenting the Tiruvāymoḻi in the context of earlier classical romantic (akam) and heroic (puṟam) Tamil poetry in order to show some of the powerful references and associations that would occur to an audience familiar with the classical Tamil tradition: the uncertainties and ultimate fulfillment of Nammāḻvār's love will be viewed against a backdrop of Tamil notions of romance and war.

The Tamil Heritage and the Works of the Āḻvārs

The bhakti movement began in South India about the sixth century C.E. when several saints wandered from temple to temple singing the praise of Viṣṇu or Śiva. The twelve devotees of Viṣṇu who are recognized as poet-saints by the Śrīvaiṣṇava community were called the āḻvārs and the sixty-three devotees of Śiva were known as nāyaṉmārs. Tirumaṅkai āḻvār and Nammāḻvār wrote over half of the four thousand verses that forms the Divya Prabandham or Sacred Collect for the Śrīvaiṣṇava community.[3] For the first time within Hinduism, devotion was expressed in a mother tongue, a "language . . . continuous with the language of one's earliest childhood and family, one's local folk and folklore."[4] Unlike Sanskrit, it was a spoken language, associated with powerful emotions, and the deity of the Tamil hymns was brought close to the worshipers by language fraught with the tender words used for beloved ones. The Tamil songs of devotion glorify the inaccessible Lord who became accessible to human beings; while the "Sanskrit" God is distant, the "Tamil" God is the distant one who makes himself close to his devotees and who is as close as the nearest temple, where he graciously abides.

Before the composition of the bhakti hymns, Tamil had a long history of sophisticated poems, grammar, and drama. A. K. Ramanujan observes the following about earlier Tamil poems:

> In their antiquity and in their contemporaneity, there is not much else in any Indian literature equal to these quiet and dramatic Tamil poems. In their values and stances, they represent a mature classical poetry: passion is balanced by courtesy, transparency by ironies and nuances of de-

> sign, impersonality by vivid detail, leanness of line by richness of implication. These poems are not just the earliest evidence of the Tamil genius. The Tamils, in all their 2,000 years of literary effort, wrote nothing better.[5]

There are many legends about the origin of this Tamil culture; almost all of them trace it back to a sage called Agastya. A late myth explains the beginning in a curious way. A divine marriage was to take place and the whole world was going to the reception. The weight of all beings was to be concentrated in one area and there was fear that the earth—imagined at the time to be a giant teeter-totter—would become permanently tilted. To maintain the balance, the sage Agastya, a gentleman of short and rather squat stature, was sent to the south of India. Agastya came, bringing with him a wife and the Tamil language that had been communicated to him by the god Śiva. According to a Buddhist version of the tale, Agastya was taught Tamil by the bodhisattva Avalokita.[6] Agastya is credited with spreading "culture" to the south; his disciple Tolkāppiyar is said to have written the first Tamil grammar *Tolkāppiyam.* The Tamil people continued the legend: Agastya started the three great *Caṅkam*s ("Academies"), involving the Tamil poets and literati. The first Caṅkam, it is said, lasted 4,440 years; the second Caṅkam is said to have lasted 3,700 years; and the third a mere 1,850 years. Agastya is also credited with dividing Tamil literature into three major categories: iyal (prose, poetry, grammar, or anything to be read); icai (that which is to be sung); and nāṭakam (that which is to be performed and acted).[7] We shall see that this division is of some significance in the early life of the bhakti poetry in the Śrīvaiṣṇava community.

The myth itself is significant in that it ascribes the beginnings of Tamil culture to Agastya, a sage mentioned as early as the Ṛig Veda, reaffirming the ironic fact that at many times in the history of the Tamil language, acceptance was sought by claiming a connection to the Sanskrit tradition, in this case, a figure in Sanskrit scripture. It is undeniable that even in the earliest written material, which is probably the original stratum of the *Tolkāppiyam,*[8] we find similarities to Sanskrit literature. The *Tolkāppiyam,* which is (in part) a Tamil grammar, is said to have many parallels to Sanskrit grammatical works.[9] The Caṅkam poems which follow chronologically have many loan myths and words from Sanskrit. And yet, Tamil literature is on the whole neither imitative of, nor derived from, early Sanskrit material. Tamil literature includes the earliest and some of the most unique compositions among the non-Āryan languages of India. Records of Tamil writing in the old Brāhmī script go back to inscriptions of the third century B.C.E.[10] The earliest extant compositions following the *Tolkāppiyam* and the other grammars are sophisticated poems known as the *Eṭṭutokai* (*Eight Anthologies*) and the *Pattuppāṭṭu* (*Ten Songs*). The earliest compositions from this corpus date back to the first to third centuries C.E. The later parts of this collection, along with the *Patineṇkīḻkaṇakku* (*Eighteen Short Classics*), which includes the didactic *Tirukkuraḷ*, were finished before the sixth century C.E.

The earliest sections of the *Eight Anthologies* and *Ten Songs* deal primarily with two themes: akam (referring to romantic love) and puṟam (frequently referring to chivalry and war).[11] The early poems were unique in that they were not religious or moralistic in tone. Zvelebil correctly comments: "What is so important about these poems is that they are the only example of Indian secular literature dating from so ancient a period."[12] And yet, these works had been lost for over a thousand years and were rediscovered in the nineteenth century primarily through the efforts of S. V. Damodaran Pillai and U. V. Swaminatha Aiyar.[13] In contradistinction to these secular poems of chivalry and romance from the classical age, the later bhakti hymns of the āḻvārs and the nāyaṉmārs have, at least since their revelation in the tenth century C.E., maintained a significant place in the piety and ritual calendar of the Vaiṣṇava and Śaiva devotees. The devotional hymns have been studied, appreciated, committed to memory, recited, enacted, enjoyed, and commented upon orally (or in writing) in every generation since the time of the preceptors.

The Caṅkam poems (also known as the poems of the classical age or the bardic corpus), dealing with romantic or heroic themes, refer to five basic situations. These situations correspond in poetry to five landscape settings (tiṇai), for each of which there are appropriate birds, flowers, times, and gods. The five basic settings for akam are love-making, waiting anxiously for a beloved, separation, patient waiting of a wife, and anger at a lover's real or imagined infidelity. These correspond to the mountainous (kuriñci), seaside (neytal), arid (pālai), pastoral (mullai), and agricultural (marutam) landscapes.[14] In these poems, trees, flowers, birds, landscapes, and gods were fitted into a symbolic mesh, each expressing a mood, attitude, or situation in love and war. A reference to the seashore, for example, meant that there was a separation between lovers; the jasmine plant indicated the patient waiting of the dutiful wife for her husband; the mountains indicated a rapturous union. A poem had an underlying structure of meaning understood by everyone in the tradition. Consider the following example. A patient wife tells her husband:

> You come from the lands by the gem-colored sea. The jasmine plant, rich in pollen and covered with thorns that are sharp as the squirrel's teeth, grows there.
>
> If this state of life should change and we are born again, may you continue to be my husband and I your beloved.
>
> (*Kuṟuntokai* 49)

Ostensibly these are the statements of a happy and dutiful wife hoping that she and her husband will be together in all their future lives. The references to the sea and the plant, however, indicate the underlying tension. The sea indicates that there has been suffering in separation; the flower, that the wife has been patiently waiting; the thorns, the sharp pain inflicted by the circumstances of the separation; the pollen, the virility and the inherent attraction of the husband. And so, we have a more complex picture: the audience understands that the wife and the husband have been separated; the behavior of the virile husband has caused her grief (which in the Tamil context would mean that he has been cohabitating with women of questionable reputation); however, she dutifully expresses her desire always to be his spouse.

In Tamil literature written between the fourth and fifth centuries C.E., there are many works authored by Buddhists and Jains. In the Tamil drama *Maṇimēkalai* (*The Jeweled Girdle*), the heroine, the daughter of a courtesan, becomes a Buddhist nun. The *Tirukkuraḷ,* a book of moral aphorisms, could have been authored by either a Jain or a Hindu. There are also many Sanskrit loanwords in these Tamil texts.[15]

Devotional poems were written between the fourth and fifth centuries C.E. A hymn in the *Paripāṭal* (included in an anthology of early classical poetry, but probably later than most other poems in that collection) addresses the deity thus:

> In fire, you are the heat; in blossoms, the fragrance;
> among the stones, you are the diamond; in speech, truth;
> among virtues, you are love; in valor—strength;
> in the Veda, you are the secret; among elements, the primordial;
> in the burning sun, the light; in moonlight, its sweetness;
> You are all, and you are the substance and meaning of all.[16]

After the seventh century C.E., the devotional movement gained momentum. The devotees of Śiva and Viṣṇu drew freely upon their Tamil heritage. Of the twelve devotee-poets of Viṣṇu, the one most revered by the Śrīvaiṣṇava community since the tenth century C.E. is Nammāḻvār,[17] a Śūdra born in a Veḷḷāla family.[18]

Nammāḻvār in Traditional Biography and Ritual

The traditional biography of Nammāḻvār as given in the thirteenth-century hagiography, *The Splendor,* lists the calendrical details of his birth and the names of his seven forefathers, emphasizing that they were all devotees of Viṣṇu.[19] The Lord at Tirukkuruṅkuṭi answered the prayers of Nammāḻvār's parents and said that he would be born as their son. The story is then picked up in the biography of Maturakavi āḻvār. The newborn child did not eat or cry. After ten days his parents took him to the temple, named him Māṟaṉ, and raised him under a sacred tamarind tree, which is reported to be an incarnation of Ananta, the cosmic serpent on which Viṣṇu reclines. The boy stayed under the tree for sixteen years and his parents were convinced that he did not speak because there was no one else as spiritually qualified as he.

Meanwhile, Maturakavi āḻvār, who was on a northern pilgrimage, saw a light in the sky; after a few days, he was convinced that the light was divine and followed it south. It went beyond Śrīraṅgam and disappeared when he reached Tirukkurukūr. Here he searched and, under the tamarind tree that never closed its leaves, he saw a sixteen-year-old boy sitting in a lotus posture with his eyes closed. This was Nammāḻvār.

To find out if the boy was conscious, Maturakavi āḻvār threw a pebble at him. Startled, Nammāḻvār opened his eyes. Maturakavi āḻvār posed a question: "If a little thing is born in the stomach of a dead thing, what will it eat and where will it lie?" This question is normally paraphrased by the Śrīvaiṣṇava community as: "When the soul (ātmā) becomes associated with a body, how will it subsist?" Nammāḻvār answered softly, breaking the silence of sixteen years: "It will feed on that and live there." This answer is variously interpreted as "it will assume an earthly body and subsist on food" or "it will be nourished by God and abide in God."[20] Whatever the interpretation, Maturakavi āḻvār was convinced of Nammāḻvār's wisdom. Subsequently, the Lord appeared before Nammāḻvār, revealed his divine nature, his handsome form, auspicious qualities, and other divine attributes. Out of the love born from this experience, Nammāḻvār burst into song. He first composed the Tiruviruttam, the Tiruvāciriyam, and the Periya Tiruvantāti which, according to *The Splendor,* have the essence of the Ṛig, Yajur, and Atharva Vedas. Finally came the Tiruvāymoḻi, which is said to contain the essential meaning of the Sāma Veda.[21] According to some accounts, Nammāḻvār lived for thirty-five years, and after his "attainment of release," Maturakavi āḻvār established festivals to honor his teacher.[22] Śrīvaiṣṇava hagiographies say that Nammāḻvār sang all his songs while immersed in yoga under a divine tamarind tree and that the presiding deities of all the various holy places appeared in front of him. The commentators on the Tiruvāymoḻi, however, speak about his going to the various places, and either "gaining union" with the Lord there, or moving on to a different place, disappointed.[23] Recent Śrīvaiṣṇava scholarship has also reiterated this and acknowledged that he must have traveled to all the shrines.[24]

Śrīvaiṣṇavas frequently refer to Nammāḻvār as "Māṟaṉ, who rendered the Vedas in Tamil."[25] In the fourteenth century, Maṇavāḷa Māmuṉi, a very important Śrīvaiṣṇava teacher and theologian, wrote:

> In that wonderful month of Vaikāci
> When the star Viśakha was ascending,
> the handsome lord of Kurukūr
> the precious lord, the true one,
> who rendered the Vedas in Tamil, was born.

I speak of the grandeur of that day
so the people of this earth may know.
(*Upadeśaratnamālai*, v. 14)

The Śrīvaiṣṇavas believe that he was the incarnation of Viṣṇu, his sacred jewel (kaustubha), and his divine commander in chief, Viśvaksena, but do not attempt to reconcile these various statements.[26] One may say that these statements were made at different times to indicate the special status of Nammāḻvār and to emphasize that he was more than just a human being. The poet was celebrated in songs composed in his honor over the centuries. A work called *Caṭakōpar antāti* attributed to the renowned Tamil poet Kampaṉ is well known in the Śrīvaiṣṇava community and is sometimes published in editions of the Sacred Collect. A hagiographical composition called *Nammāḻvār Tirutāllāṭṭu* (*Lullaby for Nammāḻvār*), composed around the thirteenth century C.E., glorifies the childhood of the poet in the medium of a folk song.

Images of Nammāḻvār are installed in almost all Śrīvaiṣṇava temples and he receives special honors several times a year. In daily worship his name is synonymous with the feet of Viṣṇu. The little crown inscribed with the feet of Viṣṇu is called Śaṭhāri, another name of Nammāḻvār, and it is this crown that is ceremoniously placed on the devotee's head to indicate the bestowal of divine grace. Nammāḻvār's role in liturgy and theology is perceived to be that of mediation between the Lord and the devotee. By becoming the master for Maturakavi āḻvār, he becomes the spiritual teacher of Nāthamuni and the rest of the Śrīvaiṣṇava community. While achieving salvation, he remains as an indispensable link between human beings and the Lord. A ritual culminating the chanting of the Tiruvāymoḻi during the annual Festival of Chanting illustrates this notion. When the penultimate decad of the Tiruvāymoḻi which describes Nammāḻvār's ascent to heaven is chanted, the image of the poet (who is dressed in white, to symbolize his death) is placed at the feet of the Lord. The poet's head is made to touch the divine feet and both are covered with tuḻāi (tulsi) leaves. The verses in Tiruvāymoḻi 10.9 are chanted twice and then the leaves are removed, and Nammāḻvār is, in a sense, returned to humanity. Having reached salvation, he is yet one with the living, drawing them to the feet of the Lord, where he abides. Through his presence and by the sacred words that he spoke—words that are considered divine, yet spoken in a human voice (*tiru vāy moḻi*)—he binds the devotee to the Lord and becomes the person in whom the divine and the human realms intersect.[27]

The Tiruvāymoḻi

Of the songs of Nammāḻvār, we have noted that the Tiruvāymoḻi has been exalted above all other works. It has 1,102 verses but is usually spoken of as being 1,000 verses long. The poem is divided into 10 sections (pattu) of about 100 verses each. Each hundred is divided into 10 decads (tiruvāymoḻi)[28] of 10 verses (pācuram) each. Thus we have:

10 sections × 10 decads × 10 verses = 1,000 verses

However, to each decad of 10 verses is added an extra verse called a phala śruti; this indicates the benefits that will ensue if one recites or even hears the poem. A hundred phala śruti verses added to the original 1,000 brings us to 1,100. There is one decad of verses (2.7) in the Tiruvāymoḻi which recounts twelve names of Viṣṇu, one in each verse, so this set is a numerical oddity, having 13 verses rather than the usual 11. This brings the total to 1,102 verses in the Tiruvāymoḻi. A special feature of the poem is that it is in the style of an antāti: that is, the last words of one verse form the opening words of the next one. This is carried on through all 1,102 verses and the last words of the very last verse of the poem are also the words with which it begins. The poem itself is like a garland woven lovingly to encircle the Lord, a point made several times by Nammāḻvār himself.

The poems were meant to be set to music and sung. Nammāḻvār says that these "thousand songs are to be spread abroad by people of the Tamil land, musicians and devotees" (1.5.11); he calls it a "garland of music" (3.2.11). He later claims that the Lord sang "songs filled with melody about himself" through Nammāḻvār (10.7.5).[29] *The Splendor* states that the preceptor Nāthamuni had them set to music after their revelation. Nāthamuni divided the collected works of the āḻvārs into icai (musical works) and iyal (that which is to be recited); and while some sections were chanted, others were set to music and performed on a regular basis. Most editions of the Sacred Collect specify the rāga in which the verses are traditionally sung. It has been an ongoing tradition for several centuries to render different versions of these songs in South Indian music and dance.[30]

The deity who is addressed in these poems—Viṣṇu—is one who is exalted in Sanskrit myth and epic; and yet, curiously enough, Viṣṇu is himself a symbol of the coalescence between Tamil and Sanskrit literatures. Nammāḻvār's poems are addressed to Tirumāl or Māyōṉ, "the dark one," the god of the mullai landscape and of Caṅkam poems. Sanskrit myths are known to Nammāḻvār, and he alludes to them frequently,[31] but it is Viṣṇu cast in the role of a king and a lover, reminiscent of the heroes of the war and love poems of the ancient Tamil, that we encounter here. Also, the devotion to the deity here is strong, vibrant, and colorful. While devotion appears in Sanskrit literature, especially the epics (which are themselves a product of both Indo-European and non-Āryan cultures), it is almost bland when compared to the variety that we encounter in the Tamil hymns. Drawing upon classical Tamil poetry, the conventions are adapted to the devotional milieu. Historically, the movement is significant; later Sanskrit literature produced in the South—like the

Bhāgavata Purāṇa—is strikingly "South Indian" and it is this Purāṇa which is very influential in the devotional movements of North India in the centuries to follow.[32]

In a curious attempt to show the continuity of Nammāḻvār's works with the classical period (just as the Śrīvaiṣṇavas strained to show its parallels to Sanskrit literature), an anachronistic tale is recounted in the thirteenth-century hagiography *The Splendor.*[33] The story goes that before Nammāḻvār could be accepted as "the lord who rendered the Vedas in Tamil," some students of the Caṅkam poets came and asked that his words be defended in a fair debate and that he should mount the "Caṅkam seat." Apparently the Caṅkam seat (caṅkappalakai) was a miraculous plank that was capable of accommodating only the most brilliant of scholars and was believed to have been granted to the ancient Caṅkam poets by Śiva. According to the story, when Nammāḻvār was invited to mount this seat, Maturakavi āḻvār replied that his master would not leave his meditation under the tree. Instead, Maturakavi wrote down the words "the feet of Kaṇṇaṉ" (10.5.1) and gave these words to the students to represent Nammāḻvār at the Caṅkam academy. When these words were tested, they were placed on one side of the caṅkappalakai, and three hundred Caṅkam poets, it is said, stood on the other side. The caṅkappalakai apparently threw off the three hundred poets and only the words of Nammāḻvār were held aloft. This miraculous event convinced the head of the Caṅkam academy of Nammāḻvār's greatness.

It is interesting that this tale was recorded in the thirteenth century when the classical poems had long ceased to be the object of any study. While there is no historic value in the anecdote (the Caṅkam academy and the poets probably existed about six or seven hundred years before Nammāḻvār), it is significant that the Śrīvaiṣṇavas did not stop at showing Sanskrit–Tamil parallels in the Tiruvāymoḻi. The story shows how highly they valued their Tamil antecedents and reflects a desire to understand the Tiruvāymoḻi as being continuous with the classical age of Tamil poetry and of a literary calibre that met with the approval of the poets of the Caṅkam academy. The heroic (puṟam) and erotic (akam) elements in Nammāḻvār's poems are striking.[34] We shall confine ourselves to showing a few important themes from earlier classical literature that are adapted to a devotional context in the Tiruvāymoḻi.

Puṟam Elements in the Tiruvāymoḻi

From the Tamil poems to the devotional literature there is a gradual transition: the generosity of the protector-king becomes the generosity of God, the protector; the chastity and exclusive love that the heroines had in love poems is applied to the exclusive love that the human has for the Lord.

Praising the King and Lord

The bard spoke of the king protecting the land ("You guard the land like the tiger watching her cub") and destroying enemies; the āḻvār speaks of the Lord vanquishing his enemies (for example, 7.4) and, more directly, conquering the āḻvār himself with his grace ("With gentle grace he conquers my heart and enters it" 9.6.5) and destroying his sins and ignorance. The bard speaks of the strong fortresses of the king; the āḻvār frequently says: "My Lord's feet are my fortress" (8.4.5). The old bard praised and delighted in the exploits of the king, singing of his gallant deeds:

> His army roars more than the seven seas.
> The elephants trumpet and thunder
> louder than the clapping rain clouds.
> Who is the victim, caught in the hands
> of this brave king . . . ?
>
> (*Puṟanāṉūṟu* 81)

Nammāḻvār exults in the victories of Viṣṇu:

> When our Lord managed
> that spectacular Bhārata war,
> what noises!
>
> Noise of well-fed wrestlers
> falling in combat,
> the jitter
> of whole armies
> of regal men,
>
> and the noises of the gods
> jostling in heaven
> to watch the fun!
>
> (7.4.5)
> (Translated by A. K. Ramanujan)[35]

Nammāḻvār praises the military prowess of Viṣṇu several times. The killing of Rāvaṇa and other demons are frequently referred to and the recollection of the Lord's vanquishing of his enemies seems to reassure the āḻvār of the Lord's might and grace.

The King's Generosity and Grace

In classical Tamil heroic poems, the bard spoke of his own poverty, praised the king's bravery and generosity, and asked the king to be generous:

"My days and years of living are many,
my life does not end."
My mother complains again and again.
My wife's body has faded; she has no peace.
In her misery, she plucks from the spinach plant on the heap
a young shoot not yet grown,...
she cooks it in saltless water....
Your fame is such
that you can make my mother and wife happy,....
giving like a cloud pouring down lightning and roaring thunder....
My whole family that now suffers from hunger
you could make happy....
I who sing you ask this gracious act of you,
O Lord of exalted fame,
born in a faultless line renowned for its victories.

(*Puṟanāṉūṟu* 159)
(Translated by George Hart)[36]

Nammāḻvār praises the actions of the Lord—creation, or any particular act of redemption or grace—and then speaks of his own human, sinful predicament and asks the Lord to bless him with a vision, to end his sins or grant that he may serve him:

Creator of the three waters and the worlds!
O Lord, with the color of the sea!
I whirl in the body that you gave me
that day; I have lost my way.
I know not when the day is
when you will cut my sins (viṉai)[37] at their roots
so the agony of these seething days will go,
and I shall reach your sacred feet.

(3.2.1)

This acknowledgment of one's helplessness and spiritual poverty is contrasted with the Lord's supremacy and power. He had the power to create the worlds; the implication is that he has the power to destroy the sins of the āḻvār. Like the king of old who is asked to give like a cloud that so generously pours down rain, the Lord is asked to shower grace on the devotee. Viṣṇu is "dark" like a life-giving cloud; he is frequently referred to as "he who is dark as a cloud" (5.2.3) or "a dark rain cloud" (10.5.8). Like rain to parched earth, his grace gives life to the poet. His generosity to his devotees is extolled and his grace is sought throughout the poem. Only he can give; indeed, he *must* give to one who is so helpless, to one who seeks his refuge and protection. This Lord burnt Laṅkā for his beloved; he will destroy his devotee's sins (3.6.2). The Lord's victories are lauded and celebrated with enthusiasm and these are followed by petitions for grace.

Guiding the Traveler to the Patron

An āṟṟuppaṭai is a "poem in which bards are directed by their fellow professionals to famous heroes who are patrons of art." [38] In the classical anthology of *Pattuppāṭṭu,* there are three long poems in this genre. The poems usually depict a bard addressing another and telling him of a certain king's wealth, prosperous lands, and generosity; he then advises the other bard to take the same road. Frequently, there are biographical details about a king, his prowess, his conquests, and benign rule; these exalted descriptions are contrasted with the minstrel's poverty and lowliness. The descriptions occur both in āṟṟuppaṭai and some other puṟam poems:

> O singer with a glowing forehead! The kuvalai plant abounds in the deep mountain pools [in his land]; . . . beetles live in its fresh blown petals. Whether it rains or not, cascades of water flow down the lofty hills . . . and irrigate large tracts of ploughed land. . . . Pari, softer than these cascades, will give you fine gifts, if you go sing to him.
>
> (*Puṟanāṉūṟu* 105)

In the *Tirumurukāṟṟuppaṭai,* one of the works in the *Pattuppāṭṭu,* but possibly later in date than the other songs in the corpus,[39] we encounter a different goal:

> For here, in the place of worldly gifts from kings and chiefs, spiritual blessings of God Muruga are received by a devotee and the worshiper directs another, who is after salvation, to approach God Muruga for the boon. The nature of God Muruga, the way one should approach him and how He blesses His devotees, the six places or shrines where He has taken his abode are all described in the poem.[40]

Instead of being guided to the king, we are directed to the deity. The journey is both outward and inward; this passage describes a part of the internal change:

> If keeping your heart pure, . . . you strive to attain the state that avoids self-conceit [of thinking yourself responsible for all good things done by you] then all your urges to action arising in your pure heart at God's will, will speedily realize [their] objective and you will quickly attain salvation for which you yearned.
>
> (*Tirumurukāṟṟuppaṭai* ll. 62–66)
>
> (Translated by Mudaliyar)[41]

Nammāḻvār writes in a similar vein, addressing his poems to Viṣṇu:

> Pull out by the roots
> thoughts of "you" and "yours."
> Reach God; there is nothing
> more right for your life.
>
> Move to his side,
> Your bondage will loosen.
> At the time your body falls,
> think of him.
>
> (1.2.3 and 9)

> He has a thousand names,
> The Wondrous One who abides in Aṉantapuram
> where flowers bloom in gardens
> and terraces loom like mountains.
> If you would go, no sins will stick to you.
> Each name is like a thousand. Say it
> and this is then a celestial city.
>
> (10.2.2)

In the religious āṟṟuppaṭai songs, the poet counsels others to control their senses and travel to a sacred place where they will receive the Lord's blessings. The Lord's grace is radiated by the sacred place that he abides in and the city or town itself seems powerful enough to destroy a pilgrim's sins.

A Localized Theology: Praising the Lord's Domain

The last verse glorifying a city of the Lord recalls another typical feature of puṟam poetry and the āṟṟuppaṭai works: a description of the wonders of a king's land.[42] In the Tamil verses of classical poetry, we find roaring cascades (the presence of water indicated prosperity in South India where drought was all too common), fertile fields that are well irrigated, lush fields of paddy and sugarcane, blossoming lotuses, and bees sucking honey from laden flowers. The waterfalls and rivers carry gems fallen from the jewels worn by people who bathe in them—obviously indicating that the king's land is filled with rich people. This is also seen in a description of Murukaṉ's domain in the *Tirumurukāṟṟuppaṭai:*

> The cataracts of the mountains look like varied waving flags of victory. . . . They spill sweet-smelling, huge honeycombs built upon lofty hills that kiss the sky. . . . The cascades gush along. . . . The falling waters bear in their bosom the pearl-bearing white tusks of huge ele-

> phants; the torrents leap along with fine gold and gems shining on their surface, washing aside glittering dusts of gold. . . . The hills abound in groves with ripening fruits. God Muruga is lord of such hills.[43]

The cities are also described in considerable detail: prosperous seaports, terraces looming like mountains, tall palaces rising to the sky; they are centers of culture where bards and courtesans flourish. In akam poetry, the place is not named. It is a landscape frozen nameless for all time in the words of the poet. In puṛam poetry, the places are specified, the land is named, the king to whom it belongs is extolled in a litany of praise. The same theme is encountered in Nammāḻvār's poetry. In the Tiruvāymoḻi over thirty-one places where there are shrines of Viṣṇu are sung about in about three hundred and seven verses;[44] in addition to these, in several phala śrutis, Nammāḻvār identifies himself as Māṛaṉ or Caṭakōpaṉ of Kurukūr—which is then described in glowing terms. We quote here just two brief examples to convey the flavor of the lines:

> . . . this primordial God stands in Tirukkurukūr
> where jeweled terraces rise like mountains. . . .
>
> (4.10.1)

> . . . [He] stands in Tirukkurukūr,
> where the red paddy grows in fertile fields
> and the lotus blossoms thrive.
>
> (4.10.6)

The significant difference between the bard and the āḻvār is that the bard requested earthly sustenance; Nammāḻvār seeks only a life with God, serving him. Nammāḻvār sings, therefore, only about Viṣṇu; he contemptuously derides anyone who will praise a human being to get material wealth.

> You are not going to like what I have to say;
> but I shall say it yet.
> Listen! I do not lend my tongue to sing
> and praise any human,
> when my Lord, my father, the mighty elephant,
> abides in Tiruvēṅkaṭam
> where the bees hum and sing.
>
> I am not a poet come here to mouth the praise
> of mere mortals,
> the Lord with a discus, the flood of goodness,
> is all for me. . . .
>
> (3.9.1 and 9)

Akam Elements in the Tiruvāymoḻi

Just as puṟam elements are incorporated in the devotional poetry of Nammāḻvār, the romantic themes of akam poems also find expression. The love poems in the Tiruvāymoḻi are dramatic and passionate and their similarities with the romantic (akam) verses are quite striking. In the recitation of early Tamil love poetry, we hear verses spoken by the mother or friend of the heroine who is languishing out of her love for the hero. These verses portray the heroine's condition and the measures taken to alleviate it; the poet sometimes adopts the stance of a lovesick heroine and speaks of "her" love for the Lord. Sometimes, the poet speaks of himself in the third person, through the words of the heroine's mother, foster mother, or girlfriend.[45]

While the akam themes are present in the Tiruvāymoḻi, two distinctions must be made. First, akam poetry should mention no names—in these poems, characters should remain nameless; and, second, the love situations should be "universal," that is, they should be situations with which many people can identify. Nammāḻvār's poetry does not conform to these rules; he is named as a person in the love poems and the love situations seem unique to the progress of his particular relationship with Viṣṇu. As in the previous sections, we shall discuss here only a few themes encountered in both classical erotic poetry and in the Tiruvāymoḻi. We shall focus on the lament of the "heroine," possession and ecstatic dancing, desperate love (riding the palmyra horse), and the sending of messengers. These are representative of a broader base of parallels seen in both classical poetry and the Tiruvāymoḻi. Out of the hundred decads in the Tiruvāymoḻi, about twenty-five are spoken from the viewpoint of a girl. We either hear Nammāḻvār as a heroine, or hear the voices of her mother or friend, lamenting the heroine's lovesick condition caused by her separation from the Lord.

The Lament of the Heroine

Where do I go from here?
    I can't stand the soft bells, the gentle breeze,
    the dark waterlily, darkness that conquers day,
    dulcet notes, jasmines, the refreshing air.
The Lord, my beguiling one,
    who creates, bores through,
    swallows and spews this earth,
    who measures here and beyond,
    who destroys the demons,
does not come.
Why should I live?

(9.9.2)

Here the longing and waiting seen in earlier Tamil poems is reflected in a familiar landscape; the jasmine, the darkness, the separation from the hero, all figure in this verse from the Tiruvāymoḻi.

Possession and Ecstatic Dancing

In classical Tamil poetry, whenever a heroine seemed to pine for her love, her family frequently thought she was possessed (usually by the god Murukaṉ). They worshiped the god with frenzied dancing and the sprinkling of wine and blood to exorcise her. Hart translates the following from the *Akanāṉūṟu:*

"If we worship the long-speared god
whose mighty hands are famed
for crushing all who do not bow to him,
she will recover,"
women who know the ancient arts said
as if it were the truth.
They arranged the place of worship,
garlanded the spear,
sang so the town resounded,
offered sacrifice,
spread lovely red millet and blood,
and worshipped Muruganੁ. . . .

(*Akanāṉūṟu* 22)

. . . they cry out the name of the god,
throwing up their hands,
and the priest makes a show on the wide floor
with his frenzied dancing. . . .

(*Akanāṉūṟu* 98)
(Translated by George Hart)[46]

In the Tiruvāymoḻi, the motif is used in a slightly different way. Here, the ecstatic dancing and worship is seen to be useless, because it is directed to the wrong god; the "friend" of the "heroine" who is diagnosed as being possessed speaks in this poem and suggests that the real cause for the "heroine's" illness is separation from Viṣṇu:

Worship the sacred feet of the Lord of the celestials,
with those who know the Vedas
and cure the disease of this girl.
Instead,
　you speak improper words,
　do improper deeds,

you sprinkle liquor, your kettle drum roars,
you dance in ecstasy.
All this is base.

(4.6.8)

The theme of ecstatic dancing (aṇaṅku āṭutal, dancing under possession) occurs several times in the Tiruvāymoḻi. Nammāḻvār sings and dances like a girl "possessed" in the early akam poetry.

There is none equal, none superior to the Lord.
My tongue sings only his songs.
My limbs dance in ecstasy (aṇaṅku).[47]
My limbs dance in ecstasy
and bow before him. . . .

(1.6.3 and 4)

Elsewhere, in a "girl" poem, the mother describes the heroine:

Dancing, dancing, her body wilting,
singing, singing, eyes pouring tears,
ever seeking, crying "Narasiṁha"
is my girl with a glowing forehead.

(2.4.1)

In other verses Nammāḻvār directs others to sing and dance passionately. One is told to worship the Lord with abandoned fervor and with tears in one's eyes (3.5, 1.10). These symptoms of ecstasy are also described in Nammāḻvār's vision of the great age to dawn when the earth swells with devotees chanting, singing, and dancing (5.2.1–10).

In a rather unique set of verses, the theme of possession appears in a different way:

"I'm the earth you see," she says.
"I'm all the visible skies," she says.
"I'm the fires,
  the winds,
  and the seas," she says.
Is it because our lord dark as the sea
  has entered her and taken her over?
How can I explain my girl
  to you who see nothing
  but this world?

(5.6.3)
(Translated by A. K. Ramanujan)[48]

In this verse, it is not separation, but an ecstatic union which makes the "heroine's" (Nammālvār's) mother speculate that her daughter is possessed by the Lord, even as in earlier poetry the heroine is perceived to be possessed by Murukan.

Desperate Love: "Riding the Palmyra Horse"

Another theme from classical poetry seen in the Tiruvāymoli is known as riding the maṭal. A man would sometimes try to force the hand of the elders to give permission for him to be united in marriage with his beloved. This act of desperation was called "riding a palmyra horse" (maṭal). The lover would mount a "horse" made of sharp palmyra leaves and announce his love for a girl in public:

> When love is ripe beyond bearing
> and goes to seed,
> men will ride even palmyra stems
> like horses; will wear on their heads
> the reeking cones of the *eṛukkam* bud
> like flowers; will draw to themselves
> the gossip of the streets;
>
> and will do worse.

(*Kuṛuntokai* 17)
(Translated by A. K. Ramanujan)[49]

In the Tiruvāymoli the theme of desperate love and riding the maṭal is encountered with a minor change of convention. Nammālvār announces his intention to ride the maṭal:

> Lifting my modesty and chastity, stealing my heart,
> the Lord of the divine ones reaches the high heavens.
> My friend, this I swear:
> I shall shock all earth,
> I shall do weird deeds,
> and ride the palmyra stem [like a horse].
> With no sense of shame, I shall ride
> that palmyra stem through every street in town
> and women from all lands will cheer me on.
> And I shall demand from my Lord,
>   who holds the discus in his splendid hand,
> a cool blossom from the tulai plant
> and adorn myself with it.

(5.3.9 and 10)

Sending Messages

One of the more common themes in Indian love poetry is the hero or heroine's sending a messenger—usually a bird, the wind, a cloud, or even bees—to carry a message of love across the streams, towns, and mountains to the beloved. Usually the physical appearance of the hero or heroine, the message of love, and detailed descriptions of towns, hills, and vales that the messenger will pass over figure prominently in the lyrics. One of the best-known works in this genre is *Meghadūta* (*The Cloud Messenger*) by Kālidāsa, written in Sanskrit around the fifth century C.E. However, Hart has convincingly shown that this theme appears in classical Tamil poetry almost two hundred years before Kālidāsa.[50] In the Sacred Collect, Āṇṭāḷ, Tirumaṅkai āḻvār, and Nammāḻvār communicate their love to the Lord through messengers; in later exegesis, the commentators take the messenger to be symbolic of a teacher who mediates between the human being and the Lord. Nammāḻvār sends messengers to inform the Lord of his love and to speak on his behalf:

> O dark bird, seeking food with your beloved mate!
> Go see the Lord who devoured all the worlds,
> The master of Tiruvaṇvaṇṭūr, the beautiful city,
> which rings with sounds of Vedic sacrifices.
> Worship his feet with your hands, and tell him
> of my excellence.
> I am his servant.
>
> (6.1.2)

The āḻvār's waiting, however, is not all in anxiety and separation. There are several verses where there is a gentle longing and which are not necessarily spoken from the viewpoint of a girl:

> You became
> water, land, fire,
> time, the soaring sky,
> The radiance
> of the sun and the moon.
> You became Śiva and Brahmā.
> Hold aloft your discus and conch
> and visit me, a sinner, some day.
> Heaven and earth
> will rejoice.
>
> (6.9.1)

A little more than a quarter of the poems are spoken with a sense of separation. There are many occasions, however, when there is an alleviation of the separation. The āḻvār speaks sometimes of a union:

Who is my companion? Frightened,
I search, sinking like a ship,
in a stormy sea of life and death.
Radiant and glorious,
bearing aloft his discus and conch,
graciously he comes to me, his servant,
and becomes one—even with me.

(5.1.9)

While this verse speaks of union, the underlying relationship between the deity and the āḻvār is seen more as that of master and servant: ". . . graciously, he comes to me, his servant (aṭiyēṉ)." In the Tiruvāymoḻi, there is a frequent and smooth shift between the āḻvār speaking as a servant and as a beloved of the Lord.

The Tiruvāymoḻi combines the literary conventions of earlier Tamil literature with mythology drawn primarily from Sanskrit texts. The voices of a heroine confessing her love or a poet praising the generosity of his king are juxtaposed with mythical allusions, philosophical and didactic statements, and an exaltation of the sacred land over which the Lord reigns. What emerges is a work which is at once majestic yet accessible, philosophical yet passionate.

In the nineteenth century, the Tamil scholar Sri U. V. Swaminatha Aiyar discovered manuscripts of the Tamil Caṅkam anthologies in a monastery. He expressed his delight thus: "There appeared in the structure of the content of that literature of the Sangam, a greatness, larger than the earth, and height higher than the sky, and a depth deeper than the sea."[51] These words are a close reflection of a classical Tamil poem in which the heroine exclaims:

Bigger than earth, certainly,
higher than the sky,
more unfathomable than the waters
is this love for this man. . . .

(*Kuṛuntokai* 3)
(Translated by A. K. Ramanujan)[52]

Centuries later, Nammāḻvār uses similar words to describe his expansive love for the Lord:

My friend,
bigger than this dense earth
and the seven seas,
higher than the skies,
is my love for the one
who has the color of the ocean. . . .

(7.3.8)

Some of these terms may be used to describe the impact of the Tiruvāymoḻi itself. For later devotees and commentators, the profundity of the Tiruvāymoḻi seems unfathomable. Since the eleventh century, the meaning and the passion of the poem have been unfolding in a commentarial tradition within the Śrīvaiṣṇava community. Just as the leitmotifs in musical compositions are developed by the orchestra as "reminiscences" to express the dramatic and psychological development of the action, the leading motifs of the Tiruvāymoḻi and their impact on the teachers and the community of devotees were developed by later commentators. These reminiscences continue to reverberate within the Śrīvaiṣṇava tradition.

3

The Vedānta in Sanskrit according to Yāmuna and Rāmānuja

The Authoritative Tradition in Sanskrit

One side of the Śrīvaiṣṇava tradition rests on the Sanskrit scriptures, both the pan-Hindu Vedas and the sectarian Vaiṣṇava Āgamas, and the succession of authoritative teachers (ācāryas) interpreting the Vedas and leading the community. The first of these ācāryas was Nāthamuni, and the traditional accounts of the ācāryas' lives begin with the story of Nāthamuni's pilgrimage to the sacred places of Lord Viṣṇu in North India.[1] Indeed, Nāthamuni had decided to settle down and spend the rest of his life in Brindavan, the boyhood home of Viṣṇu's incarnation as Krishna the Cowherd. However, Maṉṉaṉār, the image form of Lord Viṣṇu in Nāthamuni's hometown temple, appeared to Nāthamuni and ordered him to return to Tamilnāṭu. When Nāthamuni reached home he was given a position of some responsibility in Maṉṉaṉār's temple in Vīranārāyaṇapuram, and later in his life was appointed as the manager of the much larger temple of Lord Viṣṇu on the sacred island of Śrīraṅgam. The tradition attributes to Nāthamuni not only the collection, setting to music, and incorporation into the temple ritual of the hymns of the āḻvārs, but also the beginning of the distinctive philosophical tradition of the Śrīvaiṣṇavas. The names of Nāthamuni's writings are remembered, but only a few fragments survive.[2]

It was Nāthamuni's grandson Yāmuna (Āḷavantār) who wrote in Sanskrit on all the principal facets of the Śrīvaiṣṇava tradition and articulated many of the positions that would be developed by Rāmānuja. One work defends the authority of the Pāñcarātra Āgamas and the Brahmanical status of the priests who follow this ritual. Another sketches the correct understanding of Vedāntic ontology (an apparently incomplete collection of three short pieces, called collectively the *Siddhitraya*). A third summarizes the teaching of the Bhagavadgītā in thirty-two verses.[3] Yāmuna's two hymns, which will be discussed in the next chapter, mark a clear influence of the āḻvārs' hymns on devotional poetry in Sanskrit.

The most famous Śrīvaiṣṇava teacher, Rāmānuja, was the nephew of one of Yāmuna's closest disciples, Periya Tirumalai Nampi (Śrīśaila Pūrṇa), who was the father of our commentator, Tirukkurukai Pirāṉ Piḷḷāṉ. Rāmānuja was converted from his youthful adherence to a rival interpretation of Vedānta, but just too late to have been himself Yāmuna's disciple—to his bitter disappointment. Yāmuna had died just before Rāmānuja arrived, and he therefore had to learn Yāmuna's teachings secondhand from five of Yāmuna's disciples, all of whom finally acknowledged him fully as Yāmuna's spiritual heir and the new leader of the Śrīvaiṣṇava community.

Yāmuna had been unable to do more than sketch the correct interpretation of the two works that all Brahmin students of the Upaniṣads considered the keys to Upaniṣadic interpretation.[4] One was the Bhagavadgītā, even though this was strictly speaking not part of the Vedas (including the Upaniṣads), but of the great epic, the Mahābhārata. The second key text was the Brahma Sūtra (also called the Vedānta Sūtras), the systematic summary of the Upaniṣads in the brief, easily memorizable lines called sūtras (threads). Three of Rāmānuja's writings, including his longest work called the *Śrībhāṣya,* are verse-by-verse commentaries on the Vedānta Sūtras. A fourth is a more general summary of Upaniṣadic teaching (the *Vedārtha Saṁgraha*) and a fifth is a lengthy commentary on the Bhagavadgītā. Rāmānuja's equivalent to Yāmuna's hymns are three short devotional works called the *Three Gadyas.* (A modern dispute about their authorship will concern us later.) A ninth work is a manual of prescriptions for daily worship at the home shrine.[5]

Rāmānuja's effort to establish the correct interpretation of the Vedānta involves debate with all rival schools of Indian thought, but it is clear that his major debate is with a small number of other positions. For the most part he confines his criticism to those who accept the authority of the Vedas; with respect to Buddhists and Jains, he only rehearses older arguments present in the Vedānta Sūtras and the older commentaries. He spends considerably more time trying to establish that the Supreme Person, the Brahman of the Upaniṣads, is Viṣṇu rather than Brahmā or Śiva. His disciple Piḷḷāṉ follows him on this so closely, with some support from Nammāḻvār's verses, that we can wait until chapter 6 to consider that line of argument.

What is much less reflected in Piḷḷāṉ's commentary, however, is the debate with the Brahmanical schools that also assume the authority of the Vedas.[6] For Rāmānuja, as for Yāmuna, these include the followers of two rival interpreters of Vedic ritual, Kumārila and Prabhākara, and two rival interpreters of Upaniṣadic meditation, Śaṅkara and Bhāskara.[7] In the course of these debates Rāmānuja has to develop further Yāmuna's presentation of a distinctive Śrīvaiṣṇava position regarding the nature of language, of valid knowledge, and of reality. The practical debate with both ritualist schools concerned the identity of true Brahmins (dealt with extensively by Yāmuna), the appropriateness of sectarian Vaiṣṇava systems of ritual (especially that of the Pāñcarātra Āgamas), and the meaningfulness of statements concerning the nature of reality in Vedic texts (especially the Upaniṣads).

The Prabhākara School of Karma Mīmāṁsa finds the significance of Vedic texts only in the imperative mood: the injunctions to action. Indicative statements, in particular descriptions of various deities, or of the supreme Brahman, are held to be meaningful only as inducements to perform Vedic sacrifices. This interpretation puts the Karma Mīmāṁsa in diametrical opposition to all the schools of Vedānta, which regard the Vedas as providing authoritative knowledge concerning the nature of Brahman. The Vedānta began as the latter part of Vedic learning, with the "later inquiry" (uttara mīmāṁsa) following and closely connected with the "earlier inquiry" (pūrva mīmāṁsa), and the Vedāntic interpretation of particular texts makes considerable use of the Pūrva Mīmāṁsa's elaborate rules of exegesis.[8] Moreover, it is likely that at an early stage many learned Brahmins considered the Vedānta an addendum to the analysis of Vedic ritual. All those engaged in ritual performance would need the "earlier inquiry," while the "later inquiry" was of direct relevance only to those at a stage of life when they could consider ending their ritual responsibilities and possibly making a radical renunciation of their social existence, in pursuit of permanent liberation from all bodily existence. This way of combining ritual action to achieve worldly ends and meditation to reach the highest human goal is clearly articulated in Hindu treatises of social ethics (Dharma Śāstras) and is assumed by Bhāskara's socially conservative interpretation of the Vedānta Sūtras. Both Advaita Vedānta and the developing Vaiṣṇava interpretation of Vedānta rejected Bhāskara's view, but in different ways and for different reasons.[9] Śaṅkara and his followers, while accepting the authority of the Vedic social system and its ritual prescriptions for those who had not yet renounced life in society in order to seek liberation, held that the desire to seek the supreme goal overrode social duties at whatever point in life that revulsion to worldly existence arose. There was therefore no practical reason to insist on ritual analysis as a foundation for the meditation of ascetics, and Śaṅkara's sharp distinction between liberating insight and all lower forms of knowledge undercut the theoretical connection.

The Vaiṣṇava position that Yāmuna and Rāmānuja articulated stood in a more complicated relation to the conservative position of Vedic Brahmins like Bhāskara. On the one hand, they wanted to defend the caste standing and ritual qualifications of the Brahmin leadership of the community of Viṣṇu worshipers. On the other hand, they held that complete renunciation (sannyāsa) of the traditional kind was a matter of secondary importance. What was primary was a renouncing of worldly goals even when continuing one's previous occupation and ritual observance. Perhaps even more important in practice was the greatly increased involvement in non-Vedic rituals prescribed by sectarian Vaiṣṇava texts (Vaikhānasa or Pāñcarātra). For Brahmin men these rituals for the temple and the home shrine were intended to supplement Vedic observance; for all other castes and for Brahmin women these rites following the Āgamas or Tantras defined their religious existence. For serious devotees of Lord Viṣṇu, whether Brahmin or non-Brahmin, it was important that all these ritual actions, from whatever source, be undertaken in single-minded devotion to the Lord.

Although Yāmuna and Rāmānuja had both renounced their marriage ties (in Rāmānuja's case, fairly early in life) and became sannyāsīs, they led a community largely composed of married men and women continuing to carry on their social and ritual obligations.[10] The Brahmins among them had both practical and psychological reasons to affirm their continuity with the Vedic ritual tradition as well as with the Vedānta. Yet the emphasis was clearly reversed. Instead of emphasizing the ritual acts that eclipsed the deities to whom they were offered, as did the Karma Mīmāṁsa, Vaiṣṇavas kept central the Lord who inspired and enabled all acts of worship as well as receiving them as devotional offerings. It was essential that Scripture disclose the nature of this supreme Lord as well as prescribe how the Lord was to be worshiped.

Interpreting the Vedānta: Rāmānuja's Principal Doctrines

For all schools of Vedānta, there is one perfect reality, the Brahman, for this is clearly stated in the famous texts of the Upaniṣads. How this one reality is related to the evident variety and imperfection of the world we experience around us is a primary concern of Vedānta. The answer closest to the Vedic speculation on the origin of the cosmos is given by Bhāskara's "Difference and Non-difference" (Bhedābheda). Reality is one without a difference when it is tightly held together in the state before creation (more literally, "emanation"), whereas in our world, distinctions abound; this is the world of difference. Both Śaṅkara and Rāmānuja reject this cosmogonic understanding of being or reality. They both maintain that no change is possible in ultimate reality or being (sat). For Śaṅkara this means that Brahman is the sole reality or being (sat), and the differentiated reality of our ordinary practical experience is not truly real but is like a magician's trick (māyā), which vanishes once its cause is known. Thus from the vantage point of higher consciousness or insight, our everyday world is false. Rāmānuja rejects Śaṅkara's solution of two levels of knowledge, which explains the problem by reference to a change in consciousness rather than by a change in the evolving cosmos, as in Bhāskara. Both Yāmuna and Rāmānuja see the unity of ultimate reality as permanent, but regard it as unity at the essential core of a reality that in its modes or bodily expressions is always manifold.

Instead of Śaṅkara's view of illusory or false consciousness, moreover, Rāmānuja elaborates what might be considered a hyper-realistic view. No presumed knowledge is totally erroneous; what we consider errors are disordered perceptions or faulty inferences concerning something that is really there. The two worldly sources of knowledge, perception and inference, are basically trustworthy, despite the general human subjection to "beginningless ignorance." Even knowledge in dreams is real, but it is a perception of a very temporary Divine creation. The third source of valid knowledge, Scripture (śāstra), based on the eternal sounds (śabda) behind the Vedic words, does not contradict perception and inference but supplements and confirms them, providing knowledge of what is uncertain on the basis of sense perception and inferential reasoning: the unity and the specific nature of ultimate reality (Brahman).[11]

Rāmānuja rejects Śaṅkara's doctrine of two levels of truth in Scripture, maintaining that all scriptural texts are at the same level of truth; apparent discrepancies must therefore be resolved without giving more weight to some texts than to others. He resolves the contrast between the emphasis on unity in some texts and the emphasis on plurality in others by noting the synthetic principle evident in a third group of texts. According to Rāmānuja, these texts declare that in the relation between the ātmā and the body it ensouls (and likewise between a substance and its mode) there is both radical distinction and inseparable connection.

Scripture testifies to a Supreme Soul who is the inner soul of finite souls. Thus the finite soul is to the Supreme Soul as the material body is to the finite soul. This is Rāmānuja's celebrated doctrine of *śarīra-śarīri-bhāva:* the relation of the soul to the body, which corresponds to the relation between grammatical subject and predicate adjective, or substance and mode. It is the special characteristic of finite souls to be a mode in relation to God but a substance in relation to material things, which are their bodies or instruments. The entire finite universe of souls and material bodies is also the body of God. Thus God is the only ultimately substantial reality, and reality may be viewed as *viśiṣṭādvaita* (the later philosophical label for this school of Vedānta, not used by Rāmānuja): the nondual reality of that which is (internally) distinguished.

Rāmānuja defines the soul-body relation in terms of three subordinate relations, those between the support and the supported, the controller and the controlled, and the owner (śeṣī) and the owned (śeṣa).[12] It is the third relation that is most distinctive, for ownership is understood to include the obligation of the slave to serve the master and the confident expectation that the master will look after the slave. In each case it is the Supreme Soul who provides the defining instance; the finite soul's relation to its body is only a limited approximation of complete supporting, controlling, and owning its body.

Rāmānuja assumes that there are three kinds of reality: nonsentient matter (acit), sentient but finite souls (cit), and the Lord (Īśvara), who is the Supreme Soul.[13] The world consists of material bodies controlled by finite souls. While the particular bodies are temporary, the basic matter of which they consist and the souls that they embody have no beginning in time. The bondage of many souls to "beginningless karma" causes their repeated return to the world in new bodies, but the entire world of material bodies and embodied souls is intended to glorify God, that is, to express in the finite realm his power and goodness. Those who escape the ignorance induced by karma can see that the finite world is *now,* along with God's infinite world, a realm of glory (vibhūti). Despite his horror of linking God with anything defiling in the material world, Rāmānuja insists that the entire finite universe is the body of God.[14]

Finite souls and the Supreme Soul are similar but not identical in their essential natures: both have consciousness and bliss as their essential characteristics, but the finite soul is limited in its power and extent whereas the Supreme Soul is all-powerful and all-pervasive. Moreover, finite souls still bound to the material world have their secondary consciousness (that which they *possess* rather than *are*), obscured by the ignorance produced by "beginningless karma."

The Vedānta is concerned with the proper knowledge of reality in order to find liberation from this bondage. In Rāmānuja's interpretation of Vedānta both performance of social and ritual duties and knowledge of reality are auxiliary means in seeking liberation, but the chief means is bhakti (devotion), a calling to mind of God's attributes with an attitude that should become as constant as the flow of oil, as vivid and immediate as sense perception, and so emotionally gripping that the devotee feels unable to live without the pervading presence of God.[15]

The ultimate reality thus remembered in devotion is not an abstract principle but that most concrete and substantial reality who is the personal Lord, the Lord who escapes all self-confident seeking by finite souls but who chooses to become available to those who acknowledge their dependence. The Lord descends and condescends out of his great compassion to save, but those who most deeply feel their need for God's presence learn the deepest secret: the Lord also needs them. This emphasis on God's initiative along with the surprising secret that the Lord who owns everything needs his devotees' love leads to a second way of talking about the salvific process that is quite different from the first. Instead of loving devotion being the means to attaining the Lord's presence, the Lord is the means to enabling devotion that is a mutual participation of the Infinite Soul and finite souls. The end is revealed to be the means, and the means is recognized as the end. Rāmānuja seems to be able to move back and forth between the older concept of devotion as means and the implications of a radical doctrine of grace.[16]

Two Distinctions within the Divine Nature

Since all finite reality is part of the one infinite Lord, the Divine nature is all-encompassing. Rāmānuja's doctrine of God in some ways therefore includes all his teaching. The doctrine is characterized by two different kinds of distinction within the Divine nature: first, between the "inner" and "outer" sides of God's essential nature, and second, between God's supremacy (paratva) and accessibility (saulabhya).

Rāmānuja uses two terms that could be translated as "essence" or "essential nature": *svarūpa* and *svabhāva*.[17] Though he never explains the difference, his usage suggests that svarūpa refers to the interior nature of God without reference to any finite reality. God's defining attributes therefore constitute his svarūpa. These are the terms drawn from the Upaniṣads defining the soul (ātmā). Rāmānuja defines them all in such a way as to make clear that they apply primarily to the Supreme Soul and only secondarily, in a reduced sense, to finite souls. It is these attributes that are so much at the core of the Divine nature that they must be remembered in all meditations on God. The five attributes are understood as follows:

satya	true or real being;
jñāna	unlimited consciousness or "knowledge";
anantatva	infinite, free from all limitations of place, time, or particular nature;
ānanda	joy or bliss, the infinite multiplication of the bliss of the finite soul, purified of all unhappiness;
amalatva	stainlessness or purity, being "opposed to everything defiling," "free from even a trace of subjection to karma," "without the defiling qualities of matter."

Taken together, these attributes indicate that God's essential nature is an infinite and joyous self-consciousness that is externally real and flawless.[18]

All the other Divine attributes constitute God's svabhāva: his nature in relation to other entities. These include his metaphysical relation to the cosmos as ground, controller, and owner, and his active role as periodic creator, maintainer, and destroyer. They also include his "treasure trove" or "ocean" of auspicious qualities, and the various forms of his presence in the cosmos, as cosmic emanation (vyūha), occasional incarnation ("descent," avatāra), and inner controller (antaryāmin) of every soul. Sometimes, moreover, Rāmānuja speaks of the Divine svabhāva as including the eternal heavenly realm (nityavibhūti) of the Divine consorts and ministering angels and even the earthly realm of embodied souls subject to karma, known as the realm of the Lord's play (līlāvibhūti). This last aspect is definitely at a lower level, as the realm of transience and imperfection, yet even this realm is inextricably linked to God. "When Brahman is experienced as superlative bliss, there is nothing at all to be seen apart from him, since the totality of beings is included within Brahman's essential nature and the realm manifesting his glory."[19]

The other kind of distinction is the division of the Lord's attributes into those that indicate his essential lordship (īśitṛtva) or supremacy (paratva), on the one hand, and those that show his accessibility (saulabhya) to finite beings, on the other.[20] The Sanskrit word *para* is related to the English word "far," and it means both "far away" and "high above." Those Divine qualities that express "highness" or majesty include a list of "six attributes" of the Lord (Bhagavān) frequently mentioned in the Pāñcarātra Āgamas: unlimited knowledge (jñāna), untiring strength (bala), sovereignty and wealth (aiśvarya), immutability (more literally, "fortitude," vīrya), creative power (śakti), and splendor (tejas). The farness or distance of the Lord from finite beings is both a recognition of the Lord's inherent supremacy and an inability on the part of finite beings to bridge the gap, to overcome the distance between finite and Infinite. The Lord is inaccessible to all other beings, including the greatest of the lower deities, Brahmā and Śiva, even when they use such normally effective means of establishing spiritual contact as meditation or worship. Fortunately the Lord takes the initiative in overcoming the distance and makes himself easily attainable (sulabha). This easy attainability or accessibility (saulabhya) is expressed by a number of Divine attributes. Most frequently mentioned are compassion or mercy (kāruṇya or dayā), gracious condescension (sauśīlya), motherly love (vātsalya), and generosity (audārya). There are also two related qualities: concern for his creatures' welfare (literally, "good-heartedness," sauhārda) and tender (literally, "passionate") affection (anurāga).

In his Introduction to his Commentary on the Bhagavadgītā, Rāmānuja mentions these two groups of attributes.[21] There is one other attribute that he includes in both groups. This is beauty (saundarya), the extraordinary attractiveness of all the Lord's bodily forms, both in his transcendent realm and when descending into the finite realm as an incarnation (avatāra). Rāmānuja also indicates the difference between the two sides of the Divine nature in more personal and dramatic terms. On the one hand, the supreme Brahman, who is Nārāyaṇa (Viṣṇu) ever united with his Divine consort Śrī, dwells in his supreme heaven in incomparable beauty, adorned with magnificent jewels and equipped with powerful weapons. He causes the origination, continuance, and dissolution of the cosmos out of the sheer urge to self-expression, without altering his own essential nature. On the other hand, without losing his own nature the Lord repeatedly descends to earth, taking bodily forms similar to those of the creatures among whom he dwells so that they can see him and adore him. He grants the requests of his worshipers, both for worldly goods and for the supreme good of liberation from the transient world and union with him. His mighty feats rid the world of evildoers, but their deeper purpose is to captivate the hearts of his creatures and thus accomplish their salvation.

There are two levels in the Divine accessibility. In his incarnations he "becomes a mortal to benefit the universe," but he remains essentially supreme. In the Lord's longing for communion with his chosen devotees, however, his motherly love (vātsalya) overwhelms the rest of his nature and seemingly cancels his metaphysical superiority so those his own soul (ātmā) and those of his devotees depend upon and support one another. This deepest mystery of the Divine nature is only open to those rare souls who are exclusively devoted to the Lord and feel their very existence depends upon his continual presence.

The Question of Rāmānuja's Relation to the Tamil Tradition

Rāmānuja's presentation of Vedānta cites in support only those Sanskrit texts that all Brahmins would recognize as part of or closely connected to the Vedas. These include the universally acceptable Bhagavadgītā and Viṣṇu Purāṇa. Rāmānuja does quote the Pāñcarātra Āgamas, but only in the section of the *Śrībhāṣya* where he is directly defending their validity and authority.[22] Concerning the āḻvārs' poems or any other Tamil works he is completely silent.

What then are we to make of the traditional understanding that he commented on the Tiruvāymoḻi in conversations with his disciples and commissioned one of them to write a commentary? In some respects this entire book is an attempt to answer that question. Some Western scholars reject the traditional understanding completely, in particular the claim that Rāmānuja taught an alternative spiritual path to the bhaktiyoga he saw as central to Vedānta: the alternative of abject surrender to the Lord and reliance on unmerited Divine grace, called śaranāgati or prapatti. The works of Rāmānuja in which both branches of the Śrīvaiṣṇava tradition see prapatti clearly taught and exemplified are the *Three Gadyas,* "prose poems." Indeed one of them, the *Śaraṇāgati Gadya,* is believed to contain Rāmānuja's own solemn act of surrender. Recently the authenticity of the *Gadyas* has been questioned, but we believe that they are genuine.[23] They belong, however, to a different genre. They are not commentaries or philosophical arguments, but hymns in prose, and they therefore should be considered alongside the Sanskrit stotras (hymns of petition and praise) preserved by the tradition, two of them by Yāmuna and several more by a number of Rāmānuja's disciples. It is in these Sanskrit stotras that there is the most evident link between the Tamil devotion of the āḻvārs and the Sanskrit writings of the later ācāryas. After looking at these stotras in the next chapter we shall consider what we can learn from the *Gadyas* about Rāmānuja's indebtedness to the Tamil side of the Dual Vedānta.

4

Reflections of the Āḻvār Hymns in the Sanskrit Stotras

References to the Āḻvārs in Early Śrīvaiṣṇava Literature

This book is mainly concerned with the confluence of Tamil and Sanskrit traditions occurring in Piḷḷāṉ's Sanskritized Tamil (maṇipravāla) commentary on Nammāḻvār's Tamil poem. This chapter, however, is concerned with those Sanskrit writings in which the same confluence can be discussed, the hymns (stotras) in Sanskrit of Piḷḷāṉ's predecessors and contemporaries.

The Śrīvaiṣṇava community looks back to a new beginning in the life and work of Nāthamuni. As we saw earlier, the Śrīvaiṣṇava community believes that Nammāḻvār's poems were revealed to him when he was in a yogic trance. He is also said to have collected the poems of the various āḻvārs, set them to music, and instituted their recitation in Śrīvaiṣṇava temples. Nāthamuni's Sanskrit philosophical works are lost; a few sentences are quoted by later authors. The work of Nāthamuni's grandson Yāmuna constitutes the oldest Sanskrit writing produced in the community.[1]

Yāmuna's *Stotra Ratna* (*The Jewel of Hymns,* henceforth referred to as *The Jewel*) not only expresses his veneration for his grandfather, Nāthamuni, whom he acknowledges as his spiritual teacher, but also his adoration of the sage Parāśara (the traditional author of the Viṣṇu Purāṇa) and of the saint "whose feet are adorned with vakula blossoms." The saint thus described has always been identified by the Śrīvaiṣṇava community as Nammāḻvār, who referred to himself in the Tiruvāymoḻi as the one "on whose chest is the fragrant garland of makiḻ (Sanskrit: vakula) blossoms" (4.10.11). This is the earliest reference that we have to Nammāḻvār in Sanskrit literature.

Although Rāmānuja did not mention Nammāḻvār in his writings, the Śrīvaiṣṇava tradition describes his passion for the Tiruvāymoḻi and the works of the āḻvārs in many ways. The later commentaries on the Tiruvāymoḻi, as well as the thirteenth-century commentary on the Tiruppāvai by Periyavāccāṉ Piḷḷai, record distinctive interpretations of certain verses.[2] They also refer to the manner in which he understood and enjoyed them. The earliest hymn of praise written in honor of Rāmānuja by his contemporary describes him as one who was "at the feet of Nammāḻvār."[3] Other biographies of Rāmānuja confirm this. We have already noted that the Śrīvaiṣṇava community has always understood that the first commentary on the Tiruvāymoḻi by Piḷḷāṉ was written by the command, or at the very least, with the permission, of Rāmānuja. Rāmānuja's scribe and disciple, Kūrattāḻvān, does refer to Nammāḻvār as the one adorned with vakula flowers or by his Sanskrit name Parāṅkuśa in a few verses.[4]

The paucity of explicit references to the āḻvārs in early Śrīvaiṣṇava literature would be surprising and strange were it not for the evidence at another level of the community's understanding that the early theologians were strongly influenced by the hymns of the āḻvārs. The evidence comes from the stotra literature or the hymns of praise written by Yāmuna, Kūrattāḻvāṉ, and Parāśara Bhaṭṭar. These hymns (stotras) echo the phrases, images, sentiment, and the devotion seen in the Tamil verses of the āḻvārs. In some places, Tamil phrases are simply translated into Sanskrit; in others, the structure of the verses and the imagery follow patterns seen in Tamil literature. Śrīvaiṣṇava theologians even today frequently quote from the āḻvārs when they are commenting on the hymns of Yāmuna, Rāmānuja, and other teachers to show the similarity in phraseology or imagery and thus elucidate both the Tamil and Sanskrit verses in terms of each other. A systematic and detailed study of these parallels is beyond the scope of this chapter. We shall limit ourselves to a study of some striking images which show the heritage of the āḻvār poetry as reflected in the early stotras of the Śrīvaiṣṇava community. We shall focus primarily on Yāmuna's *The Jewel,* the *Gadyas* (prose poems) of Rāmānuja, and the stotras of Kūrattāḻvāṉ and Parāśara Bhaṭṭar.

The Stotra Tradition in the Śrīvaiṣṇava Community

Yāmuna, Rāmānuja, and the other teachers wrote several works of praise in Sanskrit, addressed to Viṣṇu or Śrī. The format of these verses resembles the stotras found in the Sanskrit Viṣṇu Purāṇa, but the stotras also reveal the influence of the Tamil hymns on the Sanskritic Vaiṣṇava tradition.

Yāmuna composed two stotras; one of these, *The Jewel,* was in praise of Viṣṇu; and the other, known in Śrīvaiṣṇava parlance simply as the "Four Verses" ("Catuḥśloki"), was addressed to Viṣṇu's consort Śrī. Rāmānuja, the most important Śrīvaiṣṇava teacher, wrote several philosophical works in Sanskrit and three gadyas (prose poems) in praise of Viṣṇu.[5] His scribe and disciple, Kūrattāḻvāṉ, wrote five hymns, four in praise of Viṣṇu and one in praise of Śrī.[6] Kūrattāḻvāṉ's son Parāśara Bhaṭṭar was the author of a long stotra in praise of the Lord at Śrīraṅgam and a shorter work where he glorifies Śrī.[7] A study of these works shows how the heritage of the āḻvār poetry was incorporated and preserved as part of the Śrīvaiṣṇava Sanskrit literature.

The striking areas of similarity between the works of the āḻvārs and the stotras are the assertion of exclusive devotion to Viṣṇu and a desire to serve Viṣṇu continuously; a contemplation of one's unworthiness and grief at one's sinful past; reminders to the Lord about the devotee's relationship with him; and a seeking of the Lord as one's only refuge. The stotras differ from the āḻvārs' verses, however, in some important ways. With the exception of Maturakavi āḻvār, all other āḻvārs emphasize their immediate and direct relationship with the Lord and seek refuge on the strength of that relationship. The āḻvārs depict Viṣṇu as their parent, master, lover and protector; the teachers reiterate most of these relationships.[8] While the āḻvārs focus on immediate, direct relationships, the ācāryas follow Maturakavi āḻvār in also stressing a mediate, indirect connection to the Lord, through association with their spiritual teacher and/or their association with Śrī. Maturakavi āḻvār is the only āḻvār who did not compose a hymn in honor of Viṣṇu. In his only work, "The Short Knotted String" ("Kaṇṇinuṇ Ciṟuttāmpu"), he praises his teacher Nammāḻvār. The later Śrīvaiṣṇava ācāryas share both Maturakavi āḻvār's emphasis on reverence for one's own spiritual master and the other āḻvārs' effort to seek God directly.

The Sanskrit stotras also differ from Tamil poetry in placing stronger emphasis on Śrī and in addressing some verses or occasionally entire stotras to her. We shall discuss this issue later in this chapter.

Several verses in *The Jewel* state in Sanskrit what the other āḻvārs had said earlier in Tamil. We shall focus on some of these verses and phrases now, noting the similarities in several general areas: descriptions of the Lord and his entourage, the relationship between the poet and the Lord, and the poet's feelings of sinfulness.

Descriptions of the Lord and his Attendants

The Jewel begins with lengthy expressions of reverence and surrender to Yāmuna's grandfather Nāthamuni, the sage Parāśara, and Nammāḻvār. In his description of Nammāḻvār, Yāmuna evokes familiar images used earlier by Nammāḻvār himself, as well as by Maturakavi āḻvār. Nammāḻvār describes the Lord thus in the Tiruvāymoḻi:

> Women with beautiful eyes,
> Great wealth, good sons,
> Father and mother—
> Only he
> is all these, and more.
>
> (5.1.8)

> You became
> father, mother, and children
> and all other things. . . .
>
> (7.8.1)

Maturakavi āḻvār, who, according to Śrīvaiṣṇava tradition, was the disciple of Nammāḻvār, had hailed his teacher as his "father, mother and master" (Kaṇṇinuṇ Ciṟuttāmpu, v. 4); Yāmuna pays homage to Nammāḻvār using almost the same phrases:

> I place my head before the holy feet of [Nammāḻvār] the master of our clan; the feet adorned with vakula blossoms, the feet which are to me and my descendents, for all time [as dear as one's] mother, father, wives, sons and great wealth.
>
> (*The Jewel,* v. 5)

Later, the same epithets are used for Viṣṇu: he is hailed as "the father, the mother, the beloved son, friend, and teacher" of the world (*The Jewel,* v. 60).

The Lord is also portrayed as the only refuge of human beings. The āḻvārs and Yāmuna resort to poetic hyperbole to make the point. The Lord, whether merciful or not, is still the *only* refuge:

> My Lord of Vittuvakkōṭṭu
> city surrounded by groves,
> filled with fragrant blossoms,
> A mother may push away her infant in anger,
> and yet it thinks of her loving face and weeps
> You may not dispel my grief [yet I say]
> There is no refuge other than your sacred feet.
>
> (Perumāḷ Tirumoḻi 5.1)

Yāmuna makes the same point:

> O Supreme Lord! You may reject me, but I will not leave your lotus feet; just as the child which suckles its mother's breast does not leave her even if she pushes it away. . . .
>
> (*The Jewel,* v. 26)

The āḻvārs celebrated both the Lord's supremacy and accessibility and rejoiced in the might as well as the mercy of the Lord. Nammāḻvār exulted in this paradox and Yāmuna speaks of the Lord as the supreme one and as an ocean of mercy in the same verse:

> O Lord, it is because of your glance that the three worlds exist. . . . [But you are also] our friend; . . . is it surprising that you have such affection for us?
>
> I bow (namo) before you, I salute you over and over again; you who are the very ground of speech and mind. I salute you again and again.

You have infinite powers; I salute you, I bow before you who are an ocean of boundless mercy.

(*The Jewel,* vv. 10 and 21)

Nammāḻvār had said that the Lord is extremely accessible to those with devotion but beyond the reach of others. As an example of the Lord's accessibility, he mentions the incident of Krishna stealing butter and being tied to a mortar as a punishment (1.3.1).[9] Tirumaṅkai āḻvār also refers to this incident several times and contrasts it with the Lord's elusiveness to all but his devotees. In a set of verses in the Periya Tirumoḻi, he celebrates the paradox of the Lord's supreme nature and his accessibility in an imaginary conversation between two friends:

Spanked by the cowherd lady with jet black hair,
He was tied up by a short, knotted rope, look my friend!
He was tied up by a short knotted rope, but still,
He is beyond the grasp of even the Celestials' thoughts
O cāḻalē![10]

(Periya Tirumoḻi 11.5.5)

Kūrattāḻvāṉ makes a similar contrast:

They say that you cannot be grasped by even those with pure minds; You are the supreme Lord who can cut all bonds. But we heard that you were tied by a string; were you incapable of loosening that knot?

(*Atimānuṣa Stava,* v. 36)

The attraction of the adolescent Krishna to the cowherd girls that Periyāḻvār envisaged is rendered in Sanskrit by Kūrattāḻvāṉ:

Behind the many cows, under the hanging groves,
The radiance of his sacred body glimmers.
His dark handsome head is adorned with a peacock feather.
Amidst the circles of cowherd folk,
He, whose beautiful eyes are like the red lotus,
plays his flute, sings a song and
comes dancing.
My daughter gazes at the beauty
of this cowherd boy
and is faint.

(Periyāḻvār Tirumoḻi 3.4.7)

Then,
(at the time of the festival of the dance,)[11]

Your body dark as the cloud,
eyes like petals of a lotus blossom,
a peacock feather in your hair,
hands holding aloft a flute,
your body radiant in its cowherd dress,
The fortunate ones saw you.

(*Atimānuṣa Stava,* v. 48)

Like the āḻvārs, the teachers also celebrate the Lord's "permanent" incarnation as an arcā in a holy place. The Lord at Tirumāliruñcōlai whom the āḻvārs sang about is praised by Kūrattāḻvāṉ in his *Sundarabāhu Stava.* The Sanskrit work follows the Tamil poems in (a) descriptions of the hill ("here the moonlight caresses the crests of the hill")[12]; (b) references to special incidents that are connected with Tirumāliruñcōlai ("this is the hill where the king Malayadhvaja served your feet"[13]; "this is the hill where in the midst of a lovers' quarrel the male elephant swears on the Handsome Lord")[14]; and (c) even trying to translate a Tamil pun into Sanskrit verse.[15]

Tirumaṅkai āḻvār had hailed the Lord as the "Precious One who [was] the very auspiciousness of the goddess of auspiciousness (tiruvukkum tiruvākiya celvā)" in Periya Tirumoḻi 7.7.1. Yāmuna translates this distinctive Tamil phrase into Sanskrit twice:

. . . who else but you can be the very auspiciousness (śrī) of the goddess of auspiciousness? (Śrī)

. . . You are the very auspiciousness (śrī) of the goddess of auspiciousness. . . .

(*The Jewel,* vv. 12 and 45)

Kūrattāḻvāṉ also follows the āḻvārs closely in describing the beauty of the Lord: the Lord's hair is described as being spun out of intense darkness (Nammāḻvār's TVM 7.7.9 and Kūrattāḻvāṉ's *Sundarabāhu Stava,* v. 40), while his nose is compared to a climbing plant and a limb of a kalpaka tree (TVM 7.7.2 and *Sundarabāhu Stava,* v. 45).

Yāmuna's description of Śeṣa, the serpent which serves the Lord, is like that of Poykai āḻvār. The serpent is the paradigmatic servant and is therefore called the "owned one" (śeṣa). Yāmuna's images are similar to those used by Poykai āḻvār:

The serpent is an umbrella [for the Lord] when he moves, a throne when he sits, sandals when he stands, and a bed in the large ocean. It is a brilliant lamp, a soft silk garment, a cushion for his hand. . . .

(Mutal Tiruvantāti, v. 53)

> . . . the great serpent serves you in endless ways assuming various forms; he is your dwelling, bed, seat, sandals, robes, pillow, and umbrella against rain and sun.
>
> (*The Jewel,* v. 40[16])

There are several verses of description and petition which are strikingly similar in the āḻvār poetry and in the stotras of the later teachers.[17]

The Ācāryas' Contemplation of Their Sinfulness

The sense of humility and feeling of unworthiness felt by the teachers is intense. These verses, perhaps more than others, reflect the mood of the āḻvār hymns. The āḻvārs contemplated their past sins with fear and felt unworthy to seek the Lord's grace. Yāmuna calls himself a shameless poet (*The Jewel,* v. 7) for attempting to sing of the Lord. His lines echo Periyāḻvār who said, "My tongue is not pure, I should not call you, my Lord, but my mouth knows no other name" (Periyāḻvār Tirumoḻi 5.1.1). Yāmuna says, "There is no evil deed that I have not done . . ." and later continues:

> O woe unto me, the impure, immodest, cruel creature without shame; with avarice, I long to be your servant, my Lord. . . .
>
> . . . though lowly and beastly, though I am an abode of sins which have no beginning and from which I cannot escape, I pray to you, O Sea of motherly love (vātsalya), for my fear vanishes when I think of your attributes. . . .
>
> (*The Jewel,* vv. 47 and 58)

Earlier, Tirumaṅkai āḻvār had confessed his unworthiness in several verses, of which the following is a typical example:

> Without any feeling, and with cruel mind,
> with actions filled with rage,
> wandering with packs of dogs,
> rejoicing in sport,
> I ran and roamed, destroying several lives.
>
> (Periya Tirumoḻi 1.6.2)

Kūrattāḻvāṉ continues this self-deprecation, referring to his general lack of qualifications to reach the Lord:

> . . . I am the ground of hate, pride, and avarice; I desire the wrong things; I am greedy, deluded; who am I to attain you? I have neither

> faith (śraddhā) nor devotion (bhakti), with neither the power nor even the desire to sing your praise or to bow before you; nor have I any regret for not embarking upon the right path. . . . Alas, I join the ranks of your enemies.
>
> (*Vaikuṇṭha Stava,* v. 96)

Filled with a sense of their unworthiness, both the āḻvārs and the ācāryas sought refuge at the feet of the Lord:

> I was not born in the four clans,
> I have not learnt the four good arts;
> I have not conquered my senses,
> O pure Lord! I have no fortune;
> My Lord, I have nothing to grasp
> but your twin feet.
>
> (Tiruccanta Viruttam, v. 90)

> O Perfect Lord! I have not taken the [ritual] baths
> nor kept alive the three fires as befits a brahmin,
> I am not your bhakta, O sea-colored Lord!
> How can I be happy? I cry in distress.
> Embrace me, shower your grace upon me,
> O Lord, who are in the great town of Araṅkam!
> I do not worship your golden feet all day
> with faultless words.
> I do not talk of your auspicious attributes,
> and my heart is not tinged with love.
> I feel nothing towards the Lord of Araṅkam.
> Alas! Why was I born?
>
> (Tirumālai, vv. 25 and 26)

> I have not done any [ritual] act;
> I have no intelligence;
> and yet,
> I cannot move away from you and survive.
> O king of Cirīvaramaṅkalam,
> I am not a burden on you.
>
> (5.7.1)

Yāmuna echoes this mood in *The Jewel:*

> I am not established in dharma; nor do I have knowledge of my soul; I do not have devotion (bhakti) to your lotus feet; I have nothing; I

have no other refuge (ananyagati) O protector (śaraṇya)! I take refuge at your feet.

(*The Jewel,* v. 22)

Kūrattāḻvāṉ repeats these sentiments in several places, and the following verses are striking examples:

Having no other way, no knowledge, no other refuge, I keep pleading this again and again: I am guilty, I am of a sinful nature, my mind is disturbed, but I am a vessel for your compassion.

(*Sundarabāhu Stava,* v. 132)

I have not done any good deed, nor have I any knowledge. I have no bhakti to your lotus feet. I am a vessel for your compassion.

What is the use of my ranting? I have consciously and unconsciously done every act, big and small, that can be called sin. Forgive me through your grace!

(*Vaikuṇṭha Stava,* vv. 88 and 89)

Parāśara Bhaṭṭar, the son of Kūrattāḻvāṉ, also talks of his unworthiness and lack of qualification to seek refuge with the Lord:

O Lord in Śrīraṅgam! I have always transgressed the laws that you ordained; knowingly and unknowingly, I have offended you and other devotees through thought, word and deed.

(*Śrī Raṅgarāja Stava,* v. 91)

I do not have the wealth of knowledge (jñāna), good works, or devotion; I do not have the strength to even desire you or to repent for it; O Lord of Raṅgam, with confused mind, I say: "I take refuge in you!"

(*Śrī Raṅgarāja Stava,* pt. 2, v. 89)

Submission and Surrender

It is not only in the confessions of sinfulness that we find the stotras similar to the poems of the āḻvārs. In Yāmuna's submission of himself and in his later self-conscious contemplation of his surrender we find strong similarities to Nammāḻvār's poetry. Both Yāmuna's and Nammāḻvār's verses begin with the submission of the soul, followed by the realization that the submitted soul has always belonged to the Lord who is the supreme master and owner of all. The human being has, in a sense, nothing to offer or to submit.

You mingled with my soul; and for that great aid,
I rendered my soul to you.

Can I retrieve it? You are the soul of my soul,
O Lord who devoured the seven worlds!
Who is my soul? Who am I?
You who gave it have now claimed it again.
(2.3.4)

. . . all that I am, whatever qualities I have, from this very day I offer myself at your lotus feet. . . .
O Lord, whatever is mine, whatever I am, are all truly yours. When I am awakened to this knowledge, what can I offer you?
(*The Jewel,* vv. 52 and 53)

The āḻvār and Yāmuna submit their souls to the Lord, and then feel that this is a superfluous act, since the soul has always belonged to him, and was never the property of the human being. This deep sense of being "owned" by the Lord is a theme that we see repeated throughout the Tiruvāymoḻi. And yet, Nammāḻvār surrenders himself several times to the Lord and sometimes this is accompanied by questions of its appropriateness. Yāmuna's verses are interpreted in different ways in the thirteenth century by the theologians Periyavāccāṉ Piḷḷai and Vedānta Deśika, who differ on the necessity of surrendering oneself to the Lord.

Śri in the Stotra Tradition

The Jewel is a model for later stotras of Kūrattāḻvāṉ, Parāśara Bhaṭṭar, and still later for Vedānta Deśika in the thirteenth century. Similarly, Yāmuna's "Four Verses" (Catuḥśloki), a poem written in praise of Śrī, sets the pattern for later compositions by Kūrattāḻvāṉ and Parāśara Bhaṭṭar. This genre of hymns, directly honoring Śrī, the consort of Viṣṇu, owes more to Sanskrit models found, for instance, in the later appendices of the Vedic literature (*Śrī Sūkta*) as well as in the Viṣṇu Purāṇa,[18] than to earlier āḻvār works. While the model and some descriptions of Śrī closely follow the early Sanskrit literature, it would be fair to say that these new hymns to Śrī are extremely significant in the Śrīvaiṣṇava community. They express Śrī's mercy, unbounded compassion and generosity. A verse by Parāśara Bhaṭṭar is typical:

O Mother Maithili! Even while the demon women were taunting you, you saved them from the wrath of Hanumān. Because [of this act] Rāma's [compassion] seems small, for he only protected [those . . . who] sought refuge. But you protected the demon-women at the very time they were tormenting you, even though they did not ask for protection.
(*Śrīguṇaratnakośa,* v. 50)

The theological discussions in the thirteenth century emphasize the distinction and contrast between the Lord's sense of justice and Śrī's overwhelming grace that expects no gesture from a human being. They also glorify her role as a mediator. This is one area where the influence of the āḻvārs is only indirect. All that we note in the āḻvārs' poems is the inseparable nature of Śrī's relationship to Viṣṇu and some indication (again, indirect) of her patience.

Śrī is not the only mediator for the ācāryas; they take refuge in their own teachers, who are seen as mediators in a line going back to Śrī. Listen to the words of Kūrattāḻvāṉ:

> O Varada! I am one who has sought refuge at the feet of Rāmānuja. That Rāmānuja is the light of Yāmuna's clan and Yāmuna is from the line of Nāthamuni who hails from the line of Parāṅkuśa [i.e., Nammāḻvār]. That Nammāḻvār is a servant of your consort; so I am worthy of your gaze!
> (*Varadarāja Stava,* v. 102)

Kūrattāḻvāṉ repeats several times that he takes refuge with his teacher; for him as for Yāmuna this seems to be a premise for the compassion of the Lord. Kūrattāḻvāṉ takes refuge with a teacher who is alive, just as Maturakavi āḻvār surrendered himself to Nammāḻvār. However, for Maturakavi āḻvār the surrender to his teacher seemed to preclude his seeking refuge with the Lord while for both Yāmuna and Kūrattāḻvāṉ, taking refuge with their teachers seems to be a preliminary step to seeking refuge with the Lord.

In the assertion of exclusive devotion to Viṣṇu and the repeated expression of one's desire to serve him continuously, in the meditation on their sinful past and in the seeking of the Lord as the only refuge, the ācāryas continue the fervor seen in the poetry of the āḻvārs. In the stotra literature, the Śrīvaiṣṇava community once again affirms its dual heritage of Tamil and Sanskrit texts. The bilingual Śrīvaiṣṇava ācāryas render distinctive Tamil phrases and thoughts of the āḻvārs into Sanskrit and make it available for a pan-Indian audience. The Tamil idiom is brought out in the familiar format of a Sanskrit stotra. The more popular of these stotra verses are incorporated along with the Tamil verses of the āḻvārs into temple and home rituals.

Rāmānuja's *Three Gadyas*

Rāmānuja's *Three Gadyas* share certain themes with the āḻvārs' Tamil verses and even more with the later Sanskrit hymns to Viṣṇu and to Śrī, but they also have some unique features. The most obvious one is that their devotional content is expressed in prose that shares the emotional intensity of poetry but lacks not only the formal requirements of Sanskrit verse but also its playful spirit. There is no play of images, and there is no bantering wordplay between the devotee and the divine lover. Rāmānuja's mood is one of unremitting praise. In these respects as well as in most of their vocabulary, the *Gadyas* are just like his philosophical works. They are also like those other works in their silence about the āḻvārs, whereas many of the Sanskrit stotras make either veiled or explicit acknowledgment of their indebtedness to Nammāḻvār. Since these stotras were written by the teacher whom Rāmānuja acknowledges as his master (Yāmuna) and by disciples who acknowledge the whole line of their predecessors, emphatically including Rāmānuja, we face a puzzling fact that is as true of the *Gadyas* as of Rāmānuja's other works. Rāmānuja intended his philosophical works to be convincing to an audience of Brahmin scholars outside the community, who might have been shocked by ascribing authority to Tamil poems composed by poets of various castes. The *Gadyas,* however, have always been used within the Śrīvaiṣṇava community and are little known outside it. It appears, therefore, that Rāmānuja was such a conservative Brahmin that when he was writing in Sanskrit he did not make any explicit reference to anything not written in Sanskrit.

That distinctive silence makes it all the more striking that the *Gadyas* do contain the devotional themes that we have noted in this chapter. The exclusive devotion to the Lord and the yearning for fulfillment are often accompanied in both the Tamil and the Sanskrit poems by self-denigration, confessions of sin, and appeal for the Lord's grace. The stotras differ from the āḻvārs' poems, we noted, by a greater willingness to approach the Lord through intermediaries and by much greater emphasis on the joy of serving the Lord than on the bliss of erotic union. There is a range of devotional moods among both āḻvārs and ācāryas, to be sure, and the devoted wife provides a model for devotion that encompasses eager service, passionate longing, and joyous fulfillment. Nevertheless, there is clearly a change in emphasis in the stotras, and it is one quite characteristic of Rāmānuja's devotion.

In the *Śaraṇāgati Gadya* Rāmānuja follows temple practice in first humbly approaching the goddess Śrī and gaining her blessing before making his surrender to Lord Viṣṇu (Nārāyaṇa). Rāmānuja uses Arjuna's words in the Gītā in requesting the Lord's forgiveness and Gāndhārī's words in another passage in the Māhābhārata in addressing the Lord as his "father, mother, friend, teacher, wealth, knowledge," indeed as his "all." The Lord's promises to his devotees in various scriptural passages are also brought into the "conversation." In the *Śrī Raṅga Gadya* Rāmānuja admits he does not deserve the privilege of service that he has requested since he is unable to practice bhaktiyoga and possesses no other good quality. Therefore he takes refuge at Nārāyaṇa's lotus feet. The close relation of some phrases in the *Vaikuṇṭha Gadya* to various other stotras is shown in the notes.

The Dual Vedānta to which Piḷḷāṉ gave explicit recognition in his commentary included not only the Sanskrit scriptures (Vedas, Epics, and Purāṇas) and the āḻvārs' Tamil hymns, but also the sectarian Vaiṣṇava Āgamas and the writings of the first generations of Śrīvaiṣṇava teachers. Most of these writings before Piḷḷāṉ, at least those that survived, were written in Sanskrit, and they included both philosophical works in prose and more imaginative devotional expressions in poetry. Rāmānuja's *Three Gadyas* fall in the latter category, except that they are not in verse but in prose. Rāmānuja's prayer of surrender in the *Śaraṇāgati Gadya* has a special place in this legacy. It became a model for later generations—and even more than a model, for his disciples were convinced that this prayer was answered, that the Lord accepted Rāmānuja's surrender and also accepted Rāmānuja's disciples because of their connection with him. There is little doubt that Piḷḷāṉ felt this living link through Rāmānuja, and it is therefore fitting to end this description of Piḷḷāṉ's double legacy with a condensed version of Rāmānuja's prayer of surrender .

> O you who are opposed to all filth and are entirely auspicious, your essential nature is infinite consciousness and bliss. Your unique celestial form is a treasure trove of infinite qualities. You are an ocean of auspicious qualities of matchless excellence. You are adorned with celestial ornaments and wear celestial weapons.
>
> O Nārāyaṇa, beloved consort of Śrī and of Bhūmi and Nīḷā, your feet are eternally waited upon by countless male and female attendants. You are the Lord of Vaikuṇṭha. Your sport consists in the origination, maintenance, and dissolution of the whole universe. You have eternally realized all your desires and your will is ever accomplished. You are the Supreme Brahman, the Supreme Person, who possesses the great realm of your glory.
>
> You are the refuge of the whole world. You dispel the distress of those who bow to you and are entirely an ocean of motherly love to those who lean on you for support. You always know the true nature and condition of all created beings. You totally control both animate beings and inanimate things.
>
> You are the Owner (śeṣī) of all spiritual and material entities. You are the support of the whole universe. You are the Master of the universe. You are our Master, and you are different from everything else. You are the friend of those in distress.
>
> O Nārāyaṇa united with Śrī, refuge of those without refuge, I have no other resort. I surrender myself and seek refuge at your two lotus-like feet.
>
> (*Śaraṇāgati Gadya*)

Part Two

The Commentator's Synthesis

5

The First Commentary on Nammāḻvār's Tiruvāymoḻi: Tirukkurukai Pirāṉ Piḷḷāṉ's *Six Thousand*

Introduction

Piḷḷāṉ's commentary is the briefest as well as the earliest of the written commentaries on Nammāḻvār's Tiruvāymoḻi. This first commentary, believed to have been written at the specific request of Rāmānuja, is considerably less standardized than its successors. There is great variety in the length of comments on particular verses, ranging from just a single sentence to the several pages of comment on 1.1.7, which include seventy-three quotations from Sanskrit scriptures.[1] Apart from this comment and the comment on 4.10.1, which includes seventy-one Sanskrit verses, Piḷḷāṉ's quotations from Sanskrit or Tamil texts are relatively rare, either as proof texts or as literary embellishments.

The *Six Thousand* is the earliest extant work written in the so-called maṇipravāḷa style, the name indicating that the language consists of Sanskrit "gems" mixed with Tamil "coral." The sentences have a Tamil structure and usually Tamil verbs but a great preponderance of Sanskrit nouns. Indeed the words of Sanskrit origin outnumber the Tamil words by about two to one. In the subsequent commentaries on the Tiruvāymoḻi the proportion of Sanskrit nouns decreases, but the mixed language in all of them is a reflection of the novel character of these works. Commentaries on Sanskrit works, both sacred and semi-secular, had been written for centuries. What is unusual in this case, however, is the fact that a poetic work in a language other than Sanskrit was considered by a community led by Brahmins to be of equivalent value to the Sanskrit Veda and hence as worthy of a commentary as the books of the Sanskrit Veda.

It was considered appropriate for the commentary to be in Tamil, the same language as the verses, a language not far from the ordinary speech of most of Piḷḷāṉ's non-Brahmin contemporaries. However, the particular dialect of Tamil spoken by Piḷḷāṉ and other Brahmins was quite different from this ordinary Tamil because of the large number of Sanskrit words. The language of this commentary, moreover, is that of a student familiar with Rāmānuja's lectures, and possibly with his teachings in written form. When some philosophical clarification is needed, it is provided in words similar or even identical to those of Rāmānuja, often in long phrases consisting entirely of Sanskrit nouns and adjectives. The later commentaries are also in maṇipravāḷa, but the Sanskrit is less prominent and more evenly distributed. The sentences are still heavily Sanskritized but quite recognizably Tamil.

Piḷḷāṉ's commentary thus appears to be the first written work in a style that was to become characteristic of much of the writing and speaking in the Śrīvaiṣṇava community during the subsequent centuries.[2] Piḷḷāṉ's rather peculiar mixture of Tamil and Sanskrit is also an important anticipation of the Śrīvaiṣṇava doctrine of Ubhaya Vedānta: the Dual Theology or the Theology of the Dual Veda, consisting of scriptures in both Sanskrit and Tamil.

The Structure of the Commentary

Piḷḷāṉ tries to fit his comments to the structure of the poem. Unlike the later commentators, he does not start with a general introduction, but he recognizes the obvious division into sets of decads (actually eleven verses including the phala śruti) by introducing each set before he comments on the first verse of the decad. There are also hints, however, of the tripartite division present in many Śrīvaiṣṇava (and other Vedāntic) philosophical works: tattva (reality, here ontology), hita (way or means, here soteriology) and puruṣārtha (goal of human life, here eschatology or conception of final salvation). The suggestion of this division does not come at the beginning of Piḷḷāṉ's commentary but in his introduction to some of the decads in the Tenth Hundred.[3] Wherever the exact line of division may be, it is clear that he considers most of the poem to be concerned with the means or path to salvation, and he interprets Nammāḻvār as recognizing that the truly effective means is bhaktiyoga, the concept in the Bhagavadgītā so emphasized in the commentaries of Yāmuna and Rāmānuja.

The poetic form of the Tiruvāymoḻi is known as antāti: the last word of each verse is the first word of the next verse, and the last word of the very last verse, 10.10.11, is the first word of the first verse, 1.1.1, thus completing the poetic circle. Piḷḷāṉ sees a unity in the meaning of the poem corresponding to the unbroken circle of its form. In his introduction to each decad, he tries to bring out the connection between the previous decad and the one just commencing. For example, in the Fifth Hundred he links the fourth and fifth decads with a passage discussing the relation between the praise of God in one temple and the praise of God in another temple. Then the passage between the seventh and eighth decads summarizes their similar content and notes their connection.

> Thus, the āḻvār, who is in Cirīvaramaṅkalam, could not obtain his desired goal and is sunk [in grief]. Now thinking deeply about the divine knowledge that he has gained, that is, that the Lord's sacred flowerlike feet are his way and his goal (prāpakamum prāpyamum), he becomes

calm and goes to Tirukkuṭantai. Not gaining a union with the Lord here, either, he falls down [in grief] and cries aloud.

(5.8 intro.)

The commentator interprets the poet's moving on from one sacred place to another as being caused both by his frustration and by the knowledge he has gained. The frustration at the first temple is in not gaining intimate (erotic) union with the Lord. He does, however, reflect on the knowledge he has gained that "The Lord's flowerlike feet are both my way and my goal." This knowledge, which is the basis for later Śrīvaiṣṇavas' reliance on God's grace to accomplish their salvation, has a sufficiently calming effect on the poet, as Piḷḷāṉ interprets the matter, so that Nammāḻvār goes on to another temple. There too, however, he tries to gain intimate union with the Lord and cries aloud when he is again disappointed. Even though the knowledge he has gained is considered a Divine gift, it is not enough to satisfy the poet; he continues to yearn for complete union.

Many of Piḷḷāṉ's connecting passages are more perfunctory and less illuminating than this one, for the link between decads is not always clear, and Piḷḷāṉ seeks to make his comments as brief as possible. Since he does not begin with the general introduction that starts each of the later commentaries, however, we have to attend to these connecting passages to each decad in order to discover Piḷḷāṉ's sense of the dynamic movement within the poem.

Translating Tamil into Sanskrit

Many of the distinctive features of Piḷḷāṉ's style as a commentator stem from his understanding of the scriptural authority or revelational significance of the object of his commentary. If, as his community believes, the Tiruvāymoḻi has authority comparable to the Sanskrit Vedas and expresses the same saving truth, its meaning ought to be elucidated in the precise philosophical language developed in the commentaries on the Vedas, more specifically the summing up of the meaning of the Upaniṣads in the commentaries on the Vedānta Sūtras. Piḷḷāṉ's teacher Rāmānuja had written three such commentaries, utilizing the ideas and specific terms of his Śrīvaiṣṇava predecessors Nāthamuni and Yāmuna as well as the general Vedantic vocabulary of twenty to thirty generations of previous commentators. In this case, however, Piḷḷāṉ recognizes that since the poem is in Tamil the commentary should also be in Tamil, even if the paraphrase is in a Tamil filled with Sanskrit philosophical terms.

Though two-thirds of the words are Sanskrit, the commentary is considered by the author and by the entire Śrīvaiṣṇava community to be in Tamil. Some of these Sanskrit words had already been part of Tamil for centuries, especially the Tamil of the Brahmins, but even long Sanskrit compounds are not felt to be out of place in a Tamil sentence. They are considered appropriate to express the precise meaning of the Tamil poems. The reverse is not the case, however. Words from the local vernacular are not allowed in Sanskrit writing. Sanskrit is saṁskṛta, the culturally refined or polished language, with verbal forms generated by its own special rules from its own eternal Vedic roots. It must remain pure. It is true that there was an ancient notion of a pure Tamil faithful to its own distinctive grammar and syntax, a notion that has recently been brought back in the modern Tamil cultural revival. In Piḷḷāṉ's time and cultural milieu, however, Sanskrit has greater prestige than Tamil. It is the language of revelation (śruti), of the eternal Veda. The way Piḷḷāṉ quotes from Sanskrit and Tamil sources illustrates this difference. Unlike many other commentators, Piḷḷāṉ concentrates his citations from the Sanskrit scriptures in comments on only a few verses. Most notable are the seventy-three verses in 1.1.7 in support of the doctrine that God ensouls the universe and the seventy-one verses in 4.10.1 affirming the supremacy of Viṣṇu-Nārāyaṇa.[4] In view of this imbalance and the lack of any general notion of authoritative scriptures in Tamil, the high view Piḷḷāṉ has of the Tiruvāymoḻi itself is all the more remarkable. Piḷḷāṉ only once quotes from another āḻvār's hymn the way he occasionally does from the Sanskrit scriptures, but he does occasionally quote from other verses in the Tiruvāymoḻi. This may mean that the Tiruvāymoḻi is the only Tamil poem that Piḷḷāṉ considers equivalent to the Sanskrit Vedas. However, there is one exception that should lead us to hesitate in reaching this conclusion.

This is in the paraphrase of 2.1.6, where he quotes the Lord's words given in Tirumaṅkai āḻvār's Periya Tirumoḻi 9.3.3, "O innocent girl! I shall not be separated from you." He then immediately goes on to cite a few words from two Sanskrit texts (one the words of Rāma in the Rāmāyana, the other the words of Krishna in the Gītā) that Śrīvaiṣṇavas consider key verses in the doctrine of prapatti (humble surrender to God). This strongly suggests that he considers Tirumaṅkai's verse containing the Lord's words in Tamil to have the same scriptural authority as the Sanskrit words of Rāma and Krishna respectively. A second possible exception is Piḷḷāṉ's use of the expression Tiru-pallāṇṭu ([Live for] "many auspicious years") familiar to all Śrīvaiṣṇavas. It is not clear whether Piḷḷāṉ uses the greeting with scriptural authority (Periyāḻvār's hymn) or simply as a pious expression equivalent to "Blessed be the Lord" or "God be praised."

The most characteristic linguistic shift in Piḷḷāṉ's paraphrases is from a Tamil dominated by verbs to a Tamil filled with Sanskrit compounds and nominal phrases. Piḷḷāṉ's frequent use of phrases reminiscent of Rāmānuja is one indication of his acceptance and utilization in this commentary of the views of his teacher, which we shall examine in more detail in chapter 11.

Why does Piḷḷāṉ's paraphrase seem so different from the original poem? Clearly the shift to prose and the use of Sanskrit equivalents for the Tamil words in the poem are important reasons, but there is at least one other. Piḷḷāṉ thinks that Nammāḻvār is responding to questions in the minds of his listeners. Thus Piḷḷāṉ frequently writes, "If it is asked ——, the āḻvār replies, ——."

This notion of question and answer is itself a product of the scholastic commentarial tradition, but there is no reason to suppose that Piḷḷāṉ uses this form simply as a literary device. He doubtless believes that Nammāḻvār, as a great teacher of divine truth, would anticipate the questions of those he was addressing. The fact that the poetry is dramatic or even lyrical does not prevent it, in Piḷḷāṉ's understanding, from also being didactic. This, after all, is how Brahmin scholars have treated much of the poetry in the Sanskrit scriptures, beginning with the Vedic hymns themselves.

"Translating" Poetic Images into Concepts

Interpreting poetry in prose is the task of much commentary, both aesthetic and religious. There are some examples in the Śrīvaiṣṇava tradition of poetic works commenting on and certainly inspired by earlier poetry, but generally commentary is in the language of conversation, which is prose. When conversation is used for clarification it tends to move from images to concepts. Traditional Hindu commentators did not suffer from any modern Western doubts about the possibility of translating images into concepts, but neither were they so overconfident as to allow the translation to replace the original. It is the poetry itself that has revelatory significance and salvific power. The commentary is enlightened and empowered by that poetry and therefore intends to be as faithful to its meaning as possible. It is important to emphasize this, since from our modern perspective the difference between commentary and original poem may be more evident than their affinity. Generations of Śrīvaiṣṇavas, however, have believed that the commentaries only bring out the meaning of the verses, and in particular help those who recite or listen to the verses better to savor their distinctive flavor.

One function of such a prose commentary is to spell out in greater detail the points briefly stated or alluded to in the verse. Here is a typical example:

> Worshiping the Lord,
> who runs the seven worlds alone from heaven,
> who has undecaying fortune,
> who rules with great capacity,
> who split the angry beast,
> until my hands feel comfortable.
> Praising him . . . ,
> Is there any need [unfulfilled] in seven
> generations
> for one who has the capacity to say
> garlands of words [for the Lord]?

Sing Tirupallāṇṭu ([Live for] "many auspicious years") to the Lord, who graciously wills that his rule of all the worlds should originate from [his seat] on the Primordial Serpent in the supreme heaven; who by one thousandth part of his will rules all the worlds; who has unique, eternal, faultless, unsurpassed, auspicious qualities, and is perfect in every way. In order to protect his devotees, he always destroys their enemies. With such a nature he descended to the house of Vasudeva. "Sing thus and bow in such a way that all the weariness in my hands will vanish," says the āḻvār. [He continues], "I have the great fortune to sing the Tiruvāymoḻi. Now I need nothing."

(4.5.1)

In many verses Piḷḷāṉ has difficulty conveying a poetic figure of speech in a straightforward prose "translation." Sometimes the meaning is kept but the forceful image is lost. We see this in Piḷḷāṉ's comment on 3.5.3.

To protect the cowherds and all the cows,
  from the rain and the stones,
  the Lord lifted up the mountain.
Those who do not sing continuously
  turn somersaults, dance in joy
  and spread the word of this Lord,
are worthless beings sunk deep,
toiling in miserable hell.

Those few who do not become excited (aprākṛtinga) when thinking of the one who has the great virtue (mahā guṇa) of enjoying protecting cattle and other beings who are ignorant of [God's] aid (upakārabhijña) are equal to those who experience Raurava and other hells.

(3.5.3)

The commentator here also adds an idea that was to have central importance in subsequent Śrīvaiṣṇava theology, especially in its Teṅkalai formulation. This is the idea that the Lord enjoys "protecting cattle and other creatures that do not recognize his help." The Lord enjoys helping those who are incapable of repaying him and who are not even aware of his aid. This idea is extended in the striking Teṅkalai metaphor of the mother cow's enjoyment of—indeed, frenzied excitement at—the opportunity to lick clean her newborn calf. In Nammāḻvār's verse the excitement is on the part of the devotees thinking about the sheer grace and maternal affection of such a magnificently generous Lord. If one is not moved "to turn somersaults," one really deserves no better fate than some loathsome hell.

One striking poetic term is that of the thief. Piḷḷāṉ is not shocked by the poet calling the Lord a "thief" (cf. 9.6.3 and 9.6.5, quoted in chapter 12), since in the context of Divine-human love "stealing my heart" has the same meaning as in Western romantic language. In one verse, however, the lovesick girl (representing the poet) is referred to by her mother as "my little thief," though it is she who experiences cruelty. It is interesting to see what the commentator does with this verse.

> [The words of the mother]:
> "My inner soul is parched,
>   my dear one,
>   my gracious one!"
> she cries; and then:
> "And *you* recline on the flood!"
> O, the cruelty experienced
>   by my little thief!

> Since she is grief-stricken at being separated from God and cannot bear that distress, she says, "My Kaṇṇā!" just as thirsty people say, "Water, water!" And then she says, "You recline on the floods." [The mother says], "How did this girl whose beauty is capable of conquering even the Lord become so entangled in his qualities?"
>
> (2.4.7)

The meaning of the girl's thievery is made explicit: her "beauty is capable of conquering even the Lord," but it is she who has become so "entangled" in the Lord's attractive and enthralling qualities that she cannot bear her separation from her Divine lover. Piḷḷāṉ shortens the phrase in the verse, "My inner soul is parched, my dear one, my gracious," to the short cry, "My Kaṇṇā (Krishna)!" said with the same force as the thirsty person cries "Water, water!" In this case both poet and commentator impose one image on another. Behind the Divine lover who becomes so involved with the human devotee is the all-sufficient Lord of the universe, surrounded by milk, in the midst of the cosmic flood. In this case, therefore, Piḷḷāṉ leaves out the striking phrase "my little thief" but manages to make more explicit the complicated double image of the verse.

In commenting on some verses, Piḷḷāṉ gives the symbolic or theological equivalents of the terms used in the verse. A special case of this is in his comment on 8.2.7, where the verse contains a list of names of God (Viṣṇu-Nārāyaṇa). Piḷḷāṉ indicates the meaning of this list of proper names with a list of Divine attributes or qualities, all of which also appear separately in his comments on a large number of verses.[5] This inclusion of a whole list of equivalencies occurs only rarely in Piḷḷāṉ's commentary. It is as close as he comes to a full-blown allegorical interpretation, in which each item mentioned in a particular verse has its true meaning in a higher, spiritual realm. Neither Piḷḷāṉ's commentary nor any of the three great commentaries following Piḷḷān has such a systematic allegorical scheme. Such allegory first appears in the Śrīvaiṣṇava tradition more than two centuries after Piḷḷāṉ.

In the following chapters a number of attempts at harmonization will become evident. The comments on two verses in 6.3 illustrate this tendency to resolve apparently conflicting doctrines in the verses. The most frequently utilized principle in such harmonization is to see paradoxical contraries as the diverse expressions of the Lord's cosmic body. Piḷḷāṉ repeats the words "poverty and wealth, hell and heaven . . . enmity and friendship, poison and ambrosia" in 6.3.1 as "My Lord is the inner soul (antarātmā bhūta) of poverty and wealth, hell and heaven, enmity and friendship, poison and ambrosia." Interestingly, the paraphrase of the fifth verse in the decad (6.3.5) simply restates the paradoxical list of Divine qualities: "My Lord whose form is straight and crooked, white and black, truth and lies, youth and age, new and old. . . ." In the paraphrase of the next verse (6.3.6), Piḷḷāṉ explicitly introduces his harmonizing principle:

> . . . He is the indweller of all the worlds, love and hate, Lakṣmī and anti-Lakṣmī, praise and blame; he fills all auspicious (*kalyāṇa*) and filthy (*heya*) things; and he is their inner soul. . . . he is without stain. If it is asked, how is this possible? [the āḻvār] says: It is because he has entered my filthy heart and is still not affected by the evil; he is the unsurpassed flame.
>
> (6.3.6)

The fact that the commentary is in prose and shares the concern of much prose discourse for rational precision and consistency does not mean, however, that the commentator is unaware of the poetic character of his subject or that his own comments lack affinity with that poetry.

Piḷḷāṉ is well aware, moreover, of the different dramatic voices that Nammāḻvār uses throughout the poem, and, as we shall see in chapter 8, he tries to interpret the meaning of individual verses or decads according to the specific mood of each distinct dramatic dialogue. There is one poetic image that occurs so frequently and in such important contexts that it is a crucial metaphor in the entire poem. This is the image of eating, swallowing, or even devouring. It is, indeed, so important that we shall devote all of chapter 12 to examining its ramifications.

The Commentator's View of the Poem as a Whole

Since Piḷḷāṉ does not begin his commentary with a general introduction, it is difficult to determine his overall view of the Tiruvāymoḻi. Because of his own view of the commentator's role, he tries to allow the poem to speak for itself by paraphrasing each verse and summarizing the significance of each decad.

We could therefore ask: what does Piḷḷāṉ understand Nammāḻvār to be saying through the verses themselves about the significance of the entire poem?

One place to look for such overviews is in the commentaries on the phala śrutis, the extra (usually eleventh) verse attached to each decad that, following an Indian literary convention, indicates the benefit or "fruit" (phala) from reciting or listening to the previous set of ten verses. The phala śrutis are an integral part of the poem, for they are part of the antāti chain (the first word repeating the last word or syllable of the previous verse, etc.).

A good example is 4.9.11, coming at the end of a decad full of yearning for the Lord and a plea for the Lord's gracious presence.

> These ten verses
> on the sacred feet of the Lord
> out of the thousand Tamil verses
> composed by Kurukūr Caṭakōpaṉ
> with the goal of reaching
> the sacred feet of Nārāyaṇa,
> Keśava, the radiant flame,
> will make one reach the sacred feet.
> Reach the sacred feet
> and be united with them!

> This *tiruvāymoḻi,* which praises the Lord out of the wondrous love of seeing him, will by itself cause those who recite it to obtain the Lord's feet. [The āḻvār] says: be attached to his sacred feet like the lines on them.
>
> (4.9.11)

Here the commentator adds a striking image (the unity of the lines on the feet with the feet themselves) and accurately paraphrases the apparently extravagant promise of the verse. The commentator shares the poet's confidence in the saving power of the poetic words themselves. For both author and commentator, the significance of the poem may lie not so much in the delineation of an intellectually coherent vision as in the communication of salvific power, and that power is communicated unit by unit in the very act of recitation. There may be hyperbole in the description of each specific fruit, but by such hyperbole the importance of reciting the Tiruvāymoḻi is made dramatically apparent. Near the end of the poem, for example, in a decad that describes the heavenly goal or sacred land (Tirunāṭu), Piḷḷāṉ paraphases the phala śruti as follows: "Heaven (Tirunāṭu) is under the orders of those who recite these ten verses" (10.8.11).

Piḷḷāṉ is confident that the poem he is paraphrasing and explaining is a very special one, in which the Lord inspires the poet and speaks through the poet's words. This is not because of the inclusion of discourses by the Lord, as in the Bhagavadgītā, still less because of any thundering "Thus saith the Lord" passages, as in the Hebrew prophets. The poet does speak as different persons, with different voices: these are all human voices, speaking the human language of "sweet Tamil." In several verses, however, Nammālvār clearly states his belief that the Lord is speaking through the words of his verses, that the Lord is entering and using him to sing the Tiruvāymoli. Piḷḷāṉ's comments on this subject of divine inspiration or revelation follow directly from the content of several of Nammālvār's verses.

The decad that deals most explicitly with this subject is 7.9, which is included in its entirety in Part Four. Piḷḷāṉ anticipates the content of the verses to follow in his introduction: "The Lord enters the ālvār and speaks (sings) the Tiruvāymoli through him." The first verse of the decad has been quoted in chapter 1. Piḷḷāṉ interprets Nammālvār to mean that the Lord makes the poet his own by purifying him every day, taking him as an instrument and by his omnipotence and radiance causing him to sing the Tiruvāymoli (7.9.1). By the same indwelling presence that enables the Lord to accomplish the creation, maintenance, and destruction of the world through actions of the lower gods, "He took me as an instrument and graciously sang the Tiruvāymoli" (7.9.2).

In the sixth verse Nammālvār sings, "Not just singing poems to exalt himself through the great poets who sing sweet songs, today he came so joyously, made himself [one] with me, and through me sings mighty songs about himself. My Lord of heaven!" Piḷḷāṉ's paraphrase shifts the emphasis: it is the Lord who does not sing about himself through the great poets, and the Lord is "the poet who is not limited by the Vedas or by himself." Piḷḷāṉ's paraphrase of verse 9 says that having taken Nammālvār, the Lord and the Goddess (Lakṣmī) sing the poem, and the paraphrase of verse ten includes the line, "You thus took me and graciously sang the Tiruvāymoli."

In 10.6.4 Piḷḷāṉ follows the verse closely in virtually repeating the sentiments expressed in 7.9.5 above: "Without regarding my insignificance, using me as an instrument, the Lord uttered the Tiruvāymoli. Is Heaven (Tirunāṭu) any better than my good fortune in his taking me and making me say the Tiruvāymoli?"

In the introduction to the next decad (10.7) Piḷḷāṉ puts this idea of Divine revelation in his own words: "The Lord who mingled with the ālvār and listened to the ālvār does as the ālvār said and [thus] makes himself conformable to the ālvār's words."

Although this exalted view of the Tiruvāymoli would seem to move directly towards the Śrīvaiṣṇava doctrine of Ubhaya Vedānta, Piḷḷāṉ's most extensive comment on the nature of the Vedas makes clear that the Tamil "scripture" is not simply identical with the Sanskrit scriptures. Here is his expanded paraphrase:

> The Vedas, which are transhuman and which are faultless, exalt and proclaim the soul of the Supreme Person who is difficult to obtain. [The Supreme Person] is the supreme goal and the medicine for all the sorrow of people still in transitory existence. He is also known by the human beings who with ascetic prowess, wisdom, and yogic attainment have all their sins destroyed and in whom has arisen devotion towards his sacred feet. I got to know the Lord, without there being any reason for it, says the āḻvār, that is, without any reason I have come to know him who cannot be known as he really is by the Vedas and those who know the Vedas.
>
> (9.3.3)

The emphasis in Piḷḷāṉ's comment is on the Lord and the knowledge of the Lord. It is the function of the Vedas "to make known and exalt the Supreme Person," yet Piḷḷāṉ's final sentence interpreting Nammāḻvār's words clearly states that Nammāḻvār has come to a knowledge of the Lord far superior to Vedic knowledge, for the Lord "cannot be known as he really is by the Vedas and those who know the Vedas." This would suggest that Nammāḻvār's words should supersede the Vedas. That does not happen in the Śrīvaiṣṇava tradition, but the commentarial tradition certainly lifts the Tiruvāymoḻi to a level equal to the superhuman Vedas, and, incredible as it might seem in a tradition so dominated by Brahmins, sometimes even higher than the Vedas and the entire Sanskrit tradition of sacred lore.

6

Tattva: The Fundamental Reality of God and God's World

General Statements about the Divine Nature

Although Piḷḷāṉ takes seriously his task of writing a commentary on particular verses of the Tiruvāymoḻi, he also makes a number of summary statements of Śrīvaiṣṇava doctrines. The phrases in these statements are often very close to those of his teacher Rāmānuja, and he shares Rāmānuja's tendency to turn brief doxologies into short credos. Here is one example:

> The Lord is the controller (niyantā) of meritorious (puṇya) and sinful (pāpa) deeds (karma), and of the results (phala) of deeds. He is the cause of the entire earth, has the divine form of the unsurpassed glow of a blue gem and has eyes like the lotus leaf. He is worshipped by Śeṣa (the primordial serpent) and . . . other angelic beings (sūris). Worship him with superlative bhakti, without the defects of egoism, and without being associated with anything that is distinct from him.[1]
>
> (3.5.10)

A different kind of general statement is that contained in the unique decad 2.7, which actually consists of thirteen verses, one for each of the twelve names of God (Viṣṇu), plus the usual phala śruti.[2] Interestingly, the brief introductory statement points not to the specific content of the names but to their significance for Nammāḻvār's followers: "These verses discuss the meanings relevant to the fact that because of the affection [the Lord] has for me [that is, the āḻvār] even those who are associated with me [the āḻvār] are accepted graciously by him." Here are some lines from Piḷḷāṉ's paraphrases:

> By . . . Nārāyaṇa who is Lord of all, master of the never-tiring immortals, and my master, those who are associated with me for several generations become those whose only enjoyment is the Lord.
>
> (2.7.1)

> Īśvara is the inner soul of all beings, the Lord of all the worlds and the meaning of all the Vedas.
>
> (2.7.2)

> With unsurpassed beauty . . . as one who is accessible to those who take refuge [in him], the Lord of supreme compassion entered and stayed in me, and by banishing [my] faults obstructing our union, he became my supreme enjoyment.
>
> (2.7.3)

> Thus he enters into me, . . . makes me sing and dance [proclaiming] his lordship over all, his dependence on his devotees and his essential nature. He corrects me, accepts me, and . . . even takes those connected with me, uniting them with his auspicious feet.
>
> (2.7.4)

The Supremacy of Viṣṇu-Nārāyaṇa

A major theme of the commentary, sometimes in a mood of sheer praise, sometimes in a more argumentative mood, is Nammāḻvār's exaltation of the Supreme Lord, the true God, Viṣṇu-Nārāyaṇa. We see this clearly in Piḷḷāṉ's comment on the very first verse of the poem through a paraphrase that draws heavily on Rāmānuja's language.

> The āḻvār with his holy soul experiences the Supreme Person as he really is. This is the Supreme Person who has transcendent, extraordinary, [and] divine ornaments, weapons, consorts, and attendants; and whose sport is the creation, development, [and destruction] of this universe.
>
> The āḻvār speaks as he experiences the love that arises from his being with the Lord. [The āḻvār says]: [The Lord] is wholly opposed to all faults, and [is characterized] by the statement "He who has the bliss a thousand times that of human beings" (Taittirīya Upaniṣad 2.8.1). [The Lord] is an immense ocean of infinite bliss that is multiplied a thousandfold and other auspicious attributes. He who has this bliss and other auspicious attributes further has that great quality, like gold having a fragrance, of making himself known to me, without any reason, so that there is not even a trace (literally, "whiff") of ignorance. [He arouses in] me unsurpassed bhakti toward his sacred feet. This Lord who has all auspicious attributes shows his generosity to Śeṣa, Garuḍa, and other innumerable divine beings who are naturally and wholly without fault and who have unflickering wisdom. His flowerlike feet have the inherent nature of dispelling all sorrows of his devotees. . . .
>
> (1.1.1)

Piḷḷāṉ interprets the next verse to be about the essential nature of the Lord's divine (celestial) self. The main point of these definitions is to distinguish the

Lord from all other entities and to make clear the superiority to all finite beings of the Lord who is "opposed to everything defiling" and "wholly and infinitely auspicious" (heya pratyanīka and kalyāṇaikatānatayā, two favorite phrases of Rāmānuja). The Lord

> is different from the non-sentient things that are known by our sense organs, . . . is different [lit., "of a different genus"] from the essential nature of the extremely pure soul known by the inner organ that has been made extremely pure by the practice of yoga.[3] [He] has no equal in the three times, . . . has no equal or superior, [his] essential nature is wholly wisdom and bliss, . . . [and] is my support.
>
> (1.1.2)

In a similar way Piḷḷāṉ sees the third verse as a description of

> the wealth of the universe which belongs to the Lord whose essential nature, auspicious qualities, and realm are distinct from all other entities. . . . The Lord [who] is the soul of everything, including the earth, firmament, all worlds, animate beings, and inanimate things, who is the owner of all things, who is the soul of the universe, but . . . is free from their shortcomings, . . . is pure. His . . . [dominion] is such as to control the universe which is his body, but he is different from everything.
>
> (1.1.3)

A different kind of assertion of Viṣṇu-Nārāyaṇa's supremacy is contained in those comments that speak of Lord Viṣṇu's superiority to all other deities, especially the two other deities in the trimūrti (Brahmā and Śiva) and the chief Vedic gods, Indra and Agni. Thus Piḷḷāṉ, citing a number of verses from Scripture in support, says of 1.1.8 that "this verse refutes those who hold heterodox doctrines, who identify the Lord described in Scripture with Brahmā who creates or Śiva (Rudra) who destroys." Commenting on 2.2.2, Piḷḷāṉ quotes Viṣṇu Purāṇa 1.22.21, "Except for Hari [Viṣṇu] who is the guardian of all, no one is able to protect me," and then continues, "The protector who banished the great sin (pāpa) of Rudra [that is, enabling him to lose the skull of Brahmā that had stuck to his wrist since he had cut off Brahmā's fifth head] became the lion [that is, Krishna the fierce protector] of the cowherds and, by dispelling the sin of all the worlds became the protector (savior) of all."

Another comment is more extensive and more striking:

> Praise the lotus-eyed Lord
> Who is the form of the three gods
> Who is the first among the first three
> Who removes curses

Who lies on the deep ocean
Who is the Lord of the divine beings
Whose bow burnt the beautiful Lanka and
Who destroys our sins.

> The Lord . . . is thus in the form of the trimūrti. He is the support of Brahmā, Rudra, and Indra who bring forth all the worlds. He saves them from the danger of the demons who cause grief and who steal their Vedas. He has the Sea of Milk as his abode. Being all this, with the intention of being a refuge, he descended as the son of Daśaratha [i.e., Rāma]. Though a man, by virtue of his bodily form, personal qualities, manifestations [incarnations], and deeds, he is as different from the [lower] divine beings as they are from human beings. His only enjoyment is expelling the enemies of his devotees. . . .
>
> (3.6.2)

Two other comments bring out two related facets of Piḷḷāṉ's treatment of this topic. In a comment in the first decad Piḷḷāṉ agrees that Indra and other deities do have the power to grant worldly benefits (including svarga, the lower and temporary heaven within the continuing cycle of births and deaths) to those who perform the scripturally prescribed rituals. This is because "it is the Supreme Person himself who is the inner soul of Indra and other divine beings and becomes the one propitiated by all rituals" (1.1.5). Piḷḷāṉ then goes on to give a long list of scriptural verses, many of them already quoted by Rāmānuja to establish the same point.

The second comment closely follows the sense of the verse.

> The divine beings with whom you take refuge are merely mediators of the Lord's protection. . . . When scripture says that [these gods] are worthy of being worshiped, it means only that the Supreme Person is their inner controller. He has them as his body, and he receives all [sacrificial] action (karma) and worship.[4]
>
> (5.2.7)

This comment comes in the middle of one of the most triumphal decads in the Tiruvāymoḻi, that celebrating the spread of the devotion and the breaking of the power of the present evil age (Kali Yuga). This gives the context for Piḷḷāṉ's comment three verses later in the same decad:

> Brahmā, (the four-faced one), Śiva (Paśupati), Indra, and other divine beings, by taking refuge in the Lord, become guardians of the world. So if you should also take refuge in the Lord, there would be no more Kali Yuga.
>
> (5.2.10)

The parallel between the poet and the lesser gods is taken even further in a verse already cited in chapter 5 above: Just [as the Lord existed] as the soul of Brahmā, Rudra, and other deities and caused creation and destruction, [so] "He took me as an instrument and graciously sang the Tiruvāymoḻi" (7.9.2). These gods, like human devotees, have "taken refuge" in Lord Viṣṇu to attain salvation, and the Lord is their inner controller as he is that of every soul, but what is special about Nammāḻvār's vocation, according to Piḷḷāṉ, is that, just as the Lord creates the world using Brahmā as his instrument, so he sings the Tiruvāymoḻi using the poet as his instrument.

The central theme of the last decad in the Fourth Hundred is the supremacy of Viṣṇu-Nārāyaṇa. For this reason we are including all of 4.10 in Part Four. Some of the verses and their commentaries are similar to the verses already cited. 4.10.8 closely resembles 5.2.7, which we have just quoted. A condensed version of the commentary on three of the verses is worth including here.

> "Is there a Lord other than Nārāyaṇa?" asks the āḻvār of those who are devoted to lesser gods. [He is the support, controller, and owner of these other gods and is worshiped by them] (4.10.1). But then why should Nārāyaṇa make us take refuge in other gods? . . . [He has done so because] if everyone were to be liberated, this world . . . would cease to function. Thus, to ensure the continuation of this world [the Lord has arranged] that you who have done evil deeds will . . . resort to other gods and go through births and deaths. [Now that you know this] go to the Lord immediately and take refuge in him, so you can stop the wheel of birth and death and obtain [the privilege of] loving service to the Supreme Person (4.10.6). What have you achieved by resorting to other gods from beginningless time? Leave them and take refuge with the . . . Lord.
>
> (4.10.7)

The same sentiments are expressed in Piḷḷāṉ's comment on the very last verse of the poem, the final phala śruti: "the . . . verses of Kurukūr Caṭakōpaṉ who obtained the Lord and who passionately spoke of the Lord as the inner soul of Brahmā, Rudra, and all other souls" (10.10.11).

The Divine Consorts

The self-designation Śrīvaiṣṇava, not found in any of Rāmānuja's Sanskrit writings, occurs several times in Piḷḷāṉ's Commentary. It means those who worship (or follow, or belong to) Viṣṇu in conjunction with his consort Śrī, the Auspicious One, which is another name for Lakṣmī, the goddess of wealth. In fact, Śrīvaiṣṇavas recognize three goddesses who are the consorts of Viṣṇu-Nārāyaṇa. In addition to the "Great Mother," as she is called in Tamil (Periya Pirāṭṭi), who is always recognized as the first consort, are Bhū, the goddess earth, and Nappiṉṉai, Krishna's cowherd wife in the Tamil version of the Krishna story, whose Sanskrit name is Nīḷā. Once, where the verse mentions only Śrī (Tirumakaḷ) and Bhū as the Lord's goddesses (devī), Piḷḷāṉ paraphrases "You who are the Lord (and lover, nāyakaṉ) of Lakṣmī, Bhū and Nīḷā."[5] The wives of Viṣṇu in his various incarnations or descents (avatāra) are considered incarnations of Śrī, though occasionally some distinction is made between the Goddess in her supreme form and in her incarnational form, especially as Sītā.

There is also the woman-saint Āṇṭāḷ, who is said to have been married to the image form of the Lord (Lord Raṅga) at the Śrīraṅgam Temple. Like the male āḻvārs, Āṇṭāḷ is treated as a human figure of special rank because of the Lord's special favor, and therefore worthy of worship, but she is not a fourth divine consort. Sometimes she is considered as an incarnation of Bhū. Nappiṉṉai (Nīḷā) is definitely third in rank, and might seem to be equivalent to Krishna's other wives, or to Rāma's wife Sītā, but she is frequently, though not always, mentioned with the other two divine consorts. Likewise Bhū is also the wife of the incarnation Varāha, the giant boar who rescued her (the earth) from the demons. Such inconsistencies in the scheme seem not to have troubled Piḷḷāṉ or any other Śrīvaiṣṇavas, nor does there seem to have been any problem of jealousy between the goddesses themselves, or between the goddesses on the one side and the passionate human devotees of the Lord, notably Nammāḻvār himself, on the other.

There was a later dispute among Śrīvaiṣṇavas concerning the ontological status of Śrī, the Teṅkalais holding that she is the most exalted of all finite souls, while the Vaṭakalais hold that she is a part of ultimate Godhead, and thus infinite rather than finite. This theoretical difference does not seem to have affected the practical significance of the goddesses for all Śrīvaiṣṇavas. They are almost always iconically represented along with Viṣṇu, and their favor (especially that of Śrī) is prayed for by the devotee before he or she approaches Viṣṇu himself.

One significant comment is the following.

> The radiant One,
>   infinitely blissful,
>   infinitely handsome,
> is captivated by the delightful spell of the
>   Lady of the Lotus.
> My father is infinitely wise,
>   with infinite wisdom, he acts.
> I clasped the feet of Kaṇṇaṉ who is
>   infinitely wonderful.
> I am without grief.

> [The Lord] has not [even] a touch of sorrow. He is auspicious and exceedingly radiant. Because of the love born of his constant union with Śrī, who is exceedingly tender and beautiful and possesses other fully auspicious qualities, he is excited. Because of this union he possesses unsurpassed divine knowledge. With this knowledge and Śrī he creates the world, etc. as his sport. After clasping the auspicious feet of this "Wondrous Lord of Beautiful Dvāraka," all my sorrows were expelled.
> (3.10.8)

In his very high view of Śrī, Piḷḷāṉ seems to expand the suggestion of the verse. Later Śrīvaiṣṇava theology generally associates Śrī with the salvific but not the creative work of God, possibly to make more explicit a distinction between Śrī and the various śaktis ("creative energies") conceived as consorts or partners of Lord Śiva. On the other hand, in one verse Lakṣmī and her elder sister "Anti-Lakṣmī" (that is, misfortune) are mentioned in a series of contrasting elements in the universe, in all of whom the Lord is the indweller (6.3.6). Here Piḷḷāṉ closely paraphrases the verse itself.

At the end of a decad in which the poet assumes the role of the love-sick maiden, the maiden's friend speculates, "Perhaps she is Piṉṉai; perhaps this is the Lady of the Earth; or perhaps it is the Auspicious Lady (Lakṣmī) who is reborn here?" Piḷḷāṉ paraphrases this part of the verse as follows:

> Is this girl who is drowning in the flood of her longing for the Lord, the Lady Nappiṉṉai? Or is she the Lady of the Earth? Or could she be the Great Lady (Śrī)? No, we know that it is our friend by her exceeding love.
> (6.5.10)

An important reference to Śrī by Piḷḷāṉ is in the verse he interprets as Nammāḻvār's decisive act of surrender or to "taking refuge" in the Lord (6.10.10, included in Part Four). The verse starts as follows: "O you on whose breast resides the lady of the flower who says, 'I cannot move away from him even for a second,'" and proceeds with further invocations up to the conclusion "I, your servant, who am without shelter, sat at your feet and entered [your safe haven]." Piḷḷāṉ brings these two sentences together: "I, your servant, who am without refuge and without any other goal, having the Divine Mother as the mediator (puruṣakāra), took refuge at your sacred feet" (6.10.10). In Piḷḷāṉ's commentary, the term *puruṣakāra* is used in other ways, to refer to the mediation of other deities through whom one worships Viṣṇu or the mediation of Śrīvaiṣṇavas. The comment on 6.10.10, however, is the first reference in Śrīvaiṣṇava literary tradition to the mediation of the Goddess Śrī. Full of compassion and motherly affection, Śrī might be expected to win for the suppliant the favor of the Lord in whose nature paternal love is balanced by the resolve to do justice. Because the need for such a mediator, who reinforces father love with mother love, is not made explicit until two generations after Piḷḷāṉ, his use of the term *puruṣakāra* is significant. It is not used in Yāmuna's short hymn to Śrī or even in Rāmānuja's "Hymn of Surrender" (*Śaraṇāgati Gadya*), where the suppliant takes refuge with Śrī before addressing the Lord himself in a similar act of surrender. That double surrender may have been very much in Piḷḷāṉ's mind as he interpreted Nammāḻvār's "taking refuge."

God's Relation to the Universe

From a modern historical perspective, it is not surprising that the philosophical developments during the hundreds of years between the poem and the commentary have changed the commentator's ideas as well as his vocabulary. It may be harder for us to grasp what the tradition has simply assumed: at those points where the poet is singing about the unity of God and the universe, the commentator expresses this common Hindu sense of non-duality (advaita) in the more precise if more prosaic terms of scholastic Sanskrit. It would not have occurred to Piḷḷāṉ and the later commentators, however, that the translation of the poet's words involved a metaphysical as well as a linguistic shift. It may not occur to us, unless we pay close attention, what a serious and systematic translation was going on. The whole of this book is an effort to explore this process of translation or transposition. Because the following comments express a favorite theme of Rāmānuja's, we need to take special pains to discover his disciple Piḷḷāṉ's own intentions.

Piḷḷāṉ regards the poet's Tamil words to be in perfect agreement with the meaning of the Sanskrit scriptures as expounded by Yāmuna and Rāmānuja. Of Rāmānuja's concepts concerning God's relation to the universe, the most important one, which is also most evident in Piḷḷāṉ's comments, is the analogy of the indwelling soul to the body that it animates. It is worth noting here that Piḷḷāṉ simply assumes that this analogy is well known to his readers and to Nammāḻvār.

We noted above that much of Piḷḷāṉ's philosophical position is spelled out in his paraphrases of the first three verses of the poem and that those comments are filled with the theological and philosophical terminology of Rāmānuja. When we come to the fourth verse of the first decad, which appears to be one of the most pantheistic or paradoxical verses in the whole poem, we may be surprised to see that Piḷḷāṉ's comment is very brief.

> We here and that man, this man,
>   and that other in-between,
> and that woman, this woman,
>   and that other, whoever,
>
> those people, and these,
>   and these others in-between,

this thing, that thing,
  and this other in-between, whichever,

all things dying, these things,
  those things, those others in-between,
good things, bad things,
  things that were, that will be,

being all of them,
he stands there.

[Translated by A. K. Ramanujan][6]

The previous [verses] of the *tiruvāymoḻi* are now explained. The essential nature of all the objects mentioned with various descriptive phrases is said to be that of dependence on the Lord.

(1.1.4)

Piḷḷāṉ evidently found this interpretation so self-evident that it had neither to be defended nor explained. The Tamil word that dominates this verse is the past participle *āy,* "having become," which is very frequently used in Tamil and sometimes means "as" (A. K. Ramanujan translates this as "being"). Thus the verse could be translated either (1) "having become this, this, and this, he stands" or (2) "as this, this, and this, he exists." Piḷḷāṉ seems to be following the latter course, but even to understand this interpretation we need to be aware of a concept of Rāmānuja's almost as fundamental as his concept of the soul-body relationship.

This is the relationship of substance and mode. Sometimes this is expressed in grammatical terms as the relation of the subject of a sentence to a predicate adjective. It is understood that the substance is the fundamental reality that includes but is distinct from its own adjectival qualities. Because the substance (or grammatical subject) is the foundation, the modes (or predicate adjectives) completely depend on it. Piḷḷāṉ makes this point a few verses later when he says that "coordinate predication" (sāmānādhikaraṇya) means "that the creation and movement of the earth is dependent on the Lord" (1.1.7). Piḷḷāṉ has thus put into the language of dependence Rāmānuja's doctrine that the Lord is the underlying substance qualified by a number of diverse and even opposite modes. Taking āy to mean "as," Piḷḷāṉ thus interprets Nammāḻvār to mean the Lord is qualified as quality A, as quality B, etc.

While this doctrine may be initially puzzling to us, it was not paradoxical for Piḷḷāṉ or anyone else who had accepted this notion of substance and mode in understanding the nature of God. What is paradoxical, or at least mysterious, is the Lord's disclosure, which both the poet and commentator do not emphasize until later in the poem, that the Lord is dependent on his dependents (āśritas), that is, on those persons who are not only metaphysically dependent on God but are emotionally aware of that dependence, being utterly devoted to God.

Piḷḷāṉ follows the sequence of Rāmānuja's own discussion of this subject, for Rāmānuja treats dependence as the first element in the definition of the soul's relation to its body, but expresses it as the relation of support to what is supported. His second element in that definition is what Piḷḷāṉ points to in his brief comment on verse six: "This verse says that all action (pravṛtti) and non-action (nivṛtti) of all sentient and non-sentient realities, and all other objects, are incumbent on the will of the Supreme Person (bhagavad sankalpādhinam)" (1.1.6). Here the dependence is more personal: on the Divine *will,* not just on the Divine substance.

The seventh verse illustrates Piḷḷāṉ's relation to Rāmānuja most vividly. It is by far the longest comment in the entire work, not because Piḷḷāṉ's paraphrase of the verse is so long but because he finds it necessary to support it with seventy-three scriptural quotations, most of them used by Rāmānuja for a similar purpose in his Sanskrit writings. (The verse and the entire comment preceding the quotations are translated in Part Four.) The verse itself reads as follows.

Becoming all things
spread on open space, fire,
wind, water, and earth,
he is diffused through them all.
Hidden, he pervades,
like life in a body.
The radiant scripture [speaks]
of the divine one who ate all this.

(1.1.7)

The sentence, "Hidden, he pervades, like life in a body" is one of the clearest links in the poem to Rāmānuja's celebrated doctrine that God is the hidden inner soul of the universe just as each individual soul is of its physical body. This may suggest a definite influence of Nammāḻvār's ideas on Rāmānuja's thought, something that the tradition has always assumed but that Rāmānuja does not acknowledge in his Sanskrit writings. In any case, given the importance of the soul-body doctrine to Rāmānuja, it is not surprising that Piḷḷāṉ sees this verse as summarizing what he thinks Nammāḻvār has been saying in the previous six verses. The grammatical relation between subject and predicate adjective is comparable to the relation between soul and body, which is comparable to God's pervading and ruling the five basic elements and all other finite things. This, Piḷḷāṉ says, is irrefutably established by (scriptural) authority (pramāṇa).

Piḷḷāṉ then states the nature of the Supreme Person, using phrases that could well have been dictated by Rāmānuja himself. The Lord is "different from all objects in the two states of cause and effect"; that is to say, not only is he different from the material world in its "spread out" state after creation, but also, contrary to the Bhedābheda position, he is distinct from the compact mass of finite entities before creation. The Lord is also different from all other "conscious beings, whether bound, liberated, or eternally free." Here Piḷḷāṉ refers to the notion of three kinds of finite souls: those imprisoned in the round of existence, those liberated from it, and a third category, those "angels" or divine beings who are eternal servants of the Lord.

Piḷḷāṉ then continues to define God's nature in a way that sounds very much like Rāmānuja:

> His essential nature consists of wisdom (jñāna), bliss (ānanda), and purity (amalatva). He is opposed to all filth (heya) and possesses unlimited, auspicious, glorious attributes; his pastime is the sport (līlā) of creating, protecting, and destroying the worlds; he is the soul (ātmā) of the entire universe; his body is the entire universe. He who is without any karma has as his body all souls and matter, and is their soul (ātmā). He is pure (aspṛṣṭa) and not affected by the happiness, sorrow, change, and the imperfections (doṣa) of all other things. This is the Supreme Person.
>
> (1.1.7)

Even so, when Piḷḷāṉ comes closest to *defining* the soul-body relationship, he uses only one of the three elements in Rāmānuja's definition: that the soul is the controller of the body. He does use another idea that is important to his teacher—that the soul pervades its body—but that is not part of Rāmānuja's definition. As we have seen, Piḷḷāṉ dealt with the first element of that definition (support-supported) in commenting on the previous verse, when he speaks of the soul's dependence (parādhīnam) on God. The third element (owner-owned) is as important to the disciple as to his teacher, as we shall see in chapter 10.

These slight changes suggest two facts: Piḷḷāṉ can be somewhat independent of his master Rāmānuja; and he considers his chief mentor in this commentary to be the poem's author, Nammāḻvār, for it is clear that he raises only those points that seem to him implied by each specific verse. In this case he thinks he has found a verse in which both his master and his mentor converge to disclose the truth established by the Sanskrit scriptural text concerning God's relation to the universe.

Since Piḷḷāṉ is convinced that the doctrine of God as indwelling soul in a cosmic body is Nammāḻvār's basic metaphysical position, it is natural that the central doctrine provide the key for interpreting such passages as the following one, in which God "is" or "becomes" certain parts of the universe.

Being the deeds
   that are sorrows and joys,
being the worlds,
being the oppressive hell
   where there is no happiness,
Being the sweet good heavens in the sky,
Being the many lives,
   By many entrancing marvelous (powers)
   he holds all this as joyful sport.
I have obtained him,
and now lack nothing.

> [The āḻvār] says: I have obtained him who is the inner soul of karma, which consists of both meritorious and sinful deeds, of the worlds that are the space for experiencing the consequences of karma, of the heavens and hells that result from karma, of the souls (ātmās) that experience heaven, hell, etc.; him whose sport is the origination, preservation, and dissolution of all the worlds—and now I lack nothing.
>
> (3.10.7)

A briefer statement that similarly interprets some of Nammāḻvār's paradoxical contrasts is Piḷḷāṉ's comment on 6.3.1: "My Lord is the inner soul (antarātmabhūta) of poverty and wealth, hell and heaven, enmity and friendship, poison and ambrosia." Finally, in the same vein, is the comment on 6.3.6, noted above but here quoted in full.

Being
   the three worlds
Being
   nothing,
Being
   love, being anger,
Being
   the Goddess [fortune] who dwells on the flower,
Being
   her sister [misfortune],
Being
   praise, being blame,
the Lord resides
   in the Sacred Celestial City,
   where the divine ones worship with love.
The supreme radiant flame
   abides in my mind,
   [the mind of me,] a sinner!

> He is the indweller of all the worlds, love and hate, Lakṣmī and anti-Lakṣmī [goddess of misfortune], praise and blame; he fills all auspicious and filthy things, and he is their inner soul. Being the indweller of all auspicious objects, he is not affected by any evil, and though he is the indweller of all filthy things, he is without stain. If it is asked, how is this possible? [the āḻvār] says: It is because he has entered my filthy heart and is still not affected by the evil. . . .
>
> (6.3.6)

This comment ends with Piḷḷāṉ supplying the poet's answer to the religiously important question. The proof of the Lord's capacity to indwell opposite states of being is his power to dwell "in my filthy heart."

Comments on Other "Religions" or "Philosophies" (Camayas)

Neither the poem nor the commentary is primarily polemical; there are relatively few verses that can be interpreted as refuting some other religious group or philosophical school (camaya). The term itself is of interest. It is used by the āḻvārs in a negative sense, speaking of *other* positions than one's own. Nammāḻvār uses the phrase "six camayas," which along with Sanskrit and Prakrit equivalents was used by many sects in ancient India to designate collectively the chief rival and misguided positions. Surprisingly, Piḷḷāṉ does not expand on the sentence, "He stands against the six camayas" (9.4.8) but paraphrases this as "He protected me from joining the six camayas."

If God is present in all things, it might well be asked whether Lord Viṣṇu is even immanent in rival sects, especially since Nammāḻvār believes that other deities can reward the worshiper, though finally all worship is directed to Lord Viṣṇu, the inner self of the deities worshiped. In one verse the poet says, "In each camaya He [the Lord] is not sunk [or merged]." On this Piḷḷāṉ comments as follows:

> He is connected to all objects by virtue of being their soul. Nevertheless, because he is opposed to all filth and is of a different nature from these objects, having knowledge as his essential nature, he is untouched by all the defects of all the objects which form his body. If you ask, how is this possible, [the āḻvār] says: just as it is possible for the individual soul which lives in this body to have the characteristic nature of being untouched by the defects of the body, so too is it possible for the Lord.
>
> (3.4.10)

This statement about the connection of the pure soul to the very impure material body follows very closely Rāmānuja's various statements on this subject. Here, however, the doctrine is inserted in the midst of a different topic, the superiority of Lord Viṣṇu to all other deities, and in this comment Piḷḷāṉ's intention seems to be to emphasize the negative implications of the phrase "not merged." The Lord is present in other deities and in the theological and ritual systems related to them, but the emphasis in this verse is more on the distinction than on the connection: the radical difference between the pure soul and the impure material entity it embodies.

Another verse, however, sounds more positive: "He exists as you followers of the Linga Purāṇa (that is, Śaivas), as you Jains and Buddhists, as you crafty debaters (logicians)." This Piḷḷāṉ interprets with the same soul-body analogy, but used with a positive emphasis: "God (Nārāyaṇa) is the soul of you who take your stand on the Linga Purāṇa, you followers of the Buddhist, Ulūkya [Vaiśeṣika], Nyāya, naked Jain, Sāṁkhya, and Yoga sects" (4.10.5).[7]

Piḷḷāṉ's longest comment about the six camayas is his paraphrase of a verse that asks, "When there are so many divergent views, how can we establish the truth?" The answer to this question is that the omniscient Lord has set forth in the Gītā the real meaning of the Vedic way:

> He is the person discussed in all the Vedas. . . . Since the other camayas are opposed to the Vedas, they cannot be authoritative. He revealed the six camayas to the people opposed to him and the true way to the followers of the Veda who are favorable to him in such a way that the controversy between them is resolved. He can show the real meaning of the Vedas; stand in bhaktiyoga which is a way to him.[8]
>
> (1.3.5)

The Bhagavadgītā is here given a crucial role: Lord Krishna's teaching indicates the true meaning of the Vedas. Moreover, the Gītā is understood to teach that the Lord is superior to other deities, including them and the worship offered to them in his own gracious approach to all finite beings.

There are a few verses that Piḷḷāṉ interprets as being directed against specific opposing views. This is true of the somewhat perplexing 1.1.9, which he takes to be a refutation of the Buddhist Śūnyavāda (the translation is included in Part Four). The point of the verse seems to be that even a denial of the Lord's existence affirms the Lord's existence as underlying all other forms of existence. Piḷḷāṉ explains that when the Buddhist says that God (Īśvara) does not exist, this is only attributing a negative term (non-existence) to the God whom the scriptural texts cited affirm to have the qualities of being and non-being. So Nammāḻvār concludes (according to Piḷḷāṉ's understanding): "Even when he does not seem to exist, he is the inner soul of all and therefore exists."[9]

Comments on the same subject come in the other very philosophical decad, 8.8. Piḷḷāṉ interprets the ninth verse to be speaking against advaitavāda and the tenth verse to be denouncing sāṁkhya. The first of these two verses appears to ridicule the notion of a complete merger between God and the human soul. There are two analogies that the commentator points to as fundamental in this objection. First, God's reality is so much more fundamental than that of the human soul that their qualitative difference is like that between existence and non-existence, a difference which it is impossible to overcome. Second, God and the human soul are both persons; their relation is analogous to that between finite persons, each of whom has a distinct individual reality. Here again there is a distinction in reality that cannot be denied. We have to see that Piḷḷāṉ is using these analogies in order to see why he considers the poet's ridicule to have such self-evident force. Then Piḷḷāṉ comments that "to say that the Supreme Person and the (finite) soul are one is to say that existence and non-existence are one," and that "that man is this man." But existence and non-existence could not be more opposite, and "that man cannot be this man." "The Advaitins," who hold such an untenable view, "interpret the scriptures wrongly." Piḷḷāṉ interprets Nammāḻvār as indicating through sarcasm that neither the scriptures nor common sense support the notion of a distinctionless merger of the Supreme Soul and a finite soul. Both the distinction between existence and non-existence and the distinction between one existent being and another are fundamental. They cannot be transcended. Since Nammāḻvār has a great deal to say about merger and about two becoming one, this is an important verse. However Nammāḻvār himself would have interpreted his verse in philosophical terms, the verse is a sardonic criticism of a different notion of union than that which the poet himself is trying to express. It is not unreasonable, therefore, for Piḷḷāṉ to see this verse as a criticism of the Śrīvaiṣṇavas' chief philosophical opponents.

The second of the two verses is even more difficult to interpret, especially since existence and non-existence are brought together in the Lord. It is the Lord who both "exists and does not exist" who "came and dwells in me." However transitory in this life the poet's experience of union with the Lord may be, it is clear this union produces a lasting knowledge. "Together we destroyed the knowledge that waxes and wanes like the moon or fluctuates like sunlight and darkness." Piḷḷāṉ does not seek to demonstrate but simply assumes that such "flickering" knowledge refers to the "heretic godless Sāṁkhya." It is in any case the Lord's direct self-revelation that saves the poet—in Piḷḷāṉ's interpretation—from falling victim to the wrong kind of knowledge about the soul.

It is true that the finite soul, like the Supreme Soul, has the essential nature of consciousness, but for Śrīvaiṣṇavas the distinction so emphasized in the Sāṁkhya between consciousness and material nature is secondary to another distinction that classical Sāṁkhya does not recognize, between the finite consciousness of the human soul and the infinite consciousness of God. For this reason Piḷḷāṉ calls the Sāṁkhya "godless" and also for this reason he gives the relational definition of the soul, not its essential nature of consciousness but its fundamental belonging (śeṣatva) to God as his property and its goal of intimate union (saṁśleṣa) with the Lord.

> Before that [gracious disclosure of the nature of the soul], with this goal of union, showing his unsurpassed beauty, fragrance, tenderness, youthfulness and [good] qualities, his auspicious divine ornaments and divine weapons, he entered me. . . .
>
> (8.8.10)

In the context of the entire decad, which is very much concerned with the yogic path to knowledge of the pure soul, this final statement of the finite soul's true nature as the servant or property (śeṣa) of the Lord is a fitting conclusion. Here we have no attempt at philosophical refutation, only a poem of praise to the merciful and captivating Lord.

7

God's Manifestations in the Universe

The Divine Descents

The wonder of the Lord's accessibility, a major theme in Piḷḷāṉ's commentary, is discussed in the comments on the first three verses of 1.3. Piḷḷāṉ interprets the first verse as a response to those discouraged by the āḻvār's earlier verse (1.1.2) that the Lord is not within the range of the outer sense organs or even the inner sense developed by yogis. The āḻvār answers them: "The Lord is accessible to those who wish to see him but very hard for his adversaries (to approach); this is his wonder." Then the āḻvār begins to talk about the incident that shows the extent of this accessibility. As the little boy Krishna, the Lord allows himself, when caught stealing butter, to be tied by his chest to the mortar, where he "huddles close to the stone and gazes out wistfully." Moved by the Lord's quality of accessibility, the āḻvār asks the Lord,

> If you want to show that you are dependent on those dependent on you, is it not enough to be born as their equal? Should you start trembling, bound to a mortar? O my Lord, what are you doing? Why are you doing this?[1]
>
> (1.3.1)

Meditating on this "unsurpassed accessibility" the normally calm āḻvār becomes physically agitated and in the following verse, says Piḷḷāṉ, the poet sings about the accessibility of the Lord, who disregards rank and becomes equal to his devotees. Yet when he is born he does not discard his Divine attributes. He brings with him to earth "his auspicious qualities, his complete joy, his very real [or immediately visible] form, his ability to grant liberation and his universal lordship."

Piḷḷāṉ's paraphrase of the third verse, quoted in part here, is like a brief creed or doxology:

> Nārāyaṇa, the highest human goal, who has the lordly power to create, maintain, and destroy complete worlds, who is the soul of Brahmā, Śiva, and other divine beings, as well as the soul of all conscious and

> non-conscious beings, [yet] who is indifferent to his lordly power, was born as an equal and became accessible. Can anyone comprehend this wondrous quality?[2]
>
> (1.3.3)

Commenting elsewhere on a verse (2.5.10) dealing with the impossibility of grasping the Lord's nature through ordinary categories of knowing (pramāṇa), Piḷḷāṉ emphasizes the theme of inaccessibility to others and accessibility to his devotees, even the taking of the divine bodily form desired by his devotees. He also says (in 3.6.9) that the Lord's accessibility is shown by assuming the forms imagined by mortals, not just his form in Vaikuṇṭha. In 1.7.2 he paraphrases the verse to emphasize the Lord's love towards those who take refuge in him: "though superior to Brahmā and other deities because of such auspicious qualities as his bliss, he was graciously born equal to his devotees." Moreover, commenting on 2.3.2, Piḷḷāṉ says: "Though a wondrous being who needs nothing, you are born as one equal to your devotees and are extremely accessible to them."

But he returns to the decisive contrast in his comment on 2.3.5:

> He is not to be known by those who are not his devotees, however high they may be. [But] he is supremely accessible to those who have exclusive devotion, and though I am without devotion, he became one whom I could enjoy without any effort on my part. . . .
>
> (2.3.5)

In language similar to that of Rāmānuja, Piḷḷāṉ interprets two verses dealing with the idea of avatāra.

> To kill Kaṁsa, the oppressor of the good,
> he, the first one of the Vedas,
> left his primordial form of effulgence there,
> and was born here.
> Those who do not sing of him
> and dance through the streets,
> may be learned in the chants,
> But—
> what prayer can they say?
> what kind of men are they?

> Though proclaimed by all the Vedas as the Lord of all, with the intention of expelling Kaṁsa and other demons who were the enemies of his devotees, he assumed a divine form unique to himself and was born as a

man in this world. Those who do not wander in the streets singing of the one with the great quality are of no use, however learned they may be. (3.5.5)

> Becoming human and everything else,
> The unique One, wondrously born,
> Is the Lord who belongs to the deep sea.
> Those who, without rancour, dance and praise,
> The tender fruit, the sweet juice of sugarcane
> Sweet as candy, honey, and nectar,
> Know well his goodness.

> He who is distinct from all other entities, who is not born like men under the sway of karma, who has his abode in the sea of milk, for the sake of protecting his devotees, has by his own will descended into human and other wombs in such a way that his incarnate bodies have not even a whiff of the faults of material nature.
> (3.5.6)

In these two verses Piḷḷāṉ has expanded on the references to the Lord's human form—both the wonder of the Lord's appearance in our world and the wonder of his retaining his purity within this world. But he passes over the devotees' dancing and singing the Lord's names, so important to the verse, as well as the "tasting" of the Lord's sweetness.[3]

References to specific avatāras and their deeds are frequent throughout the Tiruvāymoḻi. There are also specific "tens" celebrating the different deeds of the Lord in his avatāra forms. Significantly, he gives special attention to Rāma, even at times interpreting verses that appear to be about some other avatāra to refer to Rāma. For example, he interprets a verse in 7.7.1 about Krishna to refer to Rāma and Sītā, and he takes a whole decad, which refers to the deeds of a number of avatāras (7.5), as referring to Rāma, as the following comment reveals:

> He was beseeched by the divine beings, who wanted (the demon-king) Rāvaṇa to be destroyed, so he graciously descended as an equal to this world of human beings so dissimilar to him. If a single person was distressed, he too was extremely distressed. On the pretext of fulfilling his vow to his father, he searched out and killed all of Rāvaṇa's minions. . . . He went back to the city preparing for death because of sorrow at his absence and gave life to all animate and inanimate beings.[4]
> (7.5.2)

This emphasis on the Rāma-avatāra might be taken as an evidence of the growing ascendancy of Rāmabhakti (in the mode of humble surrender) over

Krishnabhakti (in the mode of the gopīs' erotic love) in later Śrīvaiṣṇavism. While this would seem to fit the increasing emphasis on humble surrender in Śrīvaiṣṇava doctrine and practice, Piḷḷāṉ is by no means exclusively interested in Viṣṇu's avatāra as Rāma. In general, however, Piḷḷāṉ seems to move back and forth very easily from thinking of one avatāra to thinking of another. In the previous decad (7.4), where each verse is clearly devoted to a different incarnation, Piḷḷāṉ gives equally brief space to paraphrasing each verse.

Piḷḷāṉ comments on a verse in 8.5.10 that suggests to him both celebration of the avatāra form of God and also its limitation for a devotee living in a later age.

O wondrous one who was born!
O wondrous one who fought the Bhārata war!
Great one, who became all things,
  starting with the primal elements:
  wind, fire, water, sky, and earth.
Great one, wondrous one,
  you are in all things
  as butter lies hidden in fresh milk,
you stand in all things
  and yet transcend them.
Where can I see you?

He says: O wondrous one, born in Śrī Mathura with the intention of protecting the good and destroying the evil. You reside in everything and yet do not show yourself to me. Where can I see you?

(8.5.10)

Piḷḷāṉ is right in considering "Where can I see you?" to be one of Nammāḻvār's central questions. In our present age, with no avatāra present in person, the poet must find some other way of seeing the Lord. One important means is visiting the form of the Lord incarnated at the holy shrines of Viṣṇu, and to that we now turn.

God's Presence in Holy Places

In later Śrīvaiṣṇava theology the term *arcāvatāra* (derived from the Pāñcarātra Āgamas) became the standard term for designating the image form of the Lord, that is, the descent of the Lord permanently into a consecrated image in which he is henceforth truly present. Nammāḻvār addresses many of his decads to the Lord present in some particular temple or sacred place, but does not use the term arcāvatāra or any Tamil equivalent, and Piḷḷāṉ in commenting on those many verses, does not do so either (here again in agreement with Rāmānuja).

Yet whether the Lord's presence in a particular temple should be called an avatāra or not, it is clearly a very important form of God's manifestation in the world, and it is the form that seems to make it possible for the devotee to see the Lord with his or her own eyes.

The first comment by Piḷḷāṉ we shall look at is on 10.1.4:

> To be accessible to the prayers of Brahmā and other deities desiring him, he graciously entered the ocean of milk. Similarly, to become accessible to our prayers desiring him, he graciously entered Tirumōkūr. Come let us embrace his auspicious feet.
>
> (10.1.4)

It is remarkable in the first place that Piḷḷāṉ differentiates Viṣṇu's state of yogic sleep on the milk-ocean from the Lord's presence in his highest abode (Vaikuṇṭha or Tirunāṭu) and thus seems to present this state, so central to Śrīvaiṣṇava iconography, as itself a kind of avatāra or "descent," for the sake of the lesser deities beginning with Brahmā. There is then a second level of "descent," or at least of "entry," into the temple of Tirumōkūr, for the sake of his human devotees. One of the links between the two states is that the form of the Lord is the same, that is, the consecrated image of Tirumōkūr is of Viṣṇu reclining on the primordial serpent, Ananta-Śeṣa, in the midst of the milk-ocean. Compare also 10.5.4: ". . . my Lord who with the intention of protecting the world comes to the sacred ocean of milk, and is in semislumber."

The whole of this decad concerns the Lord's presence in Tirumōkūr. If we turn back to the first verse, we might then be a little puzzled that Piḷḷāṉ comments as follows:

> There is no other goal than the Lord who has strong arms with which he long ago vanquished the enemies of his devotees. His sacred locks of hair, sacred eyes, sacred coral-like lips, and auspicious body resembling a dark cloud are beautiful and extremely enjoyable. He graciously stands in Tirumōkūr extending more affection here than he does even in heaven.
>
> (10.1.1)

Piḷḷāṉ seems to be describing the standing form of the Lord rather than the reclining form on the milk-ocean. Does this description, then, have anything to do with the specific form of the icon at Tirumōkūr? As it happens, Tirumōkūr is one of those few Śrīvaiṣṇava temples that has two central icons, one of the Lord reclining, the other standing. (A few temples also have a third: Viṣṇu in sitting position.) Thus although the Lord's presence is spoken of in connection with the sacred place and not explicitly in connection with the central image in the temple, both poet and commentator, along with the entire community, are very well aware of the specific iconic form or forms for which each major temple was famous. Piḷḷāṉ's last sentence is also important. In the forms in which he makes himself accessible, the Lord shows his affection even more clearly than he does in his supreme state.

There are a great many statements about the value of worshiping in some particular sacred place; for example, verse 3.3.6 advises: "Say *namaḥ* in Tiruvēṅkaṭam and all your sins will vanish." In 8.6.6 the verse reads: "He lives in the cool Tirukkaṭittāṉam. . . . Praise him and your grief will vanish." Piḷḷāṉ interprets this as "All this good fortune came about by resorting to Tirukkaṭittāṉam."

In 9.10.8 Piḷḷāṉ comments: ". . . just as he stands in Vaikuṇṭha, he stands in Tirukaṇṇapuram," but in 10.2.6 he goes further:

> If you ask, "Is is not the goal to go to heaven and serve our Lord?" [the āḻvār] replies: Even those who are there come to perform service in Tiruvaṉantapuram! Therefore, to do service here is itself the goal: we should come here and perform service.
>
> (10.2.6)

Here the sacred place seems to be given a higher status than heaven itself, expressing through the hyperbole of praise the real presence of the Lord in his temple and therefore the opportunity to anticipate heavenly service here on earth.

The Heart as a Holy Place

Verse 8.6.5 reads as follows:

> The very father who danced with the pots
> and who has heaven as his temple,
> while worshiped by the divine beings
> who reside in temples,
> took Tirukkaṭittāṉam as his temple.
> He also
> seized my heart as his temple.

Piḷḷāṉ's comment is very brief: "Over and above the grace of residing here and there, because of the wonder of his affection, he took Tirukkaṭittāṉam and entered my heart." However, in his comment on 8.6.10, five verses later, Piḷḷāṉ follows the verse in returning to this theme.

> The marvelous one, Nārāyaṇan, Hari, Vāmaṉaṉ,
> stands and abides with desire in my heart.

(He abides) in Tirukkaṭittāṉam,
where the wish-fulfilling groves
reverberate with the sounds
of the four sacred texts
chanted by praiseworthy scholars
well versed in the Vedas.

He stands in Tirukkaṭittāṉam that is superior among the sacred places including even heaven and the milk-ocean, but the place where he desires to abide is my heart, says [the āḻvār].

(8.6.10)

The references to the heart as a temple do not here, as in Vīra Śaiva poems, suggest a critique of temple worship, far less a rejection of it, but they do point to another important dimension of God's manifestation in the universe: his dwelling in the heart of the devotee. We see this thought in both the verse of 9.4.7 and the comment upon it.

Praising you,
ever thinking of you,
is my inner heart.
O pure one who seizes
and abides in my inner soul!
Taking the form of a Man-Lion
with your sharp claws,
You split into two
the chest of the demon.

My heart contemplates and praises the beauty and the deeds of you who graciously entered it. For this reason you became delighted. By taking it as a permanent place to reside, you graciously calmed my heart that was disturbed because it could not get a vision of you.

(9.4.7)

Here Piḷḷāṉ goes beyond the content of the verse to stress a central theme evident elsewhere in the poem: Nammāḻvār's desire for more immediate or permanent vision of the Lord than he had yet been able to secure. Piḷḷāṉ seems to suggest that the Lord's "taking this heart as a permanent place" is not so much a granting of this "sight" as it is the maximum solace that the Lord can provide the āḻvār while the āḻvār is still in his earthly body.

There is one other brief comment that gives a more exalted view of the Lord's dwelling in the āḻvār's heart. In the midst of the last decad in which Nammāḻvār takes the role of the lovesick maiden, Piḷḷāṉ comments: "The Lord considers her heart to be the supreme heaven" (9.7.5).

Qualities Expressing God's Saving and Protecting Grace

Like Rāmānuja, Piḷḷāṉ often refers to the Divine attributes collectively as an ocean (or treasure store) of auspicious qualities, and he also mentions particular qualities in paraphrasing or interpreting particular verses. There are two lists of Divine qualities that Piḷḷāṉ gives that are important in relation to God's manifesting himself in the universe and especially in his establishing a relationship with his devotees. The first is in the comment on 3.7.11:

> This verse says that the supreme goal is to be the slave of any Śrīvaiṣṇava who is captivated and enthralled by the Lord's innumerable auspicious qualities like motherly love (vātsalya), gracious condescension (sauśīlya), compassion (kāruṇya), beauty (saundarya), fragrance (saugandhya), tenderness (saukumārya), and youthfulness (yauvana).
> (3.7.11)

The second, much briefer list is in Piḷḷāṉ's comment on 4.3.6:

> The āḻvār says: You who are omniscient and almighty united with me in such a way that we could not be separated. You bear the conch, discus, and other weapons that destroy the enemies of your devotees. You have auspicious qualities like compassion, friendship, gracious condescension, etc. Even if you do not unite with me, you made me in such a way that your being became my complete enjoyment.
> (4.3.6)

Perhaps the most general quality is one not mentioned explicitly in these lists but clearly implied in the frequent references to the "nature of destroying your devotee's enemies." This quality is *rakṣakatva,* "being the protector (savior)." The noun *rakṣaṇa* is frequently translated "salvation," but the basic meaning is "protection," as one sees in the word for sandal, *pātarakṣa,* "foot-protector." Piḷḷāṉ speaks in 2.2.1 of the Lord as the "protector of all souls" and of the Lord in 1.5.8 as "protecting all devotees without perceiving their defects." (This quality is part of a later definition of vātsalya.) Commenting on 2.2.8 Piḷḷāṉ also says:

> Just as the mother who gives birth to the child also protects it, it is fitting that the one who creates also protects. Therefore for the Supreme Person who protects, the acts of creation and protection are a single act.
> (2.2.8)

Piḷḷāṉ frequently uses one of the Sanskrit nouns meaning mercy or compassion (kāruṇya, dayā, kṛpā) in interpreting the meaning of the action expressed by Tamil verbs in the verses. Two uses of kāruṇya are particularly striking.

> He who is perfect in every way, out of extreme compassion, made me, who am vile in every way, have exceeding devotion for him.
>
> (5.1.7)

> Can I not be caught in the overwhelming flood of compassion that protects the unfortunate ones and those who are devoid of any means of salvation (upāya)?
>
> (9.4.3)

Elsewhere, Piḷḷāṉ does not name the quality, but speaks in terms similar to Rāmānuja's definition of compassion or mercy (dayā): "the nature of expelling the sorrow of others because he cannot bear this suffering."[5]

> The āḻvār has been captivated by the Lord's gracious condescension, but the Lord thinks, "If I go to unite with him, he will, as before, feel unworthy and move away. To attain union with him I must separate from him, so that he will cry out his desire to unite with me; then it will be fitting to unite."
>
> (1.5.5)

Piḷḷāṉ continues his comment as an expression of Nammāḻvār's desire for God.

> To protect your devotees you were born equal to human beings. Disregarding your devotees' imperfections, you made them the objects of your grace. You banish their defects, and you even protect animals. . . . Graciously will that I, a sinner, may join your feet that are [like] flowers filled with honey.
>
> (1.5.5)

The starting point is the Lord's sauśīlya, which, according to the later definition, is the capacity of a superior to put an inferior at ease by making him forget (become unaware of) the great difference between them. There are hints of this Divine quality throughout the passage, but the main point here is separation in order to increase erotic attraction, which is a different one from that of gracious condescension. There may, however, be some connection: only the heightening of passionate desire for the beloved object will blind the devotee to the vast gulf between the devotee and the Lord. This awareness is clearly indicated by Piḷḷāṉ's comment two verses later.

> The āḻvār, who longs to see the Lord, later thinks of the Lord's superiority and his own inferiority and thinks, "Woe is me! How ignorant of me to want to see him instead of moving away. . . ."
>
> (1.5.7)

One of the most celebrated qualities of the Lord is vātsalya, the original meaning of which is the mother cow's tender love and even frenzied concern for its newborn calf. In the bhakti tradition it has two distinct meanings, for it can either indicate the devotee's taking the role of mother (or affectionate parent) with respect to the Lord (this is called the vātsalya mode of bhakti) or it can indicate the Lord's motherly love for his devotees, a love that is thought to include a forgiving or ignoring of their faults. It is vātsalya on the Lord's part with which we are here concerned, and references to it in the commentary are both frequent and important. The following comment is significant:

> When her child falls in a well, the mother, because of her excessive vātsalya, jumps in and saves it. Similarly when Earth (Pṛthivi) was sinking in the underworld, the Lord took the form of a boar and in the twinkling of an eye dived in and brought her out. . . .
>
> (7.5.5)

Piḷḷāṉ often uses the phrase, āśritavātsalya, "motherly love for the devotee." *Āśrita* means, literally, "those who have taken refuge." We might translate āśrita as "refugee" if recent English usage had not preempted the term to mean "fugitive" in a positive sense, that is, those fleeing their own countries, not because of wrongdoing, but because of the devastation of war or natural disorder. Such refugees are characterized by their searching for some refuge, which, alas, they do not always find. That āśrita is such a common term in Piḷḷāṉ's commentary shows the direction in which the Śrīvaiṣṇava community is moving, for āśrita suggests both the taking refuge at a sanctuary and the surrender to a victorious conquerer. What might seem a lowering of the devotee's status, however, is balanced by the apparently extravagant lengths to which the Lord goes to accept the "refugee" and lift him up into a state of intimate service. So in commenting on 7.10.7 Piḷḷāṉ says, "Though being 'the Lord of the never-tiring immortals,' he is a great ocean of āśritavātsalya, and because of this [quality] graciously descended to Mathura to save his āśritas. . . ." The extent of this Divine motherly love is suggested in the comment on 8.1.4: "Your quality of āśritavātsalya, expressed as divine deeds that you perform under your āśritas' commands in the divine incarnations, is my only support."

Experiencing the Lord's Beauty

Not only do the grandeur and winsomeness of his personal qualities give an impression of the Lord to the devotee, but also the fascinating beauty of his bodily form, which is represented in his consecrated images or icons. These icons, which faithfully copy textual descriptions of the Lord in a particular bodily pose, contain the very presence of the Lord. Nammāḻvār's inner vision of the Lord with his mind's eye is reinforced by his memory of his beholdings or "visions" of the Lord in image form. Piḷḷān's paraphrases of Nammāḻvār's verses retain the celebration of the Lord's beauty. One example is his comment on 2.2.5:

> The Lord has excellent qualities befitting his divine nature. This Lord's divine personality contains superior qualities; he possesses the entire universe, generated by his will, and he has beautiful auspicious eyes that befit his being the Lord of all. Can anyone know him?
>
> (2.2.5)

In his paraphrase of 10.1.1, Piḷḷāṉ writes as follows:

> There is no other goal than the Lord who has strong arms of surpassing might with which he long ago vanquished the enemies of his devotees. His sacred locks of hair, sacred eyes, sacred coral-like lips, and auspicious body resembling a dark cloud are beautiful and extremely enjoyable. He graciously stands in Tirumōkūr, extending more affection (sneha) here than he does even in heaven (Tirunāṭu)![6]
>
> (10.1.1)

The decad 8.9 is one of the dialogues between the lovesick maiden (that is, the poet) and her friend. Piḷḷāṉ introduces this dialogue as follows:

> The āḻvār speaks of himself in the guise of another, relating how the Lord, out of sheer grace, manifested his beauty, captivated him, and united with him. Then he describes the satisfaction that came about because of their union.
>
> (8.9 intro)

Commenting on the first verse Piḷḷāṉ paraphrases: "When they ask, 'Will his beauty be equal to hers?' her friend replies, 'It is in his beauty that she is caught!' "

In paraphrasing the second verse of the philosophically important decad 8.8, Piḷḷāṉ notes the crucial role of the Lord's beauty in winning Nammāḻvār's love:

> Not content with being in all the worlds, etc., he who is omniscient showed me his beauty so that I would not move away, aware of his superiority and my inferiority, and he also entered my body.
>
> (8.8.2)

Here there is another allusion to a fundamental problem in bhakti, how the Divine can be related to the human when there is a double gulf between the Supreme Person and human persons: the infinite superiority of God and the vast impurity realized by the sensitive human subject. The problem of this devotional relationship seems to be even more severe when bhakti is described in the language of erotic love. Piḷḷāṉ repeatedly states his understanding of Nammāḻvār's "solution": the gulf can only be bridged by the Lord's grace. Only the superior party can remove the psychological discomfort of the inferior party: by causing the inferior to forget the gap between them. In this case it is the overwhelming experience of the Lord's beauty that engenders that forgetfulness.

It may seem paradoxical that a tradition that puts so much emphasis on knowing God's nature and remembering God's past deeds, especially God's precious acts and appearances, should here find a solution in a double forgetting. The Lord acts as if he had forgotten the vast metaphysical difference between himself and his devotee and must so charm the human devotee that the latter is so filled with love as to forget his lowly state and hence be rid of the object of embarrassment. If bhakti here were some lower stage than the intuitive knowledge (jñāna) of union with God, there would be no paradox, but for Piḷḷāṉ, as for the entire Śrīvaiṣṇava tradition, bhakti includes jñāna. The paradox seems deliberate, even if it sometimes seems to be philosophically resolved, as in the following comment:

> Not content with captivating me with his beauty, lest there be an obstacle to continuing our union, he says [in utterly compelling fashion] that he is the meaning of that which appears as I. . . .
>
> (8.8.3)

Here the Lord's intimate disclosure, to overcome the soul's shyness in entering into a loving union, is put in terms of the fundamental Vedāntic teaching that the Lord is the Supreme Soul, the Infinite Soul within the finite soul. That basic metaphysical affinity and internal relationship might seem to make any forgetfulness unnecessary, but salvation remains a question of relationship, not metaphysical identity, and for such an improbable if not impossible relationship to be realized, the paradox of "remembering" and "forgetting" must remain.

In the following chapters we shall be looking more systematically at Piḷḷāṉ's understanding of the devotional relationship and of the necessity of the Lord's grace. Again and again that grace is manifested through the Lord's all-surpassing beauty.

8

The Devotee's Relation to God: Separation and Union

Separation and Longing

Much of the Tiruvāymoḻi uses the language of erotic love to express Nammāḻvār's relationship with God. In roughly a quarter of the entire poem, the poet uses the conventions of earlier Tamil poetry to express the alternation of separation and union between the lovers, a drama in which the Lord is the lover and the āḻvār his beloved, though the poet sometimes speaks as the young woman's mother or friend rather than as the young woman herself. The dominant mood of these poems is one of yearning and unfulfilled longing, but there are also vivid recallings of past experiences of romantic meeting and sexual union, and even rare glimpses of such union as a present experience.

Piḷḷāṉ explains why the Lord separates himself from his beloved devotee. The āḻvār's sense of unworthiness for union with the Lord would cause the poet to withdraw if the Lord did not fan his desire by creating the separation. The Lord thinks, "In order to attain union with him, I must separate from him; then he will cry out his desire."[1] The comment two verses later continues this theme:

> The āḻvār, who longs to see the Lord, later thinks of the Lord's superiority (utkarṣan) and his own inferiority and thinks, "Woe is me! How ignorant of me to want to see him instead of moving away! Those who desire kaivalya or other things have attained good fortune, for they do not desire to see him. I don't even have that [lower gift]," he says painfully.
>
> (1.5.7)

The irony in this comment is the suggestion that both kaivalya and worldly fortune have the advantage of avoiding the pain of longing and separation that is the price of a personal loving relationship with the Lord. It is important to recognize here who are included among "those who desire kaivalya." Kaivalya means the absolute isolation of an individual center of consciousness from any entanglements with material nature. Jain monks and nuns as well as yogīs following the philosophy of Sāṁkhya and classical or "royal" Yoga have this kaivalya as their goal; it means for them the realization of the full potential of the individual consciousness, untrammeled by the constraints of the physical body or even the operation of what is called the "subtle body," the mental apparatus for everyday practical thinking. According to Rāmānuja, however, followers of the rival school of Vedānta, Śaṅkara's Advaita, who say they are seeking to realize their identity with the transpersonal Brahman, are in fact also among "those who desire kaivalya," for the distinctionless consciousness they seek is only that of the individual soul separated from matter. Such an isolated individual salvation is quite attainable, Rāmānuja thought, but it is an infinitely lower good than union with the true Brahman, who is the Supreme Soul.[2] (Later Śrīvaiṣṇavas would debate among themselves whether those attaining kaivalya could move on to true union with Brahman or would be stuck for all eternity in their self-chosen isolation.)[3]

Piḷḷāṉ clearly recognizes that there is an enormous difficulty, both metaphysical and psychological, in the way of attaining such union in love. The poet-saint is precisely the one most aware of the qualitative difference between the Lord's superiority and the human devotee's inferiority, even if the devotee is a great saint. To yearn for intimate union with such a vastly superior Lord does seem ignorant, yet Piḷḷāṉ's comments throughout the poem indicate his conviction that Nammāḻvār's emotionally intense relationship with God, with its intermittent phases of separation and union, is the only path to salvation, the same path to God as the "discipline of devotion" (bhaktiyoga) in the Bhagavadgītā.

The most dramatic expressions of Nammāḻvār's desperate sense of separation and fervent longing for the Lord come in several sets of poems in which the poet takes the role of a lovesick maiden pining for her absent lover.[4] Friedhelm Hardy calls these decads the "girl poems" and finds in them the viraha (anguished separation of lovers) that he takes to be the most characteristic and authentic mode of the devotion of Nammāḻvār and the other Tamil poet-saints of Lord Viṣṇu.[5]

Piḷḷāṉ explains the dramatic context of the girl poems in his introduction to one of the sets of verses (6.2). There he emphasizes the girl's anger and depression, which are part of the erotic relationship. Since the Lord has not responded to the girl's urgent messages, she decides he has abandoned her for other women. Filled with jealous anger, she resolves not to see the Lord, "even if he does come." As Piḷḷāṉ interprets these verses, the distress is mutual: "The Lord is also depressed by the intense grief of being parted from her." He comes and pleads with her friends to serve as go-betweens, but since the girl will not change her mind, "to support his soul he looks at her playthings, touches them, and is comforted."[6]

Piḷḷāṉ comments on the extremity of the maiden's state in introducing another set of girl poems (9.5). The poet-saint, says the commentator, does not obtain "external" (that is, physical) union with the Lord; "she" is therefore depressed like a maiden who has enjoyed sexual union and is then separated from her beloved. Indeed the maiden is so depressed that she thinks that the Lord wants to "finish her off" and that even his previous act of uniting with her is to make the subsequent separation mortally wounding.[7] The maiden then goes on in her revenge to imagine that her Divine lover, when he sees that she has not totally succumbed in this separation, tells the cuckoos to praise his attractive qualities in her presence. "This is even crueler than separation itself," she thinks and imagines him saying, "thus you can finish her off."

In another set of verses (5.6), the maiden seems to be possessed in a way that bystanders interpret as the kind of trance familiar in traditional South Indian society: possession by a spirit or a village goddess. In this decad the poet uses the device of having the girl's mother describe the girl's strange actions. When others ask the mother for her explanation of her daughter's behavior, she replies, in Piḷḷāṉ's paraphrase, "I cannot diagnose her state as some specific malady, but I wonder whether the Lord has possessed her."[8] It is when expressing herself in such a state of possession that the lovesick maiden sometimes speaks as though she had assumed the identity of her Divine lover. What distinguishes this "madness" from the usual kind of spirit-possession, however, is that the girl has not slipped off into some semiconscious state of vivid hallucination. She is fully conscious, indeed sharply aware—not of her identity with her Divine lover but of their excruciatingly painful separation. It is in this state that she talks as if she were the Lord.

Most of these girl poems represent a situation similar to that of the young Krishna's girlfriends, the milkmaids (gopīs) of Brindavan. There is one set of poems (10.3, translated in Part Four) in which Nammāḻvār seems to be taking the role of a gopī, as the woman poet-saint Āṇṭāḷ does in her much-recited poem, the Tiruppāvai. This is an exception, however. In general, Nammāḻvār's lovesick maiden is the creation of a dramatic persona directly expressing his own identity as a passionate devotee of Lord Krishna, a persona modeled on classical Tamil love poetry of previous centuries. The commentator Piḷḷāṉ is aware of this distinction between the Tamil maiden and the milkmaids of Brindavan, but he draws on one element in the story of the gopīs' relation to Krishna to explain the maiden's strange behavior.

This is the gopīs' practice of consoling themselves during Krishna's absence by dramatically reenacting his presence among them. In the tradition of Krishna plays that have come down through the centuries, the concept *līlā* refers to the Lord's creation, maintenance, and destruction of the universe "in sport," to Krishna's love play or "sports" with the gopīs, to the gopīs' little "plays" in which one would take the role of the absent Krishna, and to later "plays" in which the actor taking Krishna's role is treated by the audience as a "real presence" (svarūpa) of Krishna. Piḷḷāṉ interprets the maiden's speaking as though she were the Lord of the universe to be such "play": an attempt to make bearable the absence of her Lord.

In other respects as well, Piḷḷāṉ harmonizes the specificity of the dramatic situation in a particular verse with somewhat comparable parts of the total tradition. One example is where the commentator compares the maiden's yearning for Lord Krishna with Sītā's calling out for her husband Rāma and brother-in-law Lakṣmaṇa when the demon-king Rāvaṇa held her captive in the Aśoka forest (7.7.1). In his paraphrase on another verse, Piḷḷāṉ changes the poet's "I" to "we," moving to a more general devotional attachment: "Captivated by the Lord's accessibility to his devotees and his other qualities, we become his slaves. Now we cry out that we cannot bear the agony of separation from him" (2.1.7).

A number of other verses put the devotee's longing in general and not specifically erotic terms. Piḷḷāṉ paraphrases one as follows:

> You are all; thus there is no distinction between here and the supreme Heaven (Tirunāṭu). Yet even if I know you are everything, because I cannot see you here as you are in heaven, I deem [this existence] to be hell and fear it extremely. O graciously give me your feet!
>
> (8.1.9)

In another paraphrase, Piḷḷāṉ interprets the āḻvār, because of his own loneliness in a state of separation, to be empathizing with the loneliness of the Lord:

> As a result of the āḻvār's loneliness, he thinks of the Lord's loneliness and laments, "I am of no help in his loneliness. . . . When he went out to destroy [the demons] Mārica or Kara-Dūśana, he was without a companion. He carried the conch and discus and other divine weapons himself. There was no one to follow him carrying his sword and bow. When he went alone, . . . I did not get to see and serve his sacred feet and shoulders in such a way that the yearning in my hands would vanish."
>
> (8.3.3)

Longing here means "longing to see and to serve" and is tangibly felt by "the yearning in my hands." The following verse, which includes the line, "Without seeing your captivating form I am drowning," is paraphrased as follows:

> Because there is no companion for you in that state [of the world's dissolution], and because I long to see your beautiful figure, [a desire] that is not fulfilled, I am submerged in an unfathomable flood of grief, and each moment of this dark night crawls like an aeon.
>
> (8.3.4)

To end the separation, the Lord incarnates himself in two holy shrines in the form of the reclining image of Viṣṇu, the Lord in yogic sleep on the milk-ocean, but even that does not satisfy the poet. Piḷḷāṉ paraphrases the continuing lament as follows:

> "There you do not see us with your eyes; you do not utter a word; you do not perform any divine action; you sleep all the time! Is it because you are tired after destroying the enemies of your devotees? Or because of the effort of pacing out the three worlds?" Thus he grieves, assuming that the Lord is grief-stricken.
>
> (8.3.5)

Even when the Lord "searches for me like a mother and father," the poet's sense of separation continues:

> Thus I stand in distress. Unless he comes my grief will not go. . . . He searches for me . . . and graciously comes into this world alone, [but people] do not tell him that there is a servant here who will follow him like a shadow.
>
> (8.3.7)

There is another decad, sometimes interpreted as another set of girl poems, that is more likely to be another reflection on the meeting with and longing for God in a particular place, the temple of Tirunāvāy.[9] The longing for the Lord in a particular "image-presence" is expressed by both poet and commentator throughout the set of verses, but especially in four of them. In the second verse the poet asks when he can enter the temple (Tirunāvāy) where the Lord dwells with his consorts Śrī and "young Piṉṉai." In the next verse the question is repeated while "tears flow from my eyes." In the fourth verse the poet seems to have entered the sacred precincts "longing to do unending service to you who are the enjoyment of the incomparably beautiful Nappiṉṉai." In the fifth verse his question is, "Where can I see him and drink him with my eyes?" In this verse he mentions the Lord's first two consorts, Śrī and Bhū Devī (the Goddess Earth), but Piḷḷāṉ adds the Lord's third consort (using her Sanskrit name Nīḷā instead of the Tamil Piṉṉai). And he paraphrases the question by asking, "Where can I see the Lord with these earthly eyes and become intoxicated at the sight of him . . . ?"[10]

The yearning of the devotee may seem less erotic here because he acknowledges the Lord's special relationship with his consorts, including his human wife Nappiṉṉai, but his intense yearning for physical sight of the Lord unites the apparently distinct relationships of servant and beloved. Piḷḷāṉ makes this clear in verse 6.

> [The āl̲vār asks]: O king of Cowherds! For my sake you took Tirunāvāy as your temple and abide there. I have great affection for you and desire nothing else. When can these eyes of mine see you and rejoice?
>
> (9.8.6)

In verses 7 and 8 the emphasis is on humble service, but Piḷḷāṉ's paraphrase of verse 10 illuminates the theme of erotic union again.

> And so, though I desired you and did not obtain you, [I] did not stop there. I contemplate the quality by which you came and stayed in Tirunāvāy, only to unite with me (saṁśleṣa). My mind is confused. Wondering when I can clasp you, I stand here, calling "O holy entrancing Lord!"
>
> (9.8.10)

Union: "Mingling"

In the loving relationship of devotion the apparent opposites of separation (viśleṣa) and union (saṁśleṣa) are closely linked. Not only do they alternate but each also presupposes the other. The most erotic allusions to union occur in the midst of an agonizing lament on the Lord's absence. It is the memory of the lover's past embraces that evokes both passion and jealousy, and it is the yearning anticipation of union that evokes the most vivid imagery. Piḷḷāṉ puts this dramatically in his paraphrase of the lovesick maiden's words to the bees that live on the jasmine flower adorning her hair:

> Abandoning me, he sits in Heaven under a great canopy of gems. . . . Look at him, drink from the flood of honey . . . in his hair. Ask him: A girl pines for you, she calls your name. Do you display your mercy by not thinking of her?[11]
>
> (6.8.4)

Elsewhere the girl's mother speaks, reporting that at the appointed time for their tryst, when her daughter does not obtain union with the Lord, her eyes are "filled with tears" and she cries out for him. Her daughter's grief at separation is intense: "she is extremely distressed and listless."[12]

Introducing another set of girl poems (5.5), Piḷḷāṉ says that because the girl doesn't have the patience to remember the qualities of the Supreme Lord whom she has experienced,

> her mind is in a turmoil through the night. With daybreak, however, she remembers the beauty of the Lord's city and his countless auspicious

> attributes. Yet this remembrance again kindles her love, which again leads to distress at not having gained the desired union.[13]
>
> (5.5 intro.)

The two most frequent words for union are "entering" (pukutal) and "mingling" (kalaivi). Both words may mean sexual union, but they are used by poet and commentator in a variety of devotional settings in addition to those of the lovesick heroine of Tamil classical poetry or one of Krishna's gopīs.

> He looked and stayed:
> Crushing my wild senses
> that ruled my lowly heart,
> He dwelt within it.
> I do not comprehend now
> the grace of the mighty lord
> who showered his grace on
> the elephant with mighty legs.

> He entered me; he graciously stayed in me in such a way that all my sense organs were engrossed in one attribute and were oblivious to his other attributes. Therefore I feel that there can be nothing more than this and do not consider the grace he has shown me before as any grace at all.
>
> (8.7.2)

The paraphrase leaves out a reference in the verse to a familiar story: the Lord's descending to earth for the specific purpose of rescuing his elephant devotee, Gajendra, who had been caught by a crocodile. That story suggests the extent of the Lord's grace and also a salvation that is primarily rescue or liberation. The commentator concentrates on what he takes to be the main point of the verse: the Lord's grace in entering and filling the devotee, including his "wild senses" and his lowly heart. Piḷḷāṉ glosses the phrase from the verse, "You enter inside my soul (āvi), melt it and eat it" (5.10.1), as follows: "I stood in the agony of separation and you entered the secret part of my soul (ātmā) and did not leave it. You held it in close embrace, which never seemed to end."

Elsewhere, Piḷḷāṉ shows the flexibility of the word "mingling":

> Now [the āḻvār] speaks of the manner in which [the Lord] mingled with him: "Śrī, Bhū, and Nappiṉṉai are his divine queens, the earth, the firmament, and all the worlds are his playthings; the creation, sustenance, and destruction of these worlds are his play. And now, just as that

> Kaṇṇaṉ with . . . wondrous auspicious attributes graciously perched on Mother Yaśodā's hip, he now climbs up on mine.
>
> (1.9.4)

The multiple senses of līlā, mentioned above, are evident in this paraphrase: loveplay with his heavenly queens and play in supervising the cosmic process are mentioned explicitly, and the perching of the baby Krishna on his mother's hip *and* his perching on the devotee's hip are certainly also "play" or "sport." Piḷḷāṉ seems aware, moreover, of the gradual transition between the motherly affection for Krishna as a little boy, in which the gopīs shared as older girls playing with him and carrying him around on their hip, and the gopīs' erotic yearning to "mingle" with the teenage or adolescent Krishna. Mingling seems here to apply to all the various modes of Divine activity, relating to the goddesses, to the cosmos, to Krishna's mother, and to the poet devotee. They all seem to be different ways in which the infinite Lord touches or pervades finite beings, from the most exalted to the humblest, and those different ways evoke the different modes of bhakti: reverent worship of the Lord of the universe, motherly care of the Lord coming to earth as a mischievous little boy, and passionate attachment to the Divine lover.

He discusses mingling further (in 2.3) when he says the āḻvār "talks as the Lord mingles with him, manifesting himself graciously within his life." Then he paraphrases the first verse as follows:

> The Lord whose only enjoyment is union with his devotees, whose nature (svabhāva) is to banish the enemies of his devotees, who is my master—this Lord and I mingled so that we enjoyed every kind of "taste" by this union. O my heart! You have obtained right on this earth the exclusive enjoyment of the Lord that one enjoys only in heaven. . . .
>
> (2.3.1)

He escalates the rhetoric concerning the quality of this mingling still further in another paraphrase:

> [The āḻvār] says, "He graciously mingled with me, even more completely than with the Supreme Mother who is the Goddess of all or with such divine adherents as Brahmā and Śiva, for such is his affection for me that every inch of his radiantly auspicious body he mingled with mine.
>
> (2.5.2)

This theme of mingling or intimate union is frequently related to one of the other themes of the poem, that of the Lord's inspiration of the āḻvār, which we discussed in chapter 5.[14] We see this in one of Piḷḷāṉ's introductions.

> [The āḻvār speaks] out of the unsurpassed love (prīti) born out of the union caused by his mingling with the Lord, who listened [to the āḻvār], did as he said, entered into his heart, and made himself conformable [to the āḻvār's words].
>
> (10.7)

Piḷḷāṉ continues in the same vein in his paraphrase of the first verse of this decad.

> [The āḻvār] says to those who sing songs about the Lord: when you serve [him] guard your lives. . . . He took me as an instrument and made me sing about him. Then using that as a pretext he entered into me and mingled with me.
>
> (10.7.1)

Piḷḷāṉ interprets the Lord's entering the āḻvār as an expression of the Lord's unmerited grace. Without there being any reason for the āḻvār to have obtained the Lord's grace, "the Lord together with the Supreme Mother [Śrī] came and filled my heart fully and mingled with me" (10.8.1).[15]

Mingling can also be expressed in the image of swallowing, which is important for Nammāḻvār, so important in fact that we are devoting a separate chapter to explore the different dimensions of that image. Let us, however, already look at one verse that is particularly revealing of Piḷḷāṉ's notion of union.

> By himself, he became the earth and life,
> and now he will not relinquish my flesh.
> Walking and treading
> over this earth, and in-between
> he (found) our mountain,
> and he will not relinquish
> Tirumāliruñcōlai, the jewel of the south.
> The demons are distressed by this:
> But what can I say of his grace?

> Though he enters my material body and graciously consumes my soul, he is the Lord of the entire world. He took even my material body as something that he enjoys, and he will not leave it even for a moment. Now asking, "Is there a place fit for us to have a union?" he searched and "entered" the sacred hill and there, with great love (prīti), he united with me, as he intended. Now he says, "It is this hill that made our fortune grow." Considering this sacred hill as enjoyable as my body and my life, he will not let it go. He "experiences" my life, my body, and

the sacred hill and loves them. Our enemies saw our good fortune and were crestfallen and bit the dust.

(10.7.4)

Friedhelm Hardy believes that later Śrīvaiṣṇavas lost the special emphasis of the āḻvārs' devotion, adopting the pan-Indian normative approach in which salvation lies in separating the soul or spiritual self from the physical body through systematic suppression of the senses.[16] In the concluding chapter we shall consider this and other interpretations of the historical developments after the āḻvārs. Here we want simply to note that Piḷḷāṉ's interpretation of Nammāḻvār's bhakti shares one emphasis of Hardy's own interpretation of Nammāḻvār: the Lord loves the physical body of the āḻvār as well as his soul (ātmā) in a way comparable to his love for the magnificent celestial bodies of his divine consorts, and on his part the āḻvār yearns for physical sight of the Lord's body, a sight that is provided through the image form of the Lord. But Piḷḷāṉ goes even further: the Lord has a similar physical attachment to the sacred hill. "He will not let it go." Hardy believes this notion of physical union between a finite being and the Absolute to be a metaphysical impossibility and thus an imagined experience that drives the āḻvār to the edge of madness. Hardy therefore considers the viraha poems of Nammāḻvār more realistic and more profound: the intensely painful recognition of the Lord's absence made the more poignant by the illusory memories of and heroic yearnings for the Lord's presence in the most intimate union.[17]

There is no evidence, however, that either poet or commentator believed the state of union less real than the state of separation. It is not that there were no problems for the commentators in the poet's bold assertions of a bridge between matter and spirit, finite and infinite, but the commentators considered Nammāḻvār to be celebrating the amazing reality of that connection. Piḷḷāṉ certainly recognized the rarity and the fleeting character of mingling in our present human existence, even in the existence of the poet-saint, who therefore yearns fervently for the unending communion of his heavenly goal. Yet the reality of that experience he does not doubt, nor does he miss the reflection in that momentary experience of the fundamental truth of God's presence in a physical world apparently so alien to his unblemished being. In chapter 12 we shall try to demonstrate that Nammāḻvār, as well as the later commentators on his poem, holds such a vision of the unity of God and cosmos.

Reversing the Normal Hierarchy

At the height of the devotional experience the normal one-sided dependence of the devotee on a vastly superior Lord is (or appears to be) mysteriously altered. Sometimes that unusual state is presented in terms of mutuality: a reciprocal relationship. This is the case in 4.3.8.

> You who are in my soul,
> You whose form is of radiant knowledge,
> became the beautiful seven worlds
> and everything attached to them.
> You stand such that
> My soul is yours, yours is mine.
> What can I say of this?

> He stands inside all the worlds, ruling them all. His desires are all fulfilled, and yet I am his only support. My soul is yours to command. The essence of your divine soul is mine to command—in this manner you mingled with me. He says this is how he mingled with him. Further, he says "That union being inadequate, again you mingled with me. Now what can I say?"
>
> (4.3.8)

In many other verses, however, the poet and/or the commentator go even further. The sharp hierarchical arrangements of both cosmic and social reality are reversed in the devotee's experience. The Lord is lower than the devotee; earth is higher than heaven. We saw above that the Lord's union with the āḻvār was considered more complete than that with his highest consort Śrī or with the great gods Brahmā and Śiva, here conceived as Viṣṇu's devoted servants (2.5.2). The commentator paraphrases another verse to express the same sentiment: "Even if the Great Mother (Śrī) and I should [both] take refuge at his feet today, he will show greater passion for me than for the Mother" (4.5.8). The same mood of reversal seems to be behind Piḷḷāṉ's use of a reference to Sītā as an occasion for giving her extravagant praise as the human wife of the avatāra Rāma. She is said to be "by both the beauties of her soul and her body superior to Śrī, the crowned queen of the Supreme Person and the Goddess of all" (4.2.8).

A characteristic if apparently extreme expression of this reversal is the following:

> It is as if [the āḻvār] says: The Lord cannot be separated from me even for a minute and survive; he is solely supported by me; how could he have been without me; how could he have been separated from me from time immemorial?
>
> (10.8.9)

The "as if" is reminiscent of a paraphrase of a verse in the Bhagavadgītā by Piḷḷāṉ's teacher, Rāmānuja.

> Those who worship me out of intense love because they cannot sustain their souls without worshiping me, which worship is their sole aim,

> whether they are born in a high caste or a low caste, exist within my very self provided with every happiness as though their qualities were equal to mine. "I, too, am in them" means: "I treat them as if [iva] they were my superiors." [18]

Even presuming equality with the Lord seems to deny the primary affirmation of Lord Viṣṇu's metaphysical supremacy; to place the devotee above the Lord seems both preposterous and insulting, yet here it is the Lord who makes such a strange declaration, qualified only by an "as though" or "as if" (iva in Sanskrit). In Rāmānuja's case this paradoxical reversal of values can be understood on the basis of the Lord's generosity (audārya), which is so great that he speaks with hyperbole, forgetting the great value of his own gift and treating the one who accepts it as having done him a favor. There is a self-forgetfulness on God's part that is even more prominent in the divine attribute of sauśīlya ("gracious condescension"): the conduct of a superior person who so charms those inferior to him that they are not frightened or embarrassed by his presence, for they temporarily forget his superior status. For Rāmānuja the equality or the reversal of roles is not real but "as if" or "as it were" (iva), and at least in this case Piḷḷāṉ agrees. Whether for Nammāḻvār the role reversal is real may be harder to say, but certainly for both poet and commentator, as indeed for Rāmānuja, the mutual dependence of the Lord and the devotee is the second, mysterious side of God's gracious giving of himself in love; the first side of which is the all-sufficiency of God.[19]

One recurrent type of reversal is the preferring of this world to heaven, *provided* one is already united with the Lord here and now. Piḷḷāṉ interprets Nammāḻvār to be saying in 2.9.1 that "connection with [the Lord's] feet is better than mokṣa of any kind." [20] The same point is made in Piḷḷāṉ's paraphrase of 8.10.4:

> Should we not go to blessed Vaikuṇṭha in order lovingly to serve the Lord's own people and to acquire fully the ever-increasing experience of the Lord? If this were asked, [the āḻvār] would say, "If we get that experience here, we don't lose anything by staying here!"
>
> (8.10.4)

Certain earthly "sacred places" are sometimes preferred to the preeminent heavenly "sacred place" (Tirunāṭu). "The Lord extends more affection (sneha) here than in Tirunāṭu." (10.1.1)

> Should we go to Tirunāṭu to see him? Why has he graciously come to Tirumalai nearby to stand there? So what is it to me? It is the "never-tiring immortals" who go there [Tirumalai] and serve him.
>
> (9.3.8)

Finally, Piḷḷāṉ extols the value of the Tiruvāymoḻi itself with similar sentiments of devotional reversal.

> Even if saṁsāra should come to an end and I should gain the experience of the Lord's love and share the Lord's delight in having all the worlds under his control, would all that measure up to the love I know in experiencing the Lord through the Tiruvāymoḻi?
>
> (8.10.6)

Commenting on the very last verse of the Tiruvāymoḻi (10.10.11), Piḷḷāṉ concludes: "Those who know these ten verses in which [the āḻvār's] desire was fulfilled and his thirst was quenched, though being born [as mortals], are greater than "the never-tiring immortals." There is perhaps a rhetorical flourish in this statement of the "fruit" (phala) of "knowing" the final set of verses. The pardonable exaggeration of such rhetoric is even more difficult for those outside the community to comprehend than the extravagant exaltation of the saint's spiritual state. For those inside the community, however, it is important to feel so closely connected with "our saint" (Nammāḻvār) through "inwardly digesting" his closing verses that they share in his spiritual victory. In any case there is a conscious paradox in all these reversals. It is only through the Lord's grace that any mortal, whether the poet-saint or those who meditate on his verses, can be said to be greater than "the never-tiring immortals."

9

The Means to Salvation: The Question of Upāya

Bhaktiyoga

The devotional relationship treated in the previous chapter was a fundamental fact in the lives of Nammāḻvār and the other poet-saints. For the later Śrīvaiṣṇavas, looking back admiringly at the āḻvārs and seeking to share the experience of their hymns, the devotees' relation to God was both fact and aspiration; yet their present state of spiritual life as well as the future heights to which they aspired had to be interpreted in terms of the Vedic understanding of bhakti, especially that given in the Bhagavadgītā. In both Yāmuna's short work, the "Summary of the Meaning of the Gītā" (*Gītārtha Saṁgraha*), which sums up the meaning of each chapter in a single verse, and in Rāmānuja's several hundred pages of commentary (the *Gītābhāṣya*),[1] devotion is interpreted in terms of the Gītā's category of bhaktiyoga. The Sanskrit hymns of the community, beginning with Yāmuna's own *Stotra Ratna* (*The Jewel*) and *Catuḥślokī*, indicate, however, that there are aspects of the community's understanding of bhakti that are hard to fit with the accepted definitions of bhaktiyoga. Kurattāḻvāṉ's son Parāśara Bhaṭṭar, in his commentary on the Sanskrit work *The Thousand Names of Viṣṇu* (Viṣṇusahasranāma), presents "singing of the Lord's names" as the easier and generally preferable path of bhakti, in comparison to the arduous requirements of bhaktiyoga.

In his commentary Piḷḷāṉ generally assumes that the bhakti that fills the poem is bhaktiyoga, as defined, taught, and practiced by Yāmuna and Rāmānuja. All around the edges there are questions, however, as to whether such bhaktiyoga has some easier alternative, whether bhaktiyoga is even possible for devotees who despair of their own abilities, and finally *why* as well as *how* salvation is attained. Behind the human means to salvation so carefully defined in the Sanskritic tradition is the grace of God so often celebrated in the Tamil (and later also the Sanskrit) hymns. "What is the reason for God's grace?" Piḷḷāṉ often asks, and he sees Nammāḻvār himself asking this question. In this chapter we shall look at the categories of definitions and the doubts about these definitions that Piḷḷāṉ assumes to be in Nammāḻvār's mind as well as in his. Thus the same divine-human relationship, explored in more devotional and psychological terms in the previous chapter, is here treated from the theological perspective of the early Śrīvaiṣṇava community. Its tentative definitions were sharpened and enlivened by succeeding generations and finally organized in such diverse ways as to mark, if not to precipitate, a widening rift in the community.

Piḷḷāṉ's long comment on verse 1.3.1, cited in chapter 7, begins with the assertion that "Devotion (bhakti) towards [the Lord] and detachment (vairāgya, lit., making the world distasteful) towards [worldly] things will not arise unless one can perceive the Lord with one's eyes and other sense organs." The commentator then imagines that "some dispirited people" remind the āḻvār of what he had sung at the very beginning of the poem (1.1.2) where the Lord "is not within the scope of the outer sense organs of [even] a mind made extremely pure by the practice of yoga." "One cannot approach such a person: would it be fitting to draw near to him?" According to Piḷḷāṉ, the āḻvār answers that question here: "The Lord is accessible to those who wish to see him; he is invisible [or very rarely (ariyāṉ) visible] to his adversaries." We saw the great extent of that accessibility above, but note that the very opening statement undermines the received Sanskritic tradition that bhakti is a *means* to the vision of God. It is the other way round, Piḷḷāṉ says clearly: both positive *attachment* to the Lord (one meaning of bhakti) and cultivating *detachment* from the things of this world depend on the vision of God—indeed not only vision, but a grasping of the Lord by all the sense organs. This is surely the full-blooded bhakti of the āḻvārs; but what then of the initial credo, shared by the Tamil and Sanskrit traditions, that Viṣṇu is the supremely transcendent Lord who eludes not only our ordinary external senses but even the finely honed inner sense of the yogī? Such a Lord can only be seen when and where he wills, but the wonder of it is, as Piḷḷāṉ never tires of repeating, that he does so will for those who *desire* to see him and who humbly come to him for refuge.

Later commentators, and indeed both branches of the Śrīvaiṣṇava tradition, do not want to use the term *bhaktiyoga* to designate this bhakti as a Divine gift, considering this Divinely given devotion rather as the presupposition of the alternative means of prapatti (surrender). Piḷḷāṉ follows his teacher Rāmānuja, however, in frequently considering bhaktiyoga to be synonymous with bhakti in general. Thus, in a comment cited in chapter 4, Piḷḷāṉ says, "The Lord has the great quality of making manifest the real meaning of the Vedas; stand steadfast in bhaktiyoga on his side" (1.3.5). In another comment he even goes back to the more Sanskritic interpretation of bhakti as the means:

> The full experience of the Lord that one obtains by the practice of bhaktiyoga accompanied by karmayoga and jñānayoga and by which saṁsāra is stopped—quickly and without effort I have obtained this during this present life." Thinking this the āḻvār relives in his experience the fortune that he has received.
>
> (2.3.8)

The end of this comment presents the same paradox. It is accepted that the three yogas taught in the Gītā, of which bhaktiyoga is the crown, are the means to the "experience" (anubhava) of God, but the āḻvār has acquired these difficult yogas without effort in no time at all as a Divine gift, and thus he celebrates his good fortune.

In his introduction to the fourth decad of the Tenth Hundred, Piḷḷāṉ interprets the āḻvār as there concluding his treatment of "the easy nature of bhaktiyoga that was started in the verse, 'He is accessible to those with bhakti'" (1.3.1), which is the verse with which we started above. It is remarkable, in view of all the doubts and alternatives that we have yet to explore, that Piḷḷāṉ sees more than nine-tenths of the Tiruvāymoḻi as elucidating the nature of bhaktiyoga, and what is more, believes that bhaktiyoga is easy! Piḷḷāṉ's paraphrase in the first verse of the ten (10.4.1) reiterates this understanding: though possessing the fullness of beauty, lordship, and wealth, the Lord in order to become accessible to his devotees descends to the earth and becomes their equal. "We can grasp the Lord's sacred feet by bhaktiyoga."[2]

How easy this bhaktiyoga can be is suggested by Piḷḷāṉ's paraphrase of a verse in the Ninth Hundred (9.1.7). This spiritual path is not conditional on meeting qualifications or limited to certain times or places. It is not difficult, since some remembrance of the Lord's great qualities happens automatically and Nammāḻvār assures us in this verse that the remembrance will not be fruitless. Indeed, "since this happens by itself, it will be enjoyable and esteemed."[3]

Piḷḷāṉ regards 10.4.10 as the real conclusion of the āḻvār's treatment of bhaktiyoga (despite the "postscript" in the following decad) and therefore interprets that verse as providing a summation of the topics occupying most of the entire Tiruvāymoḻi.

Immortals from all directions
  with focussed minds
worship Mādhava with incense,
  lamps, fresh flowers and water.
His feet, so fit to be worshiped
  are the refuge of his devotees.

> Having begun to talk about bhaktiyoga, [the āḻvār] goes on to talk of his having procured without reason (nirhetuka) the fortune of doing service to the Lord. The Lord fulfils the desires of Indra and others who seek his feet as refuge. They come to him controlling their inner organs, [and with minds] focussed on the Lord. . . . Indra and others bring articles that are excellent for worship. If one hold's the Lord's feet to be the only goal, one's desires will be granted graciously. There is no doubt about this. Thinking this [the āḻvār] concludes, saying that [the Lord] is to be obtained by bhaktiyoga.
>
> (10.4.10)

"Being without bhakti"—What then? Alternatives to Bhaktiyoga

To have you
is what I want for all time.
My Lord, radiant as a dark smoky gem!
Give me your hand of knowledge
So that I may approach your feet
without wasting a single minute.

(2.9.2)

In his comment on this verse, Piḷḷāṉ says: "This is the goal that I always desire. If it is asked, can you accomplish it without bhaktiyoga, [the āḻvār] replies: Graciously give me that bhaktiyoga yourself, quickly." Here it is clear that Piḷḷāṉ is considering the possibility of a distinct alternative to bhaktiyoga as a means to his final goal. It is also clear, however, that the commentator shrinks back from having the āḻvār accept such an alternative. Instead there is the seemingly evasive answer that is actually consistent with everything presented thus far: there is no alternative, but bhaktiyoga itself is not a human accomplishment but a Divine gift.

Elsewhere, however, Piḷḷāṉ seems to be willing to have the āḻvār consider some possible alternatives.

> To one whose great love of the Supreme Lord has been generated by his gracious condescension and who believes that he can destroy all obstacles, who wants to gain fortune by constantly blessing him and remaining in his presence [never parting from him], who despairs of practising bhaktiyoga because it is so difficult . . . , [the āḻvār] says: Take a flower or leaf, which is available everywhere, and perform any [act of] service to his sacred feet. Because of his unsurpassed gracious condescension he will accept it. Therefore do not be despondent at the difficulties in the way of worshiping him properly; just serve him.[4]
>
> (1.6.1)

It may be that here, too, Piḷḷāṉ stops short of admitting an alternative, but if so, then he believes that the simplest act of worship will be accepted by the Lord as bhaktiyoga. In any case, Piḷḷāṉ clearly states in another paraphrase that daily bowing to the Lord's feet or folding one's hands in reverence is a form of worship better than bhaktiyoga.

Cruel sins that cling,
constant and enduring since ages past,
will vanish in a flash;
there will be no imperfection.

> Cleanse the dirt from your inner mind;
> worship daily the graceful feet,
> the feet of our [Lord]
> that have auspiciousness.
> To die with [an act] of worship
> at the place of one's death
> is victory.

> If without any other goal, we bow before the beautiful ankles and feet of the Lord, which have auspiciousness, the karma that has accumulated from beginningless time and has constantly been a hindrance to our experiencing the Lord will vanish that very instant when we bow. Now we lack nothing; we can obtain and experience the Lord as we desire. If it is asked, if we have not done any bhaktiyoga and have not the time nor the power to do so in the last moments of our life, [is everything lost]? [the āḻvār] says: Even in the last stage but to fold one's hands in adoration, to say a single sentence, or to think [of the Lord] is better than bhaktiyoga. (1.3.8)

Along similar lines are the following comments:

> Is he thus accessible to those who merely fold their palms in reverential greeting? The answer is: for those who think he is the goal, he is accessible.
> (9.10.7)
>
> He is beyond the reach of even the divine ones and others who are his devotees but accessible to his [human] devotees. Consider him to be the only goal; only fold your hands in obeisance and all obstacles [in the path of] loving service will vanish.
> (10.5.9)

Elsewhere, however, Piḷḷāṉ questions whether salvation depends upon even such a minimal gesture. "Because my essential nature (svarūpa), sense organs, and deeds are by your will and form a body of which you are the soul (ātmā), there is no action I can do, so I do not know [even] how to bow" (8.1.8). "[When the Lord asks,] 'Can you not by yourself perform some upāya to obtain me?' [the āḻvār] replies, 'How can I with my effort obtain you who are my support?'" (8.1.5).

A similar interpretation is given of the following striking verse.

> I, a dog at your feet,
> call you with cringing heart

Like a dog wagging its short tail.
O you who held aloft the mountain,
  and protected the cattle from the rain,
I am distressed without your grace.

> "My heart does not see its unworthiness and total imperfection; it is fickle, but it desires you and does not leave you. While all my organs are so weak, you remain without speaking. Can I not be caught in the overwhelming flood of compassion that protects the unfortunate ones and those devoid of an upāya? And so I stand afraid," [the āḻvār] says.
> (9.4.3)

Here the alternative to bhaktiyoga appears to be, not another upāya, however simple, but the acknowledgment that one has no means to gain salvation and therefore must rely on the sheer mercy of the Lord. The elaboration of this stance of helplessness into a preferred means of reaching the Lord was a gradual process taking over a hundred years to develop into its two crystallized forms. In this process we see not only the cry of helplessness but also the ritual act of obeisance, both to the Lord and to the Lord's consort Śrī, which had long been recognized in both the Sanskrit and Tamil traditions as the indispensable beginning to a serious exercise of worship. The final Teṅkalai position puts slightly greater emphasis on the "I have no means" acknowledgment; the Vaṭakalai position puts more stress on the act of surrender as a minimal requirement of devotional seriousness, but both positions contain both elements. In the following section we shall look at Piḷḷāṉ's comments on both subjects, remembering that what he states is what he regards as Nammāḻvār's view: the meaning of specific verses regarding the means to salvation.

Taking Refuge with the Lord (Samāśrayaṇam)

In his introduction to 5.7 and his expanded paraphrase of three of its verses, Piḷḷāṉ develops the theme of having no upāya into what comes close to a liturgical act of surrender. (In this case, his introduction to the decad is continued with his comment on the first verse.)

O Lord who has the serpent for a bed!
  I have not done any [pious ritual] act
  I have no intelligence,
and yet
  I cannot move away from you and survive.
O King, sitting in state,
  enthroned in the city of Cirīvaramaṅkalam,
a city

filled with fertile fields of red paddy
interwoven with blossoms of lotus flowers,
I am not a burden on you!

Even though he thus imitates the nature, form, and activities of the Lord who is the Lord of all, the āḻvār does not find anything to hold onto and says, "I am separated from him and suffer so, and yet the Lord ignores me. This is because I have no upāya in the form of karmayoga, jñānayoga, and bhaktiyoga [to make it possible] for him to unite with me, but even though I do not have any of them [upāyas] I cannot survive if I am to be separated from you who are extremely enjoyable. Therefore, since you have come to the city of Cirīvaramaṅkala to make me an object [of your love], and since it does not befit you to let go of this ātmā, which is your servant, you cannot let me go. Therefore you have to make me, who am your servant (aṭiyēṉ), an object of your grace."
(5.7.1 and 5.7 intro.)

Expanding the "I am neither here nor there . . . I am nowhere" of the second verse, Piḷḷāṉ says, "I have not obtained your . . . feet. . . . In my eagerness to see you, I do not now have the patience to observe any upāya" (5.7.2). In his comment on the fifth verse Piḷḷāṉ answers the āḻvār's question to the Lord, "Is it right for me to call you?": "It is only while you are in the midst of your enemies that you should not manifest yourself. Should you be difficult to grasp even by them who desire you, . . . [even though] I cannot do any upāya that is good enough to come near your feet?" Piḷḷāṉ then imagines the Lord replying, "What more can I do? I have entered Cirīvaramaṅkala so that all those who have me as their sole enjoyment can see me with their eyes and experience me" (5.7.5).[5]

In commenting on two verses in 9.10, Piḷḷāṉ clearly seems to conceive of grasping the Lord's feet, thus taking refuge with the Lord, as an important ritual act. His first paraphrase follows the verse very closely: "Grasp the Lord as the protector, place a lotus flower at his feet, and worship him in such a way that your sinful deeds will be destroyed." Piḷḷāṉ then adds, however, "For this there is no injunction concerning the [appropriate] time."[6] The fifth verse speaks of the Lord granting heaven when they die to those who reach his feet as their refuge, and continues, "He who rules the earth from Tirukaṇṇapuram [temple] . . . is all love for his beloved ones."[7] Here Piḷḷāṉ gives a paraphrase that sounds like a ritual statement of faith for those humbly seeking the Lord's protection.

Thus [the Lord] becomes the protector, not merely in one way, but in all ways, of those who do not have the patience to take refuge in him through bhaktiyoga, but who grasp his sacred feet as the upāya. Immediately he wants to liberate them from material existence, take them to the supreme heaven, and [he] feels that he cannot survive without uniting with them. As they have been connected with matter for a long time, at the appointed time when this matter falls off by itself, the Lord graciously gives them heaven and even then, because of his affection for them, he feels that he has done nothing for them. He asks, "What can I do for them?"

(9.10.5)

Piḷḷāṉ considers Nammāḻvār's cultic act of taking refuge to occur in 6.10.10. In addition to his comment on the verse itself, he alludes to this decisive step in his introduction to 6.10. Since this set of verses is climactic for all the Śrīvaiṣṇava commentators, we are including this entire set of verses with Piḷḷāṉ's comments in Part Four. In his introduction Piḷḷāṉ states that when Nammāḻvār does not gain a vision of the Lord despite a cry "so loud that it could be heard in heaven," he concludes that "the only way to see him is to seek refuge at his sacred feet; there is no other way."

The verse 6.10.10 begins by referring to the "Lady of the Lotus" (Śrī), "who says: 'I cannot move away from him even for a second'" and ends with a definite act of surrender: "I, your servant, who am without shelter, sat at your feet and entered [your safe haven]." Piḷḷāṉ has combined these aspects of the verse in the affirmation that the Divine Mother is Nammāḻvār's mediator:

I, your servant, who am without refuge, without any other goal, having the Divine Mother as the mediator, took refuge at your sacred feet. And now, immediately, with all my obstacles gone, I, your servant, desire at all times to do all possible loving service.[8]

(6.10.10)

In a long introduction to the following decad (7.1), Piḷḷāṉ speculates as to why the Lord did not immediately take Nammāḻvār to heaven after this surrender. This introduction serves as an important postscript to 6.10, as well as establishing a connection to what follows.

Even though [the āḻvār] took refuge in the Lord and requested the Lord to sever his connection with his material body, the Lord does not do so because he covets (lobha) [the āḻvār's] auspicious body and because it is his will to use [the āḻvār] to complete the Tiruvāymoḻi. So [the āḻvār] finds himself in the midst of his sense organs, though he is quite antagonistic to the [physical] organs and worldly objects and is only disposed towards God. . . .

(7.1 intro.)

This remarkable comment sheds a great deal of light on the very special relation of the Lord to the āḻvār, in Piḷḷāṉ's view, as well as to the importance and the limitation of the poet-saint's solemn prayer of taking refuge. Since for later Śrīvaiṣṇavas Nammāḻvār's surrender is the prototypical act to secure one's salvation, it is important to note that Piḷḷāṉ uses neither the term that was to become standard, *prapatti,* nor even the expression *śaraṇāgati,* so central in Rāmānuja's *Śaraṇāgati Gadya.* Moreover, his expectation of the result of this special cultic act is not the assurance of the saint's ultimate salvation, which for him was never in doubt, but the immediate removal of Nammāḻvār from his material body to direct relationship with the Lord in the supreme heaven. Yet this does not happen; the Lord does not grant the saint's request.

The first reason may seem peculiar, if not bizarre. The Lord is greedy (lobha) for continued contact with the very physical body that the saint would like to be rid of. Of all the reversals in the devotional meditation, this may seem to outsiders the strangest, yet it is highly characteristic of Śrīvaiṣṇava theology. It is only from the standpoint of our human ignorance and sinfulness that the senses and physical existence generally are undesirable or even disgusting. From the divine standpoint the entire physical universe is part of the Lord's vibhūti, his wealth or the manifestation of his glory. Embodiment is certainly not evil: God embodies himself in every aspect of his universe. While it is true that the material bodies of human beings are tainted by sinful deeds stretching back through innumerable lifetimes, the saint who is in a special sense God's instrument has a physical body purified to such an extent that it can be enjoyed by God. In the hagiographies and ritual it is recounted of two of the saints, Āṇṭāḷ and Nammāḻvār, that they merge with the Lord's physical embodiment in the temple.

The second reason is equally important to note and is even more crucial in understanding Piḷḷāṉ's interpretation of the Tiruvāymoḻi. He conceives Nammāḻvār not only to be expressing his own heartfelt feelings but to be revealing the divine wisdom. This teaching is far from finished at the end of the Sixth Hundred. For the sake of the Lord's community on earth, it is vital for the poet-saint to remain on earth until he has completed the poem, that is, until the Lord has finished the teaching he is giving through the lips of the poet.

It remains true, however, that the very verse that Piḷḷāṉ sees as a climax of Nammāḻvār's spiritual journey is turned by the commentator's own interpretation into an apparent anticlimax. Piḷḷāṉ often asks for reasons, and here he supplies reasons for what must have appeared to his contemporaries, as well as to himself, to be a most puzzling failure of the saint's heartfelt petition and solemn act of surrender before the Lord. In the following section we turn to other examples of Piḷḷāṉ's asking, "What is the reason?" as well as to the occasions when he answers his own question: "For no reason at all."

Hetu and Nirhetuka: The Poet's Celebration of Grace and the Commentator's Question

The Tamil verses of Nammāḻvār frequently contain the word *aruḷ,* as a noun meaning "grace" and, even more often, as a verb meaning "graciously gives." Also common is its adverbial use with the verb *cey,* "to do," thus the frequent "He graciously did." This usage in Nammāḻvār and the other āḻvārs has had an impact on the speech of latter-day Śrīvaiṣṇavas as a polite and honorific adverb before various verbs. In the verses themselves, however, frequency of occurrence should not be taken merely as evidence of a linguistic convention. Aruḷ connotes the favor of a superior, often an unmerited favor, and certainly not a favor on which a suppliant can count with certainty. The meaning is thus close to "grace" in theological English. ("Grace" in the aesthetic sense is also important for Nammāḻvār, but he uses one of the many words for beauty in expressing that kind of grace.) Aruḷ in common speech refers to the gifts or the deeds of the superior person in a relationship; in the Tiruvāymoḻi that superior person is almost always God.

Piḷḷāṉ frequently asks why God did something. What reason or cause (hetu or kāraṇam) is there for God's action? He asks this especially about God's gracious actions in all his manifestations, yet because he asks this about something that often appears as a sheer, unmerited favor, he sometimes has to conclude, "Without any reason (nirhetuka)."

We see this close juxtaposition of grace and reason/cause in the comments on two significant verses. The first is the third verse of 8.8: ". . . by the grace of the highest conscious being I placed him in my mind. . . . Transcending consciousness, life, and body, . . . he himself became me." Piḷḷāṉ paraphrases this to say that the only reason for the Lord to do this is his wish to do so.

> Not content with captivating me by his beauty, lest there be any obstacle to continuing our union, he acted in a manner that I could do nothing about, saying that he is the meaning of that which appears as "I." He also graciously gave this soul its ultimate goal: the intuitive knowledge that its sole essence is being a servant at his disposal (śeṣa).[9]
>
> (8.8.3)

Commenting on the phrase, "O pure one who seizes and abides in my soul," Piḷḷāṉ paraphrases, "My heart contemplates and praises the beauty and deeds of you who graciously entered it. For this reason you became delighted. By taking this heart as a permanent dwelling, you graciously calmed my mind that was disturbed because it could not get a vision of you."[10] In one comment Piḷḷāṉ gives a straightforward answer to his own question: "The cause (kāraṇa) for mokṣa is association (sambandha) with our Lord" (2.8.2). Another answer is more paradoxical: "What is the reason (hetu)? By accident (yaddṛc-caya) I mentioned a word spoken by a follower of Śrī" (2.7.3). The emphasis may fall on the insufficiency of the reason: "The Lord . . . uses only the desire that I have to serve him as the reason" (8.10.1). This motif is elaborated in the following comment.

> I just recited the words, "The Grove and Hill of My Lord" (Tirumāliruñcōlai). There is no further reason (hetu) on my side. Thinking that I said these words in truth and using this as the reason, the Lord . . . filled my heart fully and mingled with me. . . .[11]
>
> (10.8.1)

Usually the poet speaks of grace and the commentator asks "Why?" but sometimes the poet also asks a question.

> Today he made me an object [of his grace] and kept himself inside me,
> Why did he let me go astray at all?
> He, of the City of Names, shows his grace to me
> I don't understand it.

> What is the reason (hetu) for the One in Tiruppēr today to enable me to have celestial wisdom (divyajñāna) concerning him, and to come and reside in me? What is the reason for his not having done this before? I shall ask this of him. If he is capable of answering, he will do so. . . .
>
> (10.8.9)

In commenting on the very next verse, however, Piḷḷāṉ abandons the attempt to give a substantive reason.

> The Lord, without finding an answer, says: "All that I have done for you was done, as you said, without reason (nirhetuka). Let that be. Now what can I do for you?" The āḻvār says: "I obtained your feet; I am obtaining them. Doing high service I have obtained your sacred feet. Now all that I want, my Lord, is to do service at your feet." The Lord graciously replied, "I shall fulfill your wish."
>
> (10.8.10)

Piḷḷāṉ uses the same phrase in two introductions: ". . . the āḻvār who has without reason (nirhetuka) united (saṁśleṣa) with the Lord . . ." (10.9); and: "Without reason (nirhetuka) the Lord showed me his beauty . . ." (8.9). Similar usage is found in two verses from 2.3: "Like one who without reason (nirhetukanāy) rescues a drowning person . . ."; and: "You gave yourself to me without reason (nirhetuka). Without you I have no support (dhāraka)."

Another form is the petition: "By your mercy (kṛpaiyālē) without reason (nirhetukamāka), fulfill my desire, just as you measured the world." Here Piḷḷāṉ comes very close to the later expression of nirhetuka kṛpā: "mercy for no reason at all."

We look finally at a verse in which Nammāḻvār himself speaks of "grace without reason."

> The Lord, who rules me,
> shows his grace without reason.
> He rejoices at those who do [good].
> Without allowing them to collide,
> he holds the three worlds in his stomach,
> and stands in my thoughts,
> [the thoughts of] me, a little man.
> I do not know of any other grace.

Piḷḷāṉ's paraphrase goes as follows:

> If it is asked, what is the reason (hetu) for him to come with so much affection and grandeur and graciously enter me, [the answer is,] without there being any reason (oru hetu inṟiyē), he simply did it.
>
> (8.7.8)

When God's action is conceived as utterly gracious, then to find the reason for his compassionate entry into a much-sullied world and equally-sullied soul is to discover that there is no reason, no reason in our human worthiness for such a gift, and certainly no human achievement in moral purification or ascetic prowess that would make such a Divine act "reasonable." Thus the commentator only echoes the poet in concluding, "Without there being any reason, he simply did it!"

10

The Devotee's Final Goal (Puruṣārtha)

Liberation (Vīṭu-Mokṣa)

In his paraphrase of 2.2.1, Piḷḷāṉ says that "the Lord . . . who gives mokṣa and other goals to all those who are his servants (śeṣas) . . . is the Lord of the world; there is no other Lord."[1] In the verse the equivalent word to mokṣa is vīṭu,[2] the Tamil term that for centuries had been understood as having the same meaning as mokṣa, both in its literal meaning (being set free from) and in its connotations: on the one hand referring negatively to a breaking of the bonds holding one within the world of karma-saṁsāra, and on the other hand pointing to the supreme bliss of final salvation, and, more concretely, to "heaven." The passage above makes clear that both poet and commentator accept this pan-Hindu usage, yet the mention of vīṭu or mokṣa is less frequent than that of other more specifically Śrīvaiṣṇava terms we shall be noting later in this chapter.

One meaning of the Tamil verb *viṭutal* is "to leave" or "to abandon." That word is repeated four times in one verse which Piḷḷāṉ paraphrases as follows:

> Relinquish (viṭumiṉ) everything, and having relinquished it, abandon yourself to the owner of vīṭu (heaven). Relinquish your association with all objects that are distinct from the Lord. Make a worshipful offering of your soul, for it is his property (śeṣa). When you offer it, offer to the one who possesses it. By offering we mean that the soul is his property.
> (1.2.1)

We shall come back to the importance of the second half of Piḷḷāṉ's comment in the last section of this chapter, but we should note clearly that Piḷḷāṉ follows Nammāḻvār in holding together what for the sake of clarity we are here distinguishing. On the one hand, there is the negative sense of vīṭu shared with the Hindu ascetic tradition. This abandoning of worldly objects and worldly attachments is the meaning of sannyāsa, from which one derives the general title of an ascetic, sannyāsī. On the other hand, there is the positive sense of vīṭu as a joyful offering to the Lord in worship and service of the human soul that he already owns.

The negative sense of vīṭu as discarding or abandoning is the starting point for many of the other verses in this decad, but in almost every case Piḷḷāṉ interprets the conclusion of the verse on a positive and theistic note: the establishment of a relationship with the Lord. We see this progression in the following abbreviation of his comments on the next few verses.

> When you understand that the body and other earthly things connected with this soul are temporary and have other faults, you can easily relinquish them.
>
> (1.2.2)
>
> Discard the notions of ego and individual ownership that destroy the soul. Take refuge in the Supreme Lord, who is the soul's greatest wealth.
>
> (1.2.3)
>
> [The Lord] is opposed to all filth and is wholly auspicious . . . and is the supreme object of enjoyment; therefore discard your association with worthless things and take refuge in him.
>
> (1.2.4)
>
> When you discard your association with [earthly] objects, the soul which is free from earthly nature and which has the form of happiness will manifest itself; do not get entrapped in it. If you want to know your essential nature, whose sole essence is that of being a śeṣa of the Lord, grasp our Lord at the same time you discard your association with [earthly] objects.
>
> (1.2.5)

Note the warning at the end of the last comment: Piḷḷāṉ follows Rāmānuja in believing that material attachments and finally the body itself can be abandoned, but that that achievement can turn into a terrible trap. The individual soul does have the nature of happiness which can be enjoyed in splendid isolation (kaivalya), but the individual soul might stay forever enjoying itself, instead of moving as quickly as possible to the incomparably higher goal of realizing one's own essential belonging to the Supreme Soul and participating in his joy.[3]

Here is another important verse concerning vīṭu (mokṣa).

> We swim in the waters of birth
> and other [afflictions] that flow with grief.
> These we shall overcome,
> and the cause of [obtaining] release will be
> intimate union with our unique Lord

who wears the flowering cool tuḻāi
and who removed the grief of the elephant
[caught] in the cold waters of a flowering lake.

It explains the phrase "cause of release" (vīṭu mutalām). The cause for mokṣa that is free from birth, old age, death, and all other immeasurable grief is the connection with our Lord. If it is asked, when do we see it? [the āḻvār] says: We see it in the case of Gajendrāḻvāṉ.

(2.8.2)

Mokṣa (vīṭu) is conceived as release from the sorrow of this world. It is obtained by connection with a Lord whose compassion is so great that he made a special descent to earth just to rescue his elephant devotee Gajendra from the jaws of a crocodile.

The Supreme Heaven (Tirunāṭu-Vaikuṇṭha)

Much more frequently Piḷḷāṉ speaks of the supreme goal as "heaven," not the temporary abode (svarga) in which the fruits of one's good deeds are enjoyed until the credit is exhausted and one returns in a new body to saṁsāra, but Viṣṇu's permanent home in which he is joined by his devotees. Piḷḷāṉ sometimes uses the Sanskrit term for this, *Vaikuṇṭha,* but even more frequently the Tamil term *Tirunāṭu,* the "sacred (or auspicious) land." Heaven is thus a "place," and traditional Śrīvaiṣṇava lists of the sacred places (divyadeśas) include Tirunāṭu among the hundred and eight.

Tirunāṭu is described as "the land where there is no end to goodness" (2.8.4). The most important verses concerning it come at the very end of the Tiruvāymoḻi. The last two decads of the tenth "Hundred" describe Nammāḻvār's triumphant ascent to heaven, not alone, but in the company of the Lord's devotees. Here is an abbreviation of Piḷḷāṉ's paraphrase of three of those verses.

Even the unthinking clouds, by adorning and filling the sky, applaud the Śrīvaiṣṇavas proceeding heavenwards. . . .

(10.9.1)

As some [residents of heaven] gave the fruit of their sacrifices, others worshipfully offered fragrance and lamps; some blew trumpets and conches. . . .

(10.9.6)

Like a mother overjoyed at the sight of a long absent son, [the Lord's consorts] are filled with love at seeing [the new arrivals]. . . . [and]

> come with their divine attendants, bringing . . . their greatest treasure, which is Śrī Śaṭhakōpa, along with fragrant powder, large lamps, and other auspicious articles with which to honor them.[4]
>
> (10.9.10)

Piḷḷāṉ interprets the Tamil word "treasure" (niti) in verse ten to mean Śrī Śaṭhakopa, which is the technical term for the little crown engraved with the "Lord's feet" that is ritually placed over devotees' heads at the end of Śrīvaiṣṇava worship. Śaṭhakopa is also an honorific name of Nammāḻvār, which Piḷḷāṉ sometimes uses in paraphrasing the name the poet gives himself in some of the eleventh verses (phala śrutis). Here Śaṭhakopa means the precious temple object that represents the devotees' physical link with the Lord's feet. Piḷḷāṉ here suggests that this ritual symbol is present in the heavenly temple and is used by the Lord's consorts to honor Nammāḻvār and his fellow arrivals. For Piḷḷāṉ no honor could be more appropriate, since Nammāḻvār is his saving connection with the Lord's feet.

The New Age on Earth

If heaven resembles a Śrīvaiṣṇava temple, it is because, as both poet and commentator hold, the temples and sacred precincts are holy places in which the Lord of heaven chooses to dwell. At these special places, therefore, the line between Divine space and human space almost disappears. Is the same thing true of time? Are there points at which God's time and our human time in a "fallen" world can somehow meet? On the whole both Nammāḻvār and Piḷḷāṉ accept without question the Hindu scheme of four ages (yugas) in the last of which human beings have been living for the last five thousand years. This is the degenerate age, under the spell of the demon Kali, an age in which the "cow of dharma" tries to stand on only one leg. Eventually this evil age will come to an end; the future avatāra Kalkī will usher in a new age of righteousness, and a new cycle of ages will begin. There is relatively little emphasis on the Kali Yuga (cf. 10.4.8) in the Tiruvāymoḻi and there is only one reference to the Kalkī avatāra (in 5.1.10).

There is, however, one decad (5.2) in which the verses suggest that already in the present the evil age is ending and/or that the power of Kali is coming to an end. The first verse is as follows:

> Rejoice! Rejoice! Rejoice!
> The persisting curse of life is gone,
> the agony of hell is destroyed,
> death has no place here.
> The [force of] Kali is destroyed.
> Look for yourself!
> The followers of the sea-colored Lord

swell over this earth, singing with melody,
dancing and whirling [with joy].
We see them.

(5.2.1)

This entire set of verses with Piḷḷāṉ's commentary is included in Part Four. Here is an abbreviated version of Piḷḷāṉ's paraphrase of this opening verse:

> All the sins of all the souls have gone; the hells . . . become powerless to cause torment. . . . Now the non-Vaiṣṇava people . . . are not here. Only Śrīvaiṣṇavas . . . come and fill this earth. We see them singing about and acting out the Lord's . . . qualities . . . and actions. This good fortune must become established for all eternity.[5]
>
> (5.2.1)

It is striking that the novel feature that the poet celebrates is not the intervention of a new avatāra but the spread of the devotees of Viṣṇu, singing and dancing the praises of the Lord. The new age is not simply in this world, however. Nammāḻvār says in the first verse that "the agony of hell is destroyed," which Piḷḷāṉ understands to mean that the destruction of the sins of multitudes of Viṣṇu's devotees (Śrīvaiṣṇavas) has emptied the many hells and put Yama, the god of death, out of work! Verse 3 states explicitly that this means the end of the Kali age and the dawn of the golden age. Piḷḷāṉ's interpretation is a strong one: "The age of Kali is stopped for all time and only the golden age (Kṛta Yuga) exists." The fourth verse states that the non-Vedic "religions" (camayas) are being weeded out by the host of the Lord's followers; the fifth verse makes this more emphatic: the Lord's followers will destroy those "born among demons or ungodly folk."

The sixth verse is worth quoting in full along with Piḷḷāṉ's surprisingly brief comment.

Those beloved
of the discus-wielding Lord
uproot disease, hatred, poverty,
and suffering
which kill and conquer this earth.
Singing melodiously, they jump,
dance, and fly all over this earth.
O servants [of the Lord]!
come, worship, and live.
Fix your minds [on him].

The Śrīvaiṣṇavas, whose real nature (svarūpa) is to do loving service (kaiṁkarya) to the Supreme Person who has divine weapons like the

> conch, discus, bow, etc., to repel the enemies of all the souls, enter this world. You should leave other divine beings and, with no other goal, take the Lord as refuge (āśraya); then you will live.
>
> (5.2.6)

Nammāḻvār's dramatic statement of the work of "the Lord's dear ones" is summed up in the word *kaiṁkarya,* service that implies a constant readiness to do the Lord's bidding. The emphasis of the commentary, however, is clearly on the last line of the verse; exclusive worship of the Lord, and the empowerment of devotees in the new age seems to be absent. This downplaying of the new age motif may fit the general tendencies of a later generation of Śrīvaiṣṇavas for whom the power of Kali Yuga seemed unbroken except within the liturgical space of the community at worship and the progress in the spread of the true teaching. Perhaps this liturgical emphasis is also present in Piḷḷāṉ's paraphrase of the third verse, where he says that "the Lord's followers sing with such melody that the Kali age is ended."

The latter verses of the decad introduce another theme in the triumph of the Lord and his followers: the legitimate but subordinate role of other deities, and their acceptance of the supremacy of the Lord (Viṣṇu).[6] The eighth verse states that the Lord of the gods established the lower gods, who make up his body; and it is to these gods that one makes offerings. On this Piḷḷāṉ comments, "It is the Supreme Person, the Lord of all, who graciously makes Indra and other gods, who are members of his body, the recipients of all worship and fulfill the desires of the worshipers." In the tenth verse this theme is combined with the initial emphasis on the filling of the world with the Lord's devotees.

> All over the worlds,
> the naked one (Śiva), Brahmā, Indra,
> and the hordes of immortal beings,
> worship the sacred form of Kaṇṇaṉ everywhere.
> O servants [of the Lord]!
> If you worship him,
> there will be no more age of Kali.

> Brahmā, Śiva, Indra, and other divine beings, by taking refuge in the Lord became guardians of the world. So, if you should also take refuge in the Lord, there will be no more Kali Yuga.
>
> (5.2.10)

Even though this theme of the ending of the Kali age is treated only in this one decad and is not referred to elsewhere by either poet or commentator, the biographical tradition notes the statements by some of Rāmānuja's disciples, and notably by Piḷḷāṉ, that Nammāḻvār's "prophecy" of the ending of Kali Yuga has been fulfilled by Rāmānuja.[7] Since this reference is so important in understanding the relation of Piḷḷāṉ to his teacher, Rāmānuja, we shall return to it at the beginning of chapter 11.

The Lord Himself as Goal: Modes of Union with the Lord

Piḷḷāṉ comments that the Lord "is known as the supreme goal and the medicine for all the sorrows of those still in saṁsāra" (9.3.3). In chapter 8 we saw how important union (saṁśleṣa) with the Lord is as a theme running through the entire Tiruvāymoḻi. Here we want to note three frequent physical metaphors: the eyes see the Lord, the mouth praises him, and the hands grasp his feet in supplication or surrender. The first two are included in one brief paraphrase: "Thus I got to see him and also to exalt him" (9.4.9). In the "Now I have seen his sacred flowerlike feet" (10.4.9), the first and third metaphors are contained; Piḷḷāṉ paraphrases, ". . . by his grace I saw his sacred flower[like] feet so that I could with superlative bhakti at all times do all the activities of a servant (śeṣa). As I saw his feet, all my sorrows vanished." In his comment two verses later (10.5.1), Piḷḷāṉ connects the second and third metaphors: "Those who want to obtain our Lord's sacred feet should just say the Tirumantra."

One illuminating comment reads: "If it is asked, why do you suffer so? [the āḻvār] replies: I feel (suffer) because I want to see him immediately. It is not as if I'm suffering because I haven't obtained him" (8.1.11). This could be interpreted to mean, "it's not as if I've never seen the Lord before," but we probably should take that past seeing as just one dimension of a firmly established relationship between the āḻvār and the Lord that the commentator considers also to include praising and grasping the Lord's feet. Piḷḷāṉ considers that the āḻvār has performed his decisive surrender to the Lord at the end of the Sixth Hundred and only continues to remain on earth at the Lord's will and for the Lord's pleasure.[8] Yet the impatience of the āḻvār is not diminished by his assurance. Indeed the very fact that he knows much already about the beauty of the Lord makes him desperately eager to see more, and to do so right away.

The phala śruti at the end of 4.9 says that "these ten verses . . . will make one reach the sacred feet. Come to the sacred feet and be one with them." Piḷḷāṉ interprets the āḻvār to mean: "Be as closely attached to his sacred feet as the very lines on the soles of his feet." This same theme is put in the indicative mood of calm assurance in two other verses. One reads: "He is very near to all those of you who reach his feet. Sorrows will not come near you, he will stop [further] births and rule you. . . ." Piḷḷāṉ comments as follows: "He thus banishes the sorrow and the transitory existence that is the cause for sorrow for all those who grasp his sacred feet as the goal and is accessible to them. . . ." (9.10.8). The comment on the following verse continues the same thought:

> As we thus resort to his feet, all previous and future obstacles in the way of experiencing them will go [away]; there is no doubt about this. [The āl̲vār adds:] "I have obtained his feet as both way and goal. What more do I need?" Thus he speaks of his gain.
>
> (9.10.9)

In addition to the impatient yearning for a vision of God right now, there is the repeated concern that the vision be, not fleeting, but permanent. God's positive response to that deep desire of the āl̲vār is the theme of the following verse:

> Praising you,
> ever thinking of you
> is my inner heart.
> O pure one who seizes
> and abides in my inner soul!
> Taking the form of a Man-Lion
> with your sharp claws,
> You split into two
> the chest of the demon.

> My heart contemplates and praises the beauty and deeds of you who graciously entered it. For this reason you became delighted. By taking it as a permanent place to reside, you graciously calmed my heart that was disturbed because it could not get a vision of you.
>
> (9.4.7)

Those outside the Śrīvaiṣṇava community may well be puzzled at the reference in the verse to the violent act of Viṣṇu incarnate as half-man, half-lion. In addition to the analogy between the Lord's spiritual entry into the soul and the man-lion's clawing open the chest of the demon-king Hiraṇyakaśipu, there is the well-known purpose of this frightful deed: the vindication of the king's son Prahlāda, the prototype of loyal devotion under severe adversity. Perhaps for this reason the figure of Narasiṁha, far from repelling the devotee by its violence, is conceived by Śrīvaiṣṇavas as the embodiment of masculine handsomeness or beauty. In any case, Piḷḷān̲ does not mention the man-lion incarnation in his paraphrase of the verse. What is decisive is that the Lord stills the restless heart of the āl̲vār, questing for a more immediate vision of the Lord, by entering and occupying the āl̲vār's heart.[9]

Service to the Lord

The theme of grasping the Lord's feet blends easily into a major motif in both poem and commentary: service to the Lord. The most frequent word for service (aṭimai) and servant (aṭiyēṉ) both contain the noun for foot (aṭi). Despite the originally disagreeable associations in Indian culture connected with touching someone else's feet and the degrading associations of service itself, service for Nammāḻvār is not a disagreeable chore that must be performed in order to gain the highest goal, but a privilege that is end as well as means. There is no higher goal than to serve the Lord and the Lord's devotees. (Certain other Tamil terms for service will be taken up in specific cases.)

In more than half the cases where Nammāḻvār uses aṭimai, aṭiyēṉ or some variant from the same root, Piḷḷāṉ keeps the same word or a closely related one. In other cases he uses the late Sanskrit word kaiṁkarya for service and the venerable Sanskrit term śeṣa for servant. Both words have interesting histories and reveal a great deal about the distinctive mindset of Śrīvaiṣṇavas. With all of these terms there is a common problem of translation. It could be argued that "slave" would be a more accurate translation than "servant," and "slavery" or "servitude" than service, but we have chosen the more positive English terms, partly because the religious meaning is so overwhelmingly positive. We should remember, however, that both the Sanskrit and Tamil terms convey a status that in an ordinary social context is decidedly inferior and that the term śeṣa has as one of its meanings "property that is completely at the disposal of its owner." It is precisely this degrading relationship that is transformed in the devotional context. Rāmānuja begins the conclusion to his *Vedārtha Saṁgraha* by quoting from the Laws of Manu, "Service is a dog's life," only to disagree with the venerable Hindu authority. It all depends who your master is, Rāmānuja goes on to argue. Provided you are in the service of the Supreme Master, the state of service is a higher state than the vaunted independence or isolation considered by rival religious schools as the final goal of human life.[10]

A deliberate reminder of the inferior social value of service (or slavery) is seen in the following statements by Piḷḷāṉ: "We were defeated (captured, conquered, enthralled) by the Lord's accessibility to his devotees and his other qualities, and we became his servants (or slaves, aṭimai)" (2.1.7); "O you who defeated me by your extremely captivating divine deeds and by your wondrous beauty, and made me your servant (slave)" (5.7.9). In the following statement, however, it is liberation rather than captivation that makes service possible:

> So that [our] strong bonds of attachment
> [caused by] previous deeds may be cut;

So we may serve [him] and prosper,
the strong [one],
    who held aloft the great mountain,
    abides in this temple.
Rain clouds arrive and flow
over this grove
    where the entrancing Lord dwells.
Reach that sacred hill:
that is the righteous path.

> To take us who are bound [by karma] and to make us live by doing service at his sacred feet, he, the extremely compassionate one, has come and dwelt on the sacred hill which destroys all distress; to reach this hill is the means (upāya) to do service.
>
> (2.10.4)

In 8.3.7 (cited in chapter 8), the sense is both positive and poignant: "People do not tell him that there is a servant here who will follow him like a shadow." Service as goal is clearly significant in the following:

> If you ask, "Is not the goal to go to heaven (Tirunāṭu) and serve our Lord?" [the āl̲vār] replies: Even those who are there come to perform service in Tiruvan̲antapuram! Therefore to do service here is itself the goal. . . .
>
> (10.2.6)

We have previously noted the comment, ". . . we can only do service at his sacred feet if he is the object of our eyes and other sense organs . . ." (10.5.6). Two verses later Piḷḷān̲ comments that saying the sacred name is the means to the goal of service: ". . . for those few who say this sacred name, all their obstacles will vanish and they will obtain service at his sacred feet" (10.5.8).[11]

In the same decad are two other paraphrases that use, not the Tamil word aṭimai, but the Sanskrit term kaiṁkarya.

> Those who are not qualified for bhaktiyoga should say the sacred name Mādhava. Say it with intense excitement; as you say it all the sins (pāpa) which are obstacles to your doing loving service to the Lord will be destroyed.
>
> (10.5.7)

> He is beyond the reach of even the divine ones and others who are his devotees, but accessible to his [human] devotees. Consider him to be the

only goal; only fold your hands in obeisance and all obstacles [in the path of] loving service will vanish.[12]

(10.5.9)

The Sanskrit word kaiṁkarya we have translated as "loving service." It is formed as an abstract noun from a word for service (kiṁkara) that comes from the servant's question, "What may I do" (kiṁ-karomi).[13] One other usage of kaiṁkarya clearly shows it as the goal. Commenting on 1.2.9, Piḷḷāṉ says, "Now that all the sense organs have been restrained, all the obstacles to serving the Lord will vanish. Then we shall see this present body also disappear."

Service to the Lord's Followers: Means and Goal

The devotional experience of Nammāḻvār and the other poet-saints is intensely personal, but it is not individualistic. Some kind of community of devotees is both presumed and extolled. This community is *not* given an abstract name like saṅgha or saṁpradaya until later, but service to other devotees of the Lord is highly esteemed. Piḷḷāṉ follows Nammāḻvār in using the same words to mean service with respect to God and the servants of God. Piḷḷāṉ uses both bhāgavata and Śrīvaiṣṇava to refer to the followers of the Lord. (His is the earliest written use of the latter term, which since then has been the chief designation of this particular devotional community.) Some of his uses of the name Śrīvaiṣṇava occur in different contexts than that of service. These, too, show the importance of the communal aspect of the religious life. In one case he uses Śrīvaiṣṇava to refer, not to the persons bearing that name, but to the treasure such persons share.

Keśava's followers,
for seven generations before and for seven
generations to come,
have great fortune and prosper along with us,
through the Lord, my dark gem, my adored one,
the Lord of the celestials, my god, my Nārāyaṇa.

By virtue of Nārāyaṇa, who is the Lord of all, who has wondrous beauty and other auspicious qualities, who is the master of the immortals, who is my master, those who are associated with me for several generations have become those whose only enjoyment is the Lord. By this association there will grow in us the Śrīvaiṣṇava wealth (śrī), which is to bear the mark of having the Lord as our sole enjoyment.

(2.7.1)

Reflections of the significance of the Śrīvaiṣṇava community are also evident in the following comment: "What is the use of people being born amidst

Śrīvaiṣṇavas if they do not become excited by the wondrous love that is born out of thinking of the [Lord's] passion and other virtues" (3.5.4).

In one verse, Nammāḻvār is represented as a maiden so sick with yearning and anguish that people are trying to cure her "disease" by resorting to traditional healing practices related to local spirits and village goddesses. This is noted critically in the verse with the words, "Instead of using those who know the Vedas and worshiping the auspicious feet of the celestials' Great One. . . ." Piḷḷāṉ's paraphrase substitutes "Śrīvaiṣṇavas" for "knowers of the Vedas."

> Instead of resorting to Śrīvaiṣṇavas and using them as mediators, thus curing this girl's disease, you are [engaging in mere] magic by saying improper words, performing improper rituals, sprinkling liquor, singing songs, and dancing under the influence of spirits.
>
> (4.6.8)

There is a sharp contrast here, drawn by both poet and commentator, between the healing effects of worship within the Śrīvaiṣṇava community and the assumption that psychic illness is really possession by some village spirit or goddess and is best treated by propitiating the bewitching spirit. There is a certain irony here, since in this case the bewitching possessor is the Lord himself, but the point of this particular verse is that the cure for such devotional distress is to be found in the community of "knowers of the Vedas," which Piḷḷāṉ identifies as the Śrīvaiṣṇava community.

In the midst of the exultant optimism of the verses celebrating the end of the Kali age (5.2.),[14] Piḷḷāṉ goes still further: "Śrīvaiṣṇavas make this world perfect (pūrṇa)" (5.2.8). In 8.6.6, the mood is similarly optimistic: "'Come let us praise the one who lives in Tirukkaṭittāṉam,' [the āḻvār] tells the Śrīvaiṣṇavas. He takes them and with them he praises and enjoys [the Lord]." We have noted above that at the very beginning of Nammāḻvār's triumphal ascent to heaven, Piḷḷāṉ says that the clouds and the seas applauded "the Śrīvaiṣṇavas proceeding towards heaven (Tirunāṭu)" (10.9.1), and a few verses later Piḷḷāṉ paraphrases the residents of heaven as saying, "What fortune (bhāgyam) have we gained that would account for the Śrīvaiṣṇavas of earth to come to heaven?" (10.9.9).

With this view of the Lord's followers in mind, it is easier to understand Piḷḷāṉ's apparently extreme statement in his introduction to 3.7:

> Because of the great love developing from his experience of the Lord's accessible form, [the āḻvār's] only enjoyment is to be a servant of the Lord's followers (bhāgavatas), which is the ultimate way of being the Lord's servant.
>
> (3.7 intro.)

Piḷḷāṉ has the same emphasis in his paraphrase of the phala śruti at the end of this set of verses, which states that "the supreme goal is to be the servant of any Śrīvaiṣṇava, whosoever he may be, provided he has been captivated and enslaved by the Lord's auspicious qualities" (3.7.11).

The eleven verses in the set 8.10 are particularly expressive about the goal of becoming servants (or slaves, śeṣas) of the Lord's followers. Piḷḷāṉ paraphrases these sentiments as follows:

> Though goals like wealth which are connected with Lordship abound, they cannot equal the goal of service to the Lord's followers.
>
> (8.10 intro.)
>
> I want only to be with the servants of this Lord who takes me as his servant. I do not want even the wonderful three worlds.
>
> (8.10.1)
>
> Even obtaining the Lord is not equal to service to the Lord's followers. . . .
>
> (8.10.3)
>
> Please enable me to become the servant of their servants.
>
> (8.10.9)

This last paraphrase sticks very close to Nammāḻvār's words in the verse: "I should only have the fortune of being the friend (or servant, tamar) of the friend of his faultless servants."

How are we to interpret this apparently extravagant rhetoric? It seems to be another instance of that mysterious inversion of the normal hierarchy of being, an inversion due to the Lord's gracious condescension. The Lord emphasizes his willingness to regard his devotees as higher than himself by inspiring the poet-saint to regard service to these devotees as his highest goal. We may also look at the matter from another angle. The devotee yearns for a visible and tangible connection with the Lord within this present world, and that connection is possible through the community of devotees.

It is significant that Piḷḷāṉ usually speaks of Śrīvaiṣṇavas in the plural. Much is made in Śrīvaiṣṇavism of the saving connection through the ācārya, standing in a whole line of ācāryas, as the conduit for the Lord's saving grace. Here, however, the primary emphasis is on the whole community of the Lord's devotees. In their worship this present much-flawed world is somehow transmuted into a foretaste of ultimate bliss, so to be permitted to serve them is not only an exercise of humility but a joyful entry into the heavenly precincts; it is, indeed, therefore, the devotee's highest goal. To be a servant or slave is to be a śeṣa, one who belongs to the Lord and to the Lord's community. To the implications of that belonging we now turn.

Belonging (Śeṣatva) as Metaphysical Reality and Highest Goal

We have already noted several cases, both with respect to the Lord and to the followers of the Lord, where the word for service Piḷḷāṉ uses is *śeṣatva.* Since this is the most distinctively Śrīvaiṣṇava concept of service and is the term most difficult to translate, we should try to determine what the word means for the commentator. Piḷḷāṉ no more defines this than he does the other terms he uses, but whereas in most other cases we have to wait for the commentaries of the following century to define such important theological terms as the Lord's qualities (a few are defined only a few years later by Piḷḷāṉ's younger contemporary Parāśara Bhaṭṭar), in the case of śeṣa and śeṣatva we have both definitions and extensive use of the terms by Piḷḷāṉ's teacher Rāmānuja.

The noun *śeṣa* comes from the verbal root *śeṣ,* "to leave remaining," and thus means "remainder." In the Karma Mīmāṁsa the derived meaning of "subordinate part" or "accessory" was used: "One constituent is śeṣa when it is subservient to another." Thus the śeṣī is defined as "the principal element to which other elements are śeṣas." It is in the course of a debate with the Prābhākara school of Karma Mīmāṁsa that Rāmānuja defines these terms, but his definitions themselves show that he also had in mind another meaning of śeṣa further away from the original meaning of "remnant." One of the Sanskrit grammarians writes: "Śeṣa is an object possessed, whereas the possessor is the śeṣī." Rāmānuja himself says the following:

> The śeṣa is that whose essential nature consists solely in being useful to something else by virtue of its intention to contribute some excellence to this other thing, and this other (paraḥ) is the śeṣī. Thus sacrifice . . . and the effort it entails are undertaken by virtue of the intention of obtaining its meritorious result (phala), while everything else . . . is undertaken with the intention of bringing the sacrifice . . . to a successful conclusion (siddha). In the same way, the essential nature of born slaves (garbhadāsa) and other servants is solely that they are beings who have value for their masters (puruṣa) by virtue of their intention to contribute some particular excellence to him. Likewise, the essential nature of all entities, eternal and non-eternal, intelligent and non-intelligent, is solely their value for the Lord by virtue of their intention to contribute some excellence to him.[15]

Some additional light on the relationship between śeṣī and śeṣa is shed by Rāmānuja's briefer comment in the *Śrībhāṣya:*

> . . . the chief person (pradhāna) is capable of action aimed at his servant or dependent (bhṛtya). If it is objected that in keeping his servant fed the chief person acts in his own interest, we reply, No, for the servant also acts in his own interest when he keeps his master fed.[16]

Whereas in the first definition in the *Vedārtha Saṁgraha,* the śeṣa exists only to benefit the śeṣī, here the benefit, and the interest in providing benefit, is mutual; the śeṣī also benefits the śeṣa. In the later development of the theology of prapatti (surrender as an alternative to bhaktiyoga) this second idea is crucial, for the prapanna's confidence in his salvation depends on its being the śeṣī's function to look after his śeṣa.[17] Some suggestions of this are found in the Śrīvaiṣṇava stotras we have surveyed and possibly in the work of Nammāḻvār himself.[18] Even without this emphasis on mutual benefit and mutual support, however, it is clear that the relation between śeṣī and śeṣa is personal rather than impersonal. Even with respect to the impersonal accessories ("things") needed for the sacrifice Rāmānuja uses personal language: "its intention to contribute some excellence to this other (superior, paraḥ) thing." The force of this rather awkward expression is enhanced by its repetition with respect to "slave or other servant": "their intention to contribute some particular excellence" to their master, and once again with respect to all entities in the universe: "their value for the Lord by virtue of their intention to contribute some excellence to him." To this "intention" of the śeṣa the passage from the *Śrībhāṣya* adds the further important personal dimension of mutual interest (artha).[19]

We stress the personal dimension of the śeṣī-śeṣa relation both because the literal meaning of the terms could lead to an impersonal interpretation and because the śeṣī-śeṣa relation is one of the three constituent elements in Rāmānuja's most celebrated doctrine: that the soul-body relationship is the comprehensive concept, as well as analogy, that defines the relation between the three kinds of reality—the Lord or Supreme Soul, finite conscious souls (cit), and unconscious matter (acit). The Lord is the indwelling soul of finite souls, as these souls are of their material bodies. At both levels the definition of the body is the same:

> Any substance (dravya) that an intelligent being (cetana) is able completely to control (niyantum) and support (dhārayitum) for his own purposes, and the essential nature of which is entirely subservient [or serviceable (śeṣatva)] to that intelligent self, is his body (śarīra).[20]

The definition in Rāmānuja's *Vedārtha Saṁgraha* makes exactly the same point a little differently.

> The relationship between the self and the body is: (1) that between the support and the thing supported, which is incapable of separate existence (pṛthak-siddhi-anarha); (2) that between the controller and what is controlled; and (3) that between the śeṣī and the śeṣa.[21]

In his commentary on the Gītā, Rāmānuja utilizes this definition to clarify both the relation between the Lord and "all beings" and between the finite self and its body.[22]

With these definitions in mind we can now look at some of Piḷḷāṉ's frequent uses of the terms śeṣa and śeṣatva, bearing in mind that the term is always a "translation" of a Tamil word in the particular verse meaning "servant, serve, or service/servitude."[23]

In commenting on the very first verse (1.1.1), Piḷḷāṉ glosses the verb *toḻutu* (to worship or serve), as "Serve these feet in all places, times, and conditions [as befits] a śeṣa." Later Piḷḷāṉ interprets "Conform yourself within his circle" as "to him who is the abode of all śeṣas" (1.2.6). "He is the strong heavenly home (vīṭu)" elicits the comment, "to all those who are his śeṣas" (2.2.1). The words in the verse, "Śiva and Brahmā are the bodily form (uru) of Dāmodara" leads Piḷḷāṉ to a comment much more intelligible in the light of Rāmānuja's definition of the body: "Śiva and Brahmā who are his śeṣas" (2.7.12).

Perhaps the most revealing comment of this type is the following:

> Saying, "Serve only me forever,"
> Come and reside in my mind
> without separation.
> Take me for yourself.
> My glory is in Kaṇṇaṉ having me.[24]

> He instructs the Lord to take him as a servant: "Please graciously say with your mouth, 'Serve me forever', enter and abide in my heart without losing even a second. Take me as a śeṣa, like the sandal, garland, robes, etc. This is the glory of Kaṇṇaṉ having me.
>
> (2.9.4.)

Here we see the ambiguity of śeṣa, which means both personal servant and a piece of property contributing to its owner's worth, but the same ambiguity is present in the notion of finite souls being the Lord's body; their relation to the Lord is both personal and impersonal. In the latter respect they contribute to the glory of the Lord, like the robes he wears, or the sandal or garlands that adorn him. This same meaning of the property of the Lord is reflected in a number of other comments.

One significant verse ends, "my mind, life, and body are useless; I realized this when, transcending [all], he himself became me." Piḷḷāṉ ends his comment as follows:

> Lest there be an obstacle to continuing the union, he [says compellingly] that he is the meaning of that which appears as "I". He also graciously gave this soul (ātmā) its ultimate goal: the intuitive knowledge that its sole essence is in being a śeṣa (śeṣataikarasa).
>
> (8.8.3)

Such an interpretation of "he became me" certainly reflects both Rāmānuja's definition of śeṣa and the importance attached by Rāmānuja's followers to this doctrine and to the related teaching that the Lord's presence in the finite soul is that of the indwelling Supreme Soul who supports, controls, and "owns" (śeṣitva) it. Piḷḷāṉ's comment on the very next verse (8.8.4) repeats this phrase, "its essence is solely in being a śeṣa," and then adds, in the same spirit as the comment on 2.9.4 above, "the soul is also like an anklet for God, or some other ornament."

If the devotee believes that he already belongs to God, as God's property (śeṣa), how can he offer himself to God? In later Śrīvaiṣṇava tradition, this question is felt by some Teṅkalai theologians to constitute a serious theological question demanding an unambivalent answer: No, one cannot *offer* to God what has always been his property. For Piḷḷāṉ, however, this question seems to express a teasing paradox in which the mystery of God's relation to his devotee can be sensed. Piḷḷāṉ seems to enjoy giving a number of different answers to this question.

We have already noted his comment on 1.2.1, but it is so central that we repeat it here.

> Relinquish your association with all objects that are distinct from the Lord. Make a worshipful offering of your soul, for it is his property (śeṣa). When you offer it, offer to the one who possesses it. By offering we mean that the soul is his property.
>
> (1.2.1)

Here we see an archaic notion of sacrifice, whether from Vedic or ancient Tamil sources or both, that appears quite opposite to the consequential reasoning of later Teṅkalai theologians that one cannot offer the Lord what is already his. Piḷḷāṉ shares the ancient view that you offer to a particular deity that which is appropriate to its nature and which it in some sense already possesses. Here the offering is to the Lord of All, the Supreme Soul, who already possesses finite souls as his śeṣas. In another paraphrase, Piḷḷāṉ says: "Offer yourself and all that you desire to his sacred feet and [consider them] as his possessions. You and all that you desire are his śeṣas. There is no doubt about this" (9.1.10).

There are some other comments, however, where giving the Lord what is already his no longer seems a matter of course but causes some perplexity. It is significant that the different approach is in comments on those verses where Nammāḻvār himself calls the offering of the soul some kind of repayment or compensation (kaimāṟu) to the Lord.

> You mingled with my soul and for that great aid
> I rendered my soul to you.
> Can I retrieve it? You are the soul of my soul,
> O Lord who devoured the seven worlds!
> Who is my soul? Who am I?
> You who gave have now claimed it again.

> Thus out of the intense love that came about through his union with the Lord, [the āḻvār's] good sense was lost so that instead of saying, "This soul is yours," he gave his soul to perform eternal service as a recompense (kaimāṟu) for the tremendous good that the Lord had done by mingling with him. But then [the āḻvār] perceives his essential nature as it is and says, "Who am I that gives, whose is the soul that is to be given? You have only taken this soul that since the beginning of time has been your property (śeṣa)."
>
> (2.3.4)

In his paraphrase of the similar verse 5.7.10, Piḷḷāṉ says, "if it is asked, 'Can you not give your soul (ātmā) as a recompense?' [the answer is,] 'Even my soul (āvi) is yours. Is there anything that I can do for you, who are perfect (paripūrṇa) in every way?'"[25] Here there is an additional problem for the rational theologians: the Lord is the fullness of being and lacks nothing. How can the finite self offer any gift at all? It is interesting that in this comment, unlike the previous one, Piḷḷāṉ does not use the term *śeṣa,* which functions as a solution to the theologian's problems, but instead follows the poet in letting the perplexed question stand.

In paraphrasing a verse at the end of the decad celebrating the Lord's singing the Tiruvāymoḻi through Nammāḻvār, Piḷḷāṉ takes this same theme, not as a matter of genuine perplexity but as reflective praise (literally, "experience" anubhava) of the Lord's aid.

> Thus you took me and graciously sang the Tiruvāymoḻi; for this great aid, I thought I would give my soul as recompense—but even that soul has been owned by you since the earliest times. So there is no recom-

> pense possible, neither here nor there. Saying this, he directly experiences (anubhava) the Lord's great aid.
>
> (7.9.10)

Another comment brings together the diverse facets of this dialectic between self-giving and being already owned. The first part of the verse runs, "For the great aid of placing your feet on my head . . . I, in return, caressed your shoulders and gave my life for a price. . . ." Piḷḷāṉ paraphrases:

> Even though all people in the cycle of birth and death have material things as their support, sustenance, and enjoyment, you graciously made your sacred feet my support, sustenance, and enjoyment. . . . As a recompense for this great aid I have given my soul to you . . . as [the] ultimate act of service. . . . Can I see you . . . ? Can you will that even I do not have to spend even a moment without your name?[26]
>
> (8.1.10)

The last question is a paraphrase of the last part of the verse, ". . . O you with a thousand names, I am alone, my father." The commentator has interpreted the call of adoration and the cry of loneliness, not as an answer to a presumed question, but as itself the question of the adoring and fervently yearning devotee. Here there is no puzzle of whether God may be offered what he already owns. The offering of the soul is made as the only possible recompense for a Divine grace that lifts the saint out of the normal cycle of material existence and into the different economy of grace. There one is grateful for grace received but continues to yearn for a fresh visitation, for the actual sight of God and for the continuing presence of the Divine name.[27] On the saint's part there is a conscious offering of himself to the Lord as śeṣa, with its overlapping meanings of "insignificant remainder," "disposable property," and "personal servant." From all eternity he has been such a śeṣa of the Lord, along with everything else in the universe, from the demiurge Brahmā to a blade of grass, yet he consciously and eagerly offers himself as the "ultimate śeṣa." Nammāḻvār, this saint through whose mouth the Lord himself sings, sees the life of the devotee as consisting of both longing for the Lord and belonging to the Lord. Both longing and belonging continue intertwined, even beyond the point of his formal surrender to the Lord, in the saint's poem and in his life.

Part Three

Beyond the Commentary

11

The Commentator as Disciple: Piḷḷāṉ's Relation to Rāmānuja

Piḷḷāṉ and Rāmānuja in the Śrīvaiṣṇava Tradition

For those scholars whose only knowledge of the Śrīvaiṣṇava tradition comes from the Sanskrit writings of Rāmānuja, it may seem strange that Rāmānuja is not the preeminent figure in the history of the community. For various ritual purposes Nammāḻvār is certainly more important; in other respects each appears preeminent in his own category of spiritual leadership, Nammāḻvār among the poet-saints (āḻvārs), Rāmānuja among the expositor-teachers (ācāryas). Each represents one wing of the Ubhaya Vedānta: Nammāḻvār, the Tamil Veda, and Rāmānuja, the Sanskrit Vedānta. According to the various hagiographies, Rāmānuja had to learn the correct interpretation of Nammāḻvār's verses from Yāmuna's disciples. He himself then commented on the Tiruvāymoḻi, and later appointed one of his disciples to produce the first written commentary, thereby fulfilling one of the three dying wishes of Yāmuna.[1]

In Rāmānuja's Sanskrit writings, however, there is no mention of either the Tiruvāymoḻi or any other Tamil writings. This fact does not constitute a problem for those within the tradition, but may pose difficulties for the historically-minded interpreter who approaches the hagiographic reports of Rāmānuja's sayings and doings with a modern Western skepticism or with a concern for rational consistency.

There are Tamil and Sanskrit writings, both in poetry and prose, that are attributed to some of Rāmānuja's disciples. These writings are explicitly and implicitly linked to both the Sanskrit and the Tamil streams in the tradition. Some disciples express their indebtedness to both Nammāḻvār and Rāmānuja.[2] Piḷḷāṉ's commentary does not have any opening stanza in praise of his teachers, but it makes such frequent use of so much of Rāmānuja's terminology as to suggest that its author was indeed a disciple of Rāmānuja. What kind of disciple was Piḷḷāṉ? Do his echoes of Rāmānuja's phraseology suggest his fundamental agreement with his teacher? Can we rely on Piḷḷāṉ's comments to indicate Rāmānuja's position on those points on which Rāmānuja, at least in his Sanskrit writings, is silent?

The traditional biographies consistently point out that Piḷḷāṉ was expressly commissioned by Rāmānuja to write the commentary. Piḷḷāṉ was Rāmānuja's cousin and one of his first disciples, entrusted to Rāmānuja by his father, Śrī Śaila Pūrṇa or Periya Tirumalai Nampi, who was Rāmānuja's maternal uncle. Nampi had been a disciple of Yāmuna and then had settled in the northernmost temple recognized by Śrīvaiṣṇavas, the "sacred mountain" (Tirumalai) above the small city of Tirupati. Piḷḷāṉ is said to have become a disciple of Rāmānuja at the same time as his brother Empār (Govinda Bhaṭṭar).[3]

In the earliest prose biography, *The Splendor,* composed about a century after Rāmānuja's death, Piḷḷāṉ is said to have been honored by the other disciples as Rāmānuja's "spiritual son" and to have been delegated by them to request Rāmānuja to write a commentary on the Tiruvāymoḻi and other works of the āḻvārs, and (thus) "protect" or "save" them. After considering the request Rāmānuja is said to have refused on the grounds that if he wrote a commentary, he would encourage the impression among those "dull of intellect" that "there is only this [single] meaning."

> This would be improper; the songs of the āḻvārs will increase according to the understanding of each person. [If I should write a commentary] it might seem as if I had marked a boundary for the "graciously spoken words" [Tiruvāymoḻi]. You write the commentary![4]

A later biography attributes to Piḷḷāṉ the insight that Nammāḻvār was thinking of Rāmānuja's sacred incarnation or descent (tiru avatāram) when he sang, "Behold, even Kali will be destroyed" (5.2.1).[5] This notion that Rāmānuja himself was a divine descent or partial incarnation is widely found in later Śrīvaiṣṇava tradition but is not characteristic of the earliest biography. However, the claim that Rāmānuja has fulfilled Nammāḻvār's prophecy of the destruction of Kali, the demonic power keeping our present age in thrall, is found in the ode in praise of Rāmānuja that may well have been written by one of Rāmānuja's "converts" and disciples, Amutaṉār. In the later hagiography, however, it is Piḷḷāṉ who recognizes in Rāmānuja the fulfillment of the prophecy. Rāmānuja, overjoyed with Piḷḷāṉ's words, takes him to the inner sanctum of the Śrīraṅgam temple, accepts Piḷḷāṉ as his special disciple by placing his feet on Piḷḷāṉ's head, and commissions Piḷḷāṉ to write a commentary on the Tiruvāymoḻi.

Whatever basis in accurate oral tradition these hagiographical accounts may have, it is clear from the vocabulary of Piḷḷāṉ's commentary that without attributing his interpretation to Rāmānuja explicitly, he is seeking to accomplish in a different genre what Amutaṉār had attempted in his ode: the firm linking of Rāmānuja with the āḻvārs and especially with Nammāḻvār's Tiruvāymoḻi.

In the taṉiaṉ (reverential verse) for Piḷḷāṉ composed by one of his disciples it is said, "He knew the essence of the Tamil Scriptures (drāvidāgama); he had resorted to the feet of Rāmānuja."[6] It is the link between these two statements that is our concern here. In still another hagiography, it is said that one time when Rāmānuja was meditating on the meaning of the āḻvārs' verses (prabandha), Piḷḷāṉ was having the same thoughts. When Piḷḷāṉ disclosed this, Rāmānuja was first startled and then, attributing Piḷḷāṉ's wisdom to his being part of the spiritual lineage going back to Nāthamuni (Nātha's clan), embraced him and declared, "You are my spiritual son (jñānaputra)!"[7]

In some of these hagiographies, and particularly in the last one, there is an evident concern to show that Rāmānuja had bequeathed his spiritual leadership to Piḷḷāṉ, who thereby had the right to pass this office on to his chosen disciple, and so on in each following generation. By the time of the definitive split between the Teṅkalai and Vaṭakalai groups, about two hundred years after Rāmānuja's death, the Vaṭakalai claimed that Piḷḷāṉ was Rāmānuja's successor, while the Teṅkalai gave this honor to Parāśara Bhaṭṭar, the son of Piḷḷāṉ's close associate, Kūrattāḻvāṉ. Considering the names of the two groups, there is a certain irony to these opposite claims. The northern culture (Vaṭakalai) or "Sanskritic" sub-sect claim succession from Piḷḷāṉ, who devoted himself explicitly to the Tamil Veda, and the southern culture (Teṅkalai) or "Tamil" sub-sect look back to Parāśara Bhaṭṭar, who not only did his writing in Sanskrit but is said to have been commissioned by Rāmānuja to fulfill the dying Yāmuna's wish for a commentary on the Sanskrit Thousand Names of Viṣṇu.

The stories themselves, however, are not concerned with questions of dynastic succession but with the spiritual affinity of Piḷḷāṉ with Nammāḻvār and with Rāmānuja. With the exception of a rather recent move by part of the Teṅkalai leadership to reject the authority of Piḷḷāṉ's commentary, both groups of Vaiṣṇavas have always agreed on the importance of Piḷḷāṉ, and especially on his knowing the minds of both Nammāḻvār and Rāmānuja. In a modern historical investigation such a traditional assumption can be neither unquestioningly accepted nor lightly dismissed. Certainly with our present awareness of the differences between Tamil and Sanskrit cultures it is clear what a difficult task is taken on in the Ubhaya Vedānta: *both* Sanskrit and Tamil Scriptures are said to reveal a single truth. The demonstration of this claim was the task Rāmānuja is said to have given to Piḷḷāṉ. The later Teṅkalai theologian, Maṇavāḷa Māmuṉi, strikingly affirms this link: "By the overpowering grace of Rāmānuja, Piḷḷāṉ, so wise, so clear, made translucent, with love, the inner meaning of Nammāḻvār's Vedas. This is the joyous *Six Thousand.*"[8]

Reflections of Rāmānuja's Teachings in Piḷḷāṉ's Comments

The characteristic Sanskrit phrases of Rāmānuja are so frequent in Piḷḷāṉ's comments that they seem at many points to overwhelm the Tamil framework of the sentences. Not only are many of the Tamil words in the poem glossed with Sanskrit equivalents regularly used by Rāmānuja, but at times the sentences are filled with long Sanskrit compounds very close to Rāmānuja's phraseology.

Because Piḷḷāṉ has no general introduction to his commentary, his comment on the very first verse (1.1.1) is all the more significant.

> The āḻvār with his holy soul experiences the Supreme Person as he really is. This is the Supreme Person who has transcendent, extraordinary, [and] divine ornaments, weapons, consorts, and attendants and whose sport is the creation, development, [and destruction] of this universe. The āḻvār speaks as he experiences the love that arises from his being with the Lord. . . . : [The Lord] is wholly opposed to all faults . . . [and] is an immense ocean of infinite bliss . . . and other auspicious attributes. . . . He . . . further has that great quality . . . of making himself known to me, without reason . . . such that there is not even a trace of ignorance. [He arouses in] me unsurpassed bhakti toward his sacred feet. . . . His flowerlike feet have the inherent nature of dispelling all sorrows of his devotees. Serve these feet at all places, times, and conditions [as befits] a śeṣa. [9]

> (1.1.1)

With the exception of the "without any reason" (nirhetukamāy) discussed in chapter 9, every phrase occurs prominently in Rāmānuja's writings, many of them in the following auspicious verses at the beginning of the *Vedārtha Saṁgraha* and *Śrībhāṣya* respectively.

> Obeisance to Viṣṇu, who is the treasury of auspicious qualities, which are infinite and untainted by any impurity, who is the owner (śeṣī) of all entities without exception, both spiritual and material, and who reclines on the primordial serpent Śeṣa.

> May my understanding attain the nature of devotion to the Supreme, the abode of Śrī (Lakṣmī), the Brahman who is luminously revealed in the Upaniṣads, whose sport consists in such acts as the origination, maintenance, and destruction of all the worlds, who has dedicated himself entirely to protecting and saving (rakṣā) the hosts of various kinds of creatures who bow before him. [10]

A second point of comparison is in the use of scriptural quotations. At first there seems considerable difference here, for such quotations from the Sanskrit scriptures abound in Rāmānuja's writings, whereas in Piḷḷāṉ's commentary they are found in only a few places. In particular, they are concentrated in Piḷḷāṉ's comments on 1.1.7 and 4.10.1. The relative absence of such quotations may be explained by the assumption that Piḷḷāṉ felt he was commenting on a self-authenticating and self-interpreting sacred text, whereas Rāmānuja did not write a commentary on any particular Upaniṣad. The latter's three commentaries on the Vedānta Sūtras were dealing with an authoritative summary of śruti, not with those sacred texts as such. To some extent this was also true of his commentary on the Bhagavadgītā, for even though the Gītā contained the teaching of God incarnate as Krishna, it was generally regarded by Vedantic scholars as smṛti rather than śruti, as containing the essential teaching of the Upaniṣads in a form that could be shared with women and Śudras. The Gītā needed no authentication from śruti, but the meaning of individual verses could be illumined with the aid of other scriptures, both śruti and smṛti.

The long string of scriptural citations at the end of 1.1.7 appears when Piḷḷāṉ comments on the verse that he takes to express the central metaphysical doctrine of Śrīvaiṣṇavas, the śarīra-sarīri-bhāva: God is related to all finite reality as the soul is to the body it ensouls. While Piḷḷāṉ does not mention Rāmānuja by name, it is significant that he quotes the same verses, in some cases even in the same order, as Rāmānuja when seeking to establish the scriptural basis of this central doctrine. What is equally significant is Piḷḷāṉ's agreement with Rāmānuja in what they do *not* quote as authorities. The Upaniṣadic and epic texts quoted are those that are recognized by all orthodox Brahmins, and among the Purāṇic quotations, almost all are from the Viṣṇu Purāṇa. Later Śrīvaiṣṇavas would quote with approval from the Bhāgavata Purāṇa, which soon became for Vaiṣṇavas all over India the most popular and influential of the Purāṇas. It is impossible to tell whether Rāmānuja leaves out the Bhāgavata because he does not know it, does not agree with its emphases, or considers it too sectarian to be useful evidence in arguing with scholars of other schools. In any case, it is significant that Piḷḷāṉ, who was not writing a polemical document for outsiders but a meditation for the Śrīvaiṣṇava community, either observes the same principles of citation as Rāmānuja or simply follows his actual citations in what seemed to him the most similar contexts. Here, too, he seems to be a faithful disciple.

Most of the specific doctrines of Piḷḷāṉ presented in chapters 6, 7, and 10 are in close agreement with Rāmānuja's teachings, often expressed in almost the same words. Piḷḷāṉ's comment on 3.10.10 is a brief credo reminiscent of his teacher's utterances.

> With great ease he [the Lord] pervades everything, and he rules everything. He is the cause of the universe. Knowledge is his form, and his nature is different from everything else. He is distinct from the souls he pervades; he is not held captive by the sense organs. He is untouched by the defects of the objects he pervades. He possesses a unique divine form. The celestial elements (earth, moon, sun, and planets) form his body. With his unsurpassed radiant form he descended to Vasudeva's house [to be born as Krishna]. By clasping the auspicious feet of this Lord, no harm shall ever befall me.
>
> (3.10.10)

The supremacy of the Lord, here expressed in metaphysical and devotional terms, is also put in sectarian Vaiṣṇava terms: the supreme Lord is Viṣṇu-Nārāyaṇa and the other gods, including Brahmā and Śiva, are merely his devoted servants. Piḷḷāṉ does refer to them in 5.2.7 as "mediators" (puruṣakāra), a concept that Rāmānuja does not employ. A use of that term which is more significant for future developments occurs when Piḷḷāṉ calls the Lord's consort Śrī (Lakṣmī) the "mediator."[11] Piḷḷāṉ's comments are similar to Rāmānuja's in the *Vedārtha Saṁgraha;* this includes the interpretation of the trimūrti conception, "God in three forms," in which Viṣṇu seems to be co-equal with Brahmā the creator and Śiva the destroyer. In this case Nammāḻvār's verse itself (3.6.2) poses the paradox: "Praise the lotus-eyed Lord who is the essential form of the three gods and is the first among the first three." Piḷḷāṉ simply clarifies the hierarchy: "The Lord . . . is thus in the form of the trimūrti. He brings forth Brahmā and Śiva who bring forth all the worlds." Rāmānuja's treatment of this subject is more elaborate. Nārāyaṇa is the supreme cause; scriptural references to the supremacy of Brahmā and Śiva ultimately refer to Nārāyaṇa, who is their inner soul; like Indra and other lower deities, they are only Nārāyaṇa's creaturely manifestations (vibhūti). There is the statement in the Viṣṇu Purāṇa: "That same Bhagavān-Janārdana assumes three names, Brahmā, Viṣṇu, and Śiva, to create, sustain, and destroy." To the objection that this statement tells us that the members of the trimūrtī are equal, Rāmānuja replies,

> Not so. The passage means that "Janārdana (Viṣṇu) is the inner soul of the whole phenomenal world consisting of these three deities and all other beings. The Viṣṇu with the same status as Brahmā and Śiva is a descent or incarnation (avatāra) of the Supreme Viṣṇu into the created world, by his own choice and for his own sport (līlā)."[12]

We have already noted in chapter 6 the close though not complete similarity between Rāmānuja's presentation of the soul-body relationship and that of Piḷḷāṉ. The latter does not seem to bring out what for Rāmānuja is an equivalent relation: that of an adjectival mode to its underlying substance, or in grammatical terms, of any predicate adjective to its subject (noun). Yet Piḷḷāṉ makes clear that he is grounding his understanding of the soul-body relation on the concept of coordinate predication (sāmānādhikaraṇa). "Now this coordinate predication says that the union between the universe and the Lord is that between the body and the soul" (1.1.7). The passage that follows is a summary of many basic doctrines of Rāmānuja, and it concludes with a great oddity in Piḷḷāṉ's commentary, a list of seventy-three scriptural quotations—most of them frequently cited by Rāmānuja. There is, moreover, a special reason for Piḷḷāṉ's interest in the substance-mode relation to which we have already referred in chapter 6. Piḷḷāṉ utilizes the ambiguity of the Tamil past participle *āy,* which as a verb means "having become" but frequently has the sense of "as." Piḷḷāṉ consistently chooses the latter interpretation, which means that every reference to the Lord's "having become" some other (finite) entity can be interpreted: the Lord *as* this entity. All such entities depend on the Lord just as adjectival qualities depend on their underlying substance.

Piḷḷāṉ's doctrine of the Lord's incarnation (literally, descent, avatāra) is the same as Rāmānuja's. To expel Kaṁsa and other demonic enemies of his devotees the Lord assumed a unique divine bodily form, and was born in this world as a human being. He is not born like persons determined by karma; his incarnate bodies do not have even a whiff of the faults of material nature (3.5.5 and 3.5.6). Both Rāmānuja and Piḷḷāṉ set the doctrine of incarnation in the context of the devotee's amazement at the Lord's accessibility to those he loves, even though by others, no matter how high born or skilled in yoga, he cannot be known. Piḷḷāṉ refers to the same qualities as does Rāmānuja in referring to the two sides of the divine nature: on the one hand, God is high above all finite beings, not so much distant as superior, for the Lord pervades all finite reality without being affected by that fault-ridden reality. On the other hand, God is supremely accessible to his devotees, loving them passionately; among the qualities expressing his loving nearness none is more important than the captivating beauty of his bodily form.

Piḷḷāṉ's presentation of the means (hita) to salvation seems less close to Rāmānuja than the references to God's nature, but in part this is due to a different conception of the texts on which they are commenting. Rāmānuja has a polemical concern to establish the correct interpretation of the nature of reality, though he accepts the three-fold division of subject matter into ontology (tattva), soteriology (hita) and eschatology (puruṣārtha). The same three-fold division is understood by Piḷḷāṉ, but he sees most of the poem as concerned with hita, the path to salvation, since it reflects the āḻvār's vivid experience as being on the way to and finally reaching salvation.[13] This may similarly be the explanation of the relatively greater emphasis in Piḷḷāṉ's commentary on emotional expressions of devotion to the Lord. Rāmānuja, too, has some vivid statements of the character of the devotional relationship, but they do not loom as large in most of his writing as do such sentiments in Piḷḷāṉ's effort to convey something of Nammāḻvār's "experience" (anubhava).

A final point of comparison is the significance given to service. Both Rāmānuja and Piḷḷāṉ agree that service is at once a means to salvation and a goal in itself. Service is indeed so important that we shall return to it later in the chapter.

Some Possible Differences in Emphasis

The distinctions we can clearly draw are between Piḷḷāṉ's Commentary and Rāmānuja's Sanskrit writings. Whether the historical Rāmānuja also is responsible for the *distinctive* features of Piḷḷān's interpretation, as the tradition affirms, is very difficult for the historian to determine. The fragments of Rāmānuja's interpretation of a few verses of the Tiruvāymoḻi reported in the hagiographies and later commentaries are too uncertain as evidence, but even here some differences in emphasis might indicate the distinctive personalities of teacher and disciple.

The more obvious differences between disciple and teacher relate to the distinctive character of Nammāḻvār's Tamil poetry and to the later tradition's belief that Nammāḻvār is the one through whom the Lord speaks so clearly and powerfully as to make Nammāḻvār's poem the Tamil Veda. Piḷḷāṉ's bhakti is emotional, and at many points the physical attachment—or the yearning for physical union between the Lord and the poet-saint—seems much more than a metaphor. Since Piḷḷāṉ uses so much of Rāmānuja's language, it is striking how little he uses the Vedāntic terms that Rāmānuja so closely links with bhakti: *upāsana* (meditation) and *vidyā* (meditative knowledge or insight). It is possible that this is simply because the specific Upaniṣadic paths of meditation mentioned in the Vedānta Sūtras have no obvious connection with Nammāḻvār's intense emotional expressions of devotion. It is also possible, alternatively, that Piḷḷāṉ accepts a distinction between two kinds of bhakti that his younger contemporary Parāśara Bhaṭṭar makes explicit: on the one hand, disciplined devotion (bhaktiyoga) calling for regular meditation on a series of Upanṣadic texts; on the other hand, the simple chanting of the names of God.[14] There is an obvious reason for Bhaṭṭar to make this distinction explicit, since he is writing a commentary on The Thousand Names of Viṣṇu, and it may be that his elevation of the easy bhakti, the chanting of the names of God, is a necessary rhetorical emphasis. It is striking, nonetheless, that Bhaṭṭar, who like Rāmānuja writes in Sanskrit and who acknowledges his discipleship to Rāmānuja explicitly, deemphasizes the Vedāntic bhakti that Rāmānuja spends so much time and effort to elaborate.

In Piḷḷāṉ the shift away from Vedāntic bhakti is less explicit than in Bhaṭṭar, but its most important dimension is the musing questioning that we explored in chapter 9 as to whether effort on this path of bhakti is possible if one relies totally on the Lord's grace. That questioning seems to be another approach to the same issue taken up in Yāmuna's brief summary of the Bhagavadgītā, later greatly elaborated by Rāmānuja. Krishna is understood to be teaching in the Gītā that one must abandon the idea that the self can do anything for its salvation. The climax is verse 18.66, understood by the entire Śrīvaiṣṇava tradition as the key or final verse (caramaśloka) of the Gītā. "Abandoning all duties, adopt me as your sole refuge. I shall rescue you from all sins; be not grieved!" Rāmānuja gives two interpretations, the first of which most clearly follows Yāmuna's interpretation. "All duties (dharmas)" means all the paths to mokṣa previously taught, not only karmayoga and jñānayoga but also bhaktiyoga.

"Abandoning," however, is not to be taken literally; all these disciplines are to be performed as worship pleasing to God. What is to be abandoned is the karmic "fruit" from this performance. One needs to give up the idea that such religious acts are one's own or that one is their real author. "Adopting me as your sole refuge" means recognizing that the Lord is both the actor and the One worshiped through the action, the means (upāya) as well as the goal (upeya). The Lord thus worshiped will deliver his devotees from their accumulated sins.[15]

This verse is understood by the Teṅkalai tradition to be the basis of the doctrine and practice of prapatti, which both later schools regard as an alternative to bhakti. Vedānta Deśika, articulating the Vaṭakalai position, considers Rāmānuja's interpretation of this key verse to provide only a hint of the full doctrine of prapatti as an independent means or alternative path to salvation, made clear only in Rāmānuja's *Śaraṇāgati Gadya.*

Rāmānuja's statements in his solemn prayer of Surrender in the *Śaraṇāgati Gadya,* however, do not themselves explicitly set a path of śaraṇagati or prapatti (abject surrender to the Lord) in contrast to a distinct path of bhakti, though the three later extant commentaries on Rāmānuja's *Śaraṇāgati Gadya* assume such a distinction. On this important point Piḷḷāṉ agrees with Rāmānuja. He does not spell out a path of surrender distinct from bhakti, but like Bhaṭṭar and other immediate disciples of Rāmānuja, Piḷḷāṉ moves the emphasis away from tranquil meditation on passages on the nature of Brahman in the Upaniṣads towards emotional identification with the Supreme Lord in one of his incarnate or image forms. At the same time Piḷḷāṉ shifts the emphasis from disciplined effort to acknowledgment of one's helplessness.

In both Piḷḷāṉ's and Rāmānuja's teachings there is a paradox of Divine grace, but Piḷḷāṉ's emphasis on the unmerited character of grace is greater than Rāmānuja's. The paradox from our later perspective is that Piḷḷāṉ is commenting on a poem in which every eleventh verse, following a widespread Indian convention, describes the fruit or benefit of reciting the previous ten verses. Such concern with gathering merit or spiritual benefit might seem to us as the opposite of dependence on Divine grace. Piḷḷāṉ, however, does not seem to notice any problem with these phala śrutis, perhaps because he affirms the verses' emphasis on the Divine gift (blessing) conveyed through the verses, rather than recognizing the devotee's effort in reciting them.

Perhaps "paradox" is not the right term to describe either Rāmānuja's or Piḷḷāṉ's own sense of the mysterious Divine initiative in rescuing and protecting finite beings, but both repeatedly express their amazement. In Piḷḷāṉ's case, since he is writing a commentary, it is his sense of Nammāḻvār's amazement—and occasional perplexity—at the wonder of Divine grace. He puts in the poet's mouth a question that does not occur explicitly in Rāmānuja's Sanskrit writings: how can this be? The later commentators and systematicians were to be largely concerned with that question; their inability to agree on the answer contributed to a widening split within the community of Nammālvār and Rāmānuja.

Some Possible Influences of Nammālvār's Tamil Veda on Rāmānuja's Vedānta

Although our initial concern in this chapter is with Piḷḷāṉ's interpretations, the major question for historians of the Śrīvaiṣṇava tradition is the relation between Nammālvār and Rāmānuja, that is, between Piḷḷāṉ's two most significant gurus. For Piḷḷāṉ himself the two are gurus, not in parallel but in sequence. Nammālvār is the more elevated, standing at least as close to the source of Divine revelation as the Vedic seers (ṛṣis), while Rāmānuja is his immediate teacher; Piḷḷāṉ certainly shared the traditional view that both gurus had the same insight into Divine reality, though each had his own distinctive personal experience of the Divine love.

The modern historian must attempt to reconcile the hagiographies' strong emphasis on Rāmānuja's intuitive grasp of the meaning of Nammālvār's verses with the complete silence of Rāmānuja's Sanskrit writings about any of the ālvārs. Piḷḷāṉ's commentary needs to be used positively to address this question; we should certainly not allow the commentary to obscure the historian's critical question.

One line we might pursue is to try to determine where the Rāmānuja-sounding emphases in Piḷḷāṉ's commentary are faithful to Nammālvār's meanings and where, on the contrary, the doctrinal emphases of Rāmānuja's Vedānta lead to forced interpretations of the Tiruvāymoli. Such an attempt does make a modern assumption that it is possible to penetrate behind the interpretation of this and other commentaries to the author's conscious intentions and/or (since they may not be the same) to the "grammatical sense" of the text. Contemporary Western hermeneutics is learning to be self-critical about the modern Western notion of the "original text" and is thereby regaining some appreciation of the assumption of multiple layers of meaning in medieval commentaries. Nevertheless, there are in many cases fairly clear indications, grammatical and literary-historical, of the meaning of the text itself. This is certainly the case with the verses of Nammālvār.

Despite the prominence of the image of Lord Viṣṇu reclining on the milk-ocean in South Indian Vaiṣṇava temples (as, for example, in Śrīraṅgam), the predominant picture of Viṣṇu-Nārāyaṇa in Nammālvār's poems is not of an immovable Supreme Being in yogic trance but of an active protector and savior. This same emphasis on the active lordship of Viṣṇu-Nārāyaṇa is certainly also present in the theology of Rāmānuja. Indeed, by utilizing two different terms for the essential nature of God (*svarūpa* and *svabhāva*), Rāmānuja is able to do justice both to the Upaniṣadic tradition of Brahman's nature as pure consciousness and to the active nature of God in relation to all finite beings. He does this despite an inherited philosophical language that stresses unchanging being rather than becoming and that is expressed in a host of Sanskrit substantives or nominal phrases rather than in Nammāḻvār's finite verbs.

When we look at the stance of finite beings in relation to the Lord, and in particular to the stance of the human devotees of Viṣṇu-Nārāyaṇa, a related theme is clearly present in both Nammāḻvār and Rāmānuja. This is the theme of servanthood or service. The poet's usual substitute for "I" is *aṭiyēṉ*, which can perhaps best be translated as "your servant" or "I, your servant," but which in Tamil is simply the word for servant or slave (*aṭi*), which also means "foot," with a first person singular ending.

In the latter part of chapter 10 we have already seen the prominence of this theme of service in Piḷḷāṉ's understanding of Nammāḻvār. Here, however, Nammāḻvār's own words express a theme that is equally prominent in the Sanskrit writings of Rāmānuja and is perhaps clearest where Rāmānuja is not simply commenting on a particular Sanskrit text but developing the meaning of the whole. Rāmānuja's allowing his hypothetical opponent to quote the line from the most authoritative work of jurisprudence, the Dharma Śāstra of Manu, "Service is a dog's life,"[16] is a clear enough indication that Rāmānuja knew the difficulty of persuading his proud Brahmin readers that service to God is a cardinal virtue.

Interestingly, in the oldest Tamil biography, Rāmānuja is represented as having to be reminded by his (also Brahmin) secretary Kūrattāḻvāṉ that belonging (śeṣatva) to God, which implies servitude or servanthood, is part of the definition of the finite soul.[17] According to the story, Rāmānuja was in the midst of dictating his great commentary on the Vedānta Sūtras, called the *Śrībhāṣya*. He had used a definition for the finite soul: "whose essential nature is wholly consciousness (jñānaikasvarūpa)," a definition that applies both to the Supreme Soul and to the finite soul.[18] Rāmānuja had given his brilliant and devoted secretary permission to stop writing down his statements if Rāmānuja dictated anything with which Kūrattāḻvāṉ did not agree. Nonetheless, when the latter did stop at this point, Rāmānuja became very provoked. "Sir, if *you* wish to write the commentary on the Vedānta Sūtras, you may do so," he cried, and after giving his secretary a kick he left the room. After some reflection in solitude Rāmānuja realized why his secretary had refused to continue, for the Vedāntic commentator had omitted from his definition something quite essential, the fact that the finite soul belongs to the Supreme Soul.

This is a curious story, not least because in the *Vedārtha Saṁgraha,* a work written before the *Śrībhāṣya,* Rāmānuja so frequently refers to the finite soul's being owned by God. Yet whatever the problems with historical accuracy of the story, the point would not be lost on a Tamil-speaking audience. The teacher had acted the part of an imperious master, using his foot (aṭi) to kick his disciple and servant (aṭi), which as the acknowledged guru he was no doubt entitled to do. In his definition as in his action, however, Rāmānuja momentarily forgot one of Nammālvār's central emphases: before God we are all servants. The obvious business at hand in this story is the production of Rāmānuja's magnum opus, the authoritative interpretation of the summary of the Upaniṣads. Yet the interest of the story is clearly in the lesson the teacher learns from his disciple, the master from his assistant, the professor from his secretary. In this popular strand of the Śrīvaiṣṇava tradition the Ubhaya Vedānta is affirmed and the Sanskrit scriptures are highly honored, but it is clear at many points that the crucial lesson of humility, of embodied servitude to God, is one proud Brahmins must learn from the Tamil Veda, that is, from the Śūdra saint, Nammālvār.

The close connection between the devotee and the Lord is also a theme common to Nammālvār and Rāmānuja, but there are some obvious differences in the mode of expression. The poet is more dramatic in his moving back and forth between God's presence and God's absence. The theologian frequently writes in a mood of praise for God's presence. This may seem a more distant presence than Nammālvār's intense experience of union, yet occasional comments of Rāmānuja, especially in his commentary on the Bhagavadgītā, make clear that he too knew the pain of yearning and the joy of union. The stance of servanthood (dāsya) or readiness to serve (kaiṁkarya) may seem to suggest a more distant and less intimate relationship with God than the erotic longings and satisfaction of Nammālvār's lovesick maiden, but the same intensity of emotion is there in both. The comparison here made is with the Rāmānuja we know from his Sanskrit writings. The Rāmānuja of the hagiographies is closer to Nammālvār and very close to Piḷḷān's mood in his interpretation of Nammālvār.

Rāmānuja seems especially concerned with the simultaneous reality of direct Divine-human contact and Divine purity. That concern with God's "unsulliedness" (amalatva) is a striking characteristic of Rāmānuja's writing; it is much less evident in Nammālvār's poetry. As might be expected, Piḷḷān's comments fall in between. He frequently cites Rāmānuja's characteristic epithets affirming God's utter purity, while he also shares Nammālvār's interest in the actual physical contact between the devotee and the Lord.

One important mode of the Divine presence in material objects is in consecrated images. Neither Nammālvār nor Rāmānuja use the Pāñcarātric expression *arcāvatāra,* "iconic incarnation," but Nammālvār devotes many of his verses to praising the Lord present in a particular temple and sacred place. It is mainly in his prose hymn, the *Śrī Raṅga Gadya,* that Rāmānuja has a comparable emphasis on the Lord present in a particular temple. Rāmānuja's silence in his other works is probably attributable to the character of the sources on which he is commenting. Neither the classical Upaniṣads nor the Bhagavadgītā refer to the Lord's presence at particular temples or in particular consecrated images. Since Rāmānuja interprets the Vedānta Sūtras as accepting the orthodoxy of Pāñcarātra texts, there does not seem sufficient reason to consider Rāmānuja an iconoclastic exception in the midst of the Śrīvaiṣṇava tradition, but it is worth considering the possibility that Rāmānuja and Nammāḻvār followed an ancient South Indian tradition in seeing the Lord's presence more generally in sacred places, not restricted to sacred images. The icons of village goddesses in South India right up to the present day may be one indication of this view of sacred place. Another is provided by the frequent references in temple histories (sthalapurāṇas) to the discovery of an ancient icon buried in the dirt on the site of a new temple. Through such discoveries it is possible to think of a favorite temple site as perpetually sacred or at least as going back to some specific Divine visitation. The sacredness of the place thus does not depend solely on the act of consecrating new sacred images for its temple. By the time Śrīvaiṣṇava institutions developed their characteristic medieval forms, the ritual texts of both the Pāñcarātra and Vaikhānasa Āgamas had blended in various ways with both the Vedic and āḻvār traditions, and the power of the devotee quite literally to handle the Lord in his image-form could be seen by Piḷḷai Lokācārya as a striking example of the Divine condescension: the all-powerful and all-gracious Lord places himself in the hands of his devotees.

The most complex question concerns the metaphysical relation of Nammāḻvār's and Rāmānuja's positions, for it is here that those within the community have powerfully sensed and emphatically affirmed their complete agreement while those viewing the tradition from the outside have sometimes been struck with the appearance of substantial differences. Piḷḷāṉ's commentary is a respected statement of what the tradition takes to be the same truth in both Sanskrit and Tamil Vedas. For that very reason, however, it is important to find a way to look at the distinctive metaphysical insight of Nammāḻvār that does not depend on Piḷḷāṉ's "translation" of Nammāḻvār. That we shall attempt in the next chapter.

It is worth noting here, however, that both Nammāḻvār's and Rāmānuja's metaphysical positions are related to the ancient Hindu compromise or synthesis known as Bhedābheda ("difference and non-difference"). Brahman and the universe are one in the primordial state before creation that periodically recurs as pralaya ("dissolution"). Brahman and the universe are different in the state of creation or emanation (sṛṣti). Brahman projects itself into a multitude of forms of which it remains the primordial substance. The soul seeking enlightenment thus attempts a return to the state of undifferentiated unity before creation. Such attainment of the primordial unity is possible only after death when the enlightened soul realizes itself as an undifferentiated part of the infinite consciousness. Until death the soul must live and act in a bodily form thoroughly involved in all the moral and immoral structures of the created world.

Rāmānuja criticizes the Bhedābheda for involving the pure Creator in the impurities of creation, and he seeks to demonstrate that a right understanding of the Vedic texts acknowledges that Brahman is both distinct from and inseparably connected with the universe (including all finite souls) in both the state of creation and the state of dissolution. Rāmānuja believes that a stable ontological relation of the Supreme Self to its cosmic body persists throughout the cosmic cycles of creation and dissolution. Being is more important than becoming.

Nammāḻvār appears to emphasize the element of becoming in the ancient bhedābheda position. Certainly he alludes to many of the stories about the Lord who actively creates and dramatically destroys, who can change his own form and who causes changes in all things. But as in the bhedābheda interpretation of the Vedānta, and indeed in almost all forms of ancient Indian philosophy, the cosmic "history" is chiefly important as a backdrop for meditation on the journey of the soul, which in the Vedānta means the journey to union with the primordial source of the created universe, Brahman. Piḷḷāṉ presents the Śrīvaiṣṇava belief that the same journey is described in the pithy Sanskrit aphorisms of the Vedānta Sūtras and in the dramatic Tamil verses of the Tiruvāymoḻi. According to the tradition, Piḷḷāṉ's commentary is simply the written form of the dual theology taught orally by Nāthamuni, Yāmuna, and his own teacher, Rāmānuja. Can we find our own way to comprehend the unity of the two Vedas that seemed so self-evident to Piḷḷāṉ? That is our task in the next chapter.

12

Looking Behind Piḷḷāṉ's Commentary: "Swallowing" as a Metaphor in the Poem

Union and the Theme of Swallowing

In chapters 5 through 9 we discussed the themes of the Tamil poem in the light of the earliest commentary, which was greatly influenced in words and concepts by the Sanskritic tradition. In chapters 4 and 11 we discussed the mutual influences of the Tamil and Sanskritic traditions. We turn now to the Tiruvāymoḻi itself to elucidate twin themes found in it: the union between the Lord and the universe, and the union between the Lord and the āḻvār. For Nammāḻvār, and later for Rāmānuja, God's inclusive nature establishes a fundamental connection between both cosmos and God and devotee and God. Differentiation is a reality in the cosmos and separation is a reality in the devotee's experience, but neither of these realities is fundamental or final. For Nammāḻvār and Rāmānuja, the union between the Lord and the universe, and the Lord and the devotee, is both a cosmic reality and a devotional experience.

The importance of this theme of union requires an interpretation quite different from the one that Friedhelm Hardy recently proposed. Hardy claims:

> In the ideal, the I and you would meet in complete union which . . . would imply the fulfilment of the whole person. Empirically this is clearly impossible, since a contingent being cannot 'unite' with the Absolute. . . . [A]s soon as the I opens itself to the full emotional impact of these manifestations, it is thrown into a state of emotional awareness which is felt by the Major Āḻvārs to be more 'separation' than union.[1]

Hardy repeats this point several times. He claims: "Empirically no mystic has obtained physical union with Kṛṣṇa on earth, and theologically Kṛṣṇa's nature as the Absolute precludes such a union with a contingent being."[2]

We feel that Hardy does not present the whole picture. The Tiruvāymoḻi begins and ends with statements of triumphant union between the Lord and the devotee: a cosmic reality that is realized afresh by the āḻvār in a devotional experience. One can try to show this fundamental and final unity that the poet experiences in the course of the Tiruvāymoḻi by studying one dynamic metaphor in the poem. At the base of the metaphor is the myth of Viṣṇu swallowing the universe during the time of dissolution. There are references to this story in the Mahābhārata and the Matsya Purāṇa, for example, but the Tiruvāymoḻi references are unique in mythological, philosophical, and emotional appeal, and include in their development a direct analogy to the Lord's relationship to the āḻvār.

In the first five Hundreds there are many references to Viṣṇu swallowing and spewing out the worlds and a few references to Krishna swallowing butter. At the end of the Fifth Hundred comes the first claim that the Lord swallows the poet. From then on, this second kind of swallowing increases in frequency, along with the āḻvār's claim that he, too, now swallows the Lord. As sub-themes, images of taste and food are introduced; the Lord tastes as sweet as nectar and the poet requests "the nectar of the [Lord's] mouth" (a euphemism for a kiss). A study of the images of swallowing in the poem supports our interpretation that the final reality (which is, in fact, experienced by the poet on earth) is union rather than separation. In his commentary, Piḷḷāṉ does not elaborate this image of swallowing. At times he ignores it, at times translates the relevant words into Sanskrit or Tamil, and at times interprets it as Viṣṇu's protection of the universe. Piḷḷāṉ's occasional expansions come when the reference is to the Lord's swallowing the āḻvār and he certainly does not interpret swallowing in an allegorical or esoteric way. The relative lack of prominence of the image of swallowing in Piḷḷāṉ's commentary makes it easier, without interpreting the verses in the light of his commentary, to trace the various uses of this image throughout the poem. We thus gain a vantage point independent of the commentary from which to look "behind" it at Nammāḻvār's poem itself. After that we can again consider Piḷḷāṉ's most significant "translation" of the swallowing image, which in turn clarifies the metaphysical similarities and differences between Nammāḻvār and Piḷḷāṉ's teacher, Rāmānuja.

The Lord's Swallowing of the Worlds

In the first decad of the Tiruvāymoḻi, Nammāḻvār says that the Lord has graciously bestowed wisdom and love upon him; he then proceeds in the first ten verses to talk of the intimate relationship, the sense of union between the Lord and the cosmos. Many of the themes which become fundamental and characteristic of the Śrīvaiṣṇava theology as a whole in later centuries are introduced and revealed in the first ten verses. The Lord is beyond all senses and thought; he is space, sky, fire, wind, water, earth, and what is beyond them; he is the support of everything; he is diffused in everything as life is in a body; he is all men, women, all things, all time. This is the supreme one spoken of in scripture. And this is the supreme Lord who swallowed all the worlds. He is in everything, and everything is in him.

Many of these themes, so pronounced in the theology of Rāmānuja, are best suggested and expressed in the myth referred to by Nammāḻvār—initially in the context of cosmic unity in 1.1.7, 1.1.8, and 1.1.9, and subsequently several times in the poem. The reference is to the time of dissolution when all the worlds and the entire universe are swallowed by and are inside the Lord:

> Becoming all things
> spread on open space, fire,
> wind, water, and earth,
> He is diffused through them all.
> Hidden, he pervades,
> like life in a body.
> The radiant scripture [speaks]
> of the divine one who ate all this.
>
> (1.1.7)

> Beyond the range of the divine ones' intelligence,
> He, the first one of the skies and everything thereon,
> Cause of the creator, most Supreme One, ate them all!
> He indwells; as Śiva and as Brahmā,
> He burnt the triple cities, he enlightened the immortals,
> He destroys, and then creates the worlds.
>
> (1.1.8)

Nammāḻvār refers to this event that repeats itself in the cycles of cosmic eschatology in a typically simple line, hailing the Lord as "O you who swallowed the seven worlds!" or, "O you who lie on a banyan leaf with the worlds in your stomach!" The lines bring together in a distinctive form elements from the stories recounted in the Mahābhārata (The Book of the Forest, 187 passim) and the Viṣṇu Purāṇa (VI, chapters 3 and 4).[3]

There are brief but numerous references in the writings of Nammāḻvār and the other āḻvārs to this act of dissolution. The composite picture as presented by the āḻvārs includes the following themes. Nammāḻvār refers to all of them except the first, which is mentioned at some length and several times by Tirumaṅkai āḻvār:

1. There are times of dissolution (pralaya) when the entire universe is submerged in water and floods cover the worlds.[4]
2. Viṣṇu in the form of a baby swallows/eats the worlds, the skies, and everything in between (2.2.1); or the seven worlds (2.2.7); or the three worlds (2.2.8, 10.8.2).
3. Viṣṇu keeps them in his stomach (2.3.5).

4. Viṣṇu has room to spare/is not yet satisfied (10.8.2).
5. This wonder (māyā) can not be comprehended by even the celestials (2.2.7, 6.2.5).[5]
6. Viṣṇu lies on a banyan leaf (2.2.7).[6]
7. Viṣṇu later spews out the worlds (3.4.9).

Unusual combinations of all these elements are found in the writings of the āḻvārs. While the Mahābhārata and Matsya Purāṇa contain many of these elements, they are found in the context of a particular hierophany revealed to the sage Mārkaṇḍeya, who is not mentioned by the āḻvārs (except possibly in one verse of Poykai āḻvār) in the context of dissolution.[7] The āḻvārs do not include all elements in a single reference; often only one or two of the above elements may be found in any given verse. Finally, the āḻvārs frequently mention in the same verse both swallowing (*uṇṭu*) and spewing out (*umiḻntu*) the worlds; the theme of spewing out or disgorging the worlds does not appear in the Purāṇas or the Mahābhārata.

Tiruvāymoḻi 2.2 is a decad that focuses on many of the above themes; out of eleven verses at least six allude to the various elements listed above. Consider the following verses:

Becoming the first one of fixed heaven,
and everything else,
My Lord, greater than all thought,
Gobbled up the earth and skies, all at once.
  There is no support other than Kaṇṇaṉ.[8]

(2.2.1)

The great Lord,
  his strong stomach holds
  the flood of the seven worlds.
His bed is the banyan leaf,
Who can transcend his deceptive wonder,
And know his innermost [self] as he is?

(2.2.7)

The image itself is curious in that it at once combines the Lord's supremacy and accessibility. The picture of a little child playing on a banyan leaf, floating on the waters of dissolution, and holding the universe within himself, is paradoxical, to say the least. The paradox is intensified in another verse of Nammāḻvār where he juxtaposes the Lord's act of swallowing the worlds with the one (in the incarnation as Krishna) of stealing butter from the cowherd girls and swallowing it. The contrast between might and mischief, between the all-encompassing Being who contains everything as part of the cosmic process and a divine child who steals butter for his pleasure is emphasized in this whimsical verse:

> Lord of Wonder!
> Long ago, you ate the seven worlds,
> you disgorged them and by your amazing power,
> you entered them. And then,
> you took on the mean body of the lowly human.
> Even if the mud lingered in your system,
> from your swallowing of the worlds,
> was that butter an antidote
> to dissolve the earth
> that remained in your stomach,
> [or] to avoid the afflictions of being human?
>
> (1.5.8)[9]

The picture of the Lord who contains all the worlds in his belly dynamically portrays what Rāmānuja elaborated as a key doctrine, that the universe subsists in God, being contained by him and controlled through him.

The Lord's Union with the Cosmos and the Āḻvār

The Lord not only swallows and contains the worlds, but also enters into them, pervades, and fills them.

> Deftly, without letting slip
> from his net even a tiny spot,
> He swallowed the seven worlds
> and kept them inside him.
> He entered, having entered,
> He becomes a radiant flame
> of incredible knowledge,
> slashing my grief.
> He becomes nectar.
> He does not look anywhere;
> he knows naught else [but me].
> My lotus-eyed Lord!
>
> (2.6.2)

This idea is closely associated with the Lord's act of entering and filling the āḻvār's soul. The general pervasion of the Lord throughout the universe (and the name Viṣṇu itself means "all-pervader") now becomes particular; the external presence is internally, personally, and immediately experienced. In several verses, Nammāḻvār speaks of the Lord's swallowing and pervading the worlds with the immediate act of the Lord's piercing through, entering, and filling the āḻvār's mind.

Is there anything else now that I cannot do?
He who ate the seven worlds, came with esteem
and entered inside me, his servant.
And now, he cannot move away.
Destroying the troubles that grow like weeds,
for seven generations above and below me,
He prevents them from entering fiery hells.

(2.6.7)

He who entered me,
His perfect mouth—red like the lotus.
The eyes, feet, and hands
of this radiant flame, huge as a mountain,
are lotus blossoms.
All the seven worlds are inside his stomach.
And there is nothing
that has not united within him.

(2.5.3)

The supreme Viṣṇu eating the worlds in dissolution and the accessible and playful Krishna swallowing stolen butter are both superimposed on the Lord's mingling with the āḻvār.

Long ago, he ate butter,
mixing it with his hand.
[Today] without any falsehood,
In truth, he mingled with me.

Mingling with my soul,
The Lord took it as well.
[Earlier], as a dwarf,
with subdued senses,
He took the earth.

He conquered the seven beasts,
He ate the seven worlds,
He created the beautiful heaven,
He became my very thought.

(1.8.5, 6, and 7)

Nammāḻvār closely associates the ideas of the Lord's swallowing and penetrating the worlds with his coming now and uniting with the āḻvār. The ideas are frequently presented in consecutive verses, as above, or sometimes within a single verse:

> You mingled with my soul and for that great aid,
> I rendered my soul to you.
> Can I retrieve it? You are the soul of my soul,
> O Lord who devoured the seven worlds!
> Who is my soul? Who am I?
> You who gave have now claimed it again.
>
> (2.3.4)

The erotic dimension of eating the worlds is suggested in yet another way by Nammāḻvār. He mentions two myths in a single line, thus revealing a subtle connection in his mind and creating an association in the mind of the audience. He links the myth of the Lord's swallowing and disgorging the earth with the story of Viṣṇu rescuing Earth (personified as a goddess) in his incarnation as a boar, and then marrying her.

> . . . the other day,
> You created, ate, disgorged, strode over,
> retrieved, and married Earth . . .
>
> (5.10.5)

The description of the cosmic union brought about by the Lord's swallowing the earth and the rapturous union between Viṣṇu and the āḻvār are dominated by imagery of taste and food. Consider the following verses:

> Caṭakōpaṉ sings about
> the Lord who ate the worlds,
> and who is like
> honey, milk, syrup, and nectar.
>
> (8.4.11)

> My life! You who thrive in [my] flesh!
> Rejoice! The great one of the celestials,
> Madhusūda, my Lord, took you and then,
> He and I and everything else,
> mingled totally within him.
> It was like a mixture of
> honey, milk, ghee, syrup, and nectar.
>
> (2.3.1)

He made me him so completely.
He, who precedes everyone and everything,
he, the unique one, the first one
who became himself, Śiva and Brahmā,
made me sweet as honey, milk, syrup, and nectar.
He stood in my flesh, my life, my consciousness.
I reflect on him.

(8.8.4)

The analogy used to describe and celebrate this intimate union is not without precedent in Indian literature. The *Kāma Sūtra* (*The Manual of Love*), describes the closest and most intimate union as that resembling "the mixture of milk and water."[10] One may also recall that the analogy in the Chāndogya Upaniṣad which illustrates the relationship between Brahman and ātmā uses the images of taste and food: Brahman pervades the universe and is diffused in it like salt dissolved in water.[11]

A large number of the verses which describe the Lord swallowing or eating the worlds occur within the first five hundred verses of the Tiruvāymoḻi. In these verses the Tamil verbs *viḻunki* (swallow) or *uṇ* (eat) are used. Nammāḻvār uses the verb *uṇ* most of the time. If the verb *uṇ* (to eat) is preceded by the word *uyir* (life), the phrase then has connotations of military conquest, devouring a person's life, and victorious overcoming.

Nammāḻvār uses the words for "to eat" and "to eat a life" several times in the decad 5.10. Both devouring and conquering are thus suggested by the image of Viṣṇu's swallowing the worlds. Nammāḻvār refers to the Lord (as Krishna) eating butter and sucking the life out of a demon.[12] But the most important line occurs in the first verse; the Lord abides in the āḻvār's heart and when it melts, swallows it. We give a few verses from this decad where the āḻvār remembers the various instances of the Lord's swallowing and eating, and conquering in love and in war. These acts of accessibility and supremacy include his devouring the worlds, butter, and the āḻvār, as well as the demons. The verb *uṇ* also occurs in the context of the myth of Viṣṇu churning the oceans in one of his incarnations; here he is instrumental in the divine beings' eating of (uṇ) life-giving nectar (amṛta) which makes them immortal. There are several connotations for the verb *uṇ* and Nammāḻvār plays with all of them, sometimes within one set of verses:

It's incredible—you were born! You grew up!
You showed your strength at the great battle of Bhārata!
You showed your valor to the five brothers!
The wonder of all this!
You enter my soul, stand within it, melt[13] it, and *eat* it.
O radiant flame of the sky! When can I reach you?

(5.10.1)

With innocent demeanor,
you sucked and *ate the life* of the demon woman.
With the valor of your handsome feet,
you kicked and split [the demon who appeared] as a cart.
With lotus eyes filled with tears, you stood
frightened, as your mother appeared with stick in hand,
when you *ate* stolen butter.
My heart melts.

(5.10.3)

The way in which you *consume* the life of the demons!
You assumed a deceptive form, wandered abroad,
Causing confusion, creating turmoil.
The manner in which you portrayed
[the god] with a flood of water on his hair,
as one not different from you!
These acts pierce my soul,
melt and *consume* my life.

(5.10.4)

You *consumed* the food that the cowherds placed
for the king of the divine ones to eat.
You then held up the great colorful mountain
and shielded [the cowherds] from rain.
The wonder by which the other day,
you created, ate, disgorged,
and strode over Earth;
You retrieved and married her.
My heart melts like wax on fire
when I contemplate these deeds.

(5.10.5)

My mind cannot grasp
how you stood, sat, and reclined.
I stand contemplating the wonders
of your having many and no forms.
Tell me,
O radiant one who *ate the worlds!*
How am I to think of you?

(5.10.6)

The way in which you churned those waters!
As the divine ones *ate* the nectar,
the demons were destroyed.

I am *consumed* by these wondrous acts,
and my soul melts.
Tell me,
  O Lord [who recline] on the poisonous serpent bed,
  How am I to approach you?

(5.10.10)

In 5.10.1, comes the first indication of the Lord's "eating" the āḻvār and uniting with him. It is in the hundred verses immediately following that we have the largest number of songs indicating the grief of separation. After the sixth hundred, references to the Lord's eating of the worlds begin to decrease and statements indicating that the Lord swallows the āḻvār begin to increase. The sequence of these references are given in note 33. In 9.6 alone, this sentiment is repeated seven times. The connotation of victorious conquest indicated by the phrase "eating a life" (uyir uṇṭāṉ), as well as the erotic union suggested by the act of a lover "eating-swallowing" his beloved, are all brought out in this set of verses.

With gentle grace he conquers, and enters my heart;
he sweeps me away, becomes, and eats, my life.
My father, his color dark as a cloud,
Lord of the beautiful Kāṭkarai, lush with groves.
  I am ignorant of his thieving ways.

(9.6.3)

As if he were going to show his grace,
He entered into me
  And, then, all at once,
Gobbled my body and my life!
These are the thieving ways of Kaṇṇaṉ,
  His form grows so dark!
My father, Lord of the beautiful Kāṭkarai.
Fortune grows in its very groves.

(9.6.5)

I praise Kāṭkarai, I cry, O Kaṇṇā of Kāṭkarai!
I talk of my craving, I melt when I think of him.
My life was seized. He who takes me as his servant,
The wondrous one who ate my life,
  enjoyed me.

(9.6.7)

He who seized me, came the other day
and ate up my life.

Day after day, he comes,
and devours me, so fully.
Was that the day that I became his servant?
Oh what did my dear life experience!
My father, dark as a moisture-laden cloud,
dwells in beautiful Kāṭkarai.

(9.6.8)

A. K. Ramanujan pays special attention to this decad, noting that Śrīvaiṣṇava theologians frequently consider these verses to be the very life of the Tiruvāymoḻi.[14]

The Lord had swallowed and "put away the seven worlds within him; then (as if this were not enough), he ate yogurt and butter" (4.8.11). But now the āḻvār notices that the Lord's hunger is not satisfied. He devours and gobbles up the poet himself.

With all the worlds standing within him,
he, so close, stands within them.
Lord of the beautiful Kāṭkarai,
I do not comprehend the grace
by which he ate my little life.

(9.6.4)

Where do these ideas come from? Certainly Nammāḻvār is strikingly unusual in using the metaphor of swallowing and the idea of cosmic union to suggest a personal and rapturously realized relationship with the Lord; but there are incidents of "swallowing" in earlier stories where one entity consumes another. A. K. Ramanujan has noted three important mythical events: Indra's swallowing of Vṛtra in the Vedas, the swallowing of Mārkaṇḍeya by Viṣṇu and the swallowing of the demonic sage Śukra by Śiva.[15] One may add to this list the stories of Krishna swallowing butter (which has erotic connotations),[16] and the god of fire consuming the Khāṇḍava forest in the Mahābhārata. Biardeau and Hiltebeitel have shown quite convincingly that the myth in which the Khāṇḍava ("Sugar-Candy") forest is consumed by Agni has striking parallels with the myth of dissolution (pralaya); Hiltebeitel summarizes Biardeau: ". . . the story emerges in outline as a very carefully constructed allegory of the *pralaya* and *śṛṣṭi*"; the escapees from the conflagration "symbolize the ingredients indispensible, after the *pralaya*, for a new Creation."[17]

We notice three suggestions in these episodes:

1. Swallowing denotes a conquest and overcoming, a takeover of the other entity.
2. In the Mārkaṇḍeya story, there is a description of the ultimate absorption of the universe into the Lord after the cataclysmic fires and

floods suffered by the worlds. There is also the specific instance of swallowing Mārkaṇḍeya to soothe his agitation and to comfort him. The vision of Mārkaṇḍeya within the Lord is dramatic: the entire universe is contained within Viṣṇu, and Mārkaṇḍeya is self-consciously aware of his being included and contained within the Lord.
3. As Krishna, he is the thief of butter, milk, and yogurt; he is also depicted as the thief of love. As we have seen above, the erotic significance of swallowing extends to the Lord's swallowing of Nammāḻvār.

There is a fourth implication, quite different from the three just mentioned. This is seen specifically in the story of Viṣṇu keeping the worlds in his stomach. Wendy O'Flaherty suggests that the being which swallows and then emits another person is in some ways considered female.[18] For some āḻvārs there is an element of protection in the act of containing the worlds, like that of a mother protecting an unborn infant. Tirumaṅkai āḻvār's Periya Tirumoḻi makes this point:

> At the time when the monstrous floods sweep the skies, existing as a mother, he placed you (people of the world) within his stomach, and made you live. . . .
>
> (Periya Tirumoḻi 11.6.6)

The first three implications are contained within the context of the divine-human union described by Nammāḻvār. The Lord conquers and takes over Nammāḻvār (9.6); by swallowing and uniting with him he puts an end to the time of grief and separation that the poet has suffered; the union soothes and comforts the āḻvār. The Lord often does this in secret, coming like a thief (2.2.10, 9.6.6) and stealing his heart, even as he stole butter when he incarnated as Krishna.

The Poet as Swallower and Mutual Inclusiveness

The act of swallowing is not just in one direction. Very early in the Tiruvāymoḻi (1.7.3) we hear Nammāḻvār saying that he is "drinking" (parukutal) the Lord. The taste of the Lord is as sweet as nectar; and he is addressed as nectar and as ambrosia several times in the Tiruvāymoḻi. According to Śrīvaiṣṇava hagiography, it was this appellation, in fact, that first caught the attention of Nāthamuni. When he heard the decad 5.8 sung by a group of wandering minstrels, the first phrase described the Lord as "nectar that is inexhaustible" and Nāthamuni wanted to find out more about the poem and the poet who would address the Lord in such intimate terms.[19]

The romantic-erotic suggestiveness of this term is not missing in the Tamil context. The Tamil word for "nectar," "ambrosia" is *amutu* (from the Sanskrit *amṛta,* the substance that gives immortality) and the phrase "nectar of the mouth" (Tamil *vāyamutu*) is used to mean kissing in Tamil literature.[20] This is seen in the Tiruvāymoḻi itself; Nammāḻvār identifies himself with a cowherd girl who tells Krishna:

You were gone the whole day,
grazing cows, Kaṇṇā!
Your humble words burn my soul.
Evening tramples like a rogue [elephant],
and the fragrance of the jasmine buds,
unleashing my desires,[21] blows on me.
Embrace my beautiful breasts
with the fragrance of the wild jasmine
on your radiant chest.
Give me the *nectar of your mouth!*
Adorn my lowly head
with your jeweled lotus hands.

(10.3.5)

The Tamil word *amutu* also means "food" and "enjoyment" and this word is used over and over again by Nammāḻvār. In 6.10 alone (a decad extremely important in daily ritual prayers and meditations for members of the Śrīvaiṣṇava community, and the most crucial ten in which the commentators consider Nammāḻvār to formally take refuge in the Lord),[22] the word *amutu* appears three different times. This striking set of ten verses begins with the phrase "O you whose large mouth swallowed the worlds!" (6.10.1); and in verse 3, Nammāḻvār addresses the Lord as "O nectar that enters my mind, tasting so sweet!" (6.10.3). In the following verse, he tells the Lord: "unite (puṇar, literally "to copulate") with me, so I, a sinner may reach your flowerlike feet!" In the context of these ten verses, where Nammāḻvār desires both erotic union and seeks refuge with the Lord, the analogy of eating seems to be prominent; but it is the Lord who is the food and the enjoyment, the Lord who is called by Nammāḻvār "the nectar that I, who am at your feet, desire" (6.10.7) and "My nectar forever and ever" (6.10.9). Amutu is nectar, food that gives sustenance, and food which makes one immortal. It is the source of nourishment and enjoyment, as is the Lord. Nammāḻvār says: "Kaṇṇaṉ is the food that I consume, the water that I drink, the betel that I eat" (6.7.1).

One may note in this context that the connotations of amutu are closely allied to two other words. The Sanskrit word *bhoga* (Tamil *pōkam*) means "enjoyment, pleasure, sexual enjoyment, and eating."[23] The Tamil version of the word *pōkam* is used to mean eating (as in Kampa Rāmāyaṇam 1.48) as well as sexual enjoyment (Tiruvācakam 51.3). *Parimārutal* is another Tamil word that shares the meanings of sexual and eating pleasures. This word which means "to serve food" (and it is in this sense that it is used even today by the Śrīvaiṣṇava community) also means "to copulate with" or "to exchange favors" (normally interpreted to mean those of a sexual nature). The word *parimārutal* also means "to enjoy" and "to partake of food and drink."[24]

By using the metaphor of taste and food, Nammāḻvār conveys the ideas of the sustaining and life-giving qualities of the Lord along with the erotic and sensual gratification that the Divine offers.

The reference to the Lord as food or as one who is consumed in the sacrificial and sacramental context is not new in the history of religion; what is interesting here is that the concept is being used with a strikingly erotic connotation. Early in Hindu literature, the Taittirīya Upaniṣad speaks of the highest entity Brahman as food. The sacrificer hails Brahman as food, talks of himself as food and as a singer of Brahman's praise. The mystical rapture of this person is expressed in the concluding paragraphs thus:

> Oh, wonderful! Oh, wonderful! Oh, wonderful
> I am food! I am food! I am food!
> I am a food-eater! I am a food-eater! I am a food-eater!
> I am a singer of praise, I am a singer of praise, I am a singer of praise!
> . . . .
> I, who am food, eat the eater of food!
> I have overcome the whole world![25]

The comparison with Nammāḻvār is striking because he also describes himself as singing the Lord's praise (that is, the Lord sings his own praise through Nammāḻvār). He is eaten by the Lord and the Lord becomes honey, nectar, and milk for him. However, the Upaniṣadic poet has overcome the whole world, while the Tamil poet here unites with the Lord:

> Eloquent Poets! Guard your lives with care when you serve!
> The conquering thief of Tirumāliruñcōlai, master of wonder,
> came as an entrancing poet;
> He mingled within my heart, within my life,
> and stood oblivious of everything else.
> He ate my heart, he ate my life.
> He made them over to himself; he was filled.
>
> (10.7.1)

> He ate my life fully and was filled.
> He became all worlds and all life
> and he then became me;
> he praised himself through me!
> He then became, just for me,

honey, milk, syrup, nectar,
and the king of the Tirumāliruñcōlai.

(10.7.2)

The verses talk of a mutual inclusiveness: the Lord eats the entire universe which of course contains the āl̲vār, and then becomes nectar, honey, etc., for the āl̲vār to consume. In another decad, the point of mutual inclusiveness—this time, the āl̲vār claiming that he contains in his stomach the Lord who contains the seven worlds—is brought out rather sharply in the context of a union between the Lord and the āl̲vār.

I keep within my stomach,
the dark Lord who holds
  the three worlds in his stomach;
  worlds which hold in their stomach, everyone,
  and all those rulers who protect people
  [as if guarding babies within their stomachs.]
And I make the Lord stay,
  by my will.

(8.7.9)

This "mutual cannibalism," of being filled, and filling, being contained and containing, is intensified towards the end. The unions are passionate and absorbing; the analogy of eating becomes more rapid, more intense. Nammāl̲vār and the Lord both enter and fill and contain each other.

The Lord who dwelt in the City of Names
said, "I shall not move from you!"
He entered and so filled my heart!
I have caught the Lord
whose stomach was not quite filled,
even when he ate the seven clouds, the seven seas,
the seven mountains and worlds,
  and I contain him!

(10.8.2)

He of the sacred City of Names,
He, the resident Lord of the Sacred Groves
said, "I am here to stay,"
and entered my heart filling it.
I have obtained my love,
I ate the nectar, and rejoiced.

(10.8.6)

Transfixed, he stands within my eyes.
He who is
greater than comprehension,
the subtle focus of all thought,
the sweetness of the seven notes,
Lord of the sacred City of Names,
surrounded by pavilions,
studded with colorful gems,
entered my heart.

(10.8.8)

Finally, in the last decad of the Tiruvāymoḻi, the victorious and ultimate union of the Lord and Nammāḻvār is realized and described in terms of this eating and enjoying of each other.

Just whom can I turn to,
if you let me stray outside your hold?
What is mine? Who am I?
Like red-hot iron drinking water
you drank my life to exhaustion[26] and
then, became nectar, never-ending for me.

(10.10.5)

Becoming nectar that never ends for me,
My love, you dwelt in my soul, within my life,
and ate them as if you could not have your fill.
What more can you eat?
You, dark as a kāya flower,
eyes like lotus,
lips, red as fruit,
are the beloved of the lady of the flower,
So fit for you.

(10.10.6)

Not only do the āḻvār and the Lord so consume and enjoy each other; extending the metaphor further, Nammāḻvār claims that "the thousand verses" [the entire Tiruvāymoḻi] are like milk and nectar (8.6.11).[27] And again, he says:

I, the servant
of the Lord of the immortals,
have sung garlands of words
so the beloved servants of the Lord
may eat the nectar.

(9.4.9)

The Metaphor of Swallowing and the Concept of Pervasion in the Theology of Piḷḷān and Rāmānuja

What do the commentators make of all this? Certainly they do not acknowledge "eating" as a "root" metaphor in the poem. When the āḻvār talks of the Lord eating the worlds, Piḷḷāṉ translates the word "eating" into Sanskrit in his paraphrase; sometimes he ignores it and sometimes he interprets it as "protection."[28] Occasionally he draws it out as an elaborate word picture; but the interpretation is specific to one verse and refers to the particular emotional state that the āḻvār is in, rather than providing a framework for the entire poem. For example:

> O Lord! You ate all the worlds.
> In a youthful form, you lie on the banyan leaf.
> The long darkness is with you. I drown,
> not seeing your entrancing form.

> In a youthful form, he, childish, ate all the worlds. In a mighty flood, he sleeps alone on a little leaf, without a [watchful] mother like the lady Yaśodā. Because there is no companion for you in that state and because I long to see your beautiful form—a desire not fulfilled—I am submerged in an unfathomable flood of grief. Each moment, this dark night, crawls like an aeon.
>
> (8.3.4)

Piḷḷāṉ's commentary is quite striking in its comparing the loneliness of the āḻvār and the Lord on different occasions. Sometimes Piḷḷāṉ is obviously interpreting: Yaśodā is not mentioned in the poem, but the child figure swallowing mud-earth suggests to the commentator the myth of little Krishna swallowing mud and Yaśodā's vision of the entire universe within the child's mouth.[29] The floods of dissolution become the flood of grief; the āḻvār is submerged in the latter as the worlds in the former. The time of dissolution lasts several aeons; here the loneliness makes each moment crawl like one. The comparison is striking in the commentary; the emotional state of the āḻvār is interpreted by the commentator in a creative way, but it is limited to the verse at hand.

Piḷḷāṉ, however, is not unaware of the erotic implications of the Lord's eating the āḻvār. Usually, Piḷḷāṉ simply replaces the Tamil word *uṇṭu* "eat" with the Sanskrit *bhuj* "eat, enjoy a meal" when he talks of the Lord eating the āḻvār or vice versa. However, in 5.10.1, the very first verse where the Lord eats the āḻvār, Piḷḷāṉ is explicit:

> The wonder of all this!
> You enter inside my soul (*āvi*), melt it and eat it!
> O radiant flame of the sky! . . .

> I stood in the agony of separation and you entered the secret part of my soul and did not leave it. You held it in close embrace, which never seemed to end. . . .
>
> (5.10.1)

Having made his point the very first time that the Lord eats the āḻvār, Piḷḷāṉ then simply ignores or paraphrases "eating" in Sanskrit in subsequent occurrences of the theme. Thus in the entire decad 9.6, the ten major verses of mutual cannibalism, the Tamil words *uṇṭu* "eat" and *parukutal* "drink," and *viḻuṅkutal* "swallow" are paraphrased by the word *bhuj,* the Sanskrit word for "eating" and "enjoyment." This is seen in the *Six Thousand* commentary for 9.6.3, 5, 6, 7, and 8.

Piḷḷāṉ is extremely concerned, however, about the metaphysical and philosophical implications of the Lord's eating the universe and pervading it as "life through a body" (1.1.7). Piḷḷāṉ and Rāmānuja share the concern about the relationship between the Lord and the cosmos; like 1.1.7, this is compared to the relationship between the soul/life and the body. Rāmānuja considers this relationship to be extremely important: the relationship that obtains between the Lord and the soul is like that which obtains between the soul and the body:

> The finite self (jīvātmā) has Brahman as its Self, for it is His mode (prakāra) since it is the body (śarīra) of Brahman. . . . All things having some particular structure, such as the divine form or the human form, are the modes of finite individual selves, since they are their respective bodies. This means that these physical objects, too, are ensouled by Brahman. Therefore all words naming these objects . . . first signify the objects they name in ordinary parlance, then, through these objects, the finite selves dwelling in them, and finally these words extend in their significance to denote the Supreme Self (Paramātmā) who is their Inner Controller (antaryāmī). Thus all terms do indeed denote this entire composite Being (saṁghāta). Thus [this section of Scripture] explains in detail that this entire created universe (prapañca) of intelligent and material entities has Being (sat) as its material cause, its instrumental cause, and its support (ādhāra); it is controlled (niyāmya) by Being and is the śeṣa of Being.[30]

This concept is seen earlier in the Upaniṣads; the Antaryāmi Brāhmaṇa in the Bṛhadāraṇyaka and Śvetāsvatāra Upaniṣads as well as the Taittirīya discuss this idea. In the *Gitābhāṣya,* Rāmānuja paraphrases the Lord as saying: "I pervade the universe as its Inner Controller (antaryāmī) in order to support it, and by virtue of being its Owner (*Śeṣī*). . . . I am the supporter of finite beings. . . ."[31] In the *Vedārtha Saṁgraha,* Rāmānuja explains the relationship more fully.

One of the connotations of this relationship is the closeness and inseparability of God and the universe. This relationship is mentioned by Nammāḻvār in 1.1.7:

Becoming all things
spread on open space, fire,
wind, water, and earth,
he is diffused through them all.
Hidden, he pervades,
like life (uyir) in a body.
The radiant scripture [speaks]
of the divine one who ate all this.

(1.1.7)

Piḷḷāṉ gives one of his longest comments on this verse, highlighting the nature of the body-soul relationship and giving seventy-three quotations from Sanskrit scripture to prove that this concept in the Tamil Veda is also treated in an elaborate manner in Sanskrit. We would like to suggest here that this relationship spoken of by Nammāḻvār as "diffused everywhere like life (uyir) in a body" has antecedents in classical literature, and in its flavor and use of particular words is distinctively Tamil. While we agree that the philosophical locus of Rāmānuja's account of the body-soul relationship is in Sanskrit literature, we would like to add that the Tamil simile provides a clue and an extra dimension to the understanding of a relationship that Rāmānuja perceives as both a metaphysical reality and as one filled with mutual passion.

The image is used in an akam context in earlier Tamil works and with the implication of a close, almost inseparable relationship. In the *Akaṉāṉūṟu*, a bridegroom describes his wedding and his bride:

That night she, . . .
as close to me as my body to my life (uyir)
covered herself. . . .[32]

The analogy is also used in a romantic (akam) context in the *Tirukkuraḷ* (fourth to fifth century C.E.), one of the "Eighteen Short Classics" of the classical Tamil Anthology:

The relationship (natpu) between my beloved and me is like that between body and life (uyir).

(*Tirukkuraḷ* 1122)

It should be noted that the Tamil word used for "life" is *uyir*. It is this word that is found in the akam poem, in the *Tirukkuraḷ*, and in the Tiruvāymoḻi. The Sanskrit word that would have the connotations of *uyir* is *prāṇa*. Like *prāṇa,* it is a "vital air, breath, pneuma." While in colloquial Tamil, *uyir* is used to denote "life," in the *Tirukkuraḷ* itself, the word *uyir* is used in another way, to mean "soul" (ānmā from ātmā):

> All lives (uyir) on this earth will venerate the man who has gained (or, can control) his soul (uyir).
>
> (*Tirukkuraḷ* 268)

In this context, almost all interpretations take the second occurrence of uyir to mean "soul." The same *Tirukkuraḷ* also goes on to describe the relationship between two lovers as that between body and life (uyir); the usage of the word *uyir* here being the conventional one, as found in the akam literature.

In Nammāḻvār's verse 1.1.7 then, the word *uyir* could have a double meaning: life or soul. The third line in the verse points out that this concept is found in curuti (from śruti)—a direct reference to the Sanskrit revealed literature. There is no ambiguity in the meaning and Nammāḻvār is quite clear that he is describing a relationship that was spoken of in Sanskrit literature. The commentators on this verse, in conformity with this line, interpret the word *uyir* as "soul," taking the second meaning of the word as found in the *Tirukkuraḷ*. The centrality of the theme is so pronounced in the Sanskrit Brahma (Vedānta) Sūtras that this book is referred to as Śārīrika Mīmāṁsa or "The Inquiry into the Embodied Spirit" which, in Rāmānuja's philosophy, means the Supreme soul embodied in the cosmos.

Thus both Sanskrit and Tamil representations of the body-soul relationship convey the idea of inseparability: metaphysical union between Divine and human and inseparability between two lovers. Both themes are vividly seen in the Tiruvāymoḻi. Rāmānuja and the commentators on the Tiruvāymoḻi interpret the Divine-human union as metaphysical reality; we suggest that by looking at this union from the perspective of Tamil poetry, we also apprehend the intimacy that is felt between two lovers.

The first ten verses of the Tiruvāymoḻi contain two distinct references to the Lord eating the worlds and other references to his pervading them (1.1.7 and 1.1.8). In the first hundred we hear Nammāḻvār saying that he "drinks" the Lord; later we hear him talk of the Lord "filling" him. From 5.10.1 we have references to the Lord "eating" the āḻvār—a claim made by no other āḻvār.[33] In the last ten verses of the poem we return, almost as if the poem was written thematically in the antāti style, to the idea of eating and union. The experience of union that Nammāḻvār talks about in the first ten verses of the poem is now recalled after the long travels and travails of the poet. But here, the union spoken of is not so much that between the Lord and the universe (the major theme of 1.1, expressed through the analogy of the Lord eating the worlds and pervading them), as that between the āḻvār and the Lord, who passionately "devour" each other in their all-consuming love. The triumphant union with the poet and the cosmos in the first ten verses is realized again in the last ten verses when the Lord and the āḻvār paradoxically contain and fill each other. When we look for parallels with Rāmānuja's thought it is not hard to see "swallowing" as a dynamic equivalent in the Tamil idiom of "becoming" for Rāmānuja's more static Sanskrit notions of God including the world, pervading the world, and indwelling in the world. For Nammāḻvār, the cosmic situation calls for replication in the experience of the devotee. For Rāmānuja, the devotee wants personally to feel all three dimensions of being God's body: supported, controlled, and owned by God. In the act of Nammāḻvār's being swallowed, we find an experience of this kind. God's inclusion and pervasion of the universe and the poet is then the fundamental and final reality; and this union is experienced by Nammāḻvār in the flesh, with full-blooded passion.[34]

13

Ubhaya Vedānta: Two Traditions or One?

Recapitulation: Continuity and Change in the Dual Tradition

The focus of this study has been on the first written commentary on Nammāḻvār's long poem, the Tiruvāymoḻi, composed by Tirukkurukai Pirāṉ Piḷḷāṉ, a cousin and immediate disciple of Rāmānuja. We have been concerned with the literary form and theological content of this commentary. In both form and content there is an evident effort to merge the Tamil poetic tradition of the āḻvārs with the Vaiṣṇava commentarial tradition, in Sanskrit, on the Vedānta.

The broader parameters of this study thus include the diverse traditions brought together in Piḷḷāṉ's commentary. Nammāḻvār is one of the later Vaiṣṇava Tamil poets who lived between the sixth and ninth centuries C.E. whose work has been collected and given scriptural status in the Śrīvaiṣṇava community. These poets, coming from both high and low castes, were contemporaries of a considerably larger number of Tamil poets singing in praise of Lord Śiva, and both groups of poets were heirs to an earlier tradition of Tamil poetry ascribed to a circle of court poets in Madurai known as the Tamil Caṅkam. The fragments of this "Caṅkam poetry" go back at least to the first and second century B.C.E. and thus may be the oldest extant Indian literature outside of the Sanskrit tradition. Tamil was used as a literary medium by Buddhists and Jains in the early centuries C.E., but among Hindus Tamil lacked the prestige of Sanskrit, the sacred language passed down from generation to generation by Brahmin priests and scholars.

A second literary tradition preceding and paralleling Piḷḷāṉ's commentary was the small collection of Sanskrit hymns of praise to Lord Viṣṇu and his Consorts produced in the previous two or three generations within the Śrīvaiṣṇava community. Their connection with Nammāḻvār's Tamil poem was discussed in chapter 4 above. Behind these stotras, in addition to the Tamil tradition, are the traditions of devotional and court poetry in Sanskrit.

The third important tradition behind Piḷḷāṉ is obviously the interpretation of the Vedānta articulated concisely by Yāmuna and worked out in much greater detail by Rāmānuja. The tradition of commenting on the Upaniṣads and Bhagavadgītā may have started a thousand years before Piḷḷāṉ. In any case it was crystallized before 500 C.E. in the brief and somewhat enigmatic Brahma Sūtras (Vedānta Sūtras). This in turn became the object of commentaries by each distinct school of Vedānta. Piḷḷāṉ's commentary is remarkable because it is written on a Tamil work; it consists of a paraphrase of Nammāḻvār's verses in a language that is ostensibly not a translation, since it is grammatically Tamil, but more than half the words are Sanskrit phrases, similar or identical to those used by Rāmānuja.

There is a fourth type of literary tradition that may have had some effect on Piḷḷāṉ's commentary, that of the sectarian Vaiṣṇava ritual texts known as the Āgamas, especially those of the Pāñcarātra. By a few generations after Piḷḷāṉ the influence of the Pāñcarātra Āgamas on all aspects of the Śrīvaiṣṇava tradition was marked. Yāmuna and Rāmānuja defended the orthodoxy of the Pāñcarātra texts, but it is not clear whether Rāmānuja adopts any characteristic Pāñcarātra terms. In this respect as in most others Piḷḷāṉ follows Rāmānuja's lead. It is hence all the more striking that his commentary itself is an exercise that might seem to fall outside the Brahmanical orthodoxy of Rāmānuja's Sanskrit writings. Unlike the later Śrīvaiṣṇava writers and Vaiṣṇavas of other schools, Rāmānuja restricts himself to a relatively small number of scriptural authorities, in general those that would be accepted as scriptural by conservative Brahmins in the Vedāntic tradition. As we have noted above, Piḷḷāṉ restricts himself to the texts on Rāmānuja's list in his remarkable string of seventy-three citations following his comment on 1.1.7. Yet the commentary itself is a recognition of a non-Sanskrit work composed by a non-Brahmin poet, recognition of the poem not simply as one authority among many, but as a different kind of scripture equal in status to the Sanskrit Vedas (including the Upaniṣads) themselves.

The audacity of this claim of dual scriptures is felt within the Śrīvaiṣṇava community; it is still more shockingly evident to those of rival sects and schools. It is all the more remarkable that the claim is made by the Brahmin leaders of the community. This claim, in effect, is that alongside the Sanskrit Vedas, which may not even be heard by those who are not high caste ("twice born") Hindus, there exists a Divinely inspired poem that may be heard and recited by all, a poem that is not in Sanskrit but in the mother tongue, in "sweet Tamil."

Modern scholars who do not automatically accept the traditional explanation are left with a puzzle. Nathāmuni is supposed to have instituted this dual tradition, but only a few brief quotations from his teachings have survived in later works. The only writings of his grandson Yāmuna we have are in Sanskrit, writings that include complex philosophical argumentation, hymns of praise, and a verse summary of the Gītā. While we may speculate on various influences from the Tamil tradition, there seems to be only one reference to Nammāḻvār, and that somewhat veiled, in his *Jewel of Hymns* (*Stotra Ratna*). The same absence of reference to the āḻvārs characterizes Rāmānuja's more voluminous Sanskrit works, even the more devotional pieces. How are we to understand this silence in the light of the many links made by Rāmānuja's disciples between the two Vedāntas, including the universal affirmation that Yāmuna and Rāmānuja themselves commented orally on the Tiruvāymoḻi? Can we believe that Piḷḷāṉ was commissioned by Rāmānuja to make the link between the two Vedāntas explicit, to put it down in writing?

Both the Teṅkalai and Vaṭakalai branches of the Śrīvaiṣṇava community have had no difficulty in affirming the Ubhaya Vedānta as the continuous teaching of the poet-saints and authoritative teachers (āḻvārs and ācāryas), and certainly as the teaching of Rāmānuja. In recent years, however, there have been various scholars, most of them outside the Śrīvaiṣṇava community, who have raised questions of different kinds about the reality of Ubhaya Vedānta, or, more specifically, whether Nammāḻvār, Rāmānuja, and the later commentators really taught the same doctrine or derived it from the same sources. To these questions we now turn.

Modern Scholarly Challenges to the Reality of Ubhaya Vedānta

The sharp and acrimonious debate between Indian philosophical schools in the centuries between Śaṅkara and Rāmānuja continued in commentaries and sub-commentaries for many centuries. There was an increasing tendency to rank opposing positions according to their closeness to the full truth represented by the school's own position. With the revival of Hindu learning in the nineteenth century the old scholastic debates continued, but there were in addition new Hindu movements that approached the old controversies in a new way, often with a concern for a pan-Hindu position that needed to be defended against Islam, Christianity, and Western secularism. One of the most influential spokesmen for this neo-Hindu sensibility was Swami Vivekananda, the leading disciple of Ramakrishna Paramahaṁsa. Vivekananda followed Ramakrishna's innovation of including Christian and Islamic paths among those of which something good could be said, but he also followed the earlier Advaita Vedānta in placing Advaita at the pinnacle of his pyramid. The devotional path was seen as a lower path that finally had to be superseded by those seeking the highest truth. The interpreters of the Vedānta from the standpoint of bhakti, including Rāmānuja, were praised by Vivekananda for their ardent devotion and their large-hearted intentions in trying to share the Vedānta with the masses, but Vivekananda considered the bhakti theologians to have failed to recognize the higher truth of the Upaniṣads: the Reality beyond all name and form, the Brahman who is not different from our true Self.

In the generations since Vivekananda there have been many South Indian Advaitins who have followed his approach to the teaching of Rāmānuja and his followers, notably S. Radhakrishnan and T. M. P. Mahadevan. The entire Śrīvaiṣṇava tradition is considered to affirm the path of devotion sung by the poet-saints in all parts of India and amply represented in the Sanskrit scriptures themselves, but this devotional path is not believed to contain the final truth of Vedānta expressed in the "great sayings" of the Upaniṣads and the Gītā systematized in the Vedānta Sūtras. There is only a single, not a double, Vedānta, in this view, and this Vedānta is precisely what the bhakti theologians did not grasp; they mistakenly thought the Upaniṣads were teaching the path of devotion.

This view of Vedānta and of its relation to bhakti is not so much argued as taken for granted by many modern Hindu intellectuals, including both more traditional Advaitin followers of Śaṅkara and those who have been influenced by many of the modern spokesmen for a renascent Vedānta. Certainly this modern Advaitin position is the most common understanding of Indian wisdom outside of India. Until two or three generations ago there were no Western scholars who found any reason to challenge it. Rudolf Otto records his own discovery from a Vaiṣṇava scholar in Banaras that Śaṅkara's Advaita philosophy is not "all of Hinduism."[1]

When Western scholars did begin to study Rāmānuja and other theistic interpreters of the Vedānta, it was quite natural that they should concentrate on the Sanskrit side of the Śrīvaiṣṇava tradition, and specifically on Rāmānuja's commentary on the Vedānta Sūtras. George Thibaut, who translated both Śaṅkara's and Rāmānuja's commentaries on the Vedānta Sūtras, asserts in his long introduction that Rāmānuja's interpretation is not his own innovation "but had authoritative representation already at a period anterior to Śaṅkara."[2] Thibaut concludes that in important respects the Sūtras themselves do not agree with Śaṅkara's commentary on them:

> Upon Rāmānuja's mode of interpretation—although I accept it without reserve in some important details—I look on the whole as more useful in providing us with a powerful means of criticizing Śaṅkara's explanations than in guiding us throughout to the right understanding of the text. The author of the Sūtras may have held views about the nature of Brahman, the world and the soul differing from those of Śaṅkara, and yet not agreeing in all points with those of Rāmānuja. If, however, the negative conclusions stated above should be well founded, it would follow even from them that the system of Bādārayaṇa had greater affinities with that of the Bhāgavatas and Rāmānuja than with the one of which Śankarabhāshya is the classical exponent.[3]

On the other hand, Thibaut maintains that if one is to make a philosophical system out of the unsystematic reflections of the Upaniṣads, then Śaṅkara's system is to be preferred.[4]

> While unable to allow that the Upaniṣads recognize a lower and higher knowledge of Brahman, in fact the distinction of a lower and higher Brahman, we yet acknowledge that the adoption of that distinction fur-

> nishes the interpreter with an instrument of extraordinary power for reducing to an orderly whole the heterogeneous material presented by the old theological treatises.[5]

Thibaut thus considers Śaṅkara's interpretation closer to the older Upaniṣads than that of Rāmānuja, but he sees Rāmānuja as following the theistic interpretation of the Vedānta found in both the Bhagavadgītā and the Vedānta Sūtras, which is a minority position among "Brahmanic students of philosophy" but one more genial to "the wants of the human heart, which, after all, are not so very different in India from what they are elsewhere":

> The only forms of Vedāntic philosophy which are—and can at any time have been—really popular, are those in which the Brahman of the Upaniṣads has somehow transformed itself into a being, between which and the devotee there can exist a personal relation, love and faith on the part of man, justice tempered by mercy on the part of the divinity.[6]

Thibaut's position became well known to Hindu scholars. It is not surprising that it pleased neither the followers of Śaṅkara nor those of Rāmānuja, for it denied the principle of interpretation on which all Vedāntins agree: that all three foundations (prasthānatraya) of the Vedānta teach one consistent doctrine. Advaitins are certainly not willing to concede that two of the three foundations of Vedāntic philosophy reflect devotional theism, but Thibaut's judgment about all the theistic interpretations of the Upaniṣads can be understood as making the same point as some of the newer versions of Advaita: the theistic versions of the Vedānta provide a religious path that has a much broader appeal than the lonely wisdom of Śaṅkara, but such theistic Vedānta fails to grasp the higher wisdom of the early Upaniṣads. To this view Rāmānuja and all other Vaiṣṇava interpreters of the Upaniṣads vigorously object, insisting that they are conveying the true meaning of the Upaniṣads, reformulated in the Bhagavadgītā and systematically presented in the Vedānta Sūtras.

Twenty years after Thibaut's translation the Hindu scholar V. S. Ghate, himself philosophically an Advaitin, wrote a doctoral thesis for the University of Paris in which he studied the five principal commentaries on the Vedānta Sūtras and concluded that Rāmānuja's interpretations were generally closer to the Sūtras than those of Śaṅkara though not, in Ghate's opinion, so close as the Dvaitādvaita philosophy of Nimbarka.[7] Ghate's critical conclusion is decidedly unsatisfactory for any of the traditional schools. The more systematic the interpretation, Ghate claims, the further away it is likely to be from the meaning of the Vedānta Sūtras themselves. The historian's skepticism about the supposed continuities of a religious tradition is here brilliantly expressed by a modern Indian historian. The attitude is at least equally evident in the approaches of later Western historians.

Until quite recently no Western historians of religion, nor indeed any scholars outside the community, gave any consideration to the Tamil component in Rāmānuja's philosophy. This is true even of Rudolf Otto, who was personally acquainted with A. Govindacharya, the Śrīvaiṣṇava scholar who first provided English translations over the whole range of the tradition.[8] Most European Indologists were trained in Sanskrit and not in Tamil, but their lack of scholarly interest is certainly also due to Rāmānuja's silence about the Tamil tradition. It may well be that this silence was to forestall more ancient versions of the position taken by modern Advaītins and partially concurred in by Thibaut. There is no doubt that Rāmānuja believed that his interpretation was amply supported by Vedic texts that always refer to the Supreme Brahman whose personal name is Viṣṇu-Nārāyaṇa. It was certainly difficult enough for Rāmānuja to convince Brahmin students of the Vedas of his interpretation without suggesting that the same truth was independently shown in the inspired verses of a Tamil poet!

A radical solution to the problem of Rāmānuja's silence has been proposed by the contemporary Śrīvaiṣṇava scholar Agnihothram Rāmānuja Thatachariar and has been further developed by Dr. Robert Lester.[9] This view affirms emphatically the Sanskrit side of the Ubhaya Vedānta: Rāmānuja has correctly set forth the truth of the Vedānta in the major works attributed to him, but he was a pure Vedic Brahman who would not have considered any Tamil work as scripture and in fact did not even follow the sectarian doctrine of the Pāñcarātra Āgamas. The small devotional works suggesting a closer link with temple ritual and with the later ritual of surrender are not genuine, and the entire oral tradition of Rāmānuja's learning and teaching the Tiruvāymoḻi is an invention of later Śrīvaiṣṇavas in order to claim Rāmānuja's authority for their deviations from the Vedic path.

This position rightly recognizes a difference between Rāmānuja's view of the path to salvation and those of the Teṅkalai and Vaṭakalai theologians two hundred years later. It has the advantage of explaining a number of puzzling facts, but the price is the necessity of maintaining an extensive inventiveness on the part of the subsequent tradition. The stotras attributed to Yāmuna and both poetic and prose works of Rāmānuja's disciples would also have to have been composed by later generations. That certainly is not impossible, but in view of the relative obscurity of some of these disciples, it seems improbable that the innovators of the following centuries were systematic and ingenious enough to write pseudonymous works and attribute them to Rāmānuja's disciples. Why not attribute all these later works to Yāmuna or Rāmānuja, if the aim was to lend them greater authority? One of these disciples is Piḷḷāṉ, whose writing sounds so much the way we might have expected Rāmānuja to talk in Tamil that it is remarkable that the tradition does not at least claim that the commentary on the Tiruvāymoḻi was dictated verbatim to Piḷḷāṉ, just as the *Śrībhāṣya* was dictated to Kūrattāḻvāṉ.

Agnihothram and Lester's revision of Śrīvaiṣṇava history also would require us to imagine that Yāmuna and Rāmānuja were staunch Vaiṣṇavas in the midst of a Brahmin community heavily influenced by the teaching of Śaṅkara and others, yet were not affected by the whole movement of popular Tamil Vaiṣṇavism of which the Tiruvāymoḻi is the climax. Again, this is not impossible, but it seems improbable. This radical solution of some historical puzzles seems to create even greater perplexities.

Agnihothram and Lester's arguments do force us to recognize that the modern historian cannot accept the uncritical believer's view of a completely unchanging tradition, but their approach suffers from the frequent difficulty the modern historian has in recognizing genuine continuities within a religious tradition. The more we study the positions taken in the many extant writings of Rāmānuja's immediate disciples and those of the following generations, the clearer it becomes that there was a gradual process of change, at least in emphasis, but one that differed somewhat from one author to another and from one type of work to another. Eventually the differences crystallized into two conflicting sub-schools. What all these Śrīvaiṣṇava authors seem to have in common is the intention of holding fast to both the Sanskrit and Tamil scriptures and to the traditions of commentary attached to both.

The most recent scholarly challenge to the Ubhaya Vedānta goes in a different direction and deals for the first time, among scholars outside the community, primarily with the Tamil side of the synthesis, with the poetry of the āḻvārs. This is the substantial work to which we have repeatedly referred, Friedhelm Hardy's *Viraha Bhakti*. Whereas Agnihothram and Lester see later Śrīvaiṣṇavism as overinfluenced by the Tamil tradition and abandoning the strict Vedic or Vedāntic position of Rāmānuja, Hardy sees all Śrīvaiṣṇavism, beginning with Yāmuna and Rāmānuja, as abandoning the distinctive emotional bhakti of the āḻvārs (which he holds to have been preserved in the Bhāgavata Purana and later Krishna-bhakti) and returning to the normative position of almost all Indian philosophies, in which the soul is radically distinguished from a devalued material body.[10]

In addition to an impressive marshalling of data on the history of Krishna-bhakti and a large number of insightful comments on specific works of individual āḻvārs, Hardy's interpretation has the value of reminding the modern historian of Hindu religion that there are significant changes in the Śrīvaiṣṇava tradition between the Tamil poet-saints and the organization, several centuries later, of a Brahmin-dominated community invoking their authority. The historian must recognize important differences between Nammāḻvār and Rāmānuja, and therefore also between Nammāḻvār's poem and its first written commentary by Piḷḷāṉ. This does not mean, however, that the entire commentarial tradition has to be seen as a systematic misinterpretation of the āḻvār's bhakti. Hardy follows the same style of thinking as the traditionalist if he poses an "either/or." Piḷḷāṉ's comments can be both like and unlike the text on which he is commenting. One who accepts the commentary as well as the sacred poem believes that the continuities are more important than the changes and that there is therefore an authentic tradition.

Such an affirmation of the tradition, even a critical reaffirmation of the tradition after modern historial study, is done within the community of faith and is an act of faith. What we have tried to do in this study, particularly in the previous chapter, is to show that modern literary analysis provides us with a basis for confirming the tradition's confidence in its continuity and for rejecting Hardy's characterizations of both the āḻvārs and later Śrīvaiṣṇavas, not as totally wrong, but as one-sided and therefore misleading and inadequate. The painful sense of separation from God is certainly a deeply felt experience for Nammāḻvār, but we surely misunderstand the poet if we isolate the viraha from the joy of union with God or deny the genuineness of the latter experience for the āḻvārs.

Later Śrīvaiṣṇavas certainly distinguish between their own experience and that of the āḻvārs by recognizing the special, even semi-divine, stature of their saintly predecessors. They feel themselves, however, in a continuous tradition with that experience. The path of abject surrender to the unmerited mercy of God was, after all, developed by the same commentators who loved to savor at second hand the āḻvārs' experience of God and gratefully to remember what each of their saintly predecessors had remarked about each verse. Their variety of interpretation was seen, not as undermining the reality of the devotional experience, but as testifying to its richness and its power.

Hardy does not deny Rāmānuja's connection with the Tamil tradition. Rather he suggests that Rāmānuja has reinterpreted and misinterpreted the meaning of Krishnabhakti because of his basic commitment to the ascetic worldview of the Vedānta.[11] We agree that there is a reinterpretation, indeed a profound cultural as well as linguistic translation from the earlier Tamil to a new amalgam of Sanskrit and Tamil, of Brahmin and Dravidian cultures. The translation is incomplete and the cultural streams coexist, like the celebrated distinction in color between the Blue Nile and the White Nile for many miles after they have joined. Indeed, the philosophy of the community suggests that the distinctions between streams of revelation somehow mirror the nature of reality: distinction in unity and unity in distinction. The twofold Vedānta is the doctrine of the unity of that divine reality that is internally distinguished: *viśiṣṭādvaita*.

The Widening Divide between the Teṅkalai and Vaṭakalai Traditions

Perhaps the most obvious objection to the continuing reality of Ubhaya Vedānta in the Śrīvaiṣṇava community is the division of the community into two subcommunities, the names of which suggest the two sides of Ubhaya Vedānta. *Teṅ-kalai,* meaning "southern culture," seems to refer to the Tamil tradition just as *Vaṭa-kalai,* meaning "northern culture," refers to the Sanskrit tradition. Is it then the case that the Dual Vedānta only survived a few generations and finally broke into its original component parts?

Our final answer to this question will be "No," but it has to be admitted that there are some distinctions between Vaṭakalai and Teṅkalai Śrīvaiṣṇavas that do suggest emphases on one side or the other of the attempted synthesis. The tradition of Sanskrit learning has by and large flourished more vigorously in the Vaṭakalai community. There is also a celebrated remark attributed to the Teṅkalai theologian Piḷḷai Lōkacārya that he would only teach in Tamil. Moreover, the Vaṭakalai community seems to have some closer ritual links with other Brahmins (specifically the Smārta Brahmins) than does the Teṅkalai community. One might even see in the Teṅkalai emphasis on Divine grace a reflection of the āḻvār's sentiments; conversely, in the Vaṭakalai doctrine of the divine pretext (vyāja), a hint might be seen of the Vedic emphasis on just reward according to the law of karma.

On closer scrutiny, however, these points prove to be only minor differences in emphasis. What we see in both communities is a continuing effort to affirm and to reconcile the Sanskrit and Tamil Vedas. The development for the first hundred years after Rāmānuja and Piḷḷāṉ seems to have been a common one, and the delineation of clearly distinctive and opposing positions by Piḷḷai Lokācārya (Teṅkalai) and his younger contemporary Vedānta Deśika (Vaṭakalai) was an additional hundred years later. Even then, the differences were initially between divergent scholarly positions each of which was increasingly elaborated by a group of disciples. The different initiation rituals and the social gulf between the two communities developed still more slowly, and the protracted and acrimonious litigation over the control of temples was a feature of the British colonial period, in which well-educated and socially prominent Vaṭakalai families challenged the control of most Śrīvaiṣṇava temples by Teṅkalai families. A brief survey of some of the more celebrated court reports suggests little that is characteristically "Dravidian" or "Sanskritic," let alone anything reflecting the distinctive emphases of either the Sanskrit or the Tamil Vedas. Even the scholastic formulations of opposing doctrines seem irrelevant in these disputes, which instead revolve around the issue of inherited privilege versus "fair" distribution of financial benefits and cultic honors between the two parties.[12]

There are, it seems to us, certain important differences in emphasis between the two schools that can best be understood as distinct developments of the same Ubhaya Vedānta. A modern history of later Śrīvaiṣṇavism or even of the decisive period of theological controversy has yet to be written, though more and more contributions to this historical effort are now being made. Certainly there are abundant literary materials for such a history, many of which still figure in one or other line of scholarly interpretation or cultic transmission.

The more modern the historian, the more likely it is that he or she will be struck by the changes from one generation to another, developments that were often affected by political or economic circumstances, gradual changes in the structure of society, and new cultural and religious currents. We are not denying the importance of such changes, but we want to call attention here to the Śrīvaiṣṇava community's sense of continuity with its own ancient past. To a considerable extent this was maintained through the guruparamparā, the "succession of gurus" linking the community in general and all initiated Śrīvaiṣṇavas individually (women as well as men) through their immediate ācāryas back generation by generation through Rāmānuja, Yāmuna, and Nāthamuni to Nammāḻvār, the Great Goddess Śrī and Lord Viṣṇu-Nārāyaṇa himself. This recognition of succession is both doctrine and ritual practice, and the doctrine is one expression of the affirmation of the dual tradition. The Brahmin leadership of the community notwithstanding, it is the Śūdra saint Nammāḻvār who stands in the succession between God and Goddess, on the one hand, and the founding Brahmin teachers on the other. In other respects as well the positions taken on doctrinal, ritual, and social questions in each generation are perceived within the community as affirmations of the Ubhaya Vedānta.

To a considerable extent the commentarial traditions on the Sanskrit Veda and the Tamil Veda are kept separate; hence the puzzling silence in Yāmuna's and Rāmānuja's Sanskrit writings about the āḻvārs. That separation is less pronounced in the case of Tamil commentaries, and the mixture of Sanskrit and Tamil words in a tradition in which words denote and even produce reality is a clear indication of the commentators' vivid sense of a dual perception of reality, indeed of a dual reception of revealed truth. The ritual institution of the initiation ceremony, the solemn act of surrender (called "humble approach," prapatti and "going for refuge," śaraṇāgati) is understood as an expression of the fundamental life stance required by the dual Vedānta. The twin themes of later Śrīvaiṣṇava devotion are readiness to serve the Lord and the Lord's servants, and enjoyment of the beauty of the Lord and his consorts. Both the ethics of voluntary service and the new theological aesthetics were first of all developed in the meditation on particular verses or sets of verses in the Tiruvāymoḻi.

Much of this development in the two centuries after Rāmānuja is common to the entire Śrīvaiṣṇava community; even the differing emphases were made in a conversation with all other Śrīvaiṣṇava scholars. Piḷḷai Lokācārya and Vedānta Deśika both assumed one community to whom and for whom they were teaching. What then was the distinctive difference in interpreting the Ubhaya Vedānta? It appears to us that the Teṅkalai theologians were more inclined to make a rational system out of the commentarial tradition on the āḻvārs' hymns and to insist that the more extreme metaphors be accepted as systematic doctrine. The Vaṭakalai theologians, especially Vedānta Deśika, who himself wrote a large number of works in both languages, objected to the "exaggeration in Piḷḷai Lokācārya's position," sought a balance between the Sanskrit and Tamil traditions and maintained that all the doctrines fitted together in a harmonious whole. Both positions affirmed the Ubhaya Vedānta and preserved it through scholarly traditions that continue to the present day.[13] The particular synthesis of each side was challenged by the other side, at first within a single community and later between two sub-communities that became in some parts of South India more and more separate. Outside of both sub-communities were the large community of Smārta Brahmins, officially Advaitins, and the vast majority of non-Brahmin Hindus in South India. None of them took the unique claim of Śrīvaiṣṇavas seriously, and elsewhere in India Śrīvaiṣṇavas were known as followers of Rāmānuja's interpretation of the Vedānta, the Viśiṣṭādvaita. Neither Nammāḻvār's "sweet Tamil" songs nor the claim for a Tamil Veda were widely known.

Modern Challenges to the Dual Tradition

There are at least three different challenges at present to the continuing affirmation of Ubhaya Vedānta by Śrīvaiṣṇavas. The first is the change in the social situation. The movement for Tamil cultural revival has in its most extreme form told Brahmins to "go home" to North India![14] Even outside the Tamil area where there is very little Dravidian consciousness, the change to universal suffrage and the great increase in educational opportunities for people from all castes and religious communities have ended the Brahmins' near monopoly on types of work that require some formal education. It might seem that the Śrīvaiṣṇava affirmation of a Tamil Veda would be a great advantage under these circumstances, but from the outside Śrīvaiṣṇavas are known as a Brahmin-dominated community; the body of Tamil hymns and commentaries is rarely read by other Tamils and is unintelligible for other South Indians. The Dravidian movement has been in its extreme form against all religion; at present it has some links with the non-Brahmin leadership of Tamil Śaivism. The issue is complex. Can the Brahmin and non-Brahmin Śrīvaiṣṇavas continue to feel part of the same community? Can non-Brahmins come to play a much larger leadership role comparable to their present place in Indian society? Will greater strains between Brahmins and non-Brahmins affect their acceptance of and participation in a dual tradition of Sanskrit and Tamil scriptures?

The second challenge is economic and affects all traditional religious learning in India. At a time when educated Śrīvaiṣṇavas can earn far more in factories or banks, will the traditional learning continue to be passed on from generation to generation, or can such learning by memorization be adequately replaced by modern study of texts? The tradition is dual, and each side is part of a vast literature in Sanskrit and Tamil, respectively. Will there continue to be a community of scholars familiar with both the Sanskrit Veda and the Tamil Veda?

The third challenge is spiritual and affects every religious community in the modern world. Can the claim that salvation is mediated through these scriptures and traditions remain credible and vital for religious people in an increasingly secular world? If educated members of the community continue to be religious, are they likely to adjust their practice to presently fashionable forms of worship and meditation for all educated Hindus and to adjust their theology to a pan-Hindu version of Advaita, a philosophy that claims to affirm endless variety but finally transcends the central truths as well as all the specific precepts of the Śrīvaiṣṇava tradition?

To use such words as "challenges" or "problems" may be to raise questions that are currently not of concern to most Śrīvaiṣṇavas. Finding a job or a good husband certainly are of concern. Thus far Śrīvaiṣṇavas have not voiced much fear that their traditional doctrines and institutions are threatened by the modern world. This does not mean, however, that nothing is being done about these challenges, though we are too close to the events to see whether the challenges and responses we have noted are really decisive.

There is some increase in the willingness of Brahmin Śrīvaiṣṇavas to allow non-Brahmins to play a significant role in the community. There is certainly some effort to bring Teṅkalai and Vaṭakalai Śrīvaiṣṇavas closer together to affirm their common heritage. There is also a greater awareness of the āḻvārs' hymns as a significant part of a heritage of Tamil literature that includes the Śaiva hymns of the nāyaṉmārs. The decline in traditional learning is partially compensated by the study of Śrīvaiṣṇava texts in courses on history and literature, and at a time when young men seek better paying jobs in other professions a significant number of Śrīvaiṣṇava young women are seeking to study their own scriptures and commentaries, both inside and outside the universities. Since it is also the women in educated Hindu families who have more strictly maintained traditional rites, the development of women scholar-practitioners may be of considerable importance.

The most important questions are those that can only be answered from within the Śrīvaiṣṇava community, but the "within" and "without" is also changing its meaning in the modern world, and certainly educated Śrīvaiṣṇavas are in increasing conversation, not only with other Hindus, but with many others of different religions—and of no religious persuasion—in the modern world. The aim of traditional commentary was to help the persons reciting the verses to understand their full significance in a community in which their human author could be honored, their Divine inspiration recognized, and the many facets of their Divine-human interaction explored and enjoyed.

In the case of the Śrīvaiṣṇava commentaries on the Tiruvāymoḻi, there must be an additional aim: of reconciling the high regard for this sacred poem with the corpus of Sanskrit scriptures embodied in the Hindu tradition. How can a poem by a human author be given equal status to Vedic scriptures without human authorship? In a recent article Francis Clooney has sensitively expressed the commentators' task: "to explain how the Tiruvāymoḻi is both the transcendent word of the Lord to a world of ignorance and suffering, and yet at the same time the very human word of a man in that world." [15] Clooney remarks in conclusion that modern students "in the field of modern world theology and dialogue of religions" are "in closer affinity to the commentators and thinkers of various religious traditions than to the religious poets and authors themselves . . . we like the commentators are confronted with the task of imparting a contemporary intelligibility and expression to ancient texts . . . we also must grapple with the notions of revelation and inspiration while yet seeking to preserve the very human, finite aspects of religious scripture." [16] Both intra-religious and inter-religious interpretation of sacred texts in the modern world need finally to recognize both Divine and human dimensions of scriptural inspiration and authority.

For Western students of Ubhaya Vedānta there is also a duality of traditions that provides an analogue and forms the context of their study: the continuing dialogue between "Athens and Jerusalem." Now both Indian and Western scholars are several centuries into an intellectual encounter between India and the West. This encounter has already led both to sharp clashes and to attempts at synthesis. From the many vantage points of cultural dualities within both civilizations and between them we can now look back appreciatively at the effort of Piḷḷāṉ and his successors to understand Nammāḻvār's inspired poem as the "Tamil Veda."

Part Four

Translation of Selected Decads from the Tiruvāymoḻi

1.1

1.1.1

Who is he possessing the highest good?
Who is he, who slashes ignorance,
  by graciously bestowing wisdom and love?
Who is he, the commander of the never-tiring[1] immortals?
O my mind!
  Worship his radiant feet
  that destroy all sorrow,
and rise.

The āḻvār with his holy soul experiences the Supreme Person as he really is. This is the Supreme Person who has transcendent, extraordinary, [and] divine ornaments, weapons, consorts, and attendants[2] and whose sport is the creation, development, [and destruction] of this universe.[3]

The āḻvār speaks as he experiences the love that arises from his being with the Lord. [The āḻvār says]: [The Lord] is wholly opposed to all fault, and [is characterized] by the statement "He who has the bliss a thousand times that of human beings" [Taittirīya Upaniṣad 2.8.1]. [The Lord] is an immense ocean of infinite bliss that is multiplied a thousandfold[4] and other auspicious attributes.[5] He who has this bliss and other auspicious attributes further has that great quality, like gold having a fragrance, of making himself known to me, without any reason (nirhetukamāy), so that there is not even a trace [literally, "whiff"] of ignorance. [He arouses in] me unsurpassed bhakti toward his sacred feet. This Lord who has all auspicious attributes shows his generosity to Śeṣa, Garuḍa, and other innumerable divine beings who are naturally and wholly without fault and who have unflickering wisdom. His flowerlike feet have the inherent nature of dispelling all sorrows of his devotees. Serve these feet at all places, times, and conditions [as befits] a śeṣa and live. Thus speaks [the āḻvār] to his holy soul.

1.1.2

Beyond the reach of the inner mind, freed of filth,
  full blown and rising upward,
beyond the grasp of sense organs,
  He is pure bliss and knowledge!
There is none like him
  in the past, present, and future.
He is my life!
  There is none higher than he.

[This verse] talks about the wondrous divine nature of [the Lord] who is the abode of all these [above mentioned] qualities. [This verse] also discusses the difference between that which is opposed to everything defiling and that which is wholly and infinitely auspicious.

[The āḻvār] says: O my mind! Bow before the radiant sorrow-dispelling feet of my Lord,

Who is different from the non-sentient things that are known by our sense organs;

Who is different from the essential nature of the extremely pure soul, known by the inner organ that has been made extremely pure by the practice of yoga;

Who has no equal in the three times;

Who has no equal or superior;

Whose essential nature is wholly wisdom and bliss; and

Who is my support.

1.1.3

He has this, and not that,
  precious but elusive to the mind.
The earth and the firmament are his;
  He is with form, the formless one.
In the midst of the senses, he is not of them.
  Unending, he pervades.
We have attained him who has bliss.

[This verse] talks about the wealth of the universe which belongs to the Lord whose essential nature, auspicious qualities, and glorious realm are distinct from all other entities.[6]

[The āḻvār] says: We have obtained the Lord who is the soul of everything including the earth, firmament, all worlds, animate beings and inanimate things; who is the owner (śeṣī) of all things; who is the soul of the universe, but who is free from their shortcomings; who is pure;[7] and whose [dominion] is such as to control the universe, which is his body, but who is different from everything. Oh my mind! Worship his radiant, sorrow-dispelling feet and rise.

1.1.4

We here and that man, this man,
  and that other in-between,
and that woman, this woman,
  and that other, whoever,
those people, and these,
  and these others in-between,
this thing, that thing,
  and this other in-between, whichever,

all things dying, these things,
  those things, those others in-between,
good things, bad things,
  things that were, that will be,

being all of them,
he stands there. [Translated by A. K. Ramanujan][8]

The previous [three verses] of the *tiruvāymoḻi* [i.e., this decad] are now explained. The essential nature of all the objects mentioned with various descriptive [phrases] is said to be that of dependence on the Lord.

1.1.5

Each one according to his intellect,
and in his own way,
attains his god's feet.
  These gods do not lack anything.
The Lord has determined
that each person will attain his destiny.

The āḻvār says: The key to accomplishing [good] works is dependence on the Lord.

Those men who practice rituals (karma) like Jyotishoma as a means (sādhana) [to attain] paradise (svarga) propitiate Indra and other deities to the extent of their knowledge. To fulfill their wishes they use appropriate rituals to resort [to various deities]. Those who resort to Indra and others who follow the prescriptions of the holy texts do indeed get what they desired; therefore, we can say that Indra and the other deities who are thus resorted to do not lack [the power] to fulfill their devotees' desires. It is the Supreme Person himself who is the inner soul of Indra and other divine beings and becomes the one propitiated by all rituals.

If you ask for the authority for this we have [several statements] from śruti and smṛti.

1.1.6

[He pervades] those who stand, sit, lie, and wander,
and those who do not stand, sit, lie, and wander;
He changes constantly, he is elusive to the mind,[9]
he is constant, he is unchanging;
he stands strong.

The [āḻvār] says: All action and non-action of sentient beings and non-sentient things, and all other objects are incumbent on the will of the Supreme Person.

1.1.7

Becoming all things
spread on open space, fire,
wind, water, and earth,
He is diffused through them all.
Hidden, he pervades,
like life in a body.
The radiant scripture [speaks]
of the divine one who ate all this.

In the earlier three verses it is said by sāmānādhikaraṇa [grammatical coordination, which assumes the predicate shares the substance of the subject] that the creation and movement of the earth are dependent on the Lord. Now by sāmānādhikaraṇa we say that the union between the universe and the Lord is that between the body and soul.

Just as this soul rules this body and pervades it, the Lord also pervades and rules (niyantṛ) the world, the five elements, and all other objects. This is established irrefutably by valid sources of knowledge (pramāṇa). He is different from all objects in the two states of cause and effect, as well as from the beings who are bound, free, and eternally free. His essential nature consists of wisdom, bliss, and purity. He is opposed to all filth, and possesses unlimited, auspicious, glorious attributes; his pastime is the sport of creating, protecting, and destroying the worlds; he is the soul of the entire universe; his body is the entire universe. He who is without any karma has as his body all souls and matter, and is their soul. He is pure and not affected by the happiness, sorrow, change, and the imperfections of all other things. This is the Supreme Person.

[Here there are seventy-three scriptural quotations] So say smṛti and itihāsa. These [statements] are also found in radiant revealed literature (śruti) which has not been composed by human beings and which is irrefutable. Thus, Lokāyata, Māyāvāda, Bhāskara, Yādavaprakāśa, and other sectarian viewpoints (camayam) different from the Vedas are rejected.

1.1.8

Beyond the range of the divine ones' intelligence,
He, the first one of the skies and everything thereon,
Cause of the creator, most Supreme One, ate them all!
He indwells; as Śiva and as Brahmā,
He burnt the triple cities, he enlightened the immortals,
He destroys, and then creates the worlds.

This verse refutes those who hold heterodox doctrines and who identify the Lord described in śruti with Brahmā who creates or Rudra who destroys. [Four scriptural quotations]. These sentences say: Within the egg, Brahmā was born; to this Brahmā was born Rudra. Brahmā and Rudra, born within the egg, do not know about primordial matter, intellect (mahat), egotism (ahaṁkāra), and other things outside [the egg]; they cannot create or destroy them. It is the Lord who both creates and destroys. This is stated in the following quotations. . . . Just as the Lord, by being within the four-faced one [i.e., Brahmā], instructed the immortals and by being within Rudra destroyed the triple cities, so by the same logic, he, by being within Brahmā and Rudra, creates and destroys everything within the egg. Even they do not know that it is the Lord within them who is responsible for this. By all this, says [the āḻvār], we know that our Lord is the ruler of Brahmā and Rudra.

1.1.9

If you say he exists, he does;
his forms are these forms.
If you say he does not,

his formlessness
is of these non-forms.
If he has the qualities
of existence and non-existence,
he is in two states.
He who pervades is without end.

This verse refutes the [Buddhist] śūnyavādin who clings to a wrong interpretation of the Vedas and who says: "There is no authority to be ascertained; everything is śūnya (empty). Therefore, there is no Veda, no God who is made known by the Veda or the universe which is his wealth."

We ask you, the śūnyavādin: You who insist that God does not exist, how can you declare that he exists or does not exist? Either way, we cannot establish the negative thing that you think of. If you ask how, [we say]: In this world, words of existence and non-existence, as well as self-evident ideas of existence and non-existence, are made known by being discernible [in some way]. Therefore, to say God exists is to say he is the substance qualified by existence; if not, he is the subject (or substance) qualified by non-existence. Thus when we say there are negative terms about the existence of God, we can only say they indicate his existence. Even if there are no terms of negation, we can say they are subjects qualified by non-being. These words for being and non-being (astināstirūpa padārthaṅkaḷ) are the form (rūpa) of the Lord according to the authoritative texts (pramāṇas) quoted earlier. By saying he has qualities (guṇa) of being and non-being, if you say he is (asti), he exists; if you say he is not (nāsti), he still exists. [The āḻvār] says: Even where he does not seem to be, he is the inner soul of all and therefore he exists. Thus the śūnyavādin is refuted.[10]

1.1.10

He is diffused in every drop of the cool expansive sea,
and over this expansive earth,
all the lands and all of space, not missing a spot.
He the steady one, who ate all this,
is hidden, in every shining place.
He pervades everything, everywhere.

[The āḻvār] says: Oh my mind! Worship the radiant sorrow-dispelling feet of my Lord. This Lord is in the waters of the sea, in the smallest atom, in the earth, the firmament, and the worlds. He pervades the most subtle of material objects, as well as all sentient beings, with the ease and independence with which he pervades the material world. This Lord is declared to be so by irrefutable authority.

1.1.11

These ten verses out of the thousand
composed in the right order by Kurukūr Caṭakōpaṉ
on the feet of the Great One who stands strong
in space, fire, air, water, earth;
in sound, strength, force, grace, and sustenance
[will grant] heaven.

This *tiruvāymoḻi* makes one reach the Lord who is distinguished by his [dominion] over the two realms that he has for his sport and enjoyment.[11] This meaning is suitably [proclaimed] by saying that it makes one obtain his sacred feet.

In this *tiruvāymoḻi* we find beauty of words, beauty of structure, beauty of melody, and richness of meaning. The combination of all these factors has the potential of giving birth to immense love. The [words] are not sung with any falsehood. Because of [all these reasons] "people of the Tamil land, musicians, and devotees"[12] spread the word [abroad].

The āḻvār sings out of his deep love for the Lord whose auspiciousness is unsurpassed. Because he wants [his praise] to be unbounded, he graciously sings a thousand verses about the Lord.

1.2

Introduction

Through the intense love that rises from the soul's experience of the Supreme Person, there is born [in the āḻvār] a wish to talk about, listen to, and experience the essential nature of the Lord, his qualities and glorious deeds, with those people whose exclusive enjoyment is the Lord. Since there is no soul in this world whose sole desire is to enjoy the Lord, [the āḻvār] says: We should transform them into people whose only enjoyment is the Lord, and with them experience [the glories of the Lord]. So, to those souls, he preaches bhaktiyoga, which is the way (upāya) for the sole enjoyment of the Lord.

1.2.1

Relinquish all;
having relinquished,
submit your life
to him who owns heaven.[13]

Relinquish (viṭumiṉ) everything, and having relinquished it, abandon yourself to the owner of vīṭu (heaven). Relinquish your association with all objects that are distinct from the Lord. Make a worshipful offering of your soul, for it is his property (śeṣa). When you offer it, offer it to the one who possesses it. By offering, we mean that the soul is his property.

1.2.2

Think for a moment:
your bodies inhabited by your souls[14]
last as long
as a lightning flash.

If it is asked, can we relinquish everything that we have [been associated with] for a long time? [the āḻvār says]: When you understand that the body and other earthly things connected with this soul are temporary and have other faults, you can easily relinquish them.

1.2.3

Pull out by the roots
thoughts of "you" and "yours."
Reach God; there is nothing
more right for your life.

He [the āḻvār] says: Discard the notions of ego and individual ownership that destroy the soul. Take refuge in the Supreme Lord, who is the soul's greatest wealth.

1.2.4

His form is not
that which exists
or that which does not exist.[15]
Cut your bonds;
embrace[16] that bliss
that has no end.

The āḻvār says: If what we seek as our refuge is inferior to the lowly earthly objects with which we are connected, we would find it difficult to relinquish earthly associations and cling to the other. [But this is not so; the Lord] is opposed to all filth and is wholly auspicious; he is by nature very different from animate beings and inanimate things. He is qualified by unique, auspicious qualities and is the supreme object of enjoyment; therefore, sever your connection with filthy [earthly] things and take refuge in him.

1.2.5

If you desire [heaven] after death,
loosen [earthly ties];[17]
hold fast to the Lord.
If your bonds are loosened
for sure, your life
will be in liberated.

He [the āḻvār] says: When you sever your connection with [earthly] objects, the soul which is free from earthly nature and which has the nature of happiness (sukha rūpa) will manifest itself; do not get entrapped in it. If you want to know your essential nature, which consists entirely in being a śeṣa to the Lord, grasp our Lord at the same time that you sever your connection with [earthly] objects.

1.2.6

The Lord, too, has no bonds.[18]
He exists as everything.
Without attachment,
submit yourself
to his encircling love.

If it is asked, if we grasp the Lord, will he pay attention to us; is he not the Supreme Lord? [the āḻvār replies]: Even if he is the Supreme Lord, his nature is to be a friend to all those who take refuge in him. Therefore, you can also show friendship to him and take shelter in him, who is the abode of all śeṣas.

1.2.7

Behold all, all this
beautiful wealth!
Knowing it all

to be the Lord's glory,
include yourself
within his fold.

[The āḻvār] says: If you ask, can we approach [the Lord] who has this quality of friendship, and also has this glorious universe as an instrument of his sport and has the wondrous, eternal, supreme realm (nitya vibhūti) as an instrument of his enjoyment? we say: Contemplate all this wealth and say "this is the wealth of my Lord" and without hesitation go near the Lord. Contemplate this, and serve him without hesitation.

1.2.8

Just reflect:
thought, word, and deed,
you have these three.
  Destroy them.
Submit yourself
  to the Lord's embrace.

The āḻvār says: If you ask, what shall we use to serve him, [we reply]: You do not have to acquire anything. Consider this: you have your mind, speech, and body. You have had these for a long time; [now] make them God-centered. Sever their connection with ungodly things and focus them on Divine matters.

1.2.9

Move to his side,
your bondage will loosen.
At the time your body falls,
think of him.

[The āḻvār] says: Now that all the sense organs have been restrained, all the obstacles to serving the Lord will vanish. Then we shall see this present body also disappear.

1.2.10

Infinitely good,
dazzling goal.
Without end,
his glorious fame.

Reach
Nāraṇaṉ's secure feet.

If you ask who is the Lord who is spoken of as the refuge of all, [we say]: It is Nārāyaṇa who possesses innumerable souls; whose nature is wisdom and bliss; who has eternal auspicious attributes. Take refuge with his auspicious feet that never fail and that also protect and save those who take refuge.

1.2.11

Consider carefully
these ten [songs]
from that fragrant garland
of a thousand [verses];
these words of Caṭakōpaṉ
from the beautiful Kurukūr,
a fertile [land] of lakes.

Within these thousand [verses] which describes the Lord's qualities, this *tiruvāymoḻi* understands and talks about the Lord.

4.10

Introduction

Thinking that it is preferable to die than to live with people who are not Vaiṣṇavas, he beseeches the Lord: "By your grace end [my life] as quickly as possible." The [Lord] does not do this; and so [the āḻvār] says: "Since the companionship of [the non-Vaiṣṇavas] is inevitable, let me make them Vaiṣṇavas and then live with them." And so, to these people, he proclaims the God's lordship over all (sarveśvaratva), his accessibility etc., and graciously tells them to take refuge with him. That is, [the āḻvār,] because of his union (saṁśleṣa) with the Lord, and out of the wondrous love that was born out of this union, as well as the compassion (kṛpā) that he feels for all the souls who languish without the Lord, tells them: "Take refuge in him."

4.10.1

Then, when there were no gods, no worlds, no life,
  when there was nothing,
He created Brahmā, the gods and the worlds.
  He created life.
When this primordial God stands in Tirukkurukūr,
where jewelled terraces rise like mountains,
Can you worship anyone else?

[Seventy-one quotations]

Nārāyaṇa is proclaimed by all smṛti, itihāsas, Purāṇas, and by several statements in all the Upaniṣads,

as one whose sport is to develop, preserve, and destroy Brahmā, Śiva, and all other beings, the innumerable worlds, planets etc.,

as the owner (śeṣī) of Brahmā, Rudra etc.,

as the support of all the worlds,

as one whose limbs (aṅga) are all the Vedas,

as one who is worshiped by Brahmā, Rudra, all divine beings, and all seers (ṛṣis),

as one to whom all the divine ones pay homage,

as one who is the controller (niyantṛ) of all,

as one who pervades all,

and one who is extremely accessible.

And you seek some other god as your refuge? Is there a Lord other than Nārāyaṇa? So asks the āḻvār of those who are devoted to lesser gods.

4.10.2

People of this world!
Sing, dance, and spread the word about Tirukkurukūr,
a city surrounded by beautiful palaces and towers,
where the Lord, who first created you,
and the gods you praise and worship,
The Primordial Lord, with infinite glorious qualities,
resides with love in the temple.

Statements in the Brahmā, Vāmana, Varāha, and other Purāṇas speak thus about him who created you and the gods with whom you take refuge. [Four quotations] Take refuge in the sacred city where this Lord of all who has a host of unsurpassed countless auspicious qualities (anavadhikātiśayāsaṅkhyeya kalyāṇa guṇa gaṇa)[19] graciously stands.

4.10.3

People of this world!
Say there is none but the Lord!
Speak only of his excellence.
The Supreme One of Tirukkurukūr, who the other day
created the many divine ones,
the sprawling worlds, and then
swallowed, hid, and spat them out.
He then strode over and bored through them.
The divine ones bow their heads to him.

Looking at the scriptural statements that establish Nārāyaṇa's Lordship over all and looking at his divine acts—swallowing, spitting up, striding over, and raising all the worlds—can you not know that only he is the Lord of all? There is no other God but him; if there is, says [the āḻvār], prove it by even one source of knowledge (pramāṇa).

4.10.4

Lord of Śiva, Lord of Brahmā, he is the Lord of all.
Look: He freed Śiva from the skull stuck on his hand.
This Lord stands in Tirukkurukūr,
Surrounded by splendid, majestic towers.
Why should the followers of the Liṅga [purāṇa]
Speak ill of him?

If you say that it is established by inference that Brahmā and Rudra are Lord of all, we say . . . [Three quotations]. By these scriptual quotations, we know that Nārāyaṇa is the Lord of both Rudra and Brahmā whom you declare to be superior.

4.10.5

He became and exists [as]
you, the devotees of the Linga Purāṇa,
you, the Jains, Buddhists, you crafty debaters,
and your various gods.
This is no falsehood.
This Lord flourishes in Tirukkurukūr,
[city] filled with swaying fields of paddy.
Praise him!

Nārāyaṇa is the soul (ātmā) of you who stand steadfast in the Liṅga Purāṇa, you followers of Śākya [Buddhists], Ulūkya,[20] Akṣapāda,[21] the naked Jain (Kṣapaṇa), Kapila and Patañjali sects, and all your gods. If you ask, what is the authority? [Scriptural quotations.] These are the scriptural statements. So, take refuge in him, he says.

4.10.6

If all obtained heaven, there would be no more earth,
and so he made you worship and praise other gods.
Today, your mind has been made clear.
Look at the wonder of the mighty Lord! Know him!
Know and run to him who stands in Tirukkurukūr,
  where the red paddy grows in fertile fields
  and the lotus blossoms thrive.

If you ask, thus, if Nārāyaṇa is the controller of all, why should he make us take refuge in other gods instead of making us take refuge in him alone? [the answer is]: He made you worship and praise other gods and showed you other directions; and today he clearly showed [the right path], for if everyone were to get liberated, then this earth, where people who do good and evil deeds experience the fruits of their karma, would cease to function. Thus, to ensure the continuation of this world, the omnipotent Supreme Lord himself graciously made it so that you who have done evil deeds (asat karma) will, as a result of your demerit, resort to other gods and go through births and deaths. Know all this, says the āḻvār; go immediately and take refuge in him, so you can stop the wheel of birth and death and obtain [the privilege of] loving service (kaiṁkarya) to the Supreme Person (parama puruṣa).

4.10.7

Running, rushing into several births, singing, dancing,
you worship other gods in myriad ways; you have seen it all.
Serve the Primordial Lord on whose flag is the soaring bird!
He stands in Tirukkurukūr;
  the celestial beings praise him there.

If it is asked, will we not get liberation (mokṣa) and achieve other goals if we worship other gods? the answer is: What have you achieved by resorting to other gods from beginningless time? Leave them; take refuge with the sacred feet of the flourishing Lord.

4.10.8

When Mārkaṇḍeya sought his feet as refuge,
The naked god[22] gave him life
through Nārāyaṇa's grace.
The supreme, primordial Lord stands in Tirukkurukūr,
Where cranes perch
on fences of fragrant blossoms.
How can you talk of other gods?

If it is asked, did not Mārkaṇḍeya have his wish fulfilled by taking refuge with Rudra? [the āḻvār] says: His wish was fulfilled by the grace (prasāda) of Nārāyaṇa. There, Rudra was only a mediator (puruṣakāra); therefore, what other god can you celebrate, other than Nārāyaṇa who is the Lord of all?

4.10.9

Neither the six systems that are proclaimed,
nor others like them,
can know or gauge
the Primordial Lord who resides
in cool Tirukkurukūr
amidst fertile fields of paddy.
Be wise to this, be mindful of this,
if you want to live.

[The āḻvār] says: If you want to live, leave the lowly deities and take refuge in the sacred city where the Supreme Person resides. His essential nature, [beautiful] form, and wealth of attributes cannot be tarnished by all the false doctrines preached by heretics outside the pale of the Vedas.

4.10.10

With all gods, all worlds, all else as his faultless form,
He stands radiant in Tirukkurukūr,
abundant with fertile red fields of paddy and sugar cane.
He came down to earth as [only] a little dwarf;
he is the dancer with the tall pots.
Serve him.

All the worlds which depend on him form his unique body. He exists as one whose essential nature is to hold everything.[23] It is fitting to do service to him who graciously exists in Tirukkurukūr where the red paddy and sugar cane grow in fertile fields. This is the Lord who became [just] a little dwarf and who later danced with the tall pots.

4.10.11

Those who say these ten verses from the thousand songs
Composed through the ardor of Māṟaṉ Caṭakōpaṉ—
on whose chest is the fragrant garland of makiḻ blossoms,[24]
[a poet] who comes from the beautiful city of Tirukkurukūr,
and who by his service, reached the Lord—
Will obtain the kingdom of heaven,
from which there is no return.

Those who master these ten verses out of the thousand spoken from the unsurpassed devotion (niratiśaya bhakti) for the Supreme Person by the āḻvār, whose body and essential nature of the soul is delighted by bathing in the cool ambrosia-like pool of loving service to the Lord, and whose chest is adorned with the exceedingly fragrant blossoming red flowers will retain mastery [these ten verses]; that itself is the supreme goal. If they also want the sacred land (heaven), that is also in their hands!

5.2

Introduction

He sees those who became Vaiṣṇavas [after hearing] the verses "When there were no gods . . ." [4.10]. Seeing them, [the āḻvār] is filled with unsurpassed happiness and through this happiness he sings a benediction (tirupallāṇṭu) wishing them many happy years.

5.2.1

Rejoice! Rejoice! Rejoice![25]
The persisting curse of life is gone,
the agony of hell is destroyed,
death has no place here.

The [force of] Kali is destroyed.
Look for yourself!
The followers of the sea-colored Lord
swell over this earth, singing with melody,
dancing and whirling [with joy].
 We see them.

All the sins of all the souls have gone; the hells where the fruit of these sins are experienced become powerless to cause torment; Yama is left without any work to do. Now the non-Vaiṣṇava people tormented by hells like Raurava, etc., are not here. Only Śrīvaiṣṇavas who have procured the experience of the Lord's immeasurable auspicious qualities like profundity and generosity come and fill this earth. We see them singing about and acting out the Lord's essential nature, forms, qualities, realms, and actions. This good fortune must become established for all eternity, he says.

5.2.2

We saw, we saw, we saw what is joyful to our eyes!
O servants of the Lord! Come here!
Serving, worshiping joyfully,
the followers of Mādhavaṉ,
 who wears cool tulasi leaves
 that are surrounded by humming bees,
sing with melody, dance, and spread [the word] abroad.

We saw, we saw, we saw what is joyful to our eyes. O servants [of the Lord], come here! We shall stand here serving continually. If you ask, what is all this, [the āḻvār] replies: The followers of Mādhava, who wears cool tulasi leaves surrounded by bees, now spread out all over this earth and wander about singing melodious songs.

5.2.3

The whirling age of Kali ends;
the divine ones also enter [the earth].
The golden age dawns
and floods of great joy sweep [over the land].
The followers of
 him who is dark as a cloud,
 my Lord, the sea-colored one,
Fill this earth, singing with melody.
They are all over this land.

The followers of the sea-colored one, my Lord, who is dark as a cloud, fill this earth. They sing with such melody that the age of Kali, which is the antithesis of Vaiṣṇava dharma, ends. The age of Kali is stopped for all time and only the golden age (Kṛta Yuga) exists. "The never-tiring immortals" enter here and floods of great joy sweep over the land. They worship continually and rejoice. O all you servants [of the Lord], come here!

5.2.4

Pulling out like weeds
all other religions of this earth,
becoming the followers
of the Lord who reclines on the deep sea,
they fall on the ground, sit,
rise, and sing many, many songs.
They walk, fly, bend,
acting out the drama.

All the religions (camaya) that are outside the Vedas and that are spread over the world are plucked out like weeds; the world is full of the followers of the Lord who reclines on the deep ocean. They are intoxicated with the nectar of the Supreme Person's unsurpassed auspicious attributes; they fall on the ground as if in a swoon, they rise, they sing several songs, they fly in ecstasy, and act in a way that is wonderful to watch. O servants, come here to serve continually and rejoice!

5.2.5

The followers of the Lord of heaven
dwell wondrously (māyā) on this earth.
If you are born among demons or ungodly folk
you have no chance of survival.
They will destroy you and a new age will dawn.
  There is no doubt about this.
Only this will meet my eye.

Only this will meet my eye. If you ask what? [the āḻvār] says: The followers of the Lord of Heaven spread [abroad] in an astonishing manner. They live everywhere and you non-Vaiṣṇavas find no way to live. O you who desire things other than [the Lord], you are destroyed; it is like creation being shaken. There is no doubt about this.

5.2.6

Those beloved
of the discus-wielding Lord
uproot disease, hatred, poverty,
and suffering,
which kill and conquer this earth.[27]
Singing melodiously, they jump,
dance, and fly all over this earth.
O servants [of the Lord]!
come, worship, and live.
Fix your minds [on him].

The Supreme Person has divine weapons like the conch, discus, bow, etc., to remove the afflictions of all souls. The Śrīvaiṣṇavas, whose real nature is to serve him lovingly, enter this world. You, too, should leave other divine beings and, with no other goal, take the Lord as refuge; then you will live.

5.2.7

Know that the gods whom you place in your thoughts
make you live [with help] from him.
Mārkaṇḍeya is the proof.
Do not let your minds be darkened [by doubt]:
there is no God but Kaṇṇaṉ.
Offer all you can to those beings
who are but his [outer] form.[28]

If you ask, will not Brahmā, Rudra, and other divine beings with whom we take refuge be our protectors? [the āḻvār] says: The divine beings with whom you take refuge are merely mediators of the Lord's protection. Mārkaṇḍeya also is the witness for this meaning. Nārāyaṇa is the Lord of all; there is nothing to doubt about this. Therefore, take refuge in him. If you say, scripture says that Agni, Indra, and other divine beings are worthy of being worshiped, [we reply], it means only that the Supreme Person is the inner controller of Agni, Indra, and other divine beings. He has them as his body and he receives all [sacrificial] action (karma) and worship. Therefore, [says the āḻvār], in all your acts of worship, daily and occasional rites, and optional rites to obtain personal desires (*nitya naimittika kāmya rūpa karma*), take refuge with the Supreme Person, who is the inner controller of Agni, Indra, and all divine beings.

5.2.8

It is he, the Lord of the gods, who established
[the divine ones] who make up his body.
To these [gods], one makes offerings
and enjoys [the benefits].
The followers of the Lord
who has a mole on his sacred chest
sing songs.
Without any suffering they crowd all over the land.
Worship with love and live!

If it is said, it is only by worshiping Indra and other gods with ritual acts that one gets the fruits that one desires like sons or cows, [the āḻvār replies]: It is the Supreme Person, the Lord of all, who graciously makes Indra and other gods, who are members of his body, receive all worship and fulfill the desires of the worshipers. So it is he who is the Lord of all. Since he is the Lord of all and since the world is made perfect by Śrīvaiṣṇavas whose sole enjoyment is the Lord, [the āḻvār says], without any motive [other than this enjoyment] you too should also take refuge with the Lord and live.

5.2.9

Worship with love and live.
This world is filled with servants
    who worship with desire,
    whose tongues [chant] the pure verses of the Ṛig [Veda],
    who don't deviate from the way of wisdom,[29]
    who take flowers, incense, lamps,
    sandalwood paste, and water,
and worship Achyuta with desire.

This world is now filled with beings

who recite the very pure Ṛig [Veda], which describes the Lord's nature, form, qualities, and wealth;

who, without deviating, follow the way of bhakti, carrying with them flowers, incense, lights, water, and other aids to worship the Lord, holding him to be the sole goal;

who are followers of the Lord, rendering service to him;

whose only enjoyment is the experience of the Supreme Person's deeds.

[The āḻvār] says: You should also think of the Lord as the supreme exclusive goal, do service to him, and live.

5.2.10

All over the worlds,
the naked one (Śiva), Brahmā, Indra,
and the hordes of immortal beings,
worship the sacred form of Kaṇṇaṉ everywhere.
O servants [of the Lord]!
If you worship him,
there will be no more age of Kali.

Brahmā, Śiva, Indra, and other divine beings, by taking refuge in the Lord became guardians of the world. So, if you should also take refuge in the Lord, there will be no more Kali Yuga.

5.2.11

These glorious ten verses of the thousand
[which speak of] the radiant Lord,
  the entrancing Lord,
  who shows grace to his servants,
  such that there is no more age of Kali
composed by Caṭakōpaṉ Kārimāṟaṉ,
  of the beautiful Kurukūr,
  surrounded by paddy fields,
will destroy the strains in our thoughts.

This *tiruvāymoḻi* which describes the Lord, who has the nature of graciously changing Kali Yuga to Kṛta Yuga, will (if it is the wish of his devotee) expel all the obstacles that exist in [the path] of being a Vaiṣṇava.

5.8

Introduction[30]

Thus, the āḻvār, who was in Cirīvaramaṅkalam, could not obtain his desired goal and is sunk [in grief]. Now thinking deeply (anusandittu) about the divine knowledge (divya jñāna) that he has gained, that is, that the Lord's sacred flowerlike feet are his way and his goal, he becomes calm and goes to Tirukkuṭantai. Not gaining a union with the Lord here, either, he falls down [in grief] and cries aloud.

5.8.1

O nectar that never satiates!
You cause your servant's body,
so filled with love for you,
to sway restlessly,
like the waves of a sea
dissolving the shores.[31]
I saw you, my Lord!
Radiant, you reclined with incredible beauty
in sacred Kuṭantai,
where fragrant, luxuriant
[fields] of red paddy
sway like fans,
blowing a gentle breeze [over]
rich waters.

[The āḻvār] says: You are so enjoyable that even if there were no difference between you and others, and everyone were to have equal experience of you for all time, it would still not exhaust your [glory]. By your beauty and other incomparable auspicious attributes you have made even my material body melt. So extraordinary is your servant's passion for you, yet you remain inaccessible to me. I have seen you: you reclined, radiant and incredibly beautiful, in sacred Kuṭantai where fragrant, luxuriant [fields] of red paddy sway like fans, blowing a gentle breeze over rich waters. [But] I did not see you graciously glance at me with your divine eyes, nor do I [hear] you graciously say even a word to me.

5.8.2

My Lord! My [Lord] with white form![32] My ruler!
You easily assume any splendid form that you desire.
O handsome bull!
You close your huge flowerlike eyes,
in sacred Kuṭantai,
where large red lotus blossoms
open their [petal] eyes and bloom.
What am I to do?

My Lord, your form is opposed to all that is defiling and is entirely auspicious. By your divine beauty, you captivate me and make me your servant. To protect those who seek your refuge you assume a desirable and suitable form, and are graciously born [in this world]. You are an extraordinary exalted flame.[33] Even though all the lotus flowers in Tirukkuṭantai blossom, the lotus blossoms that are your sacred eyes do not open wide. What shall I do, asks [the āḻvār].

5.8.3

What am I to do? Who is my support?
What are you doing with me?
I desire nothing
  that anyone other than you can fulfill.
You reclined in Kuṭantai
  that is surrounded by beautiful walls.
Glance at me; resolve that all the dear days
  that I, your servant, have yet to live
  shall pass with my holding your feet.

There is nothing that I can do, there is no goal other than you. Can I ever reach your sacred feet by my effort (yatna)? Look at me with grace. I do not want anything but your sacred feet, [a privilege] that should be granted only by your mercy (kṛpā) and in no other way. So, for as long as this soul exists, graciously see that it is never separated from your sacred feet.

5.8.4

Your glory spreads as far as sight,
  and then extends beyond the horizon, too;
your body includes all the worlds,
  O [Lord,] there is none comparable to you.
You recline in Kuṭantai,
  that prospers with virtuous people.
Longing to see you, I scan the skies,
  I cry, I weep, and I bow.

In distress, I cry to see you who are a great ocean of unsurpassed, extraordinary, infinite, auspicious attributes. You can captivate all souls by your beauty and by your sacred body can make them your slaves. You recline in Tirukkuṭantai that prospers with virtuous people. [Saying,] "Show yourself to me as you showed yourself to Śrī Gajendra āḻvāṉ,"[34] I scan the skies, weep, and bow [in worship].

5.8.5

I weep and I bow, I dance to see you,
I sing and I call, I search everywhere.
My sins cling to me, I cringe with shame.
[Lord] you recline in Kuṭantai
   amidst fertile, bounteous fields.
[Lord] whose eyes [bloom wide] like a red lotus flower,
show me, your devotee, [the way]
   to reach [the splendor] of your feet!

I weep to see you, I bow down to see you, I dance to see you, I sing to see you, I shriek to see you, and still I do not see you come. Not seeing you, I stand ashamed, looking at the people of this world who say evil [things] about you, and I think: this is because of my sins. O Lord who reclines in Kuṭantai amidst the fertile, bounteous fields, [Lord] with red lotus eyes, graciously think of a way for me to reach your sacred feet.

5.8.6

O king of the sky lords! Sweet music of the *yāḻ!*[35]
Nectar, fruit of the intellect, monarch of lions![36]
Cut through my ancient sins and embrace me.
How long am I to be away from you,
knowing the direction[37] [to reach] your feet,
   yet trying to fill an endless pit
   of [senses] that cannot be gratified?
You recline in Kuṭantai,
   a [town] that prospers
   with people of far-reaching fame.

You must banish my bondage and provide the means (upāya) for me to reach your sacred feet. While you do it, you must make sure that knowing about the upāya I do not get caught in it. Do it so that I do not know it is an upāya.[38] Since [the āḻvār] does not see [the Lord] fulfill his desires, he says, "Knowing the great enjoyment of union with your sacred feet, you who have a host of infinite, auspicious attributes like affection to your devotees, perfect conduct, accessibility and enjoyability, I am only enjoying these earthly objects through my corrupting sense organs. How much longer am I to be away from your sacred feet?

5.8.7

Monarch of lions, my golden flame,
dark as a cloud, eyes red,
[form that glows]
  like a coral mountain ablaze,
Lord with four shoulders!
Through your grace you took me,
  as your inseparable slave,
sacred, entrancing Lord of Kuṭantai!
[Without you] I cannot survive.
Give me your feet
  and destroy my [cycle] of births.

Through your grace, you showed me your beauty and graciously made me one who whose soul's only delight is to serve you; now I cannot survive even for a moment if I am to be separated from your sacred feet; so first give me your sacred feet and later remove my bondage.

5.8.8

Perhaps you will destroy my sorrow, perhaps not,
  but I have no support other [than you],
O Lord who hold as your weapon
  the discus with a whirling mouth,
When it is time for me to pass on,
  my body will be limp, my soul will falter;
you then must will that I should not be weak
  but clasp only[39] [the splendor] of your feet.

The [āḻvār] says: Perhaps you may destroy my sorrow, perhaps you may not. Do as your divine will pleases; I have no other refuge but you. It is to banish my sorrow that you lift aloft the sacred discus and that you recline in Tirukkuṭantai! So, before my body becomes weak and my soul falters, before this soul ceases to exist,[40] graciously, quickly, rescue me to your sacred feet.

5.8.9

Lord, consent [to my plea]; place me beneath your feet.
Leader of the chief of the strong immortal ones!
Great primeval Lord![41]
You recline, without moving, in Kuṭantai

where huge glowing gems
flash rainbows in all directions.
so the world may adore you.
O come so I may see you![42]

Telling me that this soul is only your slave, you made me one whose happiness and sadness [is incumbent] on [my] union and separation with your twin feet. Though those feet are served by your commander in chief [i.e., Viśvaksena], the leader of Śeṣa and Garuḍa, and by countless divine attendants, and though you are the Lord of all, you came to sleep [in image form] in sacred Kuṭantai so that you may be the refuge of all. O come [Lord], so I may see you!

5.8.10

You do not come,
and then you come without form [in my heart],
my Lord of entrancing form!
Nectar that never satiates,
you taste so sweet within my soul!
You ruled me so my endless sins came to an end,
Lord who dwells in Kuṭantai!
Having become your servant,
why do I still wander astray?

You come not to elate my eyes but to appear to [in] my heart; showing your exceedingly beautiful body, you became extremely beautiful to me; no one else but you could destroy the obstacles to my finding all my enjoyment with you; [since] you graciously entered Tirukkuṭantai to make me an object of [your grace], why do I who have been your servant still wander?

5.8.11

Those who [recite],
till their confusion clears,
these ten verses of a thousand
(sweeter than the melody of a flute)
spoken by Caṭakōpaṉ from Kurukūr
who took as his refuge
the feet of [the Lord]
([the Lord] who ate the breast and swallowed the life

of the demon-woman with bones
as tough as a crossbar)[43]—
[those devotees] will be loved
by doe-eyed [women].

Those who are capable of [reciting], till their confusion clears, these ten verses of the thousand, sweeter than the sounds of the divine flute played by the Lord of beautiful Dvāraka, said by Kurukūr Caṭakōpaṉ who considers as his way and his goal the flower[like] feet of the Lord whose sole pleasure is to expel the enemies of his devotees, will become enjoyable to the Lord just as the lovers of doe-eyed women are enjoyable to them.[44]

6.3

Introduction

The Lord of superlative beauty who is present in Tiruviṇṇakar has just united with [the āḻvār]. That beauty and the āḻvār's weariness in waiting for such a union combine to overcome the āḻvār's anger, which is caused by his frustrated passion and his [resolution] not to show his feelings for the Lord. Thus the āḻvār does gain union with the Lord, and that union generates such an excessive love that the āḻvār talks excitedly of seeing [the Lord] in Tiruviṇṇakar and of experiencing union with him. The āḻvār continues by describing the Lord's domain and [his] treasury of countless auspicious attributes, like beauty, which are opposed to all filth.

6.3.1

Being
poverty and wealth,
hell and heaven,
Being
enmity and friendship,
poison and ambrosia,
The great Lord, diffused everywhere,
is my ruler.

I saw him
  in the Sacred Celestial City,
a city of wealthy people.

He says: My Lord is the inner soul (antarātma bhūta) of poverty and wealth, hell and heaven, enmity and friendship, poison and ambrosia, and all the different things that have been brought forth. He is the Lord of all (sarveśvara). Being all this, my great Lord (emperumāṉ) united with me. I saw him at the Sacred Celestial City (Tiruviṇṇakar), a city filled with rich divine people who enjoy serving this Lord with love.

6.3.2

Being
  the joys and sorrows that we see,
  confusion and clarity,
Being
  punishment and grace,
  heat and shade,
The great one, rare to behold,
  is my ruler.
His is the Sacred Celestial City;
  a good city,
  surrounded by clear waters
  and waves.

[The āḻvār] enjoys the sacred city, saying that this is the sacred town of Tiruviṇṇakar, where he was able to see with his eyes, serve the Lord who is the inner soul (antarātmā) of the joys and sorrow that we perceive, disturbance (kaluṣya) and clarity, punishment and favor (nigrahānugraha), cold and heat, everything that goes forth, and that is like a womb (udyanyonya):[45] the Lord who is so rare to behold.

6.3.3

Being
  town and country,
  wisdom and idiocy;
Being
  the all-surrounding incomparable light;
Being darkness;
Being
  the earth;

Being
  the firmament;
The Lord resides
  in the Sacred Celestial City,
  surrounded by terraces
  that rise like mountains.
There is no virtue,
  other than his brilliant glory.

He says: There is no other means for existence except the incomparable compassion of the Lord who, being the controller (niyantā) of town and country, wisdom and ignorance, darkness and light, earth and sky, and everything else, resides in the Sacred Celestial City (Tiruviṇṇakar) that is surrounded by towering terraces. Saying this, he experiences (anubhava) the attribute of compassion which is the means for his existence.

6.3.4

Being
  virtue and sin,
  union and separation,
  and all of these;
Being
  memory, being forgetfulness;
Being
  existence, being non-existence;
Being none of these,
The Lord resides
  in the Sacred Celestial City
  that is surrounded by lofty mansions.
See the sweet grace of Kaṇṇaṉ,
  [Can this be] false?

He says: Being the inner controller (antaryāmī) and pervading good deeds, bad deeds and their consequences, the desired unions, separations, memory and forgetfulness, existence and non-existence (bhavābhava) and all other things, touching them, but being free from their faults (doṣa), is the Lord who is in the Sacred Celestial City surrounded by lofty mansions. By his grace (kṛpā) we can see all things that flow from the sense organs, that are the means for all goals of life (puruṣārtha) in the Sacred Celestial City.

6.3.5

Being
    crooked and straight,
    black and white,
Being
    truth and lies,
    youth and old age,
    the new and the old,
the Lord lives
    in the Sacred Celestial City
    that is surrounded by strong walls.
Look! the garden that he created forms
the three worlds of the great gods

He says: My Lord whose form (rūpa) is straight and crooked, white and black, truth and lies, youth and age, new and old, etc., is the protector of Brahmā and others as well as of all the established worlds filled with all beings.

6.3.6

Being
    the three worlds,
Being
    nothing,
Being
    love, being anger,
Being
    the Goddess [Fortune] who dwells on the flower,
Being
    her sister [Misfortune],
Being
    praise, being blame,
the Lord resides
    in the Sacred Celestial City,
    where the divine ones worship with love.
The supreme radiant flame
    abides in my mind;
    [the mind of me,] a sinner!

He says: He is the indweller (antarvartti) of all the worlds, love and hate, Lakṣmī and anti-Lakṣmī, praise and blame; he fills all auspicious (kalyāṇa) and filthy (heya) things; and he is their inner soul (ātmabhūtaṉ). Being the indweller of all auspicious objects, he is not affected by any evil (doṣa) and though he is the indweller of all filthy (heya) things, he is without stain (nirdoṣa). If it is asked, how is this possible? [the āḻvār] says: It is because he has entered my filthy heart and is still not affected by the evil (doṣa); he is the unsurpassed flame.

6.3.7

Being a supremely brilliant body;
Being a body encrusted with filth;
Hidden and manifest,
Standing erect and doing crooked deeds,
the Lord resides in the Sacred Celestial City.
The Celestial ones bow their heads,
to his feet that fulfill all desires.
These feet are our sole refuge.

He says: There is no other protection for all souls than the sacred feet of the Lord who has a divine form of exceeding radiance, who has all the filthy worlds as his body, but who is totally without filth, who is hard to know but who was born for the sake of his devotees, who unites with them and does crooked deeds towards those who are against him, and who lives in the Sacred Celestial City where the celestials bow their heads in worship.

6.3.8

Being,
  the sure refuge of the celestial ones,
Being
  wrathful destruction for the demons,
Keeping the world in the shadow of his feet,
  and not keeping them there,
the Lord who resides in the Sacred Celestial City,
  refuge of the southern direction,
is my refuge, my Kaṇṇaṉ, my father
  who has me as his servant.

He says: He has the nature (svabhāva) of banishing all the sins (pāpa) which stand as obstacles in the path of a devotee obtaining his feet and then keeps him there. The great Lord who prevents the enemies of his devotees from reaching his feet and who is death for them, resides in the

Sacred Celestial City which is the refuge of the southern direction. There he exists as my goal (prāpya), as my vision; he took me graciously as one who could do all the [service] that befits one who belongs to him and became my master.

6.3.9

Being
  my father,
Being
  my companion,
Being
  the mother who gave birth to me,
Being
  gold, gems and pearls,
  and my father,
the Lord resides in the Sacred Celestial City,
that is surrounded by glowing turrets of gold.
My father knows no equal,
he gives us the shade of his feet.

He says: Having the sacred body which has "the glow of molten gold" and unmoving; all these are his modes (prakāra). Since the Sacred Celestial City is the place where he was able to unite with me, he says, "I shall never ever leave this place" and graciously stands there. Other than this great Lord's sacred feet, we have no refuge (gati). [The āḻvār] clearly tells everyone: "Before he glanced at me [with grace], I did not have existence; since he graciously glanced at me, I exist; and so, other than he, there is no other refuge."

6.3.10

Being
  shade and sunshine,
  mean and great,
  short and tall,
Being
  all that surrounds one,
  and more,
Being none of these,
The Lord resides
  in the Sacred Celestial City,
  where bees sweetly hum and prosper.

Look! there is no support,
other than his feet.

[The Lord] is shadow and light, mean and great, short and tall, moving and unmoving; all these are his modes (prakāra). Since the Sacred Celestial City is the place where he was able to unite with me, he says, "I shall never ever leave this place" and graciously stands there. Other than this great Lord's sacred feet, we have no refuge (gati). [The āḻvār] clearly tells everyone: "Before he glanced at me [with grace], I did not have existence; since he graciously glanced at me, I exist; and so, other than he, there is no other refuge."

6.3.11

Look! O people of this world!
Those who can [recite] these ten verses
on the Sacred Celestial City,
out of the thousand
composed by Kurukūr Caṭakōpaṉ
    in praise of him who, as everyone gazed,
    kept growing in height,
will become advisors
for even the celestial ones.

He says: Not heeding the difference between devotees and non-devotees, telling all souls to look and to live, the Lord's legs grew tall in front of all eyes. Those who say this *tiruvāymoḻi* which speaks of the Lord's control of everything (sarvaniyantṛtvattai), out of the thousand verses sung by Kurukūr Caṭakōpaṉ in praise of this Lord, will be the people most respected by the "never-tiring immortals."

6.10

Introduction

And so, though [the āḻvār] calls the Lord so loudly that it could be heard in heaven, he does not obtain a vision of the Lord. He thinks: The only way (upāya) to see him is to seek refuge at his sacred feet; there is no other way. Speaking of the Lord's qualities such as compassion (kāruṇya) and motherly love (vātsalya) as his support, with the Divine Mother as the mediator, he takes refuge at the sacred feet of the Lord at Tiruvēṅkaṭam—the Lord who is the refuge of all the worlds.

6.10.1

O you
    whose large mouth ate the world!
My Lord of incomparable glory and radiant form!
O tall one,
    dear life of me, your servant,
My great Lord of the sacred Vēṅkaṭa
    that adorns this world,
Summon me, so that I,
who come from a clan of your servants,
may reach your feet.

[The āḻvār says]: You have compassion, motherly love, and countless other infinite, wonderful, auspicious qualities. By your radiance you hold up the entire world as your body and you are my sustainer. You dwell in the highest heaven, which is remote from our sense organs, [but] came to this sacred hill, which is an ornament for the entire world, and graciously stand there in order to become accessible to our senses. I am your servant and come from a family of [people] who have been your servants. For all these reasons, you must unite me with your feet.

6.10.2

O you
    whose hand holds the fiery sacred wheel
    that chops, razes, and reduces to the ground
    entire clans of wicked demons!
O king of the divine ones!
O Lord of the Sacred Vēṅkaṭa
    where blossoms of lotus, red as fire,
    grow in the muddy banks and pools.
Show your grace
    so that I, your servant,
    filled with unending love,
    may reach your feet.

If the Lord says, only when the sins which are obstacles disappear can one obtain a union with me, [the āḻvār replies]: Just as you, with your sacred discus, destroyed the demons (asuras) who were the enemies of the divine ones, who are your devotees, please destroy the obstacles which [stand between us]. Graciously make it happen that I, your servant, who am submerged in the ever-increasing, swelling flood of divine desire for all that is connected with you, may reach your sacred feet that stand on the sacred hill; the hill that is adorned and made brilliant by the rays emanating from the clusters of sun-lit lotuses that spring daintily from willowy stalks.

6.10.3

Grace is your hue,[46]
O Lord whose color is that of a beautiful cloud;
My Lord of wonder!
Nectar that seeps into my mind and tastes so sweet!
Lord of the immortal ones!
Lord of the Sacred Vēṅkaṭa,
  where the crystal[47] waterfalls crash,
  carrying gems, gold, and pearls!
My Lord! Only say the words for me,
  your servant, to reach your feet.

If you ask, should this be done without cause, [the āḻvār] says: While there are the "never-tiring immortals" for you to unite with, by sheer grace (kevala kṛpā), with your exceedingly attractive, wondrous, divine form that is similar to a dark cloud, you came, entered, filled my heart, and became very sweet to me. Similarly, again, by your grace, My Lord, graciously make me reach your sacred feet which stand on the sacred hill that is made so splendid with delightful, clear waterfalls and streams flowing with treasures of pure, radiant, diverse gems, gold, and pearls.

6.10.4

O you
  whose bow lets loose arrows that spit fire
  on the lives of the wicked demons
  who show no mercy to the world!
O husband of the supreme Śrī! O divine one!
O Lord of the Sacred Vēṅkaṭa
desired by the immortals
and the hordes of sages,
Unite[48] with me so that I a sinner

may always be at your feet
that are adorned with flowers.

He petitions: You were unable to tolerate the suffering of the world when it was assaulted by the merciless demons. So you rained fiery arrows that burnt the bodies of the demons and you saved the world from their oppression. Similarly, by your grace, make my sorrows vanish by providing an unparalleled means (upāya) meant only for me to reach your exceedingly enjoyable sacred feet. You abide with your consort on the sacred hill that is even desired by the eternal ones. Through this means, graciously enable me to join you.

6.10.5

O Victorious one!
The other day
with your bow, you knocked down the seven trees
that grew so close together.
O First One who crawled
between the two intertwined trees!
O Lord of the Sacred Vēṅkaṭa
where the rogue elephants
gather like the dense clouds!
Lord of the bow called Cārṅka!
When is the day
when I your servant
may reach your feet?

If it is asked, can a suitable means be adopted successfully, even if there is no precedent for it? he says: By one sacred arrow you felled the seven trees that were like mountains, such that the mountains and nether regions [shook] in fear. Is there anything that you cannot do? The other day you went between the two trees without harm, banished my fear, and gave me life. So when will you make me reach your feet and give me life? You graciously stand on the sacred hill which is the refuge of all beings, with innumerable divine weapons, starting with Śrī Sārṅga the bow; these weapons are capable of banishing [the fears] of all your devotees.

6.10.6

Crowds of immortal beings wonder
when they may see the twin lotus feet
that paced the worlds.

They praise and worship you every day.
O Lord of the Sacred Vēṅkaṭa
  they serve you
  with body, tongue, and mind!
When is the day
  when I your servant
may, in truth, reach your feet?

If you should ask, is it not the goal of everyone to do all kinds of service to the Lord of all who lives in the highest heaven, [the āḻvār answers]: Even the "never-tiring immortals" who live there ardently wonder, "When is the day when we can see the sacred feet of the Lord of Tiruvēṅkaṭa?" So they flock here and by thought, word, and deed do every kind of service at your sacred feet. That is also my goal; so, [tell me] when is the day that I, who eagerly want to come to the sacred hill, can really come here and serve your sacred feet with all my senses, for all time?

6.10.7

O nectar that I, your servant, desire and love![49]
Lord of the immortal ones! Master of the ferocious bird!
Great Lord, with lips like a tender fruit!
Medicine to end my sins that grow like weeds!
My great Lord of the Sacred Vēṅkaṭa!
I cannot endure
  even for a split second
  not to see your feet.

If you say, we can only obtain this goal by performing an upāya, the āḻvār says: In spite of being surrounded by the supreme angels in the highest heaven, you graciously mounted on the shoulders of Garuḍa, [whose picture] is on your victorious flag and whose essential nature is to expel the enemies of your devotees. You came to the sacred hill on his shoulder, for my sake; you banished all the hindrances on my side [that were barriers to our union]; you graciously came into my heart and through [showing me] the beauty of your corallike lips, you conquered even me who craved worldly pleasures and made me your servant. You gave me the joy of contemplating you continuously, without break, because [you knew] that my soul could not bear to survive if it was separated from you even for a moment. And since I cannot survive unless I see you, graciously show yourself to me, even though I have not performed any upāya.

6.10.8

"We have performed no austerity, fit to see your feet;
and without them we cannot survive,"
say [Śiva], the god of exquisite intelligence,
whose neck is blue,
[Brahmā], the perfect one with four faces,[50] and Indra.
Surrounded by women with sparkling eyes, they come
desiring you, O Lord of the Sacred Vēṅkaṭa.
Come, my dark entrancing Lord
to me your servant,
as you have before.

If it is asked, can you, who are without any upāya, attain [the goal] just by desiring it? [the āḻvār] says: The intelligent Śiva, Brahmā, Indra, and other divine beings come with their families and get to see you, only because they desire it. They say that even though they have no upāya, they cannot survive unless they see you. [The āḻvār] pleads: you must come to me so that I may envision you for all time. I, who am your servant, have not been able to see you and am confused and dazed because of my grief. If you do not want [to remain before me forever], could you at least come immediately and manifest yourself [briefly], just as you did to Śrī Gajendra,[51] to make me survive?

6.10.9

Seeming to come, you do not; seeming not to come, you do;
eyes like the red lotus, lips like the luscious red fruit,
Lord with four shoulders, my ambrosia, my life!
Lord of the Sacred Vēṅkaṭa where the glowing gems
negate darkness and make night seem day!
O my Lord, my Lord, I your servant,
cannot for a second move away from your feet.

You seem accessible to your enemies and yet [actually] you are very difficult [for them] to see. To your devotees you seem so distant, and yet you are so accessible. You made me one for whom your beauty is sustenance, nourishment, and enjoyment. You graciously stand, [just] for me, on the sacred hill, which is adorned by gems that emanate brilliant rays, transforming night into day. I will not be separated from your sacred feet even for a minute. For all these reasons, you must, by your mercy (kṛpā), make me, your servant, join your sacred feet.

6.10.10

O you on whose breast resides the lady of the flower
who says: "I cannot move away from him even for a second!"
Unmatched in fame, owner of the three worlds! my ruler!
O Lord of the sacred Vēṅkaṭa
 desired by the peerless immortals and sages!
 I, your servant, who am without shelter,
sat at your feet and entered [your safe haven].

You are an ocean of unbounded compassion. Because of your qualities you are my master. [You dwell] on the sacred hill that is desired even by the peerless, perfect eternal beings whose only enjoyment is to serve you and to experience your qualities in heaven. Deeming you to be "the refuge of all the worlds and all entities without distinction," I, your servant, who am without refuge, without any other goal, having the Divine Mother as the mediator (puruṣakāra) took refuge at your sacred feet. And now, immediately, with all my obstacles gone, I, your servant, desire at all times to do all possible loving service.

6.10.11

Caṭakōpaṉ who hails from Kurukūr, which has abundant paddy fields,
composed a thousand songs on the Lord who graciously says:
"O you who would serve me! Come to my feet for refuge and live!"

Those who clasp the people who hold on to these ten songs
about sacred Vēṅkaṭa, which will end [the process of rebirth],
will be enthroned with majesty in the high heavens.

To all those who have the sole desire of rendering loving service and who take refuge at his sacred feet, he gives the wealth of loving service. His devotees seek as their refuge these sacred words concerning the sacred hill, which are spoken in order to reach this incomparable Lord of Tiruvēṅkaṭa, who is characterized by motherly love. Even those who take refuge with these devotees will be crowned in the kingdom of the servants of God in heaven, and will be fortunate in being able to render service of all kinds, at all times.

7.9

Introduction

Thus, [the āḻvār] is extremely astonished while thinking deeply of the [Lord having] the wondrous form of the universe [as his body], his transcendent, extraordinary divine form, and his uniting with him. [The āḻvār] is also elated because of his great love, and with all his earlier distress being expelled, he talks of the wondrous, unsurpassed enjoyment [of his union]. As he saw it, all this was the Lord's doing; thinking about it, he exclaims, "How can he take me who am so despicable and graciously say the Tiruvāymoḻi?" He experiences the Lord's auspicious attributes such as omnipotence, gracious condescension, and motherly love. Through the excessive love that was born of this experience, in which [the Lord] took the [āḻvār] and graciously sang the Tiruvāymoḻi, [the āḻvār] now speaks.

7.9.1

What can I say of the Lord
who lifted me up for all time,
and made me himself, every day?
My radiant one, the first one,
My Lord, sings of himself,
through me, in sweet Tamil.

He takes my soul as his own; every day, he makes me extremely pure. What can I, in the end, say about his taking me as his instrument, about his omnipotence that enables me to sing the Tiruvāymoḻi, and about the exceeding radiance which was the cause for creating this work? Even if I talk of all the truths in time will I be satisfied?

7.9.2

What can I say of him,
  who unites with my sweet life today?
He makes my words, the sweet words I say,
seem as if they were mine,
[but] the wondrous one praises himself
  through his own words.
The Primary one of the three [divine] forms
says my words ahead of me.

Making even me an object [of his grace], saying that the words that I have said by my verses are mine, he took me as an instrument and graciously sang the Tiruvāymoḻi. Likewise, as the soul of Brahmā, Rudra, and other deities, he [causes] creation [and destruction]. What can I say in the end of this quality [of the Lord]?

7.9.3

Entering my tongue first,
he made clear to me that,
yes, he was the primeval one.
Would I forget any day
the father who, through my mouth,
spoke about himself
to the foremost, pure devotees
in fine sweet verse?

Yes, it is he who is the Lord of all; thus he made himself known to me as he is. Ruling my tongue and entering it, he uttered fine verses about himself, sweet to the mouth, enjoyed by "the never-tiring immortals." Will I ever forget this great favor of his?

7.9.4

The wandering Lord [intent] on protecting me
made me, an incomparable sinner, live.
Having seen his good qualities,
will I ever forget my father,
who became me and speaks of himself
in faultless verse?

[The āḻvār] says: He not only takes me as an instrument, saying poems through me, but makes the verses faultless; though I was an incomparable sinner, he takes my soul as his endless servant. Having seen the good qualities of my father who wanders, lavishing favors (naṉmai) on me, would I ever forget him?

7.9.5

When I saw his wealth,
sweet poems, worthy and good,
came about as I said them,
even though there is none comparable to me

in my lowliness.
Making me one with him,
the great one sang about himself, through me,
sweet verses that this earth celebrates.

Seeing his auspicious attributes as they really are, I sang worthy fine poems. No one can compare to my lack of goodness. He made me, who have not even a trace of a [good] quality, be like him and possess [such qualities] as omniscience and being wholly opposed to any filth. Through me he sings sweet poems with which all the worlds will praise him—how can I ever forget him?

7.9.6

Not just singing poems to exalt himself
through the great poets who sing sweet songs,
today he came so joyously, made himself [one] with me,
and through me sings mighty songs about himself.
My Lord of heaven!

Though there are many great poets within [his embrace] singing sweet poems, he does not sing about and exalt himself through them. How can I ever forget the Lord of Heaven, who came today, so happily, entered me, and sang verses which could be contained neither by the Vedas nor within himself?

7.9.7

[Known] as Kuntaṉ, the Lord of heaven
cuts through and destroys my powerful sins.
He became me; and through me
he [sang] of his own glory, as the heavenly one.
Will I ever be satisfied thinking of him,
[God] who composes graceful nectarlike songs?

[The āḻvār] says: In spite of being the master of heaven, he destroys my powerful sins, and so gets the sacred name Kuntaṉ. He makes me pure like himself, and through me composes graceful nectarlike songs, praising himself as the heavenly one. Will I ever be satisfied even if I were to experience (anubhava) him for all time?

7.9.8

Will I ever be satisfied, if I were to
to drink deep the glory of the Lord
who holds the discus in his handsome hand,
along with the earth, the skies,
the waters and all else—
The [Lord] who made me, a worthless one,
one with him, so that he may through me
utter sweet poems and obtain renown?

[The āḻvār] says: Even if I were to use all the words of the innumerable souls who dwell in this planet and all the words of "the never-tiring immortals" as means to experience (anubhava) the quality (guṇa) by which he took me and made me as one with him and sang songs, would I ever be satisfied?

7.9.9

Through me he uttered so many sweet poems,
  praising himself.
He made me [one with] him,
  me who am without forgetfulness.[52]
To celebrate this great aid,
Would I be satisfied if I were to drink deep
  in all times past and times yet to come
The glory of the handsome [Lord],
  sacred and entrancing,
Whose powers befit the occasion?

[The āḻvār] says: I am like non-sentient matter because I am not even the abode of ignorance; yet he made me like himself. Taking me, he and the Divine Mother sang the Tiruvāymoḻi. Even if I were to experience this great aid with all the means that I spoke of earlier [i.e., the words of the inhabitants of this earth and heaven, spoken of in the previous verse] for the past, present, and future ages, would I ever be satiated?

7.9.10

I thought that I would offer my life in return for his help,
but even that was not to be, for it was ever his own.
There is nothing I can do here [on earth]
or there [in heaven] for my father,

who through me sang of himself
in [fine] words and sweet verses.

Thus you took me and graciously sang the Tiruvāymoḻi; for this great aid, I thought I would give my soul as recompense—but even that soul has been owned by you since the earliest times. So there is no recompense possible, neither here nor there. Saying this, he directly experiences (anubhava) the Lord's great aid.

7.9.11

Caṭakōpaṉ from cool Kurukūr
who saw that without Tirumāl
there is no existence, anywhere,
spoke these thousand verses
here, [on earth].
Happiness will ensue
when these verses are recited,
 in any way.

The āḻvār, elated by the feeling that there is no other helper than Śrī's Lord, has uttered the *tiruvāymoḻi,* which speaks of the great act by which [the Lord] made him sing the Tiruvāymoḻi. Regardless of how they are said, [these verses] will bring about happiness.

9.8

Introduction

So he sends messengers, but still does not see the Lord coming and is depressed.

9.8.1

Is there a way for me, the wicked one,
 to get close to the sacred [city of] ships,[53]
[the city] encircled by groves,
 covered with fragrant cool flowers;

[the city] that cuts the sins of those
 who only think of keeping him in their minds?

He asks: "Is there a way (upāya) for me to approach Tirunāvāy (sacred ship), [a place] that banishes the sorrows of those who desire to have a vision of the Lord?

9.8.2

He is the husband of
 the lady of the fiery lotus,
 whose waist is slender as a liana.
He is the bridegroom of
 the young Piṉṉai with sharp piercing eyes.
When can I, his servant,
 get close to the city surrounded by groves,
 sacred city of ships,
Where the tall one dwells?

When can I reach and enter Tirunāvāy where he graciously stands with the Great Lady and with Lady Nappiṉṉai?

9.8.3

When is the day when I may get close to him?
Ceaselessly my mind wonders,
fixed on that single path without distraction.[54]
A flood of tears flows [from my eyes].
Flawless, the sacred Nāraṇaṉ dwells
 in the sacred city of ships.
I do not know on what day
 I may enter the sacred court [of the Lord].

When can I reach Tirunāvāy and be close to it? This is my only thought. Tears flow from my eyes. Still I do not know when I can enter the sacred court of Tirunāvāy where stands the sacred Nāraṇaṉ, the Lord who is opposed to all filth.

9.8.4

I do not know what days are allotted to me.
I long to render ceaseless service

at the sacred city of ships,
  [city] surrounded by groves of large fragrant flowers.
O Bridegroom of young Piṉṉai
whose large eyes pierce like a lance!

I enter this place longing to do unending service for you, who are enjoyed by the incomparably beautiful Lady Nappiṉṉai, but I do not know on what day I can serve you.

9.8.5

He is the bridegroom of the lady of the flower
  and the lady of the earth.
My dear one, the life of the world and the divine ones,
reigns over heaven [but] desires to dwell
in the sacred city of ships.
When can I see him
and drink him in with my eyes and rejoice?

The Lord of Lakṣmī, Bhūmi, and Nīḷā is the controller of all the world, from the divine ones down to every blade of grass. He abides in heaven and [yet] lovingly resides in Tirunāvāy. [The āḻvār] asks: When can I see [the Lord] with my earthly eyes and become intoxicated?

9.8.6

When may my eyes behold you and rejoice—
my king of cowherds who seizes and dwells
  in the sacred city of ships,
  [a city] surrounded by groves
  where bees [hover] over exquisite flowers?
I have become your servant; I am free from grief.

[The āḻvār asks]: O King of cowherds! For my sake, you took Tirunāvāy as your temple and abide there. I have great affection for you and desire nothing else. When can these eyes of mine see you and rejoice?

9.8.7

You took the land from Mahābali, the king,
O you who destroyed the divine ones and demons,[55]
My holy entrancing Lord! My perfect Nāraṇaṉ,

who dwells in the sacred city of ships!
Say: "He is my servant" and show me your grace!

Nārāyaṇa, the Lord with all good qualities is
he who grants the desires of his devotees,
he who is opposed to the enemies of his devotees,
he who has tender mother love (vātsalya) for his devotees,
and he who descended (avatīrṇa) to Tirunāvāy in order
to be accessible to his devotees.
Please show your mercy to me, says [the āḻvār].

9.8.8

You may not show your grace to me—
perhaps you just might
make me, who am your servant,
the focus [of your favor]
and keep me under your golden feet.
My Lord of the sacred city of ships,
give me the wit to keep you
without any confusion
in my heart.

By your grace (kṛpā) you graciously gave me the divine knowledge without a trace of ignorance about your essential nature, form, attributes, and wealth. Now again, by your mercy you may mark me and say "he is my servant," and keep me under your golden feet; or then, perhaps, you may not do so. Just graciously do as you will. So speaks [the āḻvār] to the Lord.

9.8.9

Elusive to the eyes of the divine ones,
he is the first one of the three,
and ruler of the three worlds.
The divine Lord desires and resides
in the sacred city of ships—
O, just who is it who cannot go near him now?

The Lord is inaccessible to the eyes and all other faculties of Brahmā, Rudra, and other gods. His sport is to create, protect, and destroy all the worlds from Brahmā and other gods down to every blade of grass. This

Lord likes to reside in Tirunāvāy, and is extremely accessible. How fortunate are the people who get close to Tirunāvāy! Alas, [says the āḻvār], I am unfortunate!

9.8.10

O my dark sacred Lord! When is the day
when I may come close to you?
So I call, with disturbed mind.
My great Lord, my gem-colored one,
You came to reside in
 the sacred city of ships,
 a city surrounded by groves [aglow]
 with bunches of glorious flowers.

And so, though I desired you and did not obtain you, [I] did not stop there. I contemplate the quality by which you came and stayed in Tirunāvāy, only to unite with me (saṁśleṣa). My mind is confused. Wondering when I can clasp you, I stand here, calling "O holy entrancing Lord!"

9.8.11

Those who master these ten verses
 of a thousand Tamil [poems] set to melody,
 composed by Caṭakōpaṉ from strong-walled Tirukkurukūr,
 about him who resides in the sacred city of ships,
 a city filled with terraced houses of colorful gems,
will rule this world and emit the fragrance of jasmine.

Those who say this *tiruvāymoḻi* will get to enjoy all the pleasures of this world and the next.[56]

10.3[57]

Introduction

Thus being [in a state] when [he] has united with the Lord and enjoyed (parimārutal) him, [he] sees his condition in this material world and wonders if the Lord will abandon him because of his earthly bonds. Because of this excessive fear, he is depressed. He cries out through the songs of the cowherd girls who are depressed; after they have united with and enjoyed making love with the "Handsome Lord of Dvāraka," they [fear] when the time approaches for him to go and graze the cows. They then [panic], saying, "He will leave us, to graze the cows." Even when the young girls of Tiruvāyppāṭi are with the "Handsome Lord of Dvāraka," when the time approaches for him to graze the cows, they assume that he has already gone, and feel all the grief that one feels when one is separated from him. They communicate their grief, and the cruelty of him who is parted from them, to their friends; in a similar mood the āḻvār addresses [the Lord].

10.3.1

My fragrant shoulders, slender as bamboo shoots,
have become weak, alas![58]
Blind to my pining, unheeding of my loneliness,
the koel birds coo, alas!
Peacocks mate and screech, alas!
When you go to graze the cattle,
a day seems like a thousand ages, alas!
With your lotus eyes, you pierce me, alas!
You're unfair,[59] Kaṇṇā, you're unfair!

My shoulders droop because I am separated from you. Not heeding my wasting away and my loneliness, these koel birds say your sacred name. Moreover, these peacocks mate and screech. If [the Lord should] ask, do you feel all this when I am to be away only for one morning, she [the cowherd girl/āḻvār] would reply: When you go to graze the cows, even one morning seems as long as a thousand ages; moreover, your eyes [seem] to pierce me. When I stand here separated from you and [suffering] so much, you must not be separated from us. Can it be that there is no mercy (kṛpā) even in the world that you live in? Even if there is a little mercy in this world, you have none.

10.3.2

You're unfair, Kaṇṇā, you're unfair!
When you make love and embrace my full breasts,
a tidal wave of pleasure, unchecked by our union,
rises to the firmament and soars beyond,

making my wits drown in the flood.
And then it recedes like a dream.
My passion permeates my inner life
and throbs in every cell of my body—
my soul cannot bear this burden.
If I am to be separated from you,
every time you go to graze the cows,
I shall die.

If one should ask, why does [the cowherd girl/āḻvār] feel so [distressed] even while the intense satisfaction brought about by the union still remains? [the cowherd girl] replies: That unsurpassed union has less value than a dream. Because of my extreme love for you, I feel I am ready to die if you are separated from me when you go to graze the cattle.

10.3.3

I shall die if you go to graze the cows,
for my soul is ablaze with the fire of my breath.
I have no companion:
I shall not live to see your dark body move.
When you leave me, the day never ends,
my twin eyes, shaped like kāyal fish,
swim in tears that never end.
Born in this humble state,
cowherd girls in a herder clan,
our loneliness [seems] death.

I shall die if you go to graze the cows. My soul is scorched by the fire of separation. I have no other companion, [for] I live alone expecting a relationship with you; I shall not [live], my companion, to see you come. If you move away even slightly, this morning will not end and my tears will not stop. When [suffering] this unrequited love, it is not bad to die.

10.3.4

Not feeling the loneliness suffered by the lowly ones,
and the grief of one parted from a friend,
Govinda, you seek the company of those cows in the barn,
leaving us [to lead the lives of] ascetic folk![60]
Thinking of your sweet words that flow from your lying lips,
lips as sweet as a ripened fruit,

floods of sweetness, the quintessence of soft nectar,
deluge my mind, sinner that I am, and then burn my soul!

You only hold your cows in great esteem, and go to graze them, not heeding the loneliness of us, your servants, or the great sorrow that we feel when separated from you. When [the Lord] graciously says something comforting, such sweet and passionate words as "Will I who am only supported (dhāraka) by your glances ever be separated from you?" she replies, "It is these words that destroy me as I think of them!"

10.3.5

You were gone the whole day,
grazing cows, Kaṇṇā!
Your humble words burn my soul.
Evening tramples like a rogue [elephant],
and the fragrance of the jasmine buds,
unleashing my desires, blows upon me.
Embrace my beautiful breasts
with the fragrance of the wild jasmine
upon your radiant chest.
Give me the nectar of your mouth,
and adorn my lowly head
with your jewelled lotus hands.

When he asks, "Why do you suffer so when I haven't even gone to graze the cows," she says, "Didn't you go to graze the cows? When you went to graze the cows, the whole morning ended and evening came trampling like a rogue [elephant], spreading the fragrance of jasmines that unleashed my desires.[61] To end the sorrow that I have felt from being separated from you all this long morning, make love to me,[62] make me live by your sacred words, which are like nectar (amṛtakalpamāna) and which give life to the dead (mṛtasanjīvanamāy).[63] Graciously place your beautiful sacred hands on my head so all my desires are ended."

10.3.6

Adorn our lowly heads,
O you with eyes [dark] as the deep cool sea!
There are many who would gladly massage
your splendid feet in the midst [of your work].
Be that as it may. We cannot bear to be women [without you].
My eyes are like twin lakes filled to the brim

and flow with tears that do not stop.
My heart pounds; it will break if you go to graze the cows,
and my life shall melt and burn like wax in hell.[64]

When she says again here, "Graciously keep your beautiful sacred hands on our heads, on us who are your servants, and gaze at us compassionately with your sacred eyes," he replies, "I shall only be gone for one morning to graze the cows and it is for this [short] while that I will be separated from you." She says, "Instead of grazing cows, you will be making love to the girls you desire and will be enjoying them. Can you then ask [us], should you suffer so much? Let that be; since we have been born as [people] who cannot survive without holding on to you, if we are separated from you, we shall not live. These tears will also not stop. Our hearts are feeble. So, we cannot bear it if you go to graze the cattle. Our lives will be scorched by the fire of separation."

10.3.7

My life shall burn like wax in hell.
My bright bracelets and my jewelled belt
hang loose [on my pining frame], slip, and fall.
Tears drop from my eyes
like pearls from two soft flowers;
my breasts lose color; my shoulders droop.
O you, who are the color of a priceless gem!
Your tender feet, soft as a red lotus flower,
will hurt when they trudge to graze the cattle
whose company you delight in and esteem.
What if the demons were to come near you now?

Because of the fire of separation, our lives will burn; because of our astonishing suffering, bangles and jewelled belts will loosen and fall. Because they cannot see you, my shining eyes let loose cascades of tears; my twin breasts lose their glow. More than that: you walk [through thorn bushes so] that your sacred body and your soft feet are hurt, just to delight in your cows and graze them because you hold them so dear. What will come to pass if the demons come near you now?

10.3.8

If the demons [strike] first, what then?
I ask, and my dear life is sunk in [fear].
Don't go behind the cows!

Sweat and lust mingle within me
[in such anxiety that] even our union hurts.
  Don't let go of my hand!
Show your lotus eyes, mouth, and hands,
show your golden robe to those [other] cowherd girls;
charm and captivate those young maidens you hold so dear,
with waists so frail, they seem to snap.
  Dally with them!

She says, "O Lord, I tremble, wondering what will befall if the demons were to come near you there. Don't go behind the cattle! If you go, the attachment (sneha) I have for you, my desire (abhiniveśa) which is part of my affection and which makes me feel that I cannot survive without seeing you, and the union (kalavi) we have now will all hurt. Don't let go of my hand." When he remains silent, she says, "[At least] come with those [girls] who are immersed in your beauty, girls who are so desirable, and stay within my eyesight."

10.3.9

Dally with those good women you hold so dear,
until the restlessness of your heart is removed.
We shall be surprisingly gratified.
We cannot bear our womanly nature,
  Just don't go to graze the cows!
Demons abound; they assume any form they desire;
  they shall accost you with Kaṁsa's incitement.
If you should get caught,
  awful things will come to pass,
Do heed my words, O great Lord!

Wander with those other women who are so attractive until your desires are removed. We shall deem that to be more sweet than the unions we have had. We do not want that feminine nature which cannot bear it if you unite with other women.

Many demons, who are incited by Kaṁsa and who can assume any form they desire will roam [the forests]; if you were to get caught in their hands, awful things would happen. O, heed my words, she says.

10.3.10

Awful things will come to pass, heed my words!
Those demons are strong-armed; incited by Kaṁsa,

they harass even the holy men.[65]
You relish your solitude,
you don't wander with anyone or stay with Balarāma,
so my flesh and my spirit are ablaze [with fear].
Grazing cows seems more important to you than heaven,
O Lord with tender red lips,
  our [Lord] of the herder clan!

The strong demons, including Kaṁsa, disturb even seers. My soul burns because you do not even wander with [Bala]rāma, for in his presence one cannot do mischief. When [the Lord] smilingly asks, "It is only if I were to go that you should feel afraid; what kind of affection is this?" she says, "For you, grazing cows is more important than even the Sacred Land (heaven), Lord of the cowherds! So, you did go, didn't you?"

10.3.11

These ten [verses]
  on the sacred feet, the sacred feet
  of the Lord of the cowherds,
  Lord with the tender red lips
of the thousand said by Caṭakōpaṉ,
  who lives on the banks of the Porunal,
  adorned with shells,
  in the beautiful southern Kurukūr,
were said in the [guise] of the herder girl
  who was distressed at the other herder girls
  being separated from him
  there, [in Vṛndāvana].
[These words] that were said to stop [Krishna]
  from going to graze the cows
[will have the effect] of those said by the girls.

He says, these ten verses of the thousand said on the sacred feet, the sacred feet of our Lord of cowherds, with lips red as fruit, by the good Caṭakōpaṉ from the beautiful Kurukūr, a resident on the banks of the Porunal river decorated by conches, [in the guise of] the woman who could not bear the separation felt by the cowherd girls when the [Lord] went to graze the cows, and tried to prevent him, will make one reach his sacred feet.

10.5

Introduction

This [set of verses] talks about bhaktiyoga.

10.5.1

O you who desire to obtain
Kaṇṇaṉ's feet:
think of his sacred name.
Nāraṇaṉ is the mighty refuge.

Those who want to obtain the sacred feet of our Lord should only say the Tirumantra; they will definitely reach his sacred feet.

10.5.2

Nāraṇa is my Lord;
He is the husband
of the goddess of the Earth.
He is the Cause [of all],
He, who destroyed the elephant.

If you ask, who is the Nārāyaṇa who is obtained by the tirumantra, the āḻvār replies: He is the Lord of all, the cause of this world, the destroyer of the elephant.

10.5.3

He is all the world:
he created it himself,
he bored through it,
he swallowed and spat it out;
he shall reign,
    himself.

The one who controls all the worlds, who creates, protects, [and destroys] is the one who destroyed the elephant.

10.5.4

He who reclines on the deep waters
on the serpent which has a fearful mouth:
He shall reign.
Approach him every day;
place flowers at his feet.

Obtain my Lord's auspicious feet by worshiping them daily with flowers; say the tirumantra at the sacred flower[like] feet of my Lord who lies half asleep upon the ocean of milk, having come there in order to protect the world.

10.5.5

Come near him every day.
Bring flowers
that do not wilt or fade.
Sing his name:
you can even gain release.

By saying the tirumantra, carrying flowers that do not wilt, by bowing daily before his sacred flowerlike feet, one can gain his sacred flowerlike feet. This is definite.

10.5.6

He lives in Vēṅkaṭam—
he, who has the color
of a kāya blossom.
This is Mādhava
whose mouth sucked
the breast of a demon-woman.

"The one who is on the high hill," the one who is Śrī's Lord, is he whose mouth sucked the she-demon's breast. If you say, we can only do service at his sacred feet if he is the object of our eyes and other sense organs, [the āḻvār] replies: He is the Lord, who, to become the object of all human eyes, became extremely accessible by graciously entering into and standing on the sacred hill (tirumalai).

10.5.7

Chant the name Mādhava,
repeat it;
no evil will stick [to you];
suffering will never come near.

Those who are not qualified for bhaktiyoga should say the sacred name Mādhava. Say it with intense excitement; as you say it all the sins (pāpa) which are obstacles to your doing loving service to the Lord will be destroyed.

10.5.8

Suffering will never come near you.
He has the color
of the dark rain cloud.
Those who say his name
will become immortal.

If it is asked: are we beings, imperfect as we are, qualified to say his name? the āḻvār replies: Those few who are capable of saying the sacred name are certainly highly qualified to say it. It is said that for those few who say this sacred name, all their obstacles will vanish and they will obtain service at his sacred feet.

10.5.9

Sins will not rest on them
who worship him with [passionate] desire—
[the Lord] who is beyond the reach of the immortal ones,
[the Lord] who is so accessible to his devotees.

He is beyond the reach of even the divine ones and others who are his devotees, but accessible to his [human] devotees.[66] Consider him to be the only goal; only fold your hands in obeisance and all obstacles [in the path of] loving service will vanish.

10.5.10

Strong sins, which cause darkness
and fearsome enemies will flee;
offer beautiful flowers that grow in pools
  and think of the tall Lord.

Say the tirumantra and take beautiful flowers to his sacred feet; offer them and think of him with love. Thus [the āḻvār] concludes his discussion of bhaktiyoga.

10.5.11

Those servants [of the Lord]
who say these ten verses
of the thousand spoken by Caṭakōpaṉ,
who was crowned by the tall Lord's grace,
shall also receive his grace.

Those who say this *tiruvāymoḻi* shall, like the āḻvār, obtain the Lord's grace.

10.10

Introduction

Thus the āḻvār who is with "the servants whose bliss knows no end," longingly calls [on the Lord] to see the state that he was in while in this material world.

10.10.1

O Sage! O four-faced god! O three-eyed father!
My cruel one, with eyes like the lotus and lips tender as fruit,
[Lord] dark as a gem, my thief!
Dear life of me, a lonely [soul],
You came [and placed your feet]
  on the crown of my head;
and I shall not let you go.
Lord,
  don't tantalize me even more!

"You consider as your sport the creation, protection, and destruction of all the worlds; you showed your ocean of qualities like infinite beauty, tenderness, charm, youthfulness, and immeasurable generosity. Showing such qualities as beauty, you conquered me, made me your servant, and made your qualities my support. [Thus] you filled my heart, and I shall not let you go. You shall not again reveal your qualities and actions as of old in my heart, and yet deceive me and make me forget. You must come in truth and graciously unite with me." Thinking thus, he calls loudly, with such intense desire that the Lord cannot abide in heaven unless he fulfills the āḻvār's desire.

10.10.2

Don't entrance me any more!
I swear,
  by the lady whose hair is fragrant with flowers,
  by her, who is like a garland of blossoms
  by your sacred chest!
I take a sacred oath on you,
You loved me,
  and took me without hesitation, so
  my life was one, not different from yours.
O come, beckon me to you!

Long ago when I desired to see you and felt sorrowful when I could not get to see you, you showed yourself within my heart so that I appeared to be visualizing you with my eyes. You thus alleviated my grief. You should not act like that now. Now, I swear that you should not deceive [me] by hiding yourself; I swear on her who is your unlimited wealth, who is of supreme enjoyment to you, who is esteemed even by you—the divine mother with beautiful sacred locks who dwells on your sacred body. I bind you with an oath. Instead of loathing me, who am so filled with filth, you showed your intense affection to me and graciously mingled with me in such a way that I could be said to be one with you; so it cannot be said to be [wrong] for me to swear by you. It is not enough to say that you will [fulfill my desire] in the future. Come with haste, and beckon me to you.

10.10.3

Now come call me to you, my dark, bewitching gem!
I know of no stake for my soul to lean on,
  other than you.
O First Cause, from whose navel comes the lotus flower!
[Creator] of Brahmā, Śiva, Indra,
  and all others who worship you with ardor!
O Cause of the heavens!

The [āḻvār] says: The nature, accomplishments, behavior, and wealth of Brahmā, Śiva, and other gods are dependent on your favor; therefore, I see no other way (upāya) for me to exist than you. Lord, you must yourself bring me to your sacred feet; graciously show me your divine beauty. divine beauty.

10.10.4

O you who are exquisitely fertile cosmic matter[67]!
O you who mingled inseparably within it!
O glorious flame of the skies![68]
You are Brahmā and Śiva within [this domain],
O sage who created the divine ones and human beings!
How could you abandon me with my burden
and let me stay here?

You are the support of the essential nature, condition and activity of matter (prakṛti), spirit, intellect (mahat), ego (ahaṁkāra), earth and other beings, all animate beings and inanimate things from Brahmā, Rudra, and other divine beings down to blades of grass. If *you* think that I am bearing my entire burden, it is as though you are letting me go.

10.10.5

Just whom can I turn to
if you let me stray outside your hold?
What is mine? Who am I?
Like red-hot iron consuming water
You drank my life to exhaustion[69] and
then became nectar, never-ending for me.

The [Lord] asks, "If I don't carry your burden, can't you carry it yourself?" The [āḻvār] replies, "If you let go of my hand and ignore me, then what can I ever accomplish? And with whom? Is there such a thing as I or mine for me to accomplish something? Just as a red-hot iron drinks up water and quenches its thirst, you became such inexhaustible nectar for me that all the heat vanished that had been built up by [the anguish of] my separation from you. You did all this yourself."

10.10.6

Becoming nectar that never can end for me,
My love, you dwelt in my soul, within my life,

and ate them as if you could not have your fill.
What more can you eat?
You, dark as a kāya flower,
eyes like lotus,
lips, red as fruit,
are the beloved of the lady of the flower,
so fit for you.

He [the āḻvār] says: Just as you became the one who can be enjoyed by the beautiful lady of the flower who is so fit for you, you became one whom I could enjoy. Not only that; Lord, you, with exceeding passion, graciously consumed my body and my life. Now don't let me go.

10.10.7

My love, you became the beloved
of the radiant lady of the lotus flower.
Like a blue mountain that clutches
and lifts up two crescent moons,
my father, you, as a resplendent boar,
raised your tusks, carrying [the Goddess] Earth.
O you who churned the deep blue sea!
I have obtained you,
would I now let you go?

[The āḻvār] says: You ate and enjoyed me, showing me the passion that you display to the divine mother [Śrī] and to mother earth. Now that I have obtained you, will I ever let you go?

10.10.8

I have obtained you.
Would I now let you go,
my unique exalted life?
You are the two kinds of deeds,
you are life, you are its consequence;
you are in the dense thicket
in all the three worlds.
O my first matchless seed [of creation]!
Pervading this dense thicket,
you are hidden, diffused.

[The āḻvār says]: You who are the inner soul of karma which is of the form of good and evil deeds (puṇya pāpa rūpa karmaṅkaḷ), sentient beings which enjoy their fruits and all the worlds, you who are the cause of the worlds and invisible, graciously showed yourself to me as you really are: now will I ever let go of you who are my support?

10.10.9

O unique primordial seed,
cause of the three worlds
  and everything else!
There is none your equal.
You are here, there, on everything;
  in life and matter.
You surround all that is
  vast, deep, and high,
  infinitely.
When shall I reach you,
O first one, O matchless one?

If [the Lord] should ask, you have seen me with the world as my form; what more do you desire, the [āḻvār] would reply: That is not enough for me. Even though you have the world as your form, without my being distracted by that [vision], I must see you as you are in the sacred land (heaven).

10.10.10

O supreme cosmic matter
  that surrounds, spreads wide,
  dives deep, and soars so high!
O supreme transcendent, flaming flower
  that encompasses [creation]!
O incomparable blazing fire of wisdom and bliss
  that pervades [the universe]! [70]
Greater than these was my desire
  that was quenched
  when you filled and embraced me.

Pleading in such fashion that the Lord could not deny him anything, swearing by the Divine Mother and on [the Lord] himself, compelling the Lord, he called in the voice of a devotee and the Lord graciously appeared [in front of him]. Beholding him, [the āḻvār] says: You who pervade the cosmic principles of intellect (mahat) and ego (ahaṁkāra), the primordial matter which is greater than they, the liberated souls which are greater than they, are indeed the soul of the even greater wisdom of your resolve (saṁkalpa jñāna). Greater than all these was my thirst[71]—despite your being the cause of the universe, you engulfed me so that my thirst vanished. My heart's desire was finally fulfilled.

10.10.11

Those who know these ten passionate linked [verses][72]
which conclude the thousand passionate linked [songs]
said by Kurukūr Caṭakōpaṉ
  whose craving ended,
  who attained liberation,
  who called on Ari [Viṣṇu],
[Lord] who destroys desires,
  who encompasses Ayaṉ [Brahmā] and Araṉ [Śiva]
will be born, so high.

Those who say the thousand antāti verses of Kurukūr Caṭakōpaṉ who obtained the Lord and who passionately spoke of the Lord
  as the inner soul of Brahmā, Rudra, and all other souls;
  as one who is opposed to all filth;
  as one who has unsurpassed, countless, auspicious qualities;
  as one who has a transcendent, wondrous, divine form, [as well as] jewels, weapons;
  [who is accompanied by] his consorts and followers,[73]
  as one who banishes all obstacles
and know these ten verses in which [the poet's] desire was fulfilled and his thirst was quenched—
though being born [as mortals], are greater than "the never-tiring immortals."

Notes

Full references to the works cited briefly here will be found in the Bibliography, which follows this section.

The Tiruvāymoḻi is referred to in the notes by the abbreviation TVM. Citations to parts of the poem are given, in both the text and these notes, by numbers alone to the Hundred-decad-verse in question; the abbreviation TVM is added only if confusion might arise in the particular context. Piḷḷāṉ's commentary is likewise cited by the TVM Hundred-decad-verse numbers.

Chapter 1

1. The word *vāymoḻi* also means "Veda," according to the Tamil Lexicon.

2. Nāthamuni calls the TVM a "Drāvida [Tamil] Veda" in a short verse composed in praise of the poem. This verse is recited by Śrīvaiṣṇavas everyday, prior to the ritual chanting of the TVM in daily worship.

3. One of the earliest occurrences of the concept of the Dual Vedānta is around the late eleventh or early twelfth century C.E., in a poem called *Yatirāja Vaibhavam* (*The Glory of the King of Ascetics*), written by one Āndhra Pūrṇa, in honor of his teacher, Rāmānuja. The first verse of this biographical poem describes Yāmuna, Nāthamuni's grandson, bequeathing the two-fold Vedānta to his disciple Śaila Pūrṇa, an uncle and teacher of Rāmānuja. The Sanskrit phrase used for "Dual Vedānta" is *śrutyanta yugma*. *Śrutyanta* is a synonym for "Vedānta;" both terms mean "the end of the Vedas." The word *yugma* means "confluence."

4. Norman Cutler discusses the notion of the Tamil Veda in his *Songs of Experience*, 7–10. Indira Viswanathan Peterson examines this concept in connection with the Tamil Śaiva poetry in chap. 5 of *Poems to Śiva*.

5. See Fitzgerald, "India's Fifth Veda."

6. On this issue, see Smith, "Exorcising the Transcendent," esp. 47–48.

7. *The Splendor*, 98. The *Koil Oḻuku*, a document that was compiled over several centuries and which sometimes tried to fill in the gaps for previous times when entries were not made, gives another version of how the TVM came to be held high in esteem as a Veda. According to this work, Tirumaṅkai āḻvār, one of the twelve āḻvārs, petitioned the Lord at Śrīraṅgam to have the TVM chanted in that temple and to give it equal status as a Veda. The Lord had been pleased with Tirumaṅkai āḻvār and apparently acceded to the request. In commemoration of this, the TVM is chanted once a year, over a period of ten nights starting on the eleventh day after the new moon in the

month of Mārkaḻi (December 15 to January 14). This festival is called the Festival of Chanting (adhyayanotsava) and it is significant that the Sanskrit word *adhyayana* (literally, "learning, study, especially the Vedas"), which is traditionally reserved only for the study and chanting of the Vedas, should be used in this context. *Koil Oḻuku,* trans. Hari Rao, 9–10, 33–35.

8. This set of poems is translated in Part Four.

9. *The Splendor,* 117–19.

10. The poems of the Śaiva saints are also chanted when the festival image of Śiva is taken in procession around Śaiva temples, but here, apparently, reciters of the Sanskrit scripture lead the procession while the chanters of the Tamil hymns follow behind the deity. Indira Peterson reports that this procedure is interpreted in different ways by Śaiva devotees; the Brahmins understand it to show the primacy of the Sanskrit Vedas, but others understand the Tamil recitation coming at the end of the procession as symbolizing the "final" word on the matter. See Peterson, *Poems to Śiva,* chap. 5.

The details concerning the recitation of the Tamil and Sanskrit Vedas in Śrīvaiṣṇava temples are found in *Tiruvallikkēṇi Śrī Pārtacārathi svāmi tēvastāṉa vēta atyāpaka kōṣṭi ciṟappu malar.*

11. The liturgical dimension of the TVM will be discussed in Narayanan, *The Vernacular Veda* (forthcoming).

12. Deśika, *Srimad Rahasyatrayasāram,* 1: 3 and 7.

13. Tiruvaraṅkattu Amutaṉār, a contemporary disciple of Rāmānuja, wrote a work in honor of his teacher in which he states that certain āḻvārs convey the meaning of the Vedas in Tamil. A few of these statements are given here:

> "My Lord Poykai gave in Tamil the meaning of the Vedas (maṟai)."
>
> "My Lord Pāṇ rendered into sweet Tamil the meaning of the four glorious Vedas. . . ."
>
> "Caṭakōpaṉ [Nammāḻvār], in a thousand sweet Tamil verses, gave to the world the Vedas that were beyond comprehension. . . ."
>
> ". . . The Vedas that Māṟaṉ [Nammāḻvār] established. . . ."
>
> (Tiruvaraṅkattu Amutaṉār, Irāmānuca Nūṟṟantāti (Rāmānuja Nūṟṟantāti), vv. 8, 11, 18, and 46.)

A single laudatory verse (usually called a *taṉiaṉ* in Tamil) and traditionally ascribed to Rāmānuja, refers to a short poem by Tirumaṅkai āḻvār as a Veda: "[Tirumaṅkai āḻvār] has taken all the meaning from the beautiful Vedas and without faltering, proclaimed it through the good Tamil work Tiruveḻukūṟṟirukkai, so that the world may live. . . ." In liturgical settings, taṉiaṉs are usually chanted before the recitation of the poem, and in books, printed before the text.

14. The TVM of Nammāḻvār is referred to as the Veda or Upaniṣad more often than any other work. Frequently, the TVM and the Tiruppāvai of Āṇṭāḷ, the only woman āḻvār, are singled out for this distinction and the word *upaniṣad*

is used for them. Deśika summarizes the TVM in a work called *The Gem-Necklace of the Meaning of the Tamil Upaniṣad* (*Dramidopaniṣad Tātparya Ratnāvaḷi*). Periyavāccāṉ Piḷḷai, a thirteenth-century commentator-theologian, calls the Tiruppāvai of Āṇṭāḷ a Tamil Upaniṣad. See Periyavāccāṉ Piḷḷai's commentary on v. 30 in *Tirruppāvai, Mūvayirappaṭi vyakyānam Kūṭiyatu,* 202. Chronologically, the earliest statement which compares the TVM with a Veda comes from Nammāḻvār's disciple Maturakavi āḻvār. Maturakavi refers to Nammāḻvār thus:

> He proclaimed the meaning of the Vedas that are so difficult to understand. . . .
> He sang the inner meaning of the Vedas in such a way that they became firmly established in my mind. . . .

("The Short Knotted String" vv. 8 and 9.)

Other early references to this theme are: (a) The laudatory verses on Nammāḻvār and the TVM attributed to the ācāryas Nāthamuni, Īśvaramuni, and Parāśara Bhaṭṭar; (b) Laudatory verses on Maturakavi āḻvār's "The Short Knotted String," attributed to Nāthamuni; (c) Rāmānuja Nūṟṟantāti, vv. 18, 46, and 54; and (d) Laudatory verse on the Tiruvāciriyam of Nammāḻvār, attributed to Aruḷāḷapperumāḷ Emperumāṉār.

The Splendor describes the TVM as the Sāma Veda, which is considered to be the most important of the four Vedas, and equates the other three works of Nammāḻvār with the other three Vedas, excluding all other hymns from this count. Later ācāryas, including Vedānta Deśika and Maṇavāḷa Māmuṉi, have expounded this theme at some length. Aḻakiyamaṇavāḷaperumāḷ Nāyanār in the thirteenth century and Maṇavāḷa Māmuṉi in the fifteenth century affirm that the four works of Nammāḻvār are the four Vedas and the six works of Tirumaṅkai āḻvār are like the six ancillaries to the Vedas (vedāṅgas). (See *Ācārya Hṛdayam,* sūtra 43; and *Upadeśaratnamālai,* v. 9.) Equating the six works of Tirumaṅkai āḻvār with the six ancillaries of the Vedas (vedāṅgas) is a rather strange claim, perhaps acceptable only in a limited numerical sense. On the reconciliation of these statements in recent scholarly works, see Venkatachari, *Maṇipravāḷa Literature,* 4–25 and Subbu Reddiar, *Religion and Philosophy of the Nālāyiram,* 680–93.

15. For a translation of this set of verses, see Part Four.

16. However, the authorship of these taṉiaṉs, modeled on the earlier laudatory verses in Tamil, is sometimes questioned. For a full discussion on this issue, see Venkatachari, *Maṇipravāḷa Literature,* 9–11. Other than the taṉiaṉs, we have few references to the āḻvārs in works of the early ācāryas, Yāmuna and Rāmānuja. Yāmuna was a grandson of Nāthamuni, the first ācārya, and was also the teacher of Rāmānuja's teacher. Both Yāmuna and Rāmānuja wrote only in Sanskrit. Yāmuna, in his *Jewel of Hymns,* v. 6, pays homage to "the one adorned with vakula flowers," a line that is said to refer to Nammāḻvār. Other than this, there is no formal mention of the āḻvārs in any other of his or Rāmānuja's works. Yet the Śrīvaiṣṇava biographical tradition clearly recounts stories of their involvement with the Tamil works, their efforts to institute the recitation of these hymns in temples and even the various interpretations that they gave for the verses of Nammāḻvār. Furthermore, the Sanskrit hymns of Yāmuna and the

Gadya Traya of Rāmānuja are strongly reminiscent of the sentiment of the āḻvārs. We discuss this topic in chapter 4.

17. One of the earliest Tamil commentaries was Nakkīrar's commentary on Iṛayaṉār's *Akapporuḷ* written about the eighth century C.E. This work was a commentary on the secular love poetry of the classical era. For further details, see Zvelebil, *The Smile of Murugan*, 26; for his list of the main commentaries on the Tamil grammar *Tolkāppiyam*, see 135; for his comments on the commentarial tradition in Tamil in general, 247–63.

18. In the later commentaries on the TVM (the *Twenty-four Thousand* of Periyavāccāṉ Piḷḷai and the *Thirty-six Thousand* of Vaṭakku Tiruvīti Piḷḷai), there are several verses where the special interpretation of Yāmuna is quoted. There are about thirty-five instances in these two commentaries alone where the opinions of Yāmuna are quoted. These verses are cataloged in Narayanan, *The Way and the Goal*, 179. Some of these instances are repeated in *The Splendor*.

19. *Udātta:* "High, elevated; acutely accented"; *anudātta:* "not elevated or raised, accentless" [in chanting]. Meanings taken from Apte's *The Student's Sanskrit-English Dictionary*.

20. *The Splendor*, 122 and 124. The *Koil Oḻuku*, 34, states that Nāthamuni established classes in which the TVM was taught.

21. *The Splendor*, 199–200.

22. The later commentaries are also believed to be as long as certain Sanskrit works. The *Oṉpatināyirappaṭi* (*The Nine Thousand*) was the commentary of Nañjīyar and was rewritten by Nampiḷḷai who is said to have lost the original work of his teacher. This work is said to be numerically equivalent to the *Śrībhāṣya* of Rāmānuja. The *Iṛupatinālāyirappaṭi* (*The Twenty-Four Thousand*, written in the thirteenth century by Periyavāccāṉ Piḷḷai) was said to be as long as the *Rāmāyaṇa* and the *Īṭu-Muppattārayirappaṭi* (*The Thirty-Six Thousand*) written by Vaṭakku Tiruvīti Piḷḷai, a contemporary of Periyavāccāṉ Piḷḷai, to be as long as the *Śrutaprakāśika*, the commentary on Rāmānuja's *Śrībhāṣya*.

23. Piḷḷāṉ, *The Six Thousand*, 10.9.10.

24. Venkatachari, *Maṇipravāla Literature*, 4–5 and 167–71.

25. This of course is a complex issue and we use the terms "Indo-European" and "Dravidian" in a very general sense, recognizing that neither of these are monolithic concepts. Even the earliest Indo-European literature of India is influenced by the autochthonous culture. Recently, Parpola has noted: "The Ṛgveda itself provides evidence of words and even phonological and syntactic features that indubitably spring from a Dravidian substratum and influence upon Indo-Āryan." (Parpola, "The Encounter of Religions," 26–27.) It is noted even in introductory studies on Indian culture that "the Āryans were not uninfluenced by the early inhabitants. . . . One result of this contact of Āryan and non-Āryan is evident even in the earliest stratum of the Ṛg Veda, the language of which is appreciably affected by non-Indo-European influences. . . ." (Basham, *The Wonder That Was India*, 31). In recent years, Clothey has given a brief survey of some earlier positions taken on the Āryan, pre-Āryan and non-Āryan sources of Hinduism. (See Clothey, *The Many Faces of Murukan*, 45 and 212.) In the last few years, scholars have been studying the "synthesis" of Indo-European and indigenous cultures at several levels; Solomon has written on the autochthonous heritage of Vaiṣṇava bhakti (Solomon, "Early Vaiṣṇava Bhakti and Its Autochthonous Heritage") and Zvelebil has traced the early history of devotion (Zvelebil, "The Be-

ginnings of Bhakti in South India"). Parpola has studied the complex encounter between Indian religions before 1000 B.C.E. and two distinct waves of Indo-European immigration—the earlier band known in literature as *vrātyas* and the later band the Āryans of the Ṛg Veda (Parpola, "The Encounter of Religions"). See also Hardy, *Viraha-Bhakti;* and Shekhar, *Sanskrit Drama,* esp. chap. 2, "Confluence of the Āryans and the Non-Āryan Dravidians," 14–32. The coalescence between the Sanskrit and Tamil cultures has been recognized in recent years by Clothey and Yocum in connection with the emergence of the gods Murukaṉ and Śiva as centers of Tamil devotion. Clothey, *The Many Faces of Murukaṉ,* 45–72 sees Murukaṉ as a product of a Tamil-Sanskrit coalescence. Yocum, in his excellent study of Māṇikkavācakar's Tiruvācakam, discusses the figure of Rudra-Śiva in the Vedas, bhakti in early Sanskrit sources, and the classical Tamil poems as the background to understand the Tiruvācakam. Yocum deals with the image of Śiva that Māṇikkavācakar experienced and refers to the Sanskrit myths and local tradition that inform the poet's bhakti (*Hymns to the Dancing Śiva,* 137–66). It is important to note in this connection that both the Tiruvācakam and the figure of Śiva can be seen as products of a two-fold heritage, like the Tiruvāymoḻi and the figure of Viṣṇu. The Śrīvaiṣṇava tradition takes this two-fold heritage seriously and acknowledges the dual sources very self-consciously in the commentarial tradition where the medium (that is, the maṇipravāḷa language) is itself the message. The Tiruvācakam, however, was not subject to written commentaries.

Frits Staal's article, "Sanskrit and Sanskritization," examines the word "Sanskritization," as used by Indologists and anthropologists, and the concept of Sanskritization. Staal also suggests a linguistic model for the process of Sanskritization in that the history of bhakti and the god Viṣṇu can be seen as analogous to the development of semi-*tatsama* and *tadbhāva/deśi* words respectively in the modern Indo-European languages of India. (Staal, "Sanskrit and Sanskritization," 261–75, esp. 272–75.)

26. Garuḍa is portrayed in several myths to be antagonistic to the serpent. See Śaṭhapaṭha Brāhmaṇa 3.1.13–16 and Viṣṇu Purāṇa 5.7. For a complete list of these myths see O'Flaherty, *Hindu Myths,* 332.

27. Piḷḷāṉ, *The Six Thousand,* 1.1.1.

28. Garuḍa is said to be the personification of the Vedas in Hindu mythology. Yāmuna mentions this in *Jewel of Hymns,* v. 41. In the first verse of his *Four Verses* (*Catuḥślokī*), a work written in praise of Viṣṇu's consort Śrī, Yāmuna refers to Garuḍa as the "soul of the Vedas" (vedātmā), repeating an idea found in the later sections of the Vedas themselves. The relevant verse from the Vedas is:

suparṇo 'si garutmān. Tṛvṛte śiraḥ. Gāyatri cakṣu. . . .

This line is identified by the Śrīvaiṣṇavas as Taittirīya Yajus Saṁhita 4.1.42. The Gāyatri, the most sacred verse of the Vedas for all Hindus, is likened to the eyes of Garuḍa and other parts of the Vedas are identified with the rest of Garuḍa's body. Later, in the thirteenth century, Vedānta Deśika wrote *Fifty Verses on Garuḍa* (*Garuḍa Pañcasat*), which actually contains 52 verses, and in v. 3 elaborates on this identification of Garuḍa with the Vedas in some detail. On Purāṇic identification of Garuḍa with the Vedas, see Danielou, *Hindu Polytheism,* 60–161.

29. While the Śrīvaiṣṇavas after Rāmānuja did not comment directly on the Bhagavadgītā or the Brahma Sūtras, they commented on Rāmānuja's commentary of

these works. Sudarśana Sūri wrote a commentary on the *Śrībhāṣya*, which was Rāmānuja's commentary on the Brahma Sūtras, and Vedānta Deśika wrote a commentary on Rāmānuja's commentary on the Bhagavadgītā. These later commentaries only elucidated and elaborated Rāmānuja's commentaries, which were considered to be the authoritative and only correct interpretation of the Sanskrit works. The Bhagavadgītā and the Brahma Sūtras, therefore, have had only one primary commentary. On the other hand, there have been several direct commentaries in maṇipravāḷa on the TVM. Most of the maṇipravāḷa commentaries are directly on the poem, though there are very few that comment on a commentary. The TVM and the Sacred Collect were probably at the center of many direct commentaries, primarily because they were considered to be anubhava grantha or works which could be "experienced" and "enjoyed" directly by the audience.

30. Viṣṇu, for instance, mounts and rides the Garuḍa to help the elephant whose legs are caught in the jaws of a crocodile. See Bhāgavata Purāṇa VIII.2 and VIII.3, esp. VIII.3.32.

31. Zimmer, *Myths and Symbols,* 76.

Chapter 2

1. An example of this occurs just before the E-minor theme in the development section of the first movement of Beethoven's Third Symphony (mm. 248–80). Here, the destruction of the rhythmic organization, the weakening of melodic motion, and the arrival at a harmonic impass create a musical situation bordering on chaos. Meyer, *Music: The Arts and Ideas,* 10–11.

We are indebted to Professor Reid Poole, Professor of Music, University of Florida, for his time and suggestions on the first part of this chapter.

2. Meyer, *Music,* 26.

3. There are twenty-four or twenty-five works that form part of the Sacred Collect.

Author	Work
First Thousand	
1. Periyāḻvār	Tirupallāṇṭu
2. Periyāḻvār	Periyāḻvār Tirumoḻi
3. Āṇṭāḷ	Tiruppāvai
4. Āṇṭāḷ	Nācciyār Tirumoḻi
5. Kulacēkara	Perumāḷ Tirumoḻi
6. Tirumaḻicai āḻvār	Tiruccanta viruttam
7. Toṇṭaraṭipoṭi āḻvār	Tirumālai
8. Toṇṭaraṭipoṭi āḻvār	Tirupaḷḷiyeḻucci
9. Tiruppāṇ āḻvār	Amalanātipirāṉ
10. Maturakavi āḻvār	Kaṇṇinuṇ Ciṟuttāmpu
Second Thousand	
11. Tirumaṅkai āḻvār	Periya Tirumoḻi
12. Tirumaṅkai āḻvār	Tirukkuruntāṇṭakam
13. Tirumaṅkai āḻvār	Tiruneṭuntāṇṭakam

Third Thousand	
14. Poykai āḻvār	Mutal Tiruvantāti
15. Pūtat āḻvār	Iṛaṇṭām Tiruvantāti
16. Pēy āḻvār	Mūṉrām Tiruvantāti
17. Tirumaḻicai āḻvār	Nāṉmukaṉ Tiruvantāti
18. Nammāḻvār	Tiruviruttam
19. Nammāḻvār	Tiruvāciriyam
20. Nammāḻvār	Periya Tiruvantāti
21. Tirumaṅkai āḻvār	Tiruveḻukūṟṟirukkai
22. Tirumaṅkai āḻvār	Ciriya Tirumaṭal
23. Tirumaṅkai āḻvār	Periya Tirumaṭal
Fourth Thousand	
24. Nammāḻvār	Tiruvāymoḻi
25. Tiruvaraṅkattu Amutanār	Rāmānuja Nūṟṟantāti.

We have listed twenty-five works here. The Vaṭakalai Śrīvaiṣṇavas usually count the two works of Periyāḻvār as one and call the Rāmānuja Nūṟṟantāti (twenty-fifth in this list) the last or twenty-fourth work of the corpus. The total number of works is said to be twenty-four, so as to correspond to the number of syllables in the Gayatri Mantra, the sacred line that many Hindus meditate on everyday.

4. Ramanujan, *Hymns for the Drowning*, 132.

5. Ramanujan, *The Interior Landscape*, 115.

6. For legends on Agastya and discussion on the comparatively late occurrence of his name in Tamil literature, see Zvelebil, *Tamil Literature*, 61–65; the Buddhist version is given on p. 62.

7. Zvelebil, *Tamil Literature*, 110; for a complete discussion on the Caṅkam legends and dating, fact and fiction, see 55–61. See Zvelebil, *The Smile of Murugan*, 45–64 for a discussion of works of this period.

8. Zvelebil, *Tamil Literature*, 68–71 and *The Smile of Murugan*, 130–51.

9. Zvelebil, *The Smile of Murugan*, 143.

10. Ibid., 140.

11. For translations of poems from these collections, see Hart, *Poems from the Tamil Anthologies*, and Ramanujan, *The Interior Landscape* and *Poems of Love and War*. On akam and puṛam as interpretive categories for Indian folklore, see Ramanujan, "Two Realms of Kannada Folklore."

12. Zvelebil, *Tamil Literature*, 81–82.

13. Ibid., 108–109.

14. To these five situations of love two more are added: peṛuntiṇai and kaikkilai which have no corresponding landscapes. Peṛuntiṇai indicates mismatched love and kaikkilai, unrequited love. For discussions of the landscapes, see Ramanujan, *The Interior Landscape*, 104–112; Zvelebil, *Tamil Literature*, 98–99 and *The Smile of Murugan*, 85–110.

15. For a complete list of these 102 loanwords, see Zvelebil, *The Smile of Murugan*, 169–71.

16. *Paripāṭal* III.63–68. Translated by Zvelebil in "The Beginnings of Tamil *bhakti*"; quoted by Ramanujan in *Hymns for the Drowning*, 110.

17. Literally "Our Āḻvār." This is an affectionate title given to the poet by the Śrīvaiṣṇava community. According to one of the traditional accounts, the Lord at Śrīraṅgam graciously bestowed this name upon him. *Koil Oḻuku,* 10.

18. The Veḷḷālas are landowners and are sometimes considered to be "high-caste Hindus" (Manickam, *Slavery in the Tamil Country,* 20). However, despite Burton Stein's comment that "their ubiquity and prestige . . . has been a marked feature of agrarian society until the present time" (quoted in Ramanujan, *Hymns for the Drowning,* ix), as far as the Brahmin community was concerned, Nammāḻvār was of the "fourth class," that is, a Śūdra.

19. Nammāḻvār, in 6.10.1, claims that he comes from a clan of devotees who served the Lord. The biographical account in the following pages is summarized from the lives of Nammāḻvār and Maturakavi āḻvār, as narrated in *The Splendor,* 87–101. Other biographical accounts which agree on most of the important points are in the *Divya Sūri Caritam* (circa twelfth century), the *Caramōpāya Nirṇayam* and the *Periya Tirumuṭi Aṭaivu* (fifteenth to sixteenth century). For a discussion on the sources for Nammāḻvār's biography, see Hardy, "The Tamil Veda of a Śūdra Saint." On the importance of biological ancestry to emphasize the importance of a devotee, see Narayanan, *The Way and the Goal,* 74–76.

20. Venkatachari in his foreword to Ayyangar's translation of the TVM gives both interpretations. Ayyangar, *Tiruvāymoḻi English Glossary,* xiv and xv. For a discussion of the eating symbolism, see chapter 12.

21. The equation of Nammāḻvār's works with the Vedas has only numerical significance as we noted in chapter 1. See Venkatachari, *Maṇipravāla Literature,* 42–43.

22. Arunachalam, *Nammāḻvār (varalārum nūlārāyicciyum),* 11.

23. See, for instance, Piḷḷāṉ's introduction to 6–3, translated in Part Four of this book.

24. Arunachalam, *Nammāḻvār,* 15.

25. "Vedam Tamiḻ ceyta Māṟaṉ, Caṭakōpaṉ." Māṟaṉ and Caṭakōpaṉ are other names of Nammāḻvār.

26. Arunachalam, *Nammāḻvār,* 7 and 11–12.

27. The annual Festival of Chanting will be discussed in detail in Narayanan, *The Vernacular Veda: Revelation, Recitation and Ritual,* forthcoming.

28. Piḷḷāṉ uses the word *tiruvāymoḻi* to indicate a set of eleven verses. In this book, we have spelled the word in italics and used a lower case "t" to distinguish this usage of the word from the title of the entire poem.

29. For details on the various meters used by Nammāḻvār, see Damodaran, *The Literary Value of the Tiruvāymoḻi,* 202–34 and 324–44.

30. These rāgas do not date back to more than two hundred years. Many classical singers and dancers do use sections of The Sacred Collect verses. The Tiruppāvai of Āṇṭāḷ is probably most popular with classical musicians and it has also been choreographed by leading Bharata Natyam dancers. Large segments of the Periyāḻvār Tirumoḻi have recently been set to music and performed in dance. Most of these performances are not continuous with the aṟaiyar tradition. In the Śrīvaiṣṇava community, the aṟaiyars sang and enacted certain sections from The Sacred Collect; this art was hereditary and the traditional forms of portraying most of the songs have practically vanished now. These aṟaiyars are male and the art has been confined to a few families. A few songs are regularly enacted at three of the Śrīvaiṣṇava temples, coinciding with the

annual Festival of Chanting. At this time, the entire Sacred Collect is chanted. On each day and night designated verses are remembered with their commentaries and certain verses are enacted by aṛaiyars in a traditional manner. The enactment of the TVM begins with the elucidation of 1.1.1 on Vaikuṇṭha Ekādaśi day (the eleventh day after the new moon); and the following verses are enacted by the aṛaiyars over the next nine days: 2.10.1, 3.3.1, 4.10.1, 5.5.1, 6.10.1, 7.2.1, 8.10.1, 9.10.1, and 10.10.1. Two of these verses (5.5.1 and 7.2.1) are spoken by Nammāḻvār from the viewpoint of a girl. The traditional aṛaiyar cēvai has been adapted by some Bharata Natyam dancers in recent years. In her aṛaiyar cēvai performance of some TVM verses, Mrs. Usha Narayanan portrays emotions based on traditional cues, but wears the garb of a Bharata Natyam dancer.

31. A complete list of the myths alluded to by the āḻvārs and references to the verses in the Sacred Collect are given in Narayanan, *The Way and the Goal,* Appendix 1, 153–69. For use of some Sanskrit Purāṇic stories in the TVM, see Damodaran, *Literary Value of the Tiruvāymoḻi,* chap. 8.

32. See Hardy, *Viraha-Bhakti,* 481–547; 637–52.

33. *The Splendor,* 100–101.

34. For other accounts of akam influences on Nammāḻvār, see Damodaran, *Literary Value of the Tiruvāymoḻi,* 58–127; for puṛam elements, see Cutler and Ramanujan, "From Classicism to Bhakti."

35. Ramanujan, *Hymns for the Drowning,* 8. Cutler and Ramanujan quote several varieties and categories of praise to the king, in "From Classicism to Bhakti."

36. I am quoting only fifteen scattered lines from Hart's translation of the poem in his *Poets of the Tamil Anthologies,* 171–72; two other poems (*Puṛanāṉūru* 123 and 164 on pp. 170 and 175) are also striking examples.

37. *Viṉai* literally means "action, deed, work" or "karma, as the accumulated result of deeds done in former births, of two kinds," e.g., *nal viṉai, tī viṉai.* Nal viṉai is good karma/deeds, and tī viṉai is bad karma/deeds. Sometimes, the āḻvār refers to his "two kinds of viṉai," at other times, simply refers to his "strong viṉai" (valviṉai). Viṉai may also refer to "evil deeds" and so we have translated the word as "sins," "karma," or "deed" depending on the context.

38. Zvelebil, *The Smile of Murugan,* 56.

39. The dating of the *Tirumurukāṟṟuppaṭai* is somewhat problematic. Zvelebil in *The Smile of Murugan* (1973) places it between 700–800 C.E., but, subsequently, in *Tamil Literature* (1975, p. 107) and "The Beginnings of Bhakti in South India" (1977, p. 251) places it between 250–300 C.E. "at the latest." Clothey, in *The Many Faces of Murukaṉ,* 208 n. 14, is inclined to place "the major portion of the *Tirumurukāṟṟuppaṭai* and the *Paripāṭal* somewhere in the late fourth or fifth century, with some portions of the *Tirumurukāṟṟupaṭai* possibly being even later."

40. Balakrishna Mudaliyar, *The Golden Anthology of Ancient Tamil Literature,* 2: 18.

41. Ibid. 1: 48–49.

42. On the importance of a "local deity" and a god in the immediate vicinity, see Bolle, "Speaking of a Place." Bolle says (p. 129) that ". . . unless one understands the primacy of place, the nature of the sacred in most of Hinduism remains incomprehensible, and the plurality and the variety of gods continues to form an unsolvable puzzle."

43. Mudaliyar, *The Golden Anthology of Ancient Tamil Literature,* 2: 20.

44. The twelve āl̲vārs sang about 108 places, most of them located in South India.

45. For a list of dramatis personae in Caṅkam poetry, see Ramanujan, *Interior Landscape,* 18, 112–13. In the Tiruvāymol̲i, Nammāl̲vār speaks through three characters: the heroine, the heroine's mother, and the heroine's friend.

46. Hart, *Poets of the Tamil Anthologies,* 110 and 118.

47. For a recent discussion on the concept of *aṇaṅku* in classical Tamil literature, see Rajam, "*Aṇaṅku:* A Notion Semantically Reduced to Signify Female Sacred Power."

48. Ramanujan, *Hymns for the Drowning,* 72.

49. Ramanujan, *Interior Landscape,* 27.

50. Hart, *Poems of Ancient Tamil,* 246.

51. Zvelebil, *Tamil Literature,* 109.

52. Ramanujan, *Interior Landscape,* 19.

Chapter 3

1. Our account of Nāthamuni's life is based on *The Splendor,* 114–26.

2. For a discussion on Nāthamuni as reflected in Yāmuna's works see Neevel, *Yāmuna's Vedānta and Pāñcarātra,* 195–202. Neevel also discusses the fragments from Nāthamuni's works quoted by later ācāryas in 77–82.

3. For a systematic discussion on Yāmuna, see Neevel's *Yāmuna's Vedānta and Pāñcarātra.* Narasimhachary's *Contribution of Yāmuna* contains discussions on Yāmuna as well the later commentators' interpretation of Yāmuna's works.

4. Yāmuna never did comment in detail either on the Bhagavadgīta or on the Vedānta (Brahma) Sūtras. According to Śrīvaiṣṇava hagiography, these were considered to be his unfulfilled wishes which Rāmānuja rectified several years after Yāmuna's death. *The Splendor,* 164.

5. For a discussion of the works of Rāmānuja, see Carman, *The Theology of Rāmānuja,* 15–22 and 49–64.

6. Piḷḷān̲ refers to other schools of interpretation in his comments on 1.1.7 and 4.10.5 in but does not engage in debate with them.

7. Rāmānuja refutes the Prābhākara school in his *Vedārtha Saṁgraha,* paras. 116–26. See also Lipner, *The Face of Truth,* 14–18.

8. For an account of the Pūrva Mīmāṁsa, see Clooney, *Retrieving the Pūrva Mīmāṁsa of Jaimini.*

9. Rāmānuja gives Bhāskara's view in his *Vedārtha Saṁgraha,* para. 8 and discusses this philosophy in paras. 54–57. See also Carman, *The Theology of Rāmānuja,* 110–11; and Raghavachar, *Introduction to the Vedārthasaṅgraha of Śrī Rāmānujachārya,* 61–69.

10. For an account of Rāmānuja becoming an ascetic, see Carman, *The Theology of Rāmānuja,* 31–33; and Narayanan, "Renunciation in Saffron and White Robes."

11. For further discussion see Lipner, *The Face of Truth,* 18–24; Raghavachar, *Introduction,* 7–11. Rāmānuja discusses the nature of the Vedas in his *Vedārtha Saṁgraha,* paras. 137–39.

12. Carman, *The Theology of Rāmānuja,* 127–28.

13. The expression *tattvatraya* occurs as the title of a brief treatise by the major Teṅkalai theologian Piḷḷai Lokācārya and as the fifth chapter in the larger work, *Rahasyatrayasāra,* by his younger contemporary, the leading Vaṭakalai theologian

Vedānta Deśika (see Bibliography). Lokācārya begins his treatise by stating that "the soul aspiring for salvation (*moksha*) must acquire the knowledge of the three fundamental principles at the time of attaining salvation" (M. B. Narasimha Iyengar's translation, p. 1). S. M. Srinivasa Chari has recently explained *tattvatraya* as "the three fundamental real entities—matter (*acit*), soul (*cit*) and God (Īśvara)." Rāmānuja frequently used the individual terms, but not the collective expression "three realities," perhaps because he is at such pains to emphasize that matter and finite souls are lesser realities subordinate to God. See, for example, the auspicious verse at the beginning of his *Vedārtha Saṁgraha,* quoted in chap. 11, p. 148.

14. Carman, *The Theology of Rāmānuja,* 129–33.

15. For a discussion of Rāmānuja's understanding of bhaktiyoga see Narayanan, *The Way and the Goal,* 79–87.

16. Carman, *The Theology of Rāmānuja,* 176–79, 190–98, and 257–58.

17. Ibid., 88–97.

18. Ibid., 98–108. The summary here draws on Carman, "Rāmānuja's Conception of Divine Supremacy and Accessibility," 99–100.

19. Rāmānuja, *Śrībhāṣya,* trans. Thibaut, 305.

20. On paratva and saulabhya as interpretive concepts, see Carman, *The Theology of Rāmānuja,* 77–87 and 257–58.

21. For a complete translation of the introduction and further discussion of the two groups of attributes see Carman, *The Theology of Rāmānuja,* 77–81.

22. Rāmānuja defends the Pāñcarātra Āgamas in his *Śrībhāṣya,* 2.2.43.

23. Robert Lester questions the authenticity of the *Gadyas* in "Rāmānuja and Śrī-Vaiṣṇavism: The Concept of Prapatti or Śaraṇāgati." For discussions of the authenticity of the *Gadyas,* see Carman, *The Theology of Rāmānuja,* 298–300 and 306–7; Narayanan, *The Way and the Goal,* 88–93; and Venkatachari, *Maṇipravāḷa Literature,* 96–102.

Chapter 4

1. See Neevel, *Yāmuna's Vedānta and Pañcarātra,* chap. 1 and app. 1.

2. The commentaries on the TVM alone record about fifty-seven different verses where Rāmānuja had a definite opinion or interpretation for the verses. There are other verses where he is mentioned. The verses where Rāmānuja is either mentioned or quoted in the four most authoritative commentaries are:

1.1.1	2.9.8	4.4.10	5.10.6	8.7.3	10.2.1
1.2*	2.10*	4.5.7	6.1.10	8.9.3	10.4*
1.2.9	2.10.4	4.7.5	6.7.1	9.4.3	10.6.1
1.3*	3.2.1	4.8.2	7.2.10	9.5*	10.7.1
1.4.3	3.3.6	4.10*	7.9.1	9.5.10	10.8.3
2.1.7	3.4.10	5.1.9	7.9.3	9.6.9	
2.3.1	3.6.6	5.2*	7.10.5	9.7.5	
2.3.3	3.6.8	5.2.6	7.10.11	9.8.1	
2.5.1	3.7*	5.3.6	8.4.5	9.9*	
2.7.5	4.3.5	5.10*		9.9.8	

* = introduction

3. Rāmānuja Nuṟṟantāti, v. 1.

4. Kūrattāḻvāṉ, *Sundarabāhu Stava*, v. 12; *Varadarāja Stava*, v. 102.

5. These are *Śaraṇāgati Gadya* (*Hymn of Surrender*), the *Śrī Raṅga Gadya* and *Vaikuṇṭha Gadya*. For a discussion of these Gadyas, see Venkatachari, *Maṇipravāḷa Literature*, 99–102; Carman, *The Theology of Rāmānuja*, 230–37, Narayanan, *The Way and the Goal*, 88–93.

6. The five stotras of Kūrattāḻvāṉ are *Vaikuṇtha Stava, Atimānuṣa Stava, Sundarabāhu Stava, Varadarāja Stava,* and *Śrī Stava*. For a discussion of Kūrattāḻvāṉ's works, see Narasimhachary, "The Pañcastava of Kureśvara," 57–79, and Narayanan, *The Way and the Goal*, 95–112.

7. *Śrīraṅgarāja Stava*, Pts. 1 and 2; and *Śrīguṇaratnakośa*.

8. However, it must be noted that the ācāryas never do address the Lord directly as a beloved. The eroticism is seen occasionally in a veiled manner in the physical descriptions of the Lord or in the rendering of āḻvār phraseology into Sanskrit, but we do not find verses in which the poet identifies himself as a girl pining for "her" beloved.

9. According to traditional commentaries (*The Nine Thousand, The Twenty-four Thousand*, and *The Thirty-six Thousand*) on 1.3.1, the incident of Krishna's stealing butter and being tied to a mortar is seen to be the best example that the āḻvār can give to illustrate the Lord's saulabhya or accessibility. While commenting on the following verse (1.3.2), the author of *The Thirty-six Thousand* says that after Nammāḻvār sang about this incident, he was in a trance for six months, overwhelmed at the thought of the Lord allowing himself to be bound by a silly string to a mortar.

10. These verses, in the format of a conversation, end with the refrain *cāḻal* which has no particular meaning in Tamil. Māṇikkavācakar, an important Tamil Śaivaite saint, also composed cāḻal poems. Glenn Yocum describes them as "consisting of a two-line challenge and a two-line response as the question and answer *cāḻal* game for girls; each verse ends with the exclamation *cāḻalō*" (*Hymns to the Dancing Śiva*, 214).

11. The Sanskrit phrase *rasotsava* has been translated here as "the festival of the dance." The exact words come in the verse preceding the one quoted in the text of the chapter.

12. *Sundarabāhu Stava*, v. 5. This follows 2.9.1; Tirumaṅkai āḻvār's Periya Tirumoḻi 9.9.4.

13. *Sundarabāhu Stava*, v. 128. This follows Periyāḻvār Tirumoḻi 4.2.7.

14. *Sundarabāhu Stava*, v. 8 after Periyāḻvār Tirumoḻi 4.2.5.

15. *Sundarabāhu Stava*, vv. 6 and 12 after Periyāḻvār Tirumoḻi 4.2.1. The "Anklet river" (Cilampāṟu) flows near Tirumāliruñcōlai. However, the Tamil word *cilampu* which usually means "anklet" is used occasionally to mean "mountain" as is seen in Pēyāḻvār's Mūṉṟām Tiruvantāti 89 and Kūrattāḻvāṉ uses this meaning in *Sundarabāhu Stava*, v. 12.

16. For further references see Narayanan, *The Way and the Goal*, 62–75.

17. Ibid., 178.

18. Viṣṇu Purāṇa, 1.100.117 to 133.

Chapter 5

1. See chap. 11, 148–49.

2. For a full discussion, see Venkatachari, *Maṇipravāla Literature*.

3. In his introduction to 10.4 he says that the following decad concludes the discussion of the easy nature of bhaktiyoga that the poet started to sing about in 1.3.1. This would imply that only the first two decads of the First Hundred deal with tattva and only the last six decads of the Tenth Hundred deal with puruṣārtha. However, in his introduction to the following decad (10.5) Piḷḷāṉ says that the decad talks about bhaktiyoga, and in the introduction to 10.6 he comments that in this decad Nammāḻvār relives (or experiences, anubhava) the grace that the Lord has given him. This is followed up in the introduction to 10.7 with the statement that the āḻvār speaks out of unsurpassed love (prīti), and in the introduction to 10.8 Piḷḷāṉ says that the Lord is dwelling in the āḻvār and asks, "What is the reason for the Lord showing his grace now?" Only in his introduction to 10.9 does Piḷḷāṉ say that here the āḻvār speaks "in a different statement about his ascension to heaven."

4. See discussion of 1.1.7 in chap. 6.

5. Piḷḷāṉ's list in 8.2.7 is as follows:

Māl		the one who loves his devotees (āśritavatsalaṉ)
Ari	[Hari]	the one who destroys the pain of his devotees (āśritārtiharaṉ)
Kēcavaṉ	[Keśava]	the one whose nature is to destroy those who oppose his devotees (āśritavirodhinirasana svabhāvaṉ)
Nāraṇaṉ	[Nārāyaṇa]	omnipotent (sarvaśakti)
Cī	[Śrī]	a treasury of auspicious attributes (samastakalyāṇaguṇa nidhi)
Mātavaṉ	[Mādhava]	husband of Laksmi (śriyaḥpati)
Kōvintaṉ	[Govinda]	supremely condescending (paramaśīlavāṉ)
Vaikuṇṭaṉ	[Vaikuṇṭha]	the one whose home is Vaikuṇṭha (vaikuṇṭha nilayaṉ)

Chapter 6

1. 3.5.10. Cf. also 4.5.1 cited in chap. 5, pp. 63–64, and 3.10.10 included in chap. 11, p. 149. Another striking example is 8.1.1.

Lakṣmī (Tirumakaḷ) and Bhūmi are your consorts (devī);
  other immortals serve you.
You dwell in the three worlds and rule them.
Whatever form is desired, that is your form.
I am a sinner, O you with lotus eye and coral lips,
  gem who captivates me.
My life! My master! My father who churned the
  ocean with water!
Graciously will that I may see you.

Please graciously will that I may see you, who are Lord of Lakṣmī, Bhūmi, and Nīḷā;

whose feet are attended by [the serpent] Śeṣa, Viśvaksena, Garuḍa, and various other "infinite followers";

whose līlā is the creation, sustenance, and destruction of all the worlds;
who with the object of protecting [your] devotees has an image-form that is desired by them;
who has beautiful eyes like lotus petals that fascinate all human eyes;
whose lips are like coral;
whose divine form is like a blue gem;
who is my support and my enjoyment;
whose nature is solely to fulfill the wishes of the people who bow before him.

(8.1.1)

2. The twelve names of God are: Kēcavan̲, Nārāyaṇan̲, Mātavan̲, Kōvintan̲, Viṭṭu, Matucūtanan̲, Tirivikiraman̲, Vāman̲an̲, Cirītaran̲, Irutikēcan̲, Tāmōtaran̲, Paṛpanāpan̲.

3. "Extremely pure soul" is a translation of *pariśuddhātmā,* which in modern times has been used by Protestant Christians as one translation of "Holy Spirit." It is clear that for Piḷḷān̲ the actual goal of yogic practice, whether the metaphysical assumptions are those of Sāṁkhya-Yoga, Jainism, or Śankara's Advaita, is the "extremely pure" *finite* soul detached from its material nature. Were the Brahmin pandits, many of them Vaiṣṇavas, assisting the Bible translators, having a little joke at the Protestant missionaries' expense, or was the concept of Holy Spirit given a more yogic or advaitin flavor than the missionaries realized? The Roman Catholics did not adopt this translation but simply transliterated the Latin *Spiritus Sanctus.* An alternative explanation of the Protestant translation reflects better on the pandits but rather poorly on the missionaries: they might have translated "holy" and "spirit" separately without bothering to check whether in combination these terms would have the appropriate meaning. I have discussed the use of Indian terms meaning "pure" and "auspicious" as alternative translations for "holy" in Carman, "Conclusion: Axes of Sacred Value in Hindu Society," 117–18.

4. The entire decad of 5.2 is included in Part Four.

5. 8.1.1. Periyāl̲vār mentions Rukmini, the bride of Krishna after he became king of Dvaraka, and in present day Śrīvaiṣṇava oral tradition, Rukmini is identified with Śrī. Nammāl̲vār also mentions Rukmini in 7.10.6. When the goddesses are mentioned together, Nappin̲n̲ai, the wife of the adolescent cowherd Krishna, is placed third after Śrī and Bhū, and sometimes only Śrī and Bhū are mentioned. Nammāl̲vār, however, refers frequently to the story of Nappin̲n̲ai and the seven bulls. Nammāl̲vār does not use the name Nīḷā, which is Piḷḷān̲'s standard gloss for Nappin̲n̲ai and is the name of the third consort recognized by Śrīvaiṣṇavas of Viṣṇu Nārāyaṇa. Piḷḷān̲ sometimes uses the Sanskrit Śrī as the equivalent of Nammāl̲vār's Tamil and Tirumakaḷ, but more frequently refers to the primary consort as Periya Pirāṭṭi. (See Hudson, "Pin̲n̲ai, Krishna's Cowherd Wife," 238–61; Edholm and Suneson, "The Seven Bulls and Kṛṣṇa's Marriage to Nīḷā/NappiNNai," 29–53.)

6. Translated by Ramanujan, *Hymns for the Drowning,* 3 (see also 122–26).

7. Ayyangar thinks that *Ulūkya* means *Cārvāka* (Tiruvāymol̲i English Glossary, 1: 411). Monier-Williams thinks he is a preacher of the Vaiśeṣikas.

8. The full translation of the verse and commentary of 1.3.5 is as follows:

The Lord has no beginning, no end.
He who has countless good [qualities]
explained the real way
to resolve the strife between the six systems.
Stand in the worshipful path of *tapas*
and remove the weeds of the path outside.
Know his teaching, know [him];
cut through and dry up
your sticky attachment [to the world].

If it is asked, How can we establish the reality when there are so many divergent views? [the āḻvār replies]: He who naturally possesses omniscience, and all other auspicious attributes has himself graciously set forth in Śrī Gītā the real meaning of the Way of the Vedas: that he is the person discussed in all the Vedas and their subordinate parts [aṅga] and that since the other camayas are opposed to the transhuman and faultless Veda, they cannot be valid sources of authority. He [revealed] then to the people six camayas that are averse to him and to those followers of the Vedas who are favorable to him in such a manner that the controversy between them is resolved. The Lord has this great quality of making manifest the real meaning of the Vedas; stand steadfast in bhaktiyoga on his side. Remove the weeds that are worldly objects; discard any association with them. If it is asked, How do we leave them? [the āḻvār] says: Through the Gītā that he graciously revealed, be conscious of him whose soul [ātmā] has all the auspicious attributes and discard the association with everything that is distinct from him.

(1.3.5)

9. Piḷḷāṉ seems to be closely following Rāmānuja's comment in *Śrībhāṣya* 2.2.30.

Chapter 7

1. Devotion (bhakti) towards [the Lord] and detachment towards [worldly] objects will not be born unless one can perceive the Lord with one's eyes and other sense organs. Some dispirited people say, "The Lord spoken of in the song 'Inside the mind . . .' [1.1.2] is described as one who 'is not within the scope of the outer sense organs or the mind that has been made extremely pure by the practice of yoga.' One cannot approach such a person; would it be fitting to draw oneself near to him?" The āḻvār answers them thus: The Lord is accessible to those who wish to see him. He is very elusive [lit., "rare," ariyaṉ] for his adversaries. He is invisible to some and accessible to his devotees; this is his wonder. Thinking thus [the āḻvār] begins to talk about the Lord's accessibility to his devotees: the Lord stealing the freshly churned butter, being caught and tied by his chest to the mortar, huddling close to the stone and gazing out wistfully. Contemplating this accessibility and being greatly moved by [lit., "involved with"] this great attribute of being accessible to his devotees, the āḻvār asks: If you want to show that you are dependent on those dependent on you, is it not

enough to be born and thus be equal? Should you also start trembling, bound to a mortar? O my Lord, what are you doing? Why are you doing this?

(1.3.1)

2. The āḻvār starts to talk about the Lord who thus descends (as avatāra) to the earth and becomes accessible. To gratify his sense of being accessible he becomes bound to the mortar and trembles. Contemplating this unsurpassed accessibility, the āḻvār who is not normally agitated becomes physically agitated for a long time and then graciously talks about the celebrated accessibility. In becoming accessible, the Lord does not see [regard] the superiority or inferiority of birth; he becomes equal in class to his devotee, takes innumerable births, and becomes accessible. When he is born, he does not discard his eternal auspicious qualities, his complete joy, his very real form and ability to grant liberation, his being the Lord of all and all his attributes; he brings them all and is born. Thus being both, with friendship to the devotee he gives his soul and becomes accessible.

(1.3.2)

Nārāyaṇa, the goal of the entire unsurpassed, meritorious path, higher than all the other human goals, who has dominion over the creation, preservation, and destruction of the perfect worlds, who is the soul of the perfect Brahmā, Rudra, and other divine beings and also of conscious and non-conscious beings, who is indifferent to all wealth, was born as an equal and became accessible: can anyone grasp this wondrous quality?

(1.3.3)

3. Since Piḷḷāṉ does refer to these omitted features of the two verses in his comments on many other verses, the omissions here are not because of disagreement with the poet. It may be that he considers the words he does not paraphrase to have so obvious a meaning as to require no comment. It is more likely, however, that the subjects omitted do not fit in with what he regards as the major theme of the decad.

4. For the sake of human beings,
he was born in this earth
  and suffered as never before.
He went after the demons
  who tormented [this] world
  and destroyed them.
He protected this earth
  and made it live.
Hearing of this,
  can a person born in this earth
  be a servant of anyone
  but Nāraṇa?

Is it a virtue that he made his feet the support, sustenance, and enjoyment of all the beings who lived in the sacred city when he descended? Look at his great quality by which he graciously destroyed the enemies of men, because he could not bear [to see] mankind suffer. He was beseeched by the devas who wanted Rāvaṇa to be destroyed and so he graciously descended to this world of human beings, which is so unlike his [Divine] nature, as one equal (lit., "of the same genus," sajāti) to them. If [even] a single man was distressed, he, too, was extremely distressed. On the pretext of fulfilling his father's word, he searched out and killed all the demons who were dependent on Rāvaṇa. [When Brahmā prayed for him to return,] he did not immediately set out [for heaven] but went back to the city, which because of its separation from him was preparing for death, and gave life to all animate beings and inanimate things. He then went to heaven with them. If a person with any perceptivity hears of this great quality, can he be a servant of anyone but Nārāyaṇa, the son of Daśaratha.

(7.5.2)

5. *Śrībhāṣya* 2.2.3, p. 250; Thibaut, *The Vedānta Sūtras,* 488–89; cf. Carman, *The Theology of Rāmānuja,* 189.

6. In 10.2.8 Piḷḷāṉ uses a phrase of Rāmānuja's to express the Lord's beauty: "a treasury of such auspicious qualities as beauty, tenderness, and youthfulness (saundarya lāvaṇya yauvana kalyāṇa guṇa nidhi)."

Chapter 8

1. Cf. chap. 7, p. 94.

2. *Gītābhāṣya* 7.16–17, 28–29; 8.3, 8, 13–15, 21–22. See van Buitenen, *Rāmānuja on the Bhagavadgītā,* 24 (including nn. 62 and 63) and 30–32.

3. See Śrīnivāsadāsa, *Yatīndramatadīpikā,* chap. 8, para. 16, pp. 112–13; Srinivasachari, *The Philosophy of Viśiṣṭādvaita,* 347–49; Sampatkumaran, *The Gītābhāshya of Rāmānuja,* xx, and 241n., 407.

4. See translation of 10.3 in Part Four.

5. This is the major theme of his entire book. Viraha in Nammālvar's poetry is discussed in Hardy, *Viraha-Bhakti,* 331–71. See chap. 2, pp. 27–31. Nammāḻvār is following a convention of classical Tamil love poetry, which is also followed by some of the other āḻvārs. There are one or two other decads in which Nammāḻvār identifies himself with one of the gopīs, a poetic device that, while similar in its intent, takes a different literary model and implies participating in a relationship with Krishna that is collective as well as individual.

6. She [the āḻvār] decides: Though I have been separated (viśleṣa) from him for a long time and have sent him messengers, the Lord does not come; contemplating my inferiority, he abandons me; because of his exceeding love (premātiśaya) for [other girls] he cannot survive if he is separated from them.

And so, she is depressed and filled with the anger that is felt by lovers. Because of this anger, she, with her friends, parrots, mynas, and playthings decides: "Now, even if he does come, we shall not see him" and is determined that even if [the Lord] himself comes, he cannot come close to her.

The Lord is also depressed because of the intense grief of being parted from her; he comes and though her friends do not change their minds, he approaches them, wanting them as mediators. Then he falls at her feet and [requests] that she forgive his fault (aparādha) and unite (saṁṣleṣa) [with him]. Since the parrots and mynas that are her playthings have been raised chanting his name and they are also of determined mind, he goes to them, lifts them, cajoles them to chant his name [and tries] to get some comfort. Because the lady [the āḻvār] is of determined mind, he cannot get close to her, unite with her, and live; and so without having a support for his soul, in order to gain love (lit., "to support his soul"), he lifts up her playthings, like her ball and anklets, looks at and touches them and is comforted. She glances at him from the corner of her eye and says [the following verses].

(6.2 intro.)

7. Thus he brilliantly contemplates the Lord and mentally perceives him, but when he seeks physical union and does not obtain it, he is depressed, like a lady who mingles with the Lord and is separated. He speaks his sorrow through her songs. This lady, at the time when she is separated from the Lord, hears some cuckoo birds chirp, and thinks alone: "The Lord wants to finish me off," she decides. Since he cannot do so except through separation; and separation cannot be arrived at without union with the object of separation, he unites, and then separates [from her]. He then thinks, "She is not finished even by this separation" and so he sends the cuckoos, telling them, "Talk about my guṇas in her proximity; this is even more cruel than separation; you can thus finish her off." So she thinks.

(9.5 intro.)

8. The girl is griefstricken at being separated from the Lord. Because of the overwhelming nature of that grief and her inability to bear the heartbreak (lit., "soul-tearing," ātma-dāraṇa) to console herself she resolves, like the sacred cowherd girls (gopīs) to "imitate the divine actions and works like the creation of the world by beautiful Dvāraka's Lord." She concentrates on this. Looking at her, her mother says to those who have come to enquire about her daughter, "The verses she says are astonishing. Examining her unworldly action I cannot diagnose her state as some specific malady ('such and such') other than wonder whether the Lord has possessed her."

(5.6 Intro.)

9. This set (9.8) has been included in Part Four.

10. See translation of 9.8 in Part Four.

11. The little insects that live on the jasmine flowers [adorning] her hair are her friends. She addresses them thus: "If you want to eat honey from flowers you should see the Lord who showed me a magical disappearing act (indrajālam) which he calls 'union' (saṁśleṣa). Abandoning me, he sits in Heaven (Tirunāṭu) under a great canopy of gems (tirumāmaṇimaṇṭapam) in a divine court filled with 'never-tiring immortals' and others who are his servants because of his attributes even as Lakṣmaṇa said, 'I am his servant because of his qualities.' See him; drink from the flood of honey that is contained by the sacred basil leaves in

his hair. Ask him: A girl pines for you, she calls your name. Do you display your mercy by not thinking of her?"

(6.8.4)

12. Her mother says: At the appointed time when she can see the Lord and unite with him, she does not gain the union. Her eyes are filled with tears; she cries "O Lord, O Lord." Now the grief that this tender [girl] feels is by her separation intense; she is extremely distressed; and is listless. I cannot see her walking and entering Tirukkōlur where the Lord reclines.

(6.7.7)

13. Not having the patience to remember the qualities of the Supreme Lord, whom she has experienced, her mind is in a turmoil through the night; she is extremely depressed. As soon as the day breaks, she becomes conscious; she remembers the beauty of the Lord's city; this is the Lord with good qualities whom she had earlier seen and experienced. She also remembers his countless innumerable auspicious attributes such as beauty, fragrance, softness, tenderness, youth, etc., his divine jewels, and divine weapons. The girl is distressed by the love that is born from this remembrance and the love that is connected to not having a union and wanting it. . . .

(5.5 intro.)

This introduction continues but the latter part is not relevant to our discussion.

14. Cf. chap. 5, pp. 68–69.

15. "The Hill and Grove of the Holy lord," I said,
and the Holy lord entered and filled my heart.
This is the Lord who dwells
in the southern City of Names,
where the river Kāvēri glides along
swelling with lustrous gems of brilliant hue.

I just said the words, "The Grove and Hill of my Lord Viṣṇu" (Tirumāliruñcōlai). There is no further reason (hetu) on my part [to have obtained the Lord's grace]. Thinking that I said these words in truth and using this as the reason, the Lord who usually lives in the City of Names (Tiruppēr), which lies south of the Kāvēri, the river that washes huge gems ashore, came together with the Supreme Mother, filled my heart fully, and mingled with me! O, how great is one's love!

(10.8.1)

16. Hardy, *Viraha-Bhakti,* 14–17, 46, 480.

17. Ibid., 308–71.

18. *Gītābhāṣya,* 9.29.

19. Cf. Carman, *The Theology of Rāmānuja,* chap. 15, "The Inner Mystery of God's Love," 187–198.

20. In the first song [verse], [the āḻvār] says that connection with [the Lord's] feet is better than release of any kind. He then says, "I do not have any desire for blessed Vaikuṇṭha, which is the highest goal."

(2.9.1)

Chapter 9

1. Van Buitenen, *Rāmānuja on the Bhagavadgītā* 2d ed., 9–12.

2.

Dāmodara,
His feet are the support
    [for those who walk]
    on the path of meditation (*tavaneṛi*).
He, whose color is that of a stormy cloud,
    who has eyes like a lotus flower.
    who holds the discus,
became water, sky, fire, and time.
Renowned celestials
    babble about his fame.

Despite being perfect because of his beauty, lordly power and divine wealth (or heavenly realms) with the intent of becoming accessible to [his] devotees he descended and became their equal. We can grasp this Lord's sacred feet by bhaktiyoga. There is no doubt about that.

(10.4.1)

3.

There is nothing else—
    we have said it briefly.
There is no fear
    for any life on this great earth.
Look! The thought will come by itself,
    and there is no blemish in this.
The cowherd who gave birth to us
    was born in Northern Mathura.
Learn about his faultless qualities,
and see days of prosperity.
    This is virtue.

There is no condition applying to qualification, time, or place for this. Do not grieve, thinking, "This upāya is difficult." A certain amount of remembrance will happen. If you ask, Will this not be fruitless? he says: If you do this, it will not fail. Therefore think of the qualities of the cowherd grazing cattle who was born for the sake of the devotees of Northern Madurai (Mathura), being opposed to filth and having auspicious qualities. Since this happens by itself, it will be enjoyable and esteemed.

(9.1.7)

Only a generation later, in the *Nine Thousand,* Naññīyar can no longer interpret this verse as referring to bhaktiyoga. For him the verse describes "the ease and sweetness of taking refuge in the Lord."

4. This is a condensed version of the commentary on 1.6.1. The verse is as follows:

> Singing about the Lord who knows no grief,
> O you who desire to grow,*
> Ceaselessly sprinkle pure water
> And offer incense and flowers [to the Lord].

[*The Tamil word translated "grow" is *virivatu* which literally means to expand, to bloom or blossom.]

5. I am neither here nor there. Having fallen
into the desire of seeing you, I am nowhere.
O Lord who killed Laṅka, O Lord with discus
and conch dwelling in Cirīvaramaṅkala,
show me your grace!

I have not obtained your sacred flower[like] feet; I do not have the upāya to deserve it. In my eagerness to see you I do not have the patience now to observe any upāya. In spite of that, just as you the other day banished all obstacles and [rescued] Mother (Sītā) from Rāvaṇa's garden (Aśokavana), you should now, without having any reason, banish the obstacles [hindering] your servant and show your grace to me, who am alone.

(5.7.2)

> Is it fitting for *me* to cry out to obtain [you]?
> You stand amidst your wretched enemies;
> as a cowherd you stand; you act with deceit, my dark-hued Lord!
> You [also] live in the city of Cirīvaramaṅkalam
> where the divine ones of the earth
> perform rituals and adore you.
> Even I saw that!

It is only while you are in the midst of your enemies that you should not manifest yourself! Should you be difficult to grasp [attain?] even by those who desire you? You should still fulfil my desire. If you ask, "Can you do the upāya in order to obtain your desire?" [the āḻvār] replies [says]: "I cannot do any upāya that is good enough to come near your feet." [The Lord says,] "What more can I do? I have entered Cirīvaramaṅkala so that all those who have me as their sole enjoyment can see me with their eyes and "experience me." The āḻvār replies, "Even I saw that—but that is not enough!"

(5.7.5)

6. Here is the verse, followed by the complete paraphrase:

> Approach the Entrancing Lord,
> worship him and arise!
> Your [sinful] deeds will be destroyed.
> Night and day,
> place lotus flowers at his feet.
> He, who [reclines] on the banyan leaf
> in the floods [of dissolution]
> [also] dwells in the sacred city of Kaṇṇaṉ,
> where the waves crash against the tall walls
> that surround the city.

The Lord who is the refuge of all and graciously stands in Tirukaṇṇapuram. Grasp the Lord as the protector, place a lotus flower at his feet, and worship him in such a way that your [sinful] deeds will be destroyed. For this there is no injunction concerning the [appropriate] time, he says.

(9.10.1)

7. For all those who reach his feet, the refuge,
he is the Lord who gives heaven when they die.
He, who rules the earth from Tirukaṇṇapuram,
surrounded by mighty forts,
Is all love for his beloved ones.

(9.10.5)

8. And so, though [the āḻvār] calls the Lord so loudly that it could be heard in heaven, he does not obtain a vision of the Lord. He thinks: The only way (upāya) to see him is to seek refuge at his sacred feet; there is no other way. Speaking of the Lord's qualities such as compassion (kāruṇya) and motherly love (vātsalya) as his support, with the Divine Mother as the mediator, he takes refuge at the sacred feet of the Lord of Tiruvēṅkaṭam—the Lord who is the refuge of all the worlds.

(6.10 Intro.)

> O you on whose breast resides the lady of the flower
> who says: "I cannot move away from him even for a second!"
> Unmatched in fame, owner of the three worlds! My Ruler!
> O Lord of the sacred Vēṅkaṭa
>   desired by the peerless immortals and sages!
>   I, your servant, who am without shelter,
> sat at your feet and entered [your safe haven].

You are "an ocean of unbounded compassion." Because of your qualities you are my master. [You dwell] on the Sacred Hill that is desired even by the peerless, perfect eternal beings whose only enjoyment is to serve you and experience your qualities in heaven. Deeming you to be "the refuge of all the worlds and all entities without distinction," I, your servant, who am without refuge, without any other goal, having the Divine Mother as mediator, took refuge at your sacred feet. And now, immediately, with all my obstacles gone, I, your servant, desire at all times to do all possible loving service.

(6.10.10)

9. Through his grace, I placed him in my mind—
He, who is most exalted among conscious [beings],
So that I may be close to him.
Even this [desire] was through his grace.
My mind, life, and body are useless—
I realized this when transcending [all]
He himself became me.

If it is asked, what is the reason (hetu) for the Lord to do this, [the answer is]: with only desire as a reason, he graciously did it. The āḻvār says: Look how much he has done for me. Not content with captivating me by his beauty, lest there be any obstacle to continuing our union, he acted in a manner that I could do nothing about, saying that he is the meaning of that which appears as 'I'. He also graciously gave this soul its ultimate goal: the intuitive knowledge that its sole essence is being a servant at his disposal (śeṣa).

(8.8.3)

10. For a complete translation of the verse and commentary of 9.4.7, see chap. 10, page 130.

11. I just recited the words, "The Grove and Hill of my Lord" (*Tirumāliruñcōlai*). There is no further reason (hetu) on my side. Thinking that I said these words in truth and using this as the reason, the Lord who usually lives in the City of Names (Tiruppēr) that lies north of the Kāvēri river . . . came along with the Supreme Mother, filled my heart fully, and mingled with me. O how great is one's love!

(10.8.1)

Chapter 10

1. Becoming the first one of fixed heaven,
and everything else,
My Lord, greater than all thought,
Gobbled up the earth and sky, all at once.
There is no support other than Kaṇṇaṉ.

[The āḻvār] says: "The Lord of the beautiful Dvāraka" [4.6.10] who gives mokṣa and other goals to all those who are his servants (śeṣas), the one who has auspicious qualities beyond the reach of mind and word, my master, the one who is the protector all souls is the Lord of the world; there is no other Lord. There is no doubt about this.

(2.2.1)

2. *Vīṭu:* literally, "emancipation, freedom, liberation." It also means "heaven, as the final release or liberation." Meanings taken from the *Tamil Lexicon.*

3. Cf. the discussion in chap. 8, pp. 98–99.

4. Even the unthinking clouds, by adorning and filling the sky, applaud the Śrīvaiṣṇavas proceeding heavenwards; the seas danced with their waves. [The āḻvār] says: Thus all the worlds did auspicious deeds.

(10.9.1)

As some [residents of heaven] gave the fruit of their sacrifices, others worshipfully offered fragrance and lamps; some blew trumpets and conches. Women with beautiful eyes, out of the intense love of seeing them, for there is no greater fortune than their arrival, said: "You who are the discus-bearing Lord's own people, rule this sky. This is our auspicious wish that is to be [will be] accomplished.

(10.9.6)

The strong "never-tiring immortals" with unflickering knowledge, thinking that [the Śrīvaiṣṇavas] have arrived because of their good fortune, washed their sacred feet in their own homes. Like a mother overjoyed at the sight of a long absent son, [the Lord's consorts] are filled with love at seeing [the new arrivals]. With the wonder of this love, the Divine Mother, the auspicious Goddess of the Earth, and Nappiṉṉai, who all have auspicious faces as beautiful as the full moon in the rainy season, come with their divine attendants, bringing with them their greatest treasure, which is Śrī Śaṭhakōpa, along with fragrant powder, large lamps, and other auspicious articles with which to honor them.

(10.9.10)

5. See Part Four for a translation of 5.2.
6. Cf. chap. 6, pp. 71–74 and Note 4.
7. *Caramōpaya Nirṇayam,* pp. 527–28.
8. See his introduction to 7.1 discussed in chap. 9, pp. 118–19.
9. Cf. the sentiments expressed in the verses and commentary on 3.2. 3.2.1 is discussed in chap. 2, p. 23.
10. *Vedārtha Saṁgraha,* paras. 142–44; cf. Carman, *The Theology of Rāmānuja,* 152–53.
11. See Part Four for a translation of 10.5.
12. To some extent this resembles Rāmānuja's *second* interpretation of Gītā 18.66, in which the "dharmas" to be abandoned are interpreted as expiatory rites. Arjuna is thus instructed to take refuge in the Lord without trying first to expiate his sins, with the promise that Lord Krishna himself "will remove the sins that prevent Arjuna from undertaking *bhaktiyoga.*" Carman, *The Theology of Rāmānuja,* 215–16.

13. *Nityakiṁkara,* "eternal servant" appears in Yāmuna's *Stotra Ratna,* v. 46, and in Rāmānuja's *Śrī Raṅga Gadya,* and the abstract noun *kaiṁkarya* is a key term in both the *Śrī Raṅga Gadya* and the *Saraṇāgati Gadya.* (*Kiṁkara* in secular usage has suffered the same kind of development as the English word "knave," which has changed in meaning from boy to servant to scoundrel, for *kiṁkara* in recent times is understood to mean "thief"!) Whether for that reason or not, Śrīvaiṣṇava usage has concentrated on the abstract noun *kaiṁkarya,* which we might also translated as "loving service," and which is always understood as the goal of the religious life, rather than the means to that goal. (Note Carman, *The Theology of Rāmānuja,* 221–22.) Piḷḷāṉ does once use *kiṁkara.* In 7.9.1 he says: "[The Lord] takes my soul as his own having the desire to serve (*ātmāntakiṁkaradvena*)."

14. Translated in Part Four.

15. *Vedārtha Saṁgraha,* paras. 121–22. Cf. Carman, *Theology of Rāmānuja,* 148.

16. In the Sanskrit text of *Śrībhāṣya,* 1.1.1, edited by Lacombe (*La doctrine morale et métaphysique de Rāmānuja*), this is in para. 230, p. 129. Cf. Carman, *Theology of Rāmānuja,* 149.

17. M. R. Rajagopala Ayyangar, trans., *Śrīmad Rahasyatrayasāra of Śrī Vedāntadeśika,* 30. Cf. Carman, *The Theology of Rāmānuja,* 150.

18. Cf. 5.8.8, translated in Part Four.

19. Carman, *The Theology of Rāmānuja,* chap. 11, esp. 147–49 and nn. 1–7.

20. Ibid., 127, quoting *Śrībhāṣya,* 2.1.9; Thibaut, *The Vedānta Sūtras,* 424.

21. Ibid., 128 n. 10; *Vedārtha Saṁgraha,* para. 76.

22. Ibid., 128 n. 11; *Gītābhāṣya* 10.20, 13.22, 13.28.

23. Except for his comments on the first two decads, Piḷḷāṉ does not follow Rāmānuja's frequent use of the correlative *śeṣī,* even where the Tamil term could easily be glossed in this way, especially *uṭayavaṉ* ("owner").

24. The Tamil may also be understood to mean, "my having Kaṇṇaṉ."

25.

Who gave your feet as a refuge
for me? I do not have any recompense
for you! Even my soul is yours! . . .

You graciously made it part of my nature [to know] that your sacred flower[like] feet are both the way and the goal. For this great aid I have not done anything in gratitude. If it is asked, "Can you not give your self as a recompense? [the answer is:] "Even my soul is yours. Is there anything that I can do for you, who are perfect in every way?"

(5.7.10)

26.

For my happiness, you placed your feet
on the crown of my head.
For that great aid,
I, in return, caressed [your] shoulders,
and fully gave away my life for a price.
O radiant flame!

[Lord] with a thousand shoulders
  and a thousand heads!
[Lord] with a thousand flower-like eyes—
  perfect companions for each other!
[Lord] with a thousand feet
  and a thousand names!
O great father of mine
  [of me] who am all alone!

Even though all the people who are in the cycle of birth and death have material things as their support, sustenance, and enjoyment, you graciously made your sacred feet my support, sustenance, and enjoyment. Can this great help last? The āḻvār says: "As a recompense for this great aid I have given my soul to you as your servant" and [then he] gives it with his love. He gives his soul as his ultimate act of service and says, "Can I see you who have done this great aid?" If it is asked, is it easy to see him? [the āḻvār] answers: Is it not for the devotees who desire to see him that he has innumerable divine forms and innumerable auspicious qualities? Can you will that even I do not have to spend even a moment without your name? O my Lord!

(8.1.10)

27. Cf. the last verse of Isaac Watts's great hymn, *When I Survey the Wondrous Cross:*

Were the whole realm of Nature mine,
That were an offering far too small;
Love so amazing, so divine
Demands my soul, my life, my all.

Chapter 11

1. The three dying wishes of Yāmuna have been discussed in Carman, *The Theology of Rāmānuja,* 30. See also *The Splendor,* 164–165.
2. See, for instance, Kūrattāḻvāṉ's "Sundarabāhu Stava," v. 1; "Varadarāja Stava," v. 102; "Vaikuṇṭha Stava," vv. 1 and 90; and Parāśara Bhaṭṭar's "Śrīraṅgarāja Stava (first hundred)," vv. 3 and 6.
3. Āndhra Pūrṇa, *Yatirāja Vaibhavam,* vv. 65, 77 and 78.
4. *The Splendor,* 359.
5. This decad is translated in Part Four.
6. *Caramopāya Nirṇayam,* printed with *The Splendor,* 527–28.
7. Āndhra Pūrṇa, *Yatirāja Vaibhavam,* vv. 81–82.
8. Maṉavāḷa Māmuṉi, "Upadeśaratnamālai," v. 41.
9. The commentary is given in full in Part Four.
10. *Vedārtha Saṁgraha,* para. 1; and Lacombe, *Śrībhāṣya,* 1.1.1.
11. *The Six Thousand* 6.10 intro. and 6.10.10.
12. *Vedārtha Saṁgraha,* para. 112. See also Carman, *The Theology of Rāmānuja,* 164–66.
13. From Piḷḷāṉ's introduction to 10.4, it is clear that he considers his discussion

on bhaktiyoga to have begun from 1.3. Piḷḷāṉ's commentary on the first twenty (+ two phala śrutis) verses of the TVM (1.1 and 1.2) deals with the nature of the deity and the last two sets of *The Six Thousand* (10.9 and 10.10) talk about Nammāḻvār's ascent to vaikuṇṭha. However, Piḷḷāṉ is not and, in fact, cannot be too meticulous about his scheme, because Nammāḻvār did not follow the classification that Piḷḷāṉ sees. Thus Piḷḷāṉ's comments on several verses that he has said are concerned with the means to salvation (hita) do in fact discuss tattva, i.e., the nature of God and the Divine-human relationship.

14. Parāśara Bhaṭṭar, *Bhagavadguṇadarpaṇākhyam Śrīviṣṇusahasranāmabhāṣyam,* 16–18, 23–24.

15. Rāmānuja, *Gītābhāṣya,* 18:16 in *Rāmānujagranthamāla,* ed. P. B. Annangaracariyar, 236–37.

16. *Vedārtha Saṁgraha,* para. 143.

17. See Carman, *The Theology of Rāmānuja,* 95–97.

18. Ibid., 96 and 286 n. 18. See Govindacharya, *Life of Rāmānuja,* 135–36.

Chapter 12

1. Hardy, *Viraha-Bhakti,* 466.

2. Ibid., 443.

3. The Viṣṇu Purāṇa (VI, chaps. 3 and 4), Matsya Purāṇa (chap. CLXVII) and the Mahābhārata (The Book of the Forest, 3.186) contain accounts of the annihilation of the worlds. The Mahābhārata and the Matsya Purāṇa accounts are similar and involve the adventures of the sage Mārkaṇḍeya who is roaming on the waters of dissolution. There he sees the Lord in the form of a child, under a banyan tree. The Lord swallows Mārkaṇḍeya, who sees within the Lord's belly, the earth, the oceans, mountains, etc., complete with members of the four castes fulfilling the duties that are incumbent upon them. For a hundred years he explores the entire universe within the belly of the Lord and sees no end to it.

The Viṣṇu Purāṇa's account of doomsday is more abstract and places the annihilation as part of the cycle of creation and destruction. It distinguishes between "incidental," "elemental," and "absolute" destruction. The last of these is the final liberation of the soul (mokṣa). The earlier two destructions occur at the end of each Brahmā day and at the passing of each Brahmā. For a discussion on the exact number of years after which these destructions occur (either 311,040,000,000,000 or 100,000,000,000,000,000 years), see Viṣṇu Purāṇa trans. Wilson, 494.

An abbreviated account of the Mahābhārata version of the doomsday picture is given here. The following passage is from van Buitenen's translation of The Book of the Forest, 3.186, pp. 586–88:

> Mārkaṇḍeya said: At the end of the Eon . . . when little time remains of the last thousand years, all men in general become speakers of untruth. . . .
>
> When the close of the thousand Eons has come and life has been spent, there befalls a drought of many years that drives most of the creatures . . . to their death. . . . Seven scorching suns drink up all the water in the oceans and rivers. The Fire of Annihilation then invades. . . .
>
> Wondrous-looking huge clouds rise up in the sky, . . . some are shaped like grand cities, others like elephant herds, still others black as collyrium, others in

crocodile shapes—clad in garlands of lightning, the clouds rise up. In their terrifying shapes, with their horrible echoing blasts, the clouds cover the entire expanse of the sky. . . .

Then sudden winds whirl around the skies and under their hurricane gusts the clouds are torn to shreds. And the self-existent God, drinks up these winds and lies sleeping on the Lotus of the Beginning. . . .

In this desolate mass of nothing but the ocean, . . . I alone wander about with grave concern. . . . Then one day I see in the flood of the waters a tall, wide banyan tree. I see a child sitting on a spreading branch of that tree, in a cradle made up with divine coverlets. I am greatly amazed: "How can this babe lie here, when all the world has come to an end?"

The lotus-eyed and radiant child says: "I know that you are very tired, friend, and desirous of rest: sit here, Mārkaṇḍeya Bhārgava, for as long as you wish. Enter my body, good hermit, and rest here, sir, I shall make room for you as a favor." When the child says this to me I become tired of my long life and my human estate, Bhārata. On a sudden the child opens its mouth wide, and powerlessly I am translated into it by an act of fate. And when I so suddenly enter the hollow of his mouth, O king, I behold all of earth overspread with kingdoms and cities, the rivers.

I see the ocean, teeming with fish. I see the heavens illumined by sun and moon and blazing with lights that are like sun and fire; I see the earth, king, adorned with forests. The brahmins are giving worship.

Having entered into his belly, and roaming all the quarters, I see all the hosts of Gods. . . . Whatever creature, either moving or standing, which I had seen before in the world I see again in the belly of the Large Spirit. Living off fruits I explore this entire universe inside his body for more than a hundred years, and nowhere do I see an end to his body, however far I roam while I am thinking, lord of the people.

Suddenly a wind gust expels me from the wide open mouth of the Large Spirit, he sits on the branch of that same banyan tree, holding the entire universe, where I see him of boundless luster, marked with the Śrīvatsa, while he sits in the guise of a child. With the beginning of a laugh, O hero, that radiant, Śrīvatsa-wearing, yellow-clothed child says to me, "Have you dwelled restfully today in this body of mine, good hermit Mārkaṇḍeya? Tell me!" . . .

Having witnessed the limitless power of the boundlessly august God I humbly fold my hands and approach him eagerly. I see the lotus-eyed God as the soul that has become elemental, and folding my hands and doing homage I say to him, "God, I wish to know yourself and this supernal wizardry! I entered into your body through your mouth, O lord, and saw all the worlds together in your body. . . . Faultless, lotus-eyed one, I wish to know of you why you stay here in your own person as a child. You drank up the entire universe, therefore pray tell, for what purpose does the universe survive entire within your body, blameless one? . . . For what I have seen, my lord, is greatly beyond my understanding."

It should be noted that in all the Sanskrit sources mentioned here, the situation is more complex than the brief summarizing line that the āḻvārs use so frequently: "O you who swallowed the seven worlds" or "O you who swallow and spew the worlds."

4. Tirumaṅkai āḻvār describes the time of dissolution several times. The floods are described in some detail:

> The floods of dissolution, the foaming oceans
> bubbled over and covered the seven worlds,
> the encircling mountains, everywhere.
> They swept over the eight directions
> and over the planets.
> The Lord kept all this,
> tucked inside the lower half
> of his belly
> that day.
>
> (Periya Tirumoḻi 4.4.9 [partial])

5. One of the principal themes enunciated in the account of Mārkaṇḍeya in the Mahābhārata and the Matsya Purāṇa is the wondrous power of Viṣṇu's māyā. See Wendy O'Flaherty, "Inside and Outside the Mouth of God: The Boundary between Myth and Reality," and Zimmer, *Myths and Symbols of Indian Art and Civilization,* 35–47.

The Sanskrit accounts speak of the play between reality and illusion of the vision in the mind of the sage Mārkaṇḍeya. The āḻvārs seem to be aware that there is some question whether the vision was an illusion (which is one meaning of the word māyā), because in several instances when this story is mentioned, they are at pains to add that all this is true (mey). Poykai āḻvār's Mutal Tiruvantāti v. 10 is typical: "They say that it is true (mey) that he swallowed the earth, the mountain, the seas, the wind, and the sky." The word *mey* describing this event of swallowing the worlds is repeated in Mutal Tiruvantāti vv. 34 and 69. In v. 94, Poykai āḻvār describes the Lord who reveals the worlds to the "one learned in the Vedas" as "wondrous" (māyavaṉ). Other āḻvārs also use the word *mey* "true" to describe the act of the Lord's eating the worlds (as is seen in Periya Tirumoḻi 3.1.3 and Mūṉṟām Tiruvantāti, v. 33) and sometimes call him "the wondrous one" (māyavaṉ) in that context. The āḻvārs therefore, preserve both the reality and truth (mey) of the Lord's containing the worlds in his stomach (this is not unreal) and the wondrous nature of the divine (māyā) by which all this is made possible. This is sharply seen, for instance, in Periya Tirumoḻi 3.1.3:

> Having eaten the seven worlds,
> the *wondrous* one (māyavaṉ)
> passes time on the banyan leaf.
> The *true* one (meyyāṉ)
> the Lord of the divine ones
> dwells in the place
> Tiruvayīndrapuram. . . .

6. The image of the baby Viṣṇu, lying on a banyan leaf on the waters of dissolution, is an image evoked several times by the āḻvārs. Lynn Ate has remarked that this story, along with the idea of the Lord swallowing the worlds, is one of the themes most "difficult to notate." (Ate, Periyāḻvār's "Tirumoḻi," 379.) In the Mahābhārata account

as well as in the Matsya Purāṇa account (which Ate does not mention), we read of Viṣṇu lying under a banyan tree. In oral tradition as well as in iconographic accounts, this figure of the baby Viṣṇu is identified with the baby Krishna. Gopinatha Rao (in *Elements of Hindu Iconography,* 215) summarizes the description of this image:

> "Another form in which the child Krishna is often sculptured is as lying upon a leaf of the vaṭa (Indian fig) and is hence known as the Vaṭa-patra-sāyi. This form is symbolic of God brooding over the ocean of the chaos caused after the destruction of the universe at the end of an aeon. . . ."

The similarity of this image, in principle, to that of Viṣṇu reclining on the serpent Ananta ("Without End") or Ādi Śeṣa is seen in Hindu myth. In several Śrīvaiṣṇava temples, Viṣṇu is represented in this form known as Anantaśāyin or "he who reclines on Ananta." Iconographically, a kind of the Anantaśāyin image may be classified as the Jalaśāyin variety. Gopinatha Rao (ibid., 263) describes this image as follows:

> Jalaśāyin: This aspect of Vishnu is the one conceived to be assumed by him at the end of the maha-pralaya of the great deluge of the universal dissolution. The Jalaśāyin is an image of Viṣṇu shown to be lying in the midst of waters, resting on the Adisesha, his serpent-couch. . . .

Both the images of Vaṭapatraśāyi (on the banyan leaf) and the Jalaśāyin (described above) depict Viṣṇu on the waters of dissolution. We suggest that the banyan leaf as a support of Viṣṇu evolved possibly as an alternate way of depicting Viṣṇu Anantaśāyin during the time of dissolution. Solomon, in "Early Vaiṣṇava Bhakti" indicates that the banyan tree and serpent symbolism is part of the autochthonous heritage of Vaiṣṇava bhakti.

We may also note that the banyan leaf seems to be a variant or substitue for Ananta. In the temple at Śrīvilliputtūr in South India, Viṣṇu is known as Vaṭapatraśāyin or "he who reclines on the banyan leaf." The actual image however shows him as reclining on the serpent Ananta and not on a banyan leaf as his name indicates. In fact, Soundararajan ("The Typology of the Anantaśāyi Icon," 76) says that this is one of the two shrines of the Anantaśāyi type that has full iconographic completeness, to the extent permitted by the Āgama text. Soundararajan however does not speculate as to why a Lord called "he who reclines on a banyan leaf" is depicted as reclining on a serpent. Our hypothesis that the banyan leaf is an alternate way of depicting Viṣṇu-Anantaśāyin is lent credence from the writings of two traditional Śrīvaiṣṇava theologians and commentators. Annaṅgarācāriyar writes in an appendix to his edition of the Sacred Collect: "In the end, when all the words are sunk in the sweeping floods of the great dissolution (mahāpralaya) the Lord with Śrī (Tirumāl), by the wondrous nature of his power, keeps them all in this little stomach and is in a meditational slumber (yoga nidra) on a *banyan leaf which is an aṁśa of Ādiśeṣa*" (p. 68, italics mine).

Śrī U. Ve. Uttamūr Vīrarāghavācāriyar, commenting on Periyāḻvār Tirumoḻi 2.6.6, pays special attention to the first line of the verse, "He who is on the banyan leaf, He who is on the serpent . . ." He writes (on pp. 214–15):

> Only the banyan tree was there. He (the Lord) was lying down on one of those leaves. *It is said that Ādi Śeṣa himself stood as the banyan tree.* Since he lies down on the middle of the sea on a banyan leaf (and), on a serpent, he is called "He who reclines on the ocean," "He who is of the banyan leaf," and "He who reclines on Ananta." These names apply to the first line of this verse. . . . In the same verse the āḻvār calls the Lord "He who lies in Kuṭantai" [modern Kumbakonam]. The āḻvār began the verse by calling the lord as "He who is of the banyan leaf ." The Lord reclines (on a serpent) in the form of a worshiped image (arcāvatāra) in Kumbakonam and this picture also crosses the āḻvār's mind. When the āḻvār says "He of the banyan leaf," he may also be thinking of his own native holy city, (Śrīvilliputtūr) where the Lord is called Vaṭapatraśāyi or "he who reclines on a banyan leaf." But even there, the Lord lies on Ādiśeṣa.

In myth and folklore, both the serpent and the banyan tree have been associated with conceptions of immortality and growth. The very name Ananta suggests infinity and Zimmer has discussed the symbolism of the serpent at some length. The banyan tree is described by Monier-Williams (*Religious Thought and Life in India,* 337) as follows:

> . . . Of holy trees and plants, the Vaṭa or Banyan (botanically Ficus Indica) is sacred to Kala or Time. This and the Pipal tree are supposed to enjoy a kind of immortality. When a man plants either of these trees he repeats a prayer to the following effect: "May I abide in heaven as many years as this tree continues growing on the earth." The method by which the banyan tree propagates itself is too well known to require description. . . . In the underground passage of the Allahabad fort there is the stump of a tree called the Akshaya-vaṭa or the "undecaying Banyan". . . .

While Monier-Williams relies on folk tradition in this case for his information, the Śrīvaiṣṇava theologians and commentators quoted earlier also seem to be aware of the close connection between the serpent and the banyan leaf.

7. According to Śaivaite mythology, Mārkaṇḍeya was saved from death and given the boon of a long life by the grace of the Lord Śiva. The āḻvārs allude to this story frequently (Nammāḻvār refers to it in 4.10.8) saying that it was Viṣṇu's grace that enabled Śiva to grant life to Mārkaṇḍeya. However, the myth of Mārkaṇḍeya's vision during the time of dissolution (as recorded in the Mahābhārata and in the Purāṇas) is not mentioned by the āḻvārs, except possibly Poykai āḻvār's Mutal Tiruvantāti v. 94 where he says that "the Wondrous Lord showed the seven worlds and everything else to the one learned in the Vedas."

8. The word translated as "support" in this verse is the Tamil *kaṇ* which means "eyes." The commentators have taken it to mean support, and this is in fact one of the meanings given by the Tamil Lexicon. The Lexicon however, quotes this TVM verse as the authority for its meaning. A more literal rendering would be "There are no eyes except Kaṇṇaṉ's eyes."

9. This verse is similar in sentiment to Poykai āḻvār's Mutal Tiruvantāti, v. 92. It should be mentioned at this point that art historians sometimes posit a connection between Krishna's eating butter and Viṣṇu's eating the earth as a child. Walter Spink, for

instance notes: "And in the Night of Brahmā, within the sacred Yāmuna, within the cosmic ocean, a luminous baby floats, sucking upon his toe . . . , or playing with a stolen butter ball, which represents the earthly orb . . ." (*Krishnamandala,* 106). Roy Craven makes the same point: ". . . Bal Krishna does not suck his toe in this painting but sits on a throne holding a butterball (the earth/cosmos) in his right hand . . ." ("The Sarna Collection," 69). I have neither been able to trace the origins of Spink's statement on the baby playing with the stolen butterball during the night of Brahma, nor find any textual sources which identify the orb of the earth with the orb of butter.

10. Burton, trans., *Kama Sutra,* pt. 2, chap. 2.

11. Chāndogya Upaniṣad 6.13:1 to 3. The metaphor of "eating" or "drinking" is used in an erotic context in *Harivaṁśa*, chap. 63, vv. 19, 31, 32. Hardy translates the relevant verses (*Viraha Bhakti,* 72–73):

> Those lovely cowherd women drank with their glances his charming face . . . (v. 19).
>
> Other women, with laughing faces . . . drank Kṛṣṇa with eyes wide open with emotion, without getting their fill . . . (v. 31).
>
> Other cowherd girls, eager for sexual pleasures, became thirsty when observing his face, and drank it when during the night, they had occasion to make love . . . (v. 32).

12. The reference is to the story of Pūtana, a demoness sent by Kaṁsa to kill the infant Krishna. Pūtana gave her breast which was covered with poison to Krishna, but, miraculously, Krishna, knowing her true identity, sucked her very life from her.

13. On the concept of "melting" in Māṇikkavācakar's Tiruvācakam, see Yocum, *Hymns to the Dancing Śiva,* 168–73.

14. Ramanujan, *Hymns for the Drowning,* 150–52.

15. Ibid. This is discussed under the heading of "Mutual Cannibalism."

16. See Hawley, *The Butter Thief,* 81–83, 144–50. The erotic overtones in stealing and eating butter are seen dramatically in Periyāḻvār Tirumoḻi also.

17. The reference is to the burning of the Khāṇḍava Forest, Mahābhārata I.226. The god of fire (Agni) came to Arjuna and Krishna claiming that he was starving and wanted something to eat. The Khāṇḍava forest, protected by the lord Indra (the deity presiding over rain) was donated to Fire who proceeded to swallow it, i.e., destroy it. Arjuna and Krishna protected Fire from Indra. See also Hiltebeitel, "The Burning of the Forest Myth," p. 219.

18. O'Flaherty, "Inside and Outside the Mouth of God: The Boundary Between Myth and Reality." On the element of protection see n. 28(d) below.

19. *The Splendor,* 117–18.

20. The phrase "nectar of the mouth" (vāyamutu) occurs several times in the āḻvār literature. See Periya Tirumoḻi 1.3.5, and also the distinctive erotic suggestion of Periya Tirumoḻi 6.1.2 when Viṣṇu is described as "eating the nectar (amutu) of Śrī." The erotic suggestion is then carried over into 10.4.1 of the same poem where Tirumaṅkai āḻvār claims that he is "eating you, (i.e., the Lord) or Nācciyār Tirumoḻi 2.10 where Āṇṭāḷ says that the Lord eats the vāyamutu of Sīta (in his incarnation as Rāma).

Related phrases occur in Nācciyār Tirumoḻi 7.8, 7.9, and 13.4. Among the āḻvārs,

Periyāḻvār uses this phrase very often to refer to kisses (as in Periyāḻvār Tirumoḻi 1.2.14 and 2.2.7) and also to refer to the drool from the mouth of the baby Krishna (Periyāḻvār Tirumoḻi 1.4.5, 1.5.9, etc.). It should be noted that Periyāḻvār's verses, spoken frequently from the view of Yaśoda, Krishna's foster mother, and therefore considered "maternal," are perhaps also the most erotic and that the line between maternal love and sexual passion is thin.

21. Or, "jasmine flowers, loosened from the [plants]."

22. See *The Six Thousand* 6.10 intro. and 6.10.10. See also chapter 9.

23. Meanings taken from Monier-Williams, *A Sanskrit-English Dictionary.*

24. The Śrīvaiṣṇava commentators use the word *parimārutal* to indicate the exchange of sexual favors. Piḷḷāṉ, for instance, uses it while commenting on the "mutual cannibalism" verses (quoted above). See Piḷḷāṉ's commentary on 9.6.1, 9.6.4, 9.6.9. The Tamil word *vēṭkai,* which Nammāḻvār uses in 2.1.10, 4.9.9, 9.6.7, and 10.3.8, also has a double meaning and could indicate an appetite for food or sex. Thus, *vēṭkai* in conjunction with *tuṇaivi* (companion) means "wife." When used in conjunction with *nīr* (water), the compound means "water to quench one's intense thirst." *Vēṭkainōy* or "desire-disease" (2.1.10 and 9.6.7) may mean either craving for love or for food.

25. Taittirīya Upaniṣad, 3.10.6. While commenting on this verse, Frits Staal says (in "Indian Concepts of the Body," 32):

> But it is not far-fetched to assume that "food" stands, at least in part, for the object of desire. A child wants first of all food, and if it were to inquire about brahman, the best way to explain what this concept involves is to introduce it as food, viz., the ultimate object of desire . . . at the end of the hierarchy, when explanations have also come to an end, the highest object of desire is again referred to in terms of food, which is still at the core of the eater's concern.

I am indebted to Professor Gene Thursby, University of Florida, for this reference.

26. The Tamil words are ambiguous and the line could also read thus: ". . . like red-hot iron sucking water / I drank you, my life, to exhaustion."

27. The analogy is used by modern Śrīvaiṣṇava theologians also. Thus, Sri R. Rangachari says:

> The stanzas of Nammāḻvār are not intended to be read through in a hurry. Apart from ritual recitation in centuries, each stanza has to be pondered at leisure, if we are to enjoy the nuances on a single theme. Would a person gifted with a fine palate, gulp down a cup of nectar, as if it were a bitter medicine? Would he not sip it drop by drop, relishing it more, with each drop? This applies to Śrī Deśika's Slokas too. We should enjoy each sloka separately. . . .
>
> Sri R. Rangachari, Introduction to Vedānta Deśika's *Dramiḍopaniṣad Tātparya Ratnāvaḷi and Sāra,* 2.)

28. Piḷḷāṉ deals with the verses where the concept of "eating" occurs, in one of the following ways: (a.) the Sanskrit word for eating/enjoyment (bhuj) is used; (b.) the concept is ignored in the commentary (2.3.8, 8.10.4); (c.) when the āḻvār claims that

the Lord is "eating" him, Piḷḷāṉ occasionally uses the word *saṁśleṣa* (sexual union) to describe it (10.7.2); (d.) when the Lord is described as "eating" the worlds or as keeping them within his stomach, Piḷḷāṉ calls it "protection" (2.2.1, 2.2.8, 2.3.5, 2.7.12, 3.6.1, etc.).

2.2.8 is quite explicit, noting the protective qualities of the Lord to be similar to that of a mother:

> Who but the wondrous Lord
> Who by his will creates
> the divine ones and all things
> and firmly sustains
> the three worlds within him,
> and keep and protect (us)?

> If it is asked, are not creation and protection different acts? Can we say they are but one act for the Supreme Being? the āḻvār replies: Just as the one mother who gives birth to the child also protects it, the one who creates also protects. Therefore, the Supreme One protects; the two acts of creation and protection are one act (for the Lord).
>
> (2.2.8)

(e) paraphrases and expands the Lord eating the worlds in Sanskrit words, quoting occasionally from Sanskrit sources, (as in 7.4.4, with a quote from Viṣṇu Purāṇa 4.1.84). The word for "eating" (Tamil: *uṇṭu*) is paraphrased with the Sanskrit word *cuṣa* (to suck) in this case.

29. Piḷḷāṉ is evidently thinking of the story in which Yaśodā catches her son eating mud. She asks him to open his mouth, and there sees the whole universe inside. Periyāḻvār Tirumoḻi, 1.1.6. See also Bhāgavata Purāṇa X.8.32–45.

30. *Vedārtha Saṁgraha,* 17b–18a, trans. Carman in *The Theology of Rāmānuja,* 124.

31. *Gītābhāṣya* 7.12 and 9.4, quoted in Carman, *The Theology of Rāmānuja,* 128.

32. *Akanāṉūṟu,* 136, trans. Hart in *Poets of the Tamil Anthologies,* 121.

33. Nammāḻvār is the only āḻvār to directly claim that the Lord swallows him. Tirumaṅkai āḻvār and Periyāḻvār claim that they "drink" and consume the Lord but not vice versa, to the best of my knowledge. In a review of a recent book, *Viṭṭu Chitan Viritta Tamizh* by Dr. N. Subbu Reddiar, the reviewer, Prema Nandakumar, says that "The concluding chapter deals with some of the important images (olfactory, gustatory, visual and auditory) handled in the hymns [of Periyāḻvār.]" I have not been able to get a copy of this book to check on Periyāḻvār's use of the "gustatory" image.

It is interesting to see that Glenn Yocum has noted that Māṇikkavācakar, the Śaivaite poet-saint who probably lived about the ninth century C.E. uses notions of taste and food to describe the lord Śiva in the Tiruvācakam. See Yocum, *Hymns to the Dancing Śiva,* 109–11. Yocum also mentions (ibid., 132 n. 16) that Edward Taylor (1642–1729), a pastor of a Puritan church on the Massachusetts frontier used the notions of eating and drinking. God's grace is apparently referred to as "sweet junkets," "my soul's plum cake," "sugar mill," and "honey hive." The following chart gives the references to various ways in which the "eating" and "drinking" analogy is used by Nammāḻvār in the TVM:

God Eats Butter	God Eats Worlds	Āḻvār Eats God	God Eats Āḻvār	God Eats Enemies	Misc. References
	1.1.7				
	1.1.8				
	1.1.9				
1.3.1					
1.5.1					
1.5.8	1.5.8				
		1.7.3			
1.8.5					
	1.8.7				
	1.9.4				
	1.10.5				
	2.2.1				
	2.2.6				
	2.2.7				
	2.2.8				
	2.2.10		2.2.10		
	2.2.11				
	2.3.4				
2.3.8					
	2.5.3				
	2.6.2				
	2.6.7				
	2.7.12				
	2.8.7				
					2.9.8
2.10.6					
	3.1.10				
	3.4.9				
	3.6.1				
	3.6.8				
	3.7.10				
3.8.3					
	3.10.9				
	4.2.1				
	4.3.2				
	4.3.6				
4.4.6				4.4.6	
	4.5.10				
	4.6.4				
	4.7.1				
	4.8.9				
4.8.11	4.8.11				
	4.9.8				
	4.10.3				
				5.2.6	

God Eats Butter	God Eats Worlds	Āḻvār Eats God	God Eats Āḻvār	God Eats Enemies	Misc. References
					5.2.8
				5.3.8	
	5.4.1				
	5.6.1				
	5.7.7				
		5.8.10			
				5.8.11	
	5.9.7				
			5.10.1		
				5.10.3	
				5.10.4	
	5.10.5				5.10.5
	5.10.6				
			5.10.10		5.10.10
	6.1.2				
	6.2.4				
	6.2.7				
6.2.11					
				6.4.4	
	6.4.11				
	6.6.3				
					6.6.11
		6.7.1			
	6.9.11				
	6.10.1				
	7.1.3				
	7.1.4				
		7.1.7			
	7.2.2				
				7.2.3	
	7.3.9				
	7.4.2				
	7.4.4				
			7.7.1		
7.7.2					
	8.1.5				
	8.3.4				
	8.4.11				
	8.5.5				
	8.7.8				
	8.7.9	8.7.9			
		8.8.4			
	8.9.4				
	8.10.4				
	9.1.1				

God Eats Butter	God Eats Worlds	Āḻvār Eats God	God Eats Āḻvār	God Eats Enemies	Misc. References
	9.3.2				
					9.4.9
			9.5.9		
			9.6.3		
			9.6.4		
			9.6.5		
			9.6.6		
			9.6.7		
			9.6.8		
			9.6.10		
	9.9.2				
	9.9.11				
	9.10.1				
	10.2.3				
					10.3.5
	10.4.4				
	10.5.3				
				10.5.6	
			10.7.1		
		10.7.2	10.7.2		
			10.7.3		
	10.7.6				
	10.7.9				
	10.8.2	10.8.2			
		10.8.6			
		10.10.5	10.10.5		
		10.10.6	10.10.6		

34. It is interesting to note that the metaphor of food is used in the first words said to have been uttered by Nammāḻvār. For details see chap. 2, p. 00.

Chapter 13

1. Otto, *Vischnu-Narayana,* 2.
2. Thibaut, "Introduction," *The Vedānta-Sūtras,* 34:xxii.
3. Ibid., c.
4. Ibid., cxxii.
5. Ibid., cxxiii.
6. Ibid., cxxvii.
7. Ghate, *The Vedānta,* 156–70. Ghate states the Nimbarka "is supposed to have lived a few years after Rāmānuja. The date of his death is probably 1162 A.D." (pp. 19–20), citing as his reference footnote 4 on pp. 62–63 of R. G. Bhandarkar, *Vaiṣṇavism, Saivism and Minor Religious Systems,* Encyclopedia of Indo-Aryan Research, 1913.
8. Otto, *India's Religion of Grace and Christianity Compared and Contrasted.*

See the Bibliography for the titles of Govindacharya's translations and paraphrases of traditional texts.

9. Pandit Agnihothram Rāmānuja Thatachariar's arguments are summarized in Carman, *The Theology of Rāmānuja,* 298–300 n. 1. The same note also refers to Robert Lester's unpublished Ph.D. dissertation submitted to Yale University, entitled "The Nature and Function of Patanjalian-Type Yoga as the Means to Release (Mokṣopāya) according to Rāmānuja." This dissertation has since been published as *Rāmānuja on the Yoga* (Adyar, Madras: The Adyar Library and Research Centre, 1976). See also Lester's article, "Rāmānuja and Śrī-Vaiṣṇavism" read at the Fifth International Conference-Seminar of Tamil Studies, Madurai, 1981, and his article "Rāmānuja and Śrī-Vaiṣṇavism: The concept of Prapatti or Śaraṇāgati," *History of Religions* 5: 266–82. Carman's entire chap. 17, entitled "Rāmānuja's Relation to his Successors: The Problem of the Gadyas" (212–37) considers issues related to the points raised; see also 306–7 n. 54.

10. Hardy, *Viraha-Bhakti,* esp. 13–17, 36–38, 436–80, 489, 546–47, 579–83.

11. Ibid., 479–80.

12. For a full discussion, see Appadurai, *Worship and Conflict under Colonial Rule.*

13. This is discussed in Vasudha Narayanan's Ph.D. dissertation "Bhakti and Prapatti in the Śrīvaiṣṇava Tradition," which is expected to be published under the title, *The Widening Divide.* See also Mumme, "The Theology of Maṉavālamāmuri."

14. Cf. Carman, "Report from South India," in *Religious Situation: 1968,* edited by Donald R. Cutler (Boston: Beacon Press, 1968), 395–434.

15. Clooney, "Divine Word, Human Word," 5.

16. Ibid., 14.

Part Four

1. *Ayarvu aṟum.* The word *ayarvu* may be translated as "fatigue, forgetfulness, or sorrow." All these meanings are given by Uttamūr Vīrarāghavācāriyar in his commentary on this verse.

This phrase is quoted frequently by Piḷḷāṉ and is used to describe the "immortal ones" who serve Viṣṇu.

2. This list is an abbreviated version of Rāmānuja's description of Viṣṇu. See, for instance, *Gītābhāṣya,* "Introduction"; *Vedārthasaṁgraha* ed. van Buitenen, para. 127. (All subsequent references also cite the paragraph numbers in van Buitenen's text and translation.)

3. *Nikhila jagad udaya vibhava ādi līlanāy.* Rāmānuja frequently uses this phrase. See *Gītābhāṣya,* "Introduction," *Vedārtha Saṁgraha,* para. 13.

4. Piḷḷāṉ employs a phrase that Rāmānuja uses in the description of bliss. See *Śrībhāṣya* 1.1.13.

5. *Asaṅkhyeya kalyāṇa guṇa mahodadhi.* Perhaps the most frequently used phrase by Rāmānuja in talking about God. See, for instance, *Gītābhāṣya,* "Introduction."

6. *Svetara samasta vastu vilakṣana svarūpa.* The same phrase is used by Rāmānuja. See *Vedārtha Saṁgraha,* para. 1 *Śrībhāṣya* 2.1.23; seen with a slight variation in *Gītābhāṣya* 2.29.

7. The major thrust of the first few paragraphs of *Vedārtha Saṁgraha* (pp. 1–2) is

to talk about (a) the Lord's "purity and opposition to all filth," and (b) his distinct nature, separated from spirit and matter while being their inner controller. Piḷḷāṉ address both these points early in the commentary.

Piḷḷāṉ, in his comment on 1.1.3, talks of the Lord being the inner soul [of the universe which is his body], the owner (séṣī), and the controller. The same list is used by Rāmānuja in *Gītābhāṣya* 10.20, 13.22, and 13.28. Rāmānuja adds one more term of description in his commentary and says that the Lord is the support (ādhāra) of everyone and everything.

8. Ramanujan, *Hymns for the Drowning,* 3.

9. Or, "It is difficult to comprehend him as having one nature."

10. Piḷḷāṉ uses terms very like Rāmānuja's in his refutation of the śunyavādin. See *Śrībhāṣya* 2.2.30.

11. "Instruments of sport and enjoyment" (*līlopakaraṇa, bhōgopakaraṇa*). Phrase used often by Rāmānuja, *Vedārtha Saṁgraha* para. 132.

12. Phrase from TVM 1.5.11.

13. *Vīṭu:* Literally, "emancipation, freedom, liberation." It also means "heaven, as the final release or liberation." Meanings taken from the *Tamil Lexicon.*

14. The second line may also be translated as "gold, life, body."

15. "That which exists or that which does not exist." Commentators interpret these lines as "that which is sentient and that which is non-sentient."

16. *Pulku,* which has been translated as "embrace," is a rather unusual Tamil word. All later commentators discuss this term and say it means "to take refuge."

17. All the later commentators interpret the lines "if you desire heaven after death, loosen earthly ties" as "Destroy the experience of kaivalya which your soul will enjoy when you gain liberation from the body."

18. Commentators say that the Lord is bound to his devotees.

19. This is a phrase used frequently by Rāmānuja.

20. Ulūkya is sometimes understood to be the school of materialism (Cārvāka). Others like Monier-Williams think that it is the name of a preacher of the Vaiśeṣika school.

21. Sri Satyamurti Ayyangar, in his *Tiruvāymoḻi English Glossary* (p. 411), says that "Akṣapāda" is a school of Logic or Nyāya.

22. A reference to Śiva.

23. *Ajahat svabhāvaṉāy.* Ajahat is "not dropping or losing."

24. Makiḻ blossoms are known as vakuḷa in Sanskrit.

25. *Polika:* from *poli,* "to be abundant, overflow, to be auspicious, to live long, to shine." The common factor is the happiness or joy of auspiciousness, wealth or long life, and so I have taken the liberty of translating the word as "rejoice."

26. Or, "the [old] age will be displaced."

27. *Koṉṟu uyir uṇṇum . . .* The phrase *uyir uṇṇum* literally means "to eat [one's] life," i.e., to conquer or overwhelm. See chapter 12 for the connotations of "eating" and "swallowing."

28. The Tamil word *mūrti* is translated as "form."

29. *Jñāna Vīti* has been translated as "the way of wisdom."

30. This introduction is a typical example of Piḷḷāṉ's finding a connection between two sets of verses.

According to Śrīvaiṣṇava tradition, Nāthamuni heard this set of songs and was so overcome by its beauty that he wanted to retrieve the other "thousand verses."

31. Or, "you make my body wander like water, melt, and dissolve." The word *karai* can be translated as "melt" or as "bank, shore."

32. *Veḷḷai mūrti:* literally, "white form or image."

33. Piḷḷāṉ has interpreted the Tamil words *eḻil ēṟē* ("O handsome bull") as *dipti yuktan. Dipta* in Sanskrit may mean flame or lion and *dipti* is splendor or radiance. I have translated *dipti* as flame in the commentary.

34. Gajendra Āḻvāṉ is the name given by the Śrīvaiṣṇavas to the elephant-king Gajendra, whose legs were caught by a crocodile. Gajendra took refuge with Viṣṇu, who appeared in the sky, riding his mount Garuḍa and quickly hurled his discus and destroyed the crocodile. See Bhāgavata Purāṇa, VIII.2 and VIII.3.

35. *Yāḻ:* a stringed instrument of the lute family.

36. Literally "bull among lions." Interpreted by commentators as "best" or "king" of the lions.

37. *Ūḻ.* Literally, "rule, old karma." I have translated it in a general way as "direction."

38. Piḷḷāṉ carefully paraphrases the āḻvār as saying that the Lord should successfully execute a "means" for the āḻvār to get salvation, without him knowing about it. If the āḻvār knows that he is undertaking a "means" (*upāya*) to attain the goal, this may count as self-effort and possibly compromise the Lord's independence and initiative in the process of redemption. Piḷḷāṉ wants the Lord to take full responsibility to accomplish the *upāya* without making the āḻvār feel self-conscious that he is practising a "way" which will accomplish a goal. The thought of the thirteenth-century ācārya, Piḷḷai Lōkācārya, a leading theologian of the Teṅkalai community, is very close to Piḷḷāṉ's position on this issue. For a discussion of this issue in Teṅkalai Śrīvaiṣṇava literature, see Mumme, *The Theology of Maṇavāḷamāmuni,* 140–66; and Rajagopalan, "The Śrīvaiṣṇava Understanding of *Bhakti* and *Prapatti,*" 352–63.

39. I have translated the Tamil word *oruṅkutal* as "only." *The Tamil Lexicon* gives the meaning as "to be concentrated, to have singleness of aim or purpose," but refers to this TVM verse as the authority for this meaning.

40. *Ivvātma muṭivataṟku muṉṉē* . . . Literally, "before this soul ends." This phrase may be understood as an intense plea, with the āḻvār stating that his soul may cease to exist if he does not obtain the feet of the Lord.

41. *Mūrti:* literally, "form, image."

42. Or, "Come to see me."

43. *Uḻalai:* literally, "crossbar." The *Tamil Lexicon* also states that this is a "block of wood suspended from neck of cattle to prevent straying."

44. The last line of the verse promises that those who recite these verses will become the beloved of doe-eyed women and the commentators interpret this in different ways. Piḷḷāṉ says that the Lord will enjoy those who [recite] these songs like a doe-eyed woman enjoying her lover and in a later commentary (*The Nine Thousand*), Nañjīyar says that those who [recite] will be appreciated ("enjoyed") by other Śrīvaiṣṇavas.

45. Piḷḷāṉ uses Sanskrit terms for all the Tamil words to indicate polarities. Some of these words have slightly different connotations; the Tamil *kalakkam,* "confusion, agitation," for instance, is translated as *kaluṣya,* which means "disturbance," but also "turbid, dirty" and "foul." The Tamil *taṉmai,* which means "grace, gentleness," is

translated by the Sanskrit *anugraha* ("favor," "grace"). He also introduces a new word which is not in the verse: *udanyonya,* which means "everything in the womb and what issues from it."

46. *Vaṇṇam* has been translated as "hue" in the text of the poem. The Tamil word means "color, pigment" and also "nature, characteristic or quality."

47. *Teḷ:* literally, "extremely clear, shining."

48. *Puṇar-tal:* literally, "to join, unite, to copulate; union of lovers, appropriate to Kuriñci, one of the five landscapes." *Kuriñci* denotes the landscape of hills (see chap. 2) and the reference here to the Vēṅkata hill makes the landscape suitable for the act of union.

49. The words translated as "desire and love" and *mēvu-tal* and *amar-tal.* Both words mean desire; *mēvu-tal* also means to eat, to love or to be united with. Commentators usually paraphrase it as "to enjoy."

50. A reference to Brahmā the creator.

51. See n. 30.

52. Uttamūr Vīrarāghavācāriyar, a twentieth-century commentator, paraphrases the words *maṟappu ilā,* which we have translated as "without forgetfulness," as "not having even a [trace of] a good quality, like having had intelligence and later not having it."

53. Nammāḻvār talks about the city of Tirunāvāy in this entire decad. *Tiru* = Sacred, *nāvāy,* ships, boats, rafts etc.; hence I have taken the liberty of translating it as "Sacred [city] of ships." At least one contemporary commentator pays attention to the name of the city and writes: "*Nāvāy* means 'boat.' Since even the city, like the Lord, [provides] the way to cross the sea of life and death, [the poet] says that it cuts through [our] sins" (Uttamūr Vīrarāghavācāriyar, commentary on TVM 9.8.1).

54. I have translated the Tamil words *kavayil inṟi* (literally, "not on a forked path") as "single path." The words imply that the poet only thinks of reaching the sacred city and no other thought distracts him.

55. I have translated the Tamil phrase *tēvācura ceṟṟavanē* literally as "you who destroyed the divine ones and the demons." Piḷḷāṉ, however, interprets this rather loosely.

56. The phrase "emit the fragrance of jasmine" in the text of the verse is interpreted by the commentators as meaning "to enjoy the pleasures of heaven." The fragrance of jasmine is associated with the Lord and the implication is that one acquires this fragrance by intimate association with him.

57. This set of verses is spoken by the āḻvār in the guise of a cowherd girl who swears that she will die if Krishna leaves her to graze cows in the morning. At times we see a single cowherd girl talking and, in other places, she seems to represent a whole group of girls who feel the grief of separation. In the distress and confusion of the impending separation, "she" speaks as though Krishna had already gone for the whole day (verse 5), though he is standing in front of her.

58. This verse has the refrain *ālō* occurring five times. It is an exclamation of sorrow and grief and has no exact meaning. I have translated it as "alas" to indicate the agony felt by the cowherd girl.

59. *Takavu illai:* literally, "suitability, fitness, worthiness, mercy, kindness, justice, equity, impartiality, morality, virtue." We have translated it as "unfair" but commentators, like Piḷḷāṉ, interpret the word as "without grace (*kṛpā*)."

60. *Turavu:* "relinquishment, renunciation of the pleasures of life, asceticism." Uttamūr Vīrarāghavācāriyar interprets this line as "leaving us to be like ascetics (*sannyāsīs*)."

61. I have translated the phrase *piṇi aviḻ mallikai* as "the jasmine that unleashed my desires." *Piṇi* means both "desire" and "buds" and so one may either translate it as I have, or as "the jasmine buds that are loosened." Nañjīyar clearly interprets *piṇi aviḻ* as loosening or unleashing of flower buds in his *Nine Thousand* commentary.

62. *Pulki:* literally, "to copulate."

63. Notice that some of the erotic nature of the verse is obscured by this line. The āḻvār's plea to "give me the nectar of your mouth" is interpreted by Piḷḷāṉ as "sacred words which are like nectar."

64. The word *aḻal* can mean great fire or hell.

65. *Tavattavar:* literally, "those performing *tapas.*"

66. Piḷḷāṉ is somewhat inscrutable at this point; later commentaries believe that the divine ones are his devotees, but are devoted to him so as to realize other wishes; to them the Lord is still distant. He is, however, very close to those āśritas who worship him with no other goal in mind.

67. *Pāḻē:* primordial matter or soul; commentators take it as both and say that it is that which is capable of growth; that which has potential for creation.

68. Commentators take the two words "flame" (*cōti*) and "skies" (*amparam*) to mean fire and ether and as indicative of the other three primordial categories, water, earth and air.

69. The Tamil words being ambiguous, the line could read:

. . . like red-hot iron sucking water,
I drank you, my life, to exhaustion.

70. This verse is marked by repetition of words. The word *cūḻntu* occurs five times and I have translated it as "surrounds," "encompasses," "pervades," "filled" and "embraced." The word *periya* ("big") occurs four times and I have rendered it as "supreme," "incomparable" and "great."

71. *Viṭāi:* literally, "thirst, desire, weariness."

72. The word translated as "linked" is *antāti* ("end-beginning"). This is the style in which the last word of a verse becomes the first word of the next one.

73. This is a condensed rendering of Rāmānuja's favorite litany and description of Viṣṇu. Piḷḷāṉ began his commentary with a similar description and ends it by recapitulating the essential points.

Bibliography

Editions of the Sacred Collect, Commentaries on the Tiruvāymoḻi, and Translations

Editions of the Tiruvāymoḻi in The Sacred Collect

Aṇṇaṅgarācāriyar, P. B., ed. *Nālāyira tivviyap pirapantam.* Kāñci: V. N. Tēvanātaṉ, 1971.

Reṭṭiyār, K. Vēṅkaṭacāmi, ed. *Nālāyira tivviyappirapantam.* Madras: Tiruvēṅkaṭatāṉ Tirumaṉṟam, 1981.

Tamil Scholars, eds. *Śrī Tivyap pirapantam.* 4 vols. Madras: Murray and Company, 1956.

Commentaries on the Tiruvāymoḻi

Aṇṇaṅgarācāriyar, P. B., ed. *Tiruvāymoḻi.* 10 vols. Kāñci, 1949–1963.

———, ed. *Pakavat Viṣayam.* 4 vols. [With Nañjīyar's *Nine Thousand,* Periyavāccāṉ Piḷḷai's *Twenty-four Thousand,* and Vaṭakku Tiruvīti Piḷḷai's *"Īṭu" Thirty-Six Thousand* Commentaries.] Kāñci, 1975–76.

Balasundara Nayakar, K. *Īṭṭurai Āṟāychi and Commentary on Tiruvāymoḻi* (*For Agapporuḷ stanzas only*). Parts 1 and 2. Tirupati: Tirumala-Tirupati Devasthanam Press, 1956–1958.

Kiruṣṇasvāmi Ayyaṅkār, S., ed. *Bhagavad Viṣayam.* 10 vols. [With Tirukkurukai Pirāṉ Piḷḷāṉ's *Six Thousand,* Nañjīyar's *Nine Thousand,* Periyavāccāṉ Piḷḷai's *Twenty-four Thousand,* and Vaṭakku Tiruvīti Piḷḷai's *"Īṭu" Thirty-Six Thousand* Commentaries.] Madras: Nobel Press, 1924–1930.

Rāmānujācāriyār, P. S., and A. A. Mātavācāryaṉ, eds. *Nammāḻvār aruḷiceyta Tiruvāymoḻi.* [For the first four hundred verses, with Piḷḷāṉ's *Six Thousand,* Śrīsākṣātsvāmi's *Twenty-four Thousand* and *Captārtam,* Vedānta Deśika's *Dramiḍopaniṣad Tātparya Ratnāvaḷi,* and Śrī Vētānta Rāmānuja Mahātēcikaṉ's *Pakavat-Viṣaya Sāram.*] 2 vols. Srirangam: Śrīraṅgam Śrīmatāṇṭavaṉ Ācramam, 1986–87.

Uttamūr Vīrarāghavācāriyar. *Nammāḻvār aruḷiceyta Tiruvāymoḻi, prabandha rakṣai.* 4 vols. Madras: Visishtadvaita Pracharini Sabha, 1970–1978.

Translations

Kurattalvar Aiyengar, N. *A Free Translation of Tiruvaimoli of Sathakopa (Ten Parts).* Sri Penukonda Alvar Sannadhi Series no. 4. Trichinopoly: The Vakulabharanam Press, 1929.

Ramanujan, A. K. *Hymns for the Drowning: Poems for Viṣṇu by Nammāḻvār.* Princeton: Princeton University Press, 1981.

Satyamurti Ayyangar. *Tiruvāymoḻi English Glossary.* 2 vols. Bombay: Ananthacharya Indological Research Institute, 1981.

General Bibliography

Āndhra Pūrṇa. *Yatirāja Vaibhavam.* Śrīvaiṣṇava granthamāla 1. Bombay: Śrī Kāñci Prativādi Bhayaṅkaram Maṭha Publications, 1979.

Aṇṇaṅgarācāriyar, P. B., ed. *Tiruppāvai, Mūvāyirappaṭi Āṛāyirappaṭi Vyākyānaṅkaḷ Kūṭiyatu.* Kāñci: Śrī P. B. Aṇṇaṅgarācāriyar Publications, 1970.

———, ed. *Stotramāla.* Kāñci, 1974.

Appadurai, Arjun. *Worship and Conflict under Colonial Rule.* New Delhi: Orient Longman, 1983.

Appasamy, A. J. *The Theology of Hindu Bhakti.* Bangalore: The Christian Literature Society Press, 1970.

Apte, Vaman Shivram. *The Student's Sanskrit English Dictionary.* New Delhi: Motilal Banarsidass, 1982.

Arunachalam, M. *Nammāḻvār, Varalāṛum Nūlāṛaycciyum.* Srirangam: Śrīraṅgam Śrīnivāsa Tātācāriyar svāmi ṭirust veḷiyīṭu, 1984.

Ate, Lynn M. "Periyāḻvār's 'Tirumoḻi': A Bāla Kṛṣṇa Text from the Devotional Period in Tamil Literature." Ph.D. diss., University of Wisconsin, 1978.

Balakrishna Mudaliyar, R. *The Golden Anthology of Ancient Tamil Literature.* 3 vols. Tirunelveli and Madras: The South Indian Saiva Siddhanta Works Publishing Society, Tinnevelly Ltd. 1959–60.

Balasubramaniam, R. *The Mysticism of Poygai Alvar.* Madras: Vedanta Publications, 1976.

Basham, A. L. *The Wonder That Was India.* London: Macmillan & Co., 1954.

Bashyam, K. *Saranaagati gadya with English Translation of the Text and its Commentary by Srutaprakaasika Acharya.* Madras: Visishtadvaita Pracharini Sabha, 1964.

Bhāgavata Purāṇa, The. Translated by Ganesh Vasudeo Tagare. 5 vols. Delhi: Motilal Banarsidass, 1976–78.

Bhatt, S. R. *Studies in Rāmānuja Vedānta.* New Delhi: Heritage Publishers, 1975.

Blackburn, Stuart, and A. K. Ramanujan. *Another Harmony: New Essays on the Folklore of India.* Berkeley and Los Angeles: University of California Press, 1986.

Bolle, Kees. "Speaking of a Place." In *Myths and Symbols: Essays in Honor of Mircea Eliade,* edited by J. M. Kitagawa and C. M. Long, 127–39. Chicago: University of Chicago Press, 1969.

Bryant, Kenneth. *Poems to the Child-God: Structures and Strategies in the Poetry of Sūrdās.* Berkeley and Los Angeles: University of California Press, 1978.

Burton, Richard. *The Kama Sutra of Vatsyayana.* New York: E. P. Dutton and Co., 1962.

Carman, John B. "Rāmānuja's Conception of Divine Supremacy and Accessibility." *Ānvīkṣikī*: Research Bulletin of the Centre of Advanced Study in Philosophy (Banaras Hindu University) 1 (1968): 96–130.

———. *The Theology of Rāmānuja: An Essay in Interreligious Understanding*. New Haven and London: Yale University Press, 1974.

———. "Rāmānuja's Contemporaneity." *Śrī Rāmānuja Vāṇi* 1 (1978): 37–45.

———. "Hindu Bhakti as a Middle Way." In *The Other Side of God: A Polarity in World Religions,* edited by Peter L. Berger, 182–207. Garden City, NY: Anchor Books, 1981.

———. "Conceiving Hindu 'Bhakti' as Theistic Mysticism." In *Mysticism and Religious Traditions,* edited by Steven Katz, 191–225. New York: Oxford University Press, 1983.

———. "Conclusion: Axes of Sacred Value in Hindu Society." In *Purity and Auspiciousness in Indian Society,* edited by John B. Carman and Frederique Marglin, 109–120. International Studies in Sociology and Social Anthropology 43. Leiden: E. J. Brill, 1985.

———. *Majesty and Mercy: Contrasts and Harmonies in the Concept of God* [tentative title]. Grand Rapids: Eerdman Publications. Forthcoming.

Caramōpāya Nirṇayam. See Nayanāräccāṉ Piḷḷai.

Champakalakshmi, R. *Vaiṣṇava Iconography in the Tamil Country*. New Delhi: Orient Longmans, 1981.

Clooney, Francis X. "Unity in Enjoyment: An Exploration into Nammāḻvār's Tamil Veda and its Commentators." *Śrī Rāmānuja Vāṇi* 6 (1983): 34–61.

———. "Divine Word, Human Word: The Śrīvaiṣṇava Exposition of the Character of Nammāḻvār's Experience as Revelation." In *In Spirit and In Truth: Festschrift for Ignatius Hrudayam,* 155–68. Madras, 1985.

———. "Sacrifice and Its Spiritualization in the Christian and Hindu Traditions: A Study in Comparative Theology." *Harvard Theological Review* 78 (1985): 361–80.

———. *Retrieving the Pūrva Mīmāṁsa of Jaimini*. De Nobili Research Series, vol. 17. Vienna: Indological Institute of the University of Vienna. Forthcoming.

Clothey, Fred. *The Many Faces of Murukaṉ: The History and Meaning of a South Indian God*. The Hague: Mouton, 1978.

Craven, Roy C., Jr. "The Sarna Collection: Indian Reverse Painting on Glass." *Arts of Asia* 13 (1980): 67–77.

Cutler, Norman. *Consider Our Vow: An English Translation of Tiruppāvai and Tiruvempāvai*. Madurai: Muttu patippakam, 1979.

———. "The Poetry of the Tamil Saints." Ph.D. diss., University of Chicago, 1980.

———. *Songs of Experience*. Bloomington: Indiana University Press, 1987.

———. See also A. K. Ramanujan and Norman Cutler.

Damodaran, G. *The Literary Value of the Tiruvaymoli*. Tirupati: Sri Venkateswara University, 1978.

Danielou, Alain. *Hindu Polytheism*. Bollingen Series 73. New York: Pantheon Books, 1964.

Divyasūri Caritam. See Garuḍa Vāhana Paṇḍita.

Edholm, Erik Af, and Carl Suneson. "The Seven Bulls and Kṛṣṇa's Marriage to Nīḷa/NappiNNai in Sanskrit and Tamil Literature." *Temenos* 8 (1972): 29–53.

Fitzgerald, James. "India's Fifth Veda: The Mahābhārata's Presentation of Itself." *Journal of South Asian Literature* 20 (1980): 125–40.

Garuḍa Vāhana Paṇḍita. *Divyasūri Caritam*. Translated into Hindi by Paṇḍita Mādhavācharya. Edited by T. A. Sampath Kumaracharya and K. K. A. Venkatachari. Bombay: Ananthacharya Research Institute, 1978.

Ghate, V. S. *The Vedānta: A Study of the Brahma-Sūtras with the Bhāṣyas of Śaṁkara, Rāmānuja, Nimbarka, Madhva, and Vallabha*. Poona: Bhandarkar Oriental Research Institute, 1960.

Gopalakrishna Naidu. *Lord Venkateswara and Alwars*. Tirupati: Tirupati Devasthanam, n.d.

Gopalan, L. V. *Sir Vaishnava Divya Desams (108 Tirupatis)*. Madras: Visishtadvaita Pracharini Sabha, 1972.

Gopinatha Rao, T. A. *Elements of Hindu Iconography*. New York: Paragon Books Reprint Corp., 1968.

Govindacharya, Alkondavilli. *Sri Bhagavad Gita with Sri Ramanujacharya's Visistadvaita Commentary*. Madras: Vaijayanti Press, 1898.

———. *The Divine Wisdom of the Dravida Saints*. Madras: C. N. Press, 1902.

———. *Holy Lives of the Azhwars*. Mysore: G. E. Press, 1902.

———. *The Life of Ramanujacharya*. Madras: S. Murthy and Co., 1906.

———. "The Artha-Pancaka of Pillai Lokacarya." *Journal of the Royal Asiatic Society* (1910) 565–97.

———. "The Astadasa-Bhedas, or the Eighteen Points of Doctrinal Differences Between the Tengalais (Southerners) and the Vadagalais (Northerners) of the Visistadvaita Vaisnava School, South India." *Journal of the Royal Asiatic Society* (1910): 1103–12.

Hardy, Friedhelm. "Mādhavendra Pūri: A link between Bengal Vaiṣṇavism and South Indian Bhakti." *Journal of the Royal Asiatic Society* (1974): 23–41.

———. "Ideology and Cultural Contexts of the Śrīvaiṣṇava Temple." *The Indian Economic and Social History Review* 14 (1977): 119–51.

———. "The Tamil Veda of a Śūdra Saint: The Śrīvaiṣṇava Interpretation of Nammāḻvār." In *Contribution to South Asian Studies*, edited by Gopal Krishna, vol. 1, 28–87. Delhi: Oxford University Press, 1979.

———. *Viraha-Bhakti: The Early History of Kṛṣṇa Devotion in South India*. Delhi: Oxford University Press, 1983.

Hari Rao, V. N., ed. and trans. *Koil Oḻugu: The Chronicle of the Srirangam Temple with Historical Notes*. Madras: Rochouse and Sons, 1961.

Hart, George L., III. "The Nature of Tamil Devotion." In *Aryan and Non-Aryan in India*, edited by Madhav N. Deshpande and Peter Hook, 11–33. Ann Arbor: Michigan Papers on South and South East Asia, no. 14, 1979.

———. *The Poems of Ancient Tamil: Their Milieu and Sanskrit Counterparts*. Berkeley: University of California Press, 1975.

———. *The Poets of the Tamil Anthologies*. Princeton: Princeton University Press, 1979.

Hawley, John Stratton. *Krishna, The Butter Thief*. Princeton: Princeton University Press, 1983.

Hiltebeitel, Alf. "The Burning of the Forest Myth." In *Hinduism: New Essays in the History of Religions*, edited by Bardwell L. Smith, 208–24. Leiden: E. J. Brill, 1982.

Hooper, J. S. M. *Hymns of the Āḻvārs*. Calcutta: Association Press, 1929.

Hudson, Dennis. "Bathing in Krishna." *Harvard Theological Review* 78 (1980): 539–66.

———. "Piṉṉai, Krishna's Cowherd Wife." In *The Divine Consort: Rādha and the Goddesses of India,* edited by John S. Hawley and Donna Wulff, 238–61. Berkeley: Berkeley Religious Studies Series, 1982.

———. "Āṇṭāḷ's Enjoyment of God." Typescript.

———. "The Vaiṣṇava Temple with Three Floors for Icons." Typescript.

Hume, Robert Ernest. *The Thirteen Principal Upanishads*. London: Oxford University Press, 1931.

Jagadeesan, Nainar. *History of Śrī Vaishṇavism in the Tamil Country: Post-Rāmānuja*. Madurai: Koodal Publishers, 1977.

Jewel, The. See Yāmuna.

Kampaṉ. "Caṭakōpar Antāti." In *Nālayira Tivviyappirapantam,* edited by K. Vēṅkaṭacāmi Reṭṭiyār, 132–44. Madras: Tiruvēṅkaṭattāṉ Tirumaṉṟam, 1981.

Kaylor, R. David. "The Concept of Grace in the Hymns of Nammāḻvār." *Journal of the American Academy of Religion* 44 (1976): 649–60.

Kaylor, R. D., and K. K. A. Venkatachari. *God Far, God Near: An Interpretation of the Thought of Nammāḻvār.* Bombay: Ananthacharya Indological Research Institute Series, no. 5 (Supplement), 1981.

Kōyil Kantāṭaināyaṉ. *Periya Tirumuṭi Aṭaivu*. In *Āṟayirappaṭi Guruparamparāprabhāvam,* edited by S. Kiruṣṇasvāmi Ayyaṅkār. Tirucci: Puttūr Agrahāram, 1975.

Krishnaswami Iyengar, S. *Early History of Vaiṣṇavism in South India*. London: Oxford University Press, 1920.

———. *History of Tirupati*. 2 vols. Tirupati: Tirumalai Tirupati Devasthanam, 1940–41.

Kumarappa, Bharatan. *The Hindu Conception of the Deity as Culminating in Rāmānuja*. London: Luzac, 1934.

Kūrattāḻvāṉ, "Vaikuṇṭha Stava," "Varadarāja Stava," "Atimānuṣa Stava," "Śrī Stava," and "Sundarabāhu Stava." In *Stotramāla,* edited by P. B. Aṇṇaṅgarācāriyar, 15–42. Kāñci, 1974.

Lacombe, Olivier. *L'Absolu selon le Védânta: Les notions de Brahman et d'Atman dans les systèmes de Cankara et Râmânoudja*. Paris: Librairie Orientaliste Paul Geuthner, 1937.

———. *La doctrine morale et métaphysique de Rāmānuja*. [Text and French translation, with notes, on Sribhasya 1.1.1] Paris: Adrien-Maisonneuve, 1938.

Lester, Robert. "Rāmānuja and Śrī-Vaiṣṇavism: The Concept of *Prapatti* or *Śaraṇāgati*." *History of Religions* 5 (1966): 266–82.

———. *Rāmānuja on the Yoga*. Madras: Adyar Library and Research Centre, 1976.

———. "Rāmānuja and Śrī-Vaiṣṇavism (in the light of the *Āṟāyirappaḍi* to Nammāḻvār's *Tiruvāymoḻi*.)" Paper presented in the Fifth International Conference-Seminar of Tamil Studies, Madurai, South India, January 4–10, 1981.

Lipner, Julius. *The Face of Truth: A Study of Meaning and Metaphysics in the Vedāntic Theology of Rāmānuja*. Albany: State University of New York Press, 1986.

Lott, Eric. *God and the Universe in the Vedāntic Theology of Rāmānuja*. Madras: Ramanuja Research Society, 1976.

Maṉavāḷa Māmuni. "Upatēcarattiṉamālai [Upadeśaratnamālai]." In *Nālāyira tivviyap pirapantam*. Edited by P. B. Aṇṇaṅgarācāriyar, 604–13. Kāñci: V. N. Tēvanātaṉ, 1971.

Mangala Murugesan. *Sangam Age*. Madras: Thendral Pathipakam, 1982.

Manickam, S. *Slavery in the Tamil Country: A Historical Overview*. Madras: The Christian Literature Society, 1982.

Matsya Purāṇam, The. Translated by A Talgudar of Oudh. New York: A. M.-S. Press, 1974.

Meenakshisundaran, T. P. "Saranagati." In *The Munshi Indological Felicitation Volume*. *Bharatiya Vidya*, 20–21 (1960–61), 182–91.

Meyer, Leonard. *Music, The Arts, and Ideas*. Chicago: University of Chicago Press, 1967.

Monier-Williams, Monier. *A Sanskrit English Dictionary*. Oxford: Clarendon Press, 1974.

———. *Religious Thought and Life in India: Vedism, Brahmanism and Hinduism*. New Delhi: Oriental Books Reprint Corp., 1974.

Mumme, Patricia Yvonne. "The Theology of Maṉavāḷamāmuni: Toward an Understanding of the Teṅkalai-Vaṭakalai Dispute in Post-Rāmānuja Śrīvaiṣṇavism." Ph.D. diss., University of Pennsylvania, 1983.

———. "Grace and Karma in Nammāḻvār's Salvation." *Journal of the American Oriental Society* 107 (1987): 257–66.

Muthuratna Mudaliyar, S., ed. *Nammāḻvār Tiruttālāṭṭu*. Tanjore: Tañcāvūr Carasvati Mahāl Publications, no. 43, 1951.

Narayanan, Vasudha. "The Goddess Śrī: Blossoming Lotus and Breast Jewel of Viṣṇu." In *The Divine Consort: Rādha and the Goddesses of India*, edited by John S. Hawley and Donna Wulff, 224–37. Berkeley: Berkeley Religious Studies Series, 1982.

———. "Arcāvatāra: On Earth, as He is in Heaven." In *Gods of Flesh, Gods of Stone*, edited by Joanne P. Waghorne and Norman Cutler in association with Vasudha Narayanan, 53–66. Chambersburg: Anima Publications, 1985.

———. "Hindu Devotional Literature: the Tamil Connection." *Religious Studies Review* 12 (1985): 12–20.

———. *The Way and the Goal*. Washington: Institute for Vaishnava Studies and Cambridge, Mass.: Center for the Study of World Religions (Harvard University), 1987.

———. "Reciprocal Gratitude—Human and Divine Acts of Thanksgiving." In *Spoken and Unspoken Thanks: Some Comparative Soundings*, edited by John B. Carman and Frederick Streng. Cambridge, Mass.: Center for the Study of World Religions (Harvard University) and Dallas: Center for World Thanksgiving. Forthcoming.

———. *The Vernacular Veda: Revelation, Recitation, and Ritual*. Columbia: University of South Carolina Press. Forthcoming.

———. "Renunciation in Saffron and White Robes." In *Monastic Life in the Christian and Hindu Traditions*, edited by Austin B. Creel and Vasudha Narayanan. Lewiston: Edwin Mellen Press. Forthcoming.

Narasimhachary, M. *Contribution of Yāmuna to Viśiṣṭādvaita*. Madras: Prof. M. Rangacharya Trust, 1971.

———. "The Pañcastava of Kureśvara." In *Papers of Seminar on Sanskrit Literature*, 57–79. Bombay: Ananthacharya Indological Institute, 1980.

Nayanārāccāṉ Piḷḷai. *Caramōpāya Nirṇayam*. In *Āṛāyirappaṭi Guruparamparāprabhāvam*, edited by S. Kiruṣṇasvāmi Ayyaṅkār. Tirucci: Puttūr Agrahāram, 1975.

Neevel, Walter G. *Yāmuna's Vedānta and Pāñcarātra: Integrating the Classical with the Popular*. Missoula: Scholars Press, 1977.

O'Flaherty, Wendy. *Hindu Myths*. Harmondsworth: Penguin Books, 1975.

———. "Inside and Outside the Mouth of God: The Boundary between Myth and Reality." *Daedalus* (Spring 1980): 93–125.

Otto, Rudolf. *Vischnu-Nārāyana*. Texte zur Indischen Gottesmystik I. Jena: Eugen Diderichs, 1917.

———. *India's Religion of Grace and Christianity Compared and Contrasted*. London: S. C. M. Press, 1930.

Parameswaran, Mangalam R. "The Twofold Vedānta of Śrīvaiṣṇavism." Master's thesis, University of Manitoba, 1981.

Parāśara Bhaṭṭar. *Bhagavadguṇadarpaṇākhyam Śrīviṣṇusahasranāmabhāṣyam*. [The Commentary on the Thousand Names of Viṣṇu.] Edited by P. B. Aṇṇaṅgarācāriyar. Kāñci, 1964.

———. *Tiruneṭuntāṇṭakam Vyākyāṉam*. Edited by P. B. Aṇṇaṅgarācāriyar. Kāñci, 1970.

———. "Śrīraṅgarājastavam" and "Śrīguṇaratnakośa." In *Stotramāla*, edited by P. B. Aṇṇaṅgarācāriyar, 43–62.

———. *Sri Vishnu Sahasranama with the Bhashya of Sri Parasara Bhattar*. Edited and Translated by A. Srinivasa Raghavan. Madras: Sri Visishtadvaita Pracharini Sabha, 1983.

Parpola, Asko. "The Encounter of Religions in India, 2000–1000 B.C." *Temenos* 12 (1976): 21–36.

Parthasarathi, Vanamala. "Evolution of Rituals in Viṣṇu Temple Utsavas, with special reference to Śrīraṅgam, Tirumalai and Kāñci." Ph.D. diss., University of Bombay, 1983.

Periyavāccāṉ Piḷḷai. *Stotraratna Vyākyāṉam, Catuccloki Vyākyāṉam, Jitante Stotra Vyākyāṉam*, edited by K. Śrīnivāsa Ayyaṅkār. Tirucci: Puttūr Agrahāram, 1948.

———. *Katya Vyākyāṉaṅkaḷ*. Edited by S. Kiruṣṇasvāmi Ayyaṅkār. Tirucci: Puttūr Agrahāram, 1976.

———. See also Aṇṇaṅgarācāriyar, P. B.

Peterson, Indira Viswanathan. "Singing of a Place: Pilgrimage and Poetry in Tamil Saivaite Hagiography." *Journal of the American Oriental Society* 102 (1982): 69–90.

———. *Poems to Śiva*. Princeton: Princeton University Press. Forthcoming.

Piḷḷai Lōkācārya. *Śrīvacana Bhūṣaṇam*. In *Śrīmatvaravaramunīntra krantamālai*, edited by P. B. Aṇṇaṅgarācāriyar. Kāñci, 1966.

———. *Tattva traya of Lokacharya, A Manual of Visishtadvaita*. Translated by M. B. Narasimha Iyengar. Madras: M. C. Krishnan, 1966.

Piṉpaḻakiya Perumāḷ Jīyar. *Āṛāyirappaṭi Guruparamparāprabhāvam*. Edited by S. Kiruṣṇasvāmi Ayyaṅkār. Tirucci: Puttūr Agrahāram, 1975.

Puliyūr Kēcikaṉ, ed. *Tolkāppiyam*. Madras: Parinilayam, 1986.

Raghavachar, S. S. *Introduction to the Vedārthasaṅgraha of Śrī Rāmānujācharya*. Mangalore: Mangalore Trading Assn., 1973.

———. "Vishṇu Sahasranāma Bhāsya of Śrī Parāsara Bhaṭṭa." In *Papers of Seminar on Sanskrit Literature*. Bombay: Ananthacharya Research Institute, 1979.

Rajagopala Ayyangar, M. R., trans. *Śrīmad Rahasyatrayasāra of Śrī Vedāntadeśika*. Kumbakonam: Agnihothram Ramanuja Thathachariar [Publication], 1956.

Rajagopalan, Vasudha [Narayanan]. "The Śrīvaiṣṇava Understanding of *Bhakti* and *Prapatti:* The Āḻvārs to Vedānta Deśika." Ph.D. diss., University of Bombay, 1978.

Rajam, V. S. "*Aṇaṅku:* A Notion Semantically Reduced to Signify Female Sacred Power." *Journal of the American Oriental Society* 106 (1986): 257–72.

Rāmānuja. *Śrībhāṣya, Vedārtha Saṁgraha, Gītābhāṣya, Gadya traya*. In *Rāmānujagranthamāla*. Edited by P. B. Aṇṇaṅgarācāriyar. Kāñci, 1974.

———. *The Gitabhashya of Ramanuja*. Edited and translated by M. R. Sampatkumaran. Madras: Prof. M. Rangacharya Memorial Trust, 1969.

———. *Rāmānuja's Vedārtha Saṃgraha*. Edited and translated by J. A. B. van Buitenen. Poona: Deccan College, 1956.

———. *Vedārtha-Saṅgraha*. Translated by S. S. Raghavachar. Mysore: Sri Ramakrishna Ashrama, 1968.

———. *Vedartha Sangraha of Ramanuja*. Translated by M. R. Rajagopala Ayyangar. Chromepet (Madras): published by the author, 1956.

Ramanujachari, R. "Nathamuni, His Life and Times." *Journal of the Annamalai University* 9 (June 1940): 267–77.

———. "Ubhaya Vedanta." In *Seventh Centenary Souvenir of Nigamantha Mahadesikan*, 45–57. Bangalore: Srimad Andavan of Periya Ashramam, 1968.

Ramanujan, A. K. *Interior Landscape: Love Poems from a Classical Tamil Anthology*. Bloomington: Indiana University Press, 1967.

———. "Form in Classical Tamil Poetry." In *Symposium on Dravidian Civilization*, edited by Andrie F. Sjoberg, 74–104. Austin: Asian Series of the Center for Asian Studies, 1971.

———. "Karma in Bhakti with Special Reference to Nammāḻvār and Basavaṇṇa." Paper presented at the ACLS/SSRC Workshop on Karma in Post-Classical Texts, Pendle Hill, Pennsylvania, October 1980.

Ramanujan, A. K., and Norman Cutler. "From Classicism to Bhakti." In *Essays in Gupta Culture*, edited by Bardwell Smith, 177–214. Delhi: Motilal Banarsidass, 1983.

Rangachari, K. *The Sri Vaishnava Brahmans*. Madras: Bulletin of the Madras Government Museum, 1931.

Rangachari, R., trans. *Dramidopanisad Tatparya Ratnavali and Sara*. Madras: Vedanta Desika Research Society, 1974.

Rangacharya, V. "Historical Evolution of Sri Vaishnavism." In *The Cultural Heritage of India*, vol. 2, pp. 66–103. Calcutta: Sri Ramakrishna Centenary Committee, n.d.

Raṅkanāta Mutaliyār, ed. *Śrī Vaiṣṇavam*. Madras, 1937.

Shekhar, I. *Sanskrit Drama: Its Origin and Decline*. Leiden: E. J. Brill, 1960.

Singer, Milton, ed. *Krishna: Myths, Rites, and Attitudes*. Honolulu: East-West Center Press, 1966.

Six Thousand, The. See Tirukkurukai Pirāṉ Piḷḷāṉ.

Smith, Brian K. "Exorcising the Transcendent: Strategies for Defining Hinduism and Religion." *History of Religions* 27 (1987): 32–55.

Smith, H. Daniel. "Pāñcarātra Literature in Perspective." *Journal of Ancient Indian History* 12 (1978–79): 45–58.

Solomon, Ted. "Early Vaiṣṇava Bhakti and its Autochthonous Heritage." *History of Religions* 10 (1971): 32–48.

Soundararajan, K. V. "The Typology of the Anantaśāyi Icon." *Artibus Asiae* 29 (1969): 67–84.

Spink, Walter M. *Krishnamandala: A Devotional Theme in Indian Art.* Ann Arbor: The University of Michigan Center for South and Southeast Asian Studies, 1971.

Splendor, The. See Piṉpaḻakiya Perumāḷ Jīyar.

Srinivasa Chari, S. M. *Fundamentals of Viśiṣṭādvaita Vedānta: A Study Based on Vedāntadeśika's Tattva-mukta-kalapa.* New Delhi: Motilal Banarsidass, 1988.

Srinivasachari, P. N. *The Philosophy of Viśiṣṭādvaita.* Madras: Adyar Library, 1943.

Śrīnivāsadāsa. *Yatīndramatadīpika.* Translated by Swami Adidevananda. Madras: Sri Ramakrishna Math, 1949.

Srinivasa Raghavan, A. "Mystic Symbolism in the Works of the Alwars." In *Proceedings of the First Conference and Seminar on Tamil Studies.* Kuala Lumpur, 1969.

Subbu Reddiar, N. *Philosophy of the Nālāyiram with Special Reference to Nammāḻvār.* Tirupati: Sri Venkateswara University, 1977.

———. *Viṭṭu Chithaṉ Viritta Tamizh.* Madras: Paari Nilayam, 1987.

Staal, J. F. "Sanskrit and Sanskritization." *The Journal of Asian Studies* 22 (1963): 261–75.

———. "Indian Concepts of the Body." *Somatics* (Autumn/Winter 1983–84): 31–41.

Tamil Lexicon. 6 vols. Madras: Madras University Press, 1982–83.

Tamil Scholars. *Kuṟuntokai.* Madras: Murray and Co., 1957.

———. *Pāṭṭum Tokaiyum.* Madras: Murray and Co., 1958.

Thani Nayagam, Xavier S. *Nature in Ancient Tamil Poetry.* Tutucorin: Tamil Literature Society, n.d.

Thibaut, George. *The Vedānta Sūtras with the Commentary of Rāmānuja.* Sacred Books of the East, vol. 48. Oxford: Clarendon Press, 1903.

Tirukkurukai Pirāṉ Piḷḷāṉ. "Āṟayirappaṭi Vyākkyāṉam." In *Bhagavad Viṣayam,* edited by Śrī S. Kiruṣṇasvāmi Ayyaṅkār, 10 vols. Madras: Nobel Press, 1924–1930.

Tiruvaḷḷuvar. *Tirukkuṟaḷ.* Edited and translated by V. R. Ramachandra Dikshitar. The Adyar Library Series, no. 68. Madras: The Adyar Library, 1949.

Tiruvallikkēṇi Śrī Pārtacārathi svāmi tēvastāṉa vēta atyāpaka kōṣṭi cirappu malar [Śrī Pārthasārathi Temple Veda-Reciters' Felicitation Volume]. Madras, 1985.

Uttamūr Vīrarāghavācāriyar. *Upaya Vētānta Krantamālai, Periyāḻvār aruḷiceyta tivyaprapantam, Periyāḻvār Tirumoḻi prapantarakṣai eṉṉum uṟaiyuṭan.* Madras: Visishtadvaita Pracarini Sabha, 1975.

van Buitenen, J. A. B. *Yāmuna's Āgama Prāmāṇyam.* Madras: Ramanuja Research Society, 1971.

———. *Ramanuja on the Bhagavadgīta.* Delhi: Motilal Banarsidass, 1974.

———, ed. and trans. *The Mahābhārata.* Vols. 1–3. Chicago and London: University of Chicago Press, 1973–78.

Varadachari, K. C. *Alvars of South India.* Bombay: Bharatiya Vidya Bhavan, 1970.

Vedanta Desika. *Śrīmad Rahasya Traya Sāram.* Edited by Śrī Rāmatēcikācāriyar. 2 vols. Kumbakonam: Opilliyappaṉ Sanniti, 1961.

———. "Garuḍa Pañcāśat." In *Stotrāṇi.* Bombay: Sri Vedanta Desika Sampradaya Sabha, 1964.

———. *Dramidopanisad Tatparya Ratnavali and Sara*. Translated by R. Rangachari. Madras: Vedanta Desika Research Society, 1974.

———. *Catuḥślokibhāṣyam, Stotraratnabhāṣyam, Gadyatrayabhāṣyañca*. Madras: Sri Vedantha Desika Seventh Centenary Trust, n.d.

Venkatachari, K. K. A. *The Maṇipravāḷa Literature of the Śrī Vaiṣṇava Ācāryas*. Bombay: Ananthacarya Research Institute, 1978.

Wilson, H. H., trans. *The Viṣṇu Purāṇa: A System of Hindu Mythology and Tradition*. Calcutta: Punthi Pustak, 1961.

Yāmuna. "Catuḥśloki" and "Stotra Ratna." In *Stotramāla*, edited by P. B. Aṇṇaṅgarācāriyar. Kāñci, 1974.

Yamunacharya, M. *Ramanuja's Teachings in His Own Words*. Bombay: Bharatiya Vidya Bhavan, 1963.

Yocum, Glenn. "Shrines, Shamanism, and Love Poetry: Elements in the Emergence of Popular Tamil Bhakti." *Journal of the American Academy of Religion* 41 (1973): 3–17.

———. *Hymns to the Dancing Śiva: A Study of Māṇikkavācakar's Tiruvācakam*. New Delhi: Heritage Publishers, 1982.

Young, Katherine. "Beloved Places (Ukantaruḷiṉanilaṅkaḷ): The Correlation of Topography and Theology in the Śrīvaiṣṇava Tradition of South India." Ph.D. diss., Montreal: Mcgill University, 1978.

Zimmer, Heinrich. *Myths and Symbols of Indian Art and Civilization*. Bollingen Series 6. Princeton: Princeton University Press, 1974.

Zvelebil, Kamil. *The Smile of Murugan*. Leiden: E. J. Brill, 1973.

———. *Tamil Literature*. Vol. 10, fasc. 1 of *A History of Indian Literature*. Wiesbaden: Otto Harrassowitz, 1974.

———. *Tamil Literature*. Leiden: E. J. Brill, 1975.

———. "The Beginnings of Tamil *bhakti* in South India." *Temenos* 13 (1977): 233–57.

General Index

References are to discussions of the subjects cited, with the exception of certain words or names which are simply mentioned in the verse or commentary quoted. These are of interest as examples of Tamil versions of Sanskrit names or of the emphasis given certain epithets. Such words include, for example, "auspicious attributes," Caṭakōpaṉ, feet, Kaṇṇa(ṉ), sacred names, and sacred places.

ācārya(s), 3, 6, 7, 8, 9–10, 34, 42, 45, 48, 50, 54; as mediators, 53, 135. *See also* Rāmānuja
accessibility (saulabhya) of the Lord, 39, 40, 41, 46, 47, 86, 87, 90, 91, 101, 151, 162, 269n.18, 270n.9; to his devotees, 71, 112, 113, 115, 129, 132, 251, 274n.2. *See also* inaccessibility
acit (nonsentient matter), 38, 55, 72, 87, 137
Advaita Vedānta, 36, 83, 99, 182, 191
Advaitin(s), 84, 183, 184, 190
Āgamas, 4, 34, 36, 54, 181. *See also* Pāñcarātra Āgamas
Agnihothram Rāmānuja Thatachariar, 185, 186, 296n.9
akam (romantic) poetry, 14, 16, 21, 26, 29. *See also* tiṇai; Tiruvāymoḻi
Akanāṉūṟu, the, 28, 177
Aḻakiyamaṇavāḷaperumāḷ Nāyanār, 261n.14
Āḷavantār. *See* Yāmuna
āḻvār(s), 3, 34, 42, 48, 50, 52, 154; and Tamil heritage, 14–17; devotion of, 107, 183; poems of, 20, 22, 44, 45, 46, 51, 53, 54; references in early Śrīvaiṣṇava literature to, 43–44. *See also* Nammāḻvār; union
amalatva. *See* purity
Amutaṉār, 146
ānanda (joy or bliss), 40
aṇaṅku āṭutal. *See* possession
Ananta-Śeṣa, 18, 64, 70, 71, 168, 195, 271n.1; and sea of milk, 73, 88, 90, 92, 212, 250; as paradigmatic servant, 48, 49, 220; iconography of, 11–12, 288–89n.6; in temples, 90, 102, 116, 154, 216
anantatva (infinite), 40
Āndhra Pūrṇa, 259n.3
Āṇṭāḷ, 31, 75, 100, 119, 290n.20. *See also* Tiruppāvai, the
antaryāmī. *See* inner controller
antāti (end-beginning) xvi, 20, 60, 67, 257
anurāga (tender affection). *See* Divine attributes
aṟaiyar cēvai, 267n.30
aṟaiyars, 266n.30
Āṟāyirappaṭi, the. See *Six Thousand Paṭi*s
arcāvatāra (iconic incarnation), 48, 89, 102, 156, 289n.6
āṟṟuppaṭai, 24, 25. See also *Tirumurukāṟṟuppaṭai*
arul. *See* grace
āśraya (refuge), 128
āśrita (those who have taken refuge), 78, 95
āśritavātsalya (motherly love for the devotee), 95
Ate, Lynn, 287n.6
aṭimai. *See* service
Atimānuṣa Stava, the, 47, 48
ātmā (finite soul or souls), 39, 40, 41, 117, 166, 178; and body, 18, 38. *See also* soul
audārya (generosity). *See* Divine attributes
auspicious attributes or qualities, 41, 50, 71, 72, 80, 93, 103, 105, 133, 135, 148, 212, 217, 277n.13. *See also* Divine attributes
avatāra (incarnation or descent), 40, 41, 86–89, 151; āḻvārs as, 6, 18; as boar

Maṇavāḷa Māmuṉi, 7, 18, 147, 261 n.14
Māṇikkavācakar, 263 n.25, 270 n.10, 292 n.33
Maṇimēkalai (*Jeweled Girdle*), the, 17
maṇipravāla (gems and corals, Sanskritized Tamil), xii, xv, 10, 11, 43, 59, 60
Manu. *See* Laws of Manu
Māṟaṉ (Nammāḻvār), 17, 18, 26, 210
Mārkaṇḍeya, 162, 209, 213, 285–86 n.3, 287 n.5, 289 n.7; swallowed by Viṣṇu, 169, 170
maṭal (riding a palmyra horse), 30
Maturakavi āḻvār, 5, 7, 17, 18, 19, 21, 45, 46, 53, 261 n.14
māyā, 37, 162, 212, 287 n.5
Māyāvāda, 199
Māyōṉ. *See* sacred names
means. *See* way
mediator(s), 54; other deities as, 73, 150, 213; Rāmānuja as, 55; Śrīvaiṣṇavas as, 134. *See also* ācārya; puruṣakāra; Śrī
mercy: appeal for, 232; ocean of, 47; of Śrī, 52. *See also* Divine attributes
milkmaids. *See* gopīs
mokṣa (viṭu). *See* liberation
motherly love (vātsalya). *See* Divine attributes
Mudaliyar, 24
Murukaṉ (Muruga), 24, 25, 26, 30, 263 n.25

Nakkīrar, 262 n.17
Nālāyira Tivyap Pirapantam. *See* Sacred Collect of Four Thousand Verses
Nammāḻvār, 3, 4, 10, 17, 19, 21, 23, 30, 44, 45, 51, 53, 54; and Piḷḷāṉ, 35, 60, 61, 63, 66, 67, 69, 84, 126; and Rāmānuja, 154; and the Lord, 13, 20, 22, 23, 25, 31, 32, 71; ascent to heaven of, 134, 285 n.13; as gopī, 100, 242–48, 275 n.5; as incarnation of the Lord, 18; as instrument of the Lord, 5, 68, 70, 74, 119, 125, 140, 152, 172, 237; in Śrīvaiṣṇava tradition, 17–19, 110, 145; mentioned by Yāmuna, 43; use of phrase "six camayas", 82; viraha poems of, 107. *See also* surrender; Tiruvāciriyam; Tiruvāymoḻi
Nammāḻvār Tirutāllāṭṭu (*Lullaby for Nammāḻvār*), the, 19
Nañjīyar, 8, 279 n.3, 298 n.44, 300 n.61
Nappiṉṉai, 75, 76, 102, 104, 239, 240, 282 n.4; and the seven bulls, 272 n.5. *See also* consort(s)
Nāraṇa(ṉ), 205, 239, 240, 249, 274 n.3
Narasimhachary, M., 268 n.3
Narasiṁha. *See* avatāra
Nārāyaṇa(ṉ) (Viṣṇu), 41, 54, 67, 91, 133, 150, 205, 206, 207, 208. *See also* Lord; Viṣṇu
Nāthamuni, 4, 34, 43, 45, 53, 147, 158, 170, 181; and recovery of lost poems, 4–10, 20
nāyaṉmārs, 14, 16, 191
Neevel, Walter G., 268 n.2, 269 n.1
Nīḷā, 55, 75, 240, 271 n.1, 272 n.5. *See also* consort(s)
Nimbarka, 184, 295 n.7
Nine Thousand Paṭis, the, 10, 262, 278–79 n.3, 298 n.44, 300 n.61
nirhetuka (without reason), 113, 120, 121, 122, 148

obeisance, 115, 116, 148, 251
O'Flaherty, Wendy, 170
Otto, Rudolph, 183, 185
ownership. *See* śeṣa; śeṣī

Pāñcarātra Āgamas, the, 34, 35, 36, 41, 42, 89, 157, 185; orthodoxy defended by Yāmuna and Rāmānuja, 181, 269 n.22
paradoxical contraries, 66, 80–82
Parāṅkuśa (Nammāḻvār), 44
Parāśara, 43, 45
Parāśara Bhaṭṭar, 44, 51, 52, 111, 136, 152, 261 n.14
paratva. *See* supremacy
Paripāṭal, the, 17, 267 n.39
Patineṇkīḻkaṇakku. See *Eighteen Short Classics*
Pattuppāṭṭu. See *Ten Songs*
Periya Tirumalai Nampi (Śrī Śaila Pūrṇa), 8, 34, 146
Periya Tirumoḻi, the, 62, 170
Periya Tirumuṭi Aṭaivu, the, 266 n.19
Periyāḻvār, 47, 62, 272 n.5, 291 n.20
Periyāḻvār Tirumoḻi, the, 47, 49, 266 n.30
Periya Tiruvantāti, the, 18
Parpola, Asko, 262 n.25
Periyavāccāṉ Piḷḷai, 8, 43, 52, 261 n.14, 262 n.18. See also *Twenty-Four Thousand Paṭis*
Perumāḷ Tirumoḻi, the, 46, 47
Peterson, Indira Viswanathan, 259 n.4
phala śruti(s), 20, 26, 60, 67, 70, 74, 126, 129, 135, 153
pilgrimage centers. *See* sacred places
Piḷḷai Lokācārya, xii, 157, 188, 189, 190, 268 n.13, 298 n.38

Piḷḷāṉ, Tirukkurukai Pirāṉ. *See* Tirukkurukai Pirāṉ Piḷḷāṉ
Piṉṉai. *See* Nappiṉṉai
play. *See* sport
possession, 28, 30; dancing under, 29, 134; spirit possession, 100, 134
Poykai (āḻvār), 6, 287n.5, 289n.7
Prabhākara, 35–36, 136, 268n.7
pralaya. *See* dissolution
prapatti (humble surrender to God), xii, 42, 62, 112, 119, 137, 153, 189. *See also* bhaktiyoga, alternatives to; grace; śaranāgati; surrender
prayer: for gods' favor, 75; of surrender, 55; of taking refuge, 119
prīti (unsurpassed love), 106
propitiation, 73, 197
protection (rakṣana), 93. *See also* devotee(s), Lord as protector of
puṟam (heroic) poetry, 14, 16, 26, 27. *See also* Tiruvāymoḻi
Puṟanāṉūṟu, the, 22, 23, 24
Purāṇa(s), the, 4, 54, 162, 206; Bhāgavata, 21, 149, 186; Liṅga, 83, 207, 208; Matsya, 160, 162, 187n.5, 285n.3; Viṣṇu Purāṇa, the, 10, 42, 43, 44, 52, 72, 149, 150, 161
purity, 40, 80, 82, 88, 156, 272n.3
puruṣakāra (mediator), 76–77, 209, 233. *See also* mediator(s)
puruṣārtha (eschatology or goal of human life), 60, 151. *See also* goal
Pūrva Mīmāṁsa, 36, 268n.8
Pūtana. *See* Krishna

Radhakrishnan, S., 182
Rajam, V. S., 268n.47
Rāma, 62, 75, 88, 89, 101, 108, 279n.5; destroys Laṅka, 73
Rāmabhakti, 88
Ramakrishna Paramahaṁsa, 182
Rāmānuja, 3, 12, 54, 157–58, 268n.5; and Bhagavadgītā, 108–9, 138, 149, 282n.12; and Nammāḻvār, 128–29, 145, 154; and Piḷḷāṉ, 8, 44, 59, 60, 62, 79, 80, 145; and Śaṅkara, 38, 99, 184; and the Tiruvāymoḻi (oral commentary on), 145, 182, 269n.2; and Vedānta, 39, 180, 185; and Yāmuna, 34–35, 36; as avatāra, 146; as mediator, 53, 55; doctrine of, 36, 37f., 40, 41, 154; in Śrīvaiṣṇava tradition, 145; language of, 61, 71, 136, 139; relation of disciples to, 53, 55, 70; relation to Tamil tradition, question of, 42; Sanskrit writings of, 74, 145, 154. See also *Gadyas*; *Gītābhāṣya*; *Śrībhāṣya*; *Vedārtha Samgraha*
Rāmānuja Nūṟṟantāti, 261n.14, 265n.3, 270n.3
Ramanujan, A. K., 14, 78, 169, 266n.18, 267n.35, 268n.45
Rāmāyaṇa, the, 62
reality, xiii, 38, 60, 79, 137, 151, 159; three realities, 269n.13
reason (hetu), 121. *See also* nirhetuka
refuge, 45, 51, 189; ācāryas as, 53; in other gods, 74; Lord as, 50, 55, 113, 128; with Śrī, 77, 95; with the Lord, 53, 70, 74, 116–22, 124, 171, 202, 208. *See also* feet of the Lord; prapatti; śaraṇāgati
renunciation (sannyāsa), 36
revelation, 5, 61, 67, 68, 74, 154; language of, 62
Rudra, 73, 74, 199, 207, 209, 213, 235, 241. *See also* Śiva
Rukmini, 272n.5. *See also* consort(s)

śabda (eternal sounds), 38
Sacred Celestial City. *See* sacred places, Tiruviṇṇakar
Sacred Collect of Four Thousand Verses, the, 6, 8, 14, 19, 20, 31, 266–67n.30
sacred names, 132, 141, 272n.2; chanting of, 251; Dāmodara, 138, 278n.2; Hari, 91; Keśava, 67, 133; Kuntaṉ, 236; Mādhava(ṉ), 113, 132, 211, 250, 251; Madhusūda(ṉ), 165; Maṉṉaṉār (Viṣṇu), 5, 34; Māyōṉ, 20; Piḷḷāṉ's interpretation of, 271n.5; Raṅga, 75; Tirumāl, 20, 238, 288n.6. *See also* Thousand Names of Viṣṇu
sacred places, 125, 157; Araṅkam, 50; Brindavan, 34; Cirīvaramaṅkala(m), 50, 60, 116, 117, 215, 279n.5; Kāṭkarai, 168, 169; Śrīraṅgam, 12, 18, 34, 44, 51, 75, 259n.7; Śrīvilliputtūr, 288–89n.6; Tirukaṇṇapuram, 91, 117, 280nn. 6, 7; Tirukkaṭittāṉam, 91, 92, 134; Tirukkōlur, 277n.12; Tirukkurukūr, 5, 18, 26, 67, 74, 201, 206–10, 215, 220, 221, 227, 238, 242, 248, 257; Tirukkuṟuṅkuṭi, 17; Tirukkuṭantai, 61, 216–21, 289n.6; Tirumāliruñcōlai, 48, 106, 121, 172, 173, 277n.15, 281n.11; Tirumōkūr, 90, 96;

Index to Verses and Commentary

Tiruvāymoḻi verses

The Six Thousand